The Earliest Christian Mission
to 'All Nations' in the
Light of Matthew's Gospel

The Earliest Christian Mission to 'All Nations' in the Light of Matthew's Gospel

James LaGrand

WILLIAM B. EERDMANS PUBLISHING COMPANY
GRAND RAPIDS, MICHIGAN / CAMBRIDGE, U.K.

First published 1995 by
Scholars Press
© 1995 University of South Florida

This edition published 1999 by
Wm. B. Eerdmans Publishing Co.
255 Jefferson Ave. S.E., Grand Rapids, Michigan 49503 /
P.O. Box 163, Cambridge CB3 9PU U.K.
All rights reserved

Printed in the United States of America

04 03 02 01 00 99   7 6 5 4 3 2 1

Library of Congress Cataloging-in-Publication Data
LaGrand, James 1941-
The earliest Christian mission to 'all nations' in the
Light of Matthew's Gospel / James LaGrand.
p.   cm. — (University of South Florida international
studies in formative Christianity and Judaism ; v. 1)
Includes bibliographical references.
ISBN 0-8028-4653-X (alk. paper)
1. Missions — Biblical teaching. 2. Bible. N.T. Matthew —
Criticism, interpretation, etc. 3. Great Commission (Bible)
4. Missions — History — Early church, ca. 30-600. I. Title.
II. Series.
BV2073.L27   1995
226 — dc21   98-53605
                                                 CIP

To the memory of Markus Barth
(1915-1994)

CONTENTS

Abbreviations	*page x*
Acknowledgments	*xi*
Author's Note	*xii*
Foreword	*xiii*

1. INTRODUCTION	1
A. Harnack and 'the Tübingen School'	1
B. Key Terms in Current Discussions	6
C. Aim of the Present Study	14

Part One ISRAEL AND THE NATIONS

2. MODERN TERMS AND CONCEPTS: PROBLEMS AND CHALLENGE	17
A. Conceptual Analysis	20
B. Linguistics	23
C. The Several Israels and Various Nationalities	31
D. The Threat of Expert Opinion	43
3. IDENTIFICATION IN ANCIENT SOURCES	47
A. Hebrew Bible	47
B. Septuagint and Apocrypha	65
4. USAGE IN NEAR-CONTEMPORARY LITERATURE	75
A. Pseudepigrapha and Qumran	76
B. Philo and Josephus	82
C. Paul in his own account and Luke's	86
D. Other NT writings and the Didache	92
5. LATER TRAJECTORIES OF THE CONCEPTS	95
A. Syriac Christianity	96
B. Rabbinic Judaism	98

Part Two JESUS AND THE NATIONS

6. LIVING TRADITIONS IN THE BACKGROUND OF THE GOSPEL — 105

    A. The Multiple Tradition about Jesus — 105
    B. Scriptures as Background and Directives — 113
    C. Messianic Expectations (Matthew 10.5b-6) — 126

7. PROSELYTIZING (Matthew 23.15) — 145

    A. "Scribes and Pharisees" — 147
    B. "A Single Proselyte" — 149
    C. "More Divided Than Yourselves" — 154

8. THE NATIONS IN THE DESIGN OF THE GOSPEL: SIGNALS OF THINGS TO COME — 157

    A. Arguments from Design — 158
    B. Presentation — 169

9. THE NATIONS IN THE DESIGN OF THE GOSPEL: PROCLAMATION IN WORD AND DEED — 187

    A. Call to Discipleship — 188
    B. Instructions for the First Mission — 194
    C. Parables — To Know the Mysteries — 200
    D. Mighty Acts and the Sign of Jonah — 203
    E. Two Exceptional Responses to Non-Israelites — 207

10. THE NATIONS IN THE DESIGN OF THE GOSPEL: ESTABLISHMENT OF THE KINGDOM — 211

    A. The Messiah's Death — 212
    B. The Resurrection of the Lord — 225

11. THE GREAT COMMISSION (Matthew 28.16-20) — 235

    A. Textual and Literary Criticism — 236
    B. Sayings of the Risen Jesus — 240
    C. Preparation for Pentecost — 244

12. CONCLUSION — 249

    A. The Single People of God — 251
    B. Israel's Messiah, Lord of the Nations — 251

MAPS

    A. The Land of Israel *ca.* AD 30   16
    B. The World of the Messianic Mission *ca.* AD 35   102

SELECT BIBLIOGRAPHY

    A. Texts & Translations   253
    B. Resources for Analysis   255
    C. Monographs: Commentaries and Studies   257

INDEX

    A. Ancient Texts Cited   269
    B. Authors   282
    C. Subjects   288

ABBREVIATIONS

ABD	*Anchor Bible Dictionary*
ANRW	*Aufstieg und Niedergang der römischen Welt*
Antiq	*Josephus' Jewish Antiquities*
APOT	R.H. Charles' ed. *The Apocrypha and Pseudepigrapha*
BA	*Biblical Archeologist*
BASOR	*Bulletin of the American Schools of Oriental Research*
BJRL	*Bulletin of the John Rylands Library*
CBQ	*Catholic Biblical Quarterly*
ExpT	*Expository Times*
HJP	*History of the Jewish People*
HTR	*Harvard Theological Review*
IDB	*Interpreter's Dictionary of the Bible*
JBL	*Journal of Biblical Literature*
JJS	*Journal of Jewish Studies*
JSJ	*Journal for the Study of Judaism in the Persian, Hellenistic, and Roman Period*
JSNT	*Journal for the Study of the New Testament*
JTS	*Journal of Theological Studies*
LXX	Septuagint including Apocrypha
NovT	*Novum Testamentum*
NTS	*New Testament Studies*
TDNT	*Theological Dictionary of the New Testament*
USQR	*Union Seminary Quarterly Review*
War	*Josephus' Jewish War*
ZNW	*Zeitschrift für die neutestamentliche Wissenschaft*

Translations are the author's except where otherwise noted.

Dates in brackets [ ] represent the time of first publication, the edition upon which the quoted translation is based, *or* the year the work achieved definitive form.

ACKNOWLEDGMENTS

I am debtor to persons and institutions in several nations for the challenge and opportunity to undertake this work, which was begun many years ago. For the shape of the thesis, I owe most to Professor Markus Barth. My personal debt to Professor and Mrs. Barth extends in many directions. Professor Bo Reicke also had a formative influence on my work in relating theology to history, and especially for the dating of documents and events in the NT era.

Formulation of the basic questions for this study began with my participation in the Wycliffe Bible Translators' Summer Institute in Linguistics, Norman, Oklahoma, and in my association with the CMS missionaries in Zaria, Nigeria, 1963-65. An Ecumenical Scholarship from the British Council of Churches and a Centennial Missions Scholarship from the Christian Reformed Church in North America sponsored the academic research which I began in Sheffield and Cambridge, England. Dr. John J. Vincent and Dr. David Hill supervised the first stage of this study. Professor Herman Ridderbos and Professor W.C. van Unnik gave me direction and encouragement through their published work and conversations in their homes in the Netherlands.

Membership in the Tyndale Fellowship for Biblical Research in Cambridge and the invitation to participate in Professor Morna Hooker's 1976-77 New Testament Seminar introduced me to many of the scholars whose published work is the basis for much of the present study. I am especially indebted to three of the younger New Testament scholars who were in Cambridge that year, Dr. Seyoon Kim, Dr. Brian McNeil, and Dr. William Schutter.

Besides the *Öffentliche Bibliothek der Universität* Basel, several libraries in England, Canada, and the U.S.A. supported my research. Special thanks to Herr Jakob Tschopp, Mrs. Alice Harrison at AST, and Dr. Ken Sawyer at the Jesuit-Krauss-McCormick Library.

Paul and Jennifer Jenkins, Christian Deutsch, and others in the Basel Mission gave me more help than I would have dared to ask —and I often asked more than is allowed by European or American conventions.

Jacob Neusner's proposal that I publish this work in the new series "International Studies in Formative Christianity and Judaism" makes me bold to acknowledge here my heavy debt to his published work. My immediate debt is to Dr. James F. Strange, the editor of this series. Thanks to my son Paul and his friend Mark Turner for help with the index.

Dr. John Ngusha Orkar and other members of the congregations I served, in Halifax and Chicago, encouraged me to step into the sometimes threatening field of Biblical Studies to attempt clarification (for myself and for them) of "the faith once for all delivered to the saints".

James LaGrand
Lutheran School of Theology at Chicago
Rosh Hashanah, 1995

AUTHOR'S NOTE TO PAPERBACK EDITION

"It is characteristic of twentieth-century scholarship to assume that persons at the greatest distance in time from historical events can see and understand them most clearly." This ironic classroom observation by Jaroslav Pelikan continues to chasten me. If I were to re-write this book now I would be more concerned to canvass the literature written between AD 135 and 1950 than to concentrate on publications of the last five or ten years. In fact, I have made only minor typographical corrections which do not change the pagination of the text. Nevertheless, I should note here that valuable reflections on ancient Israel and Jesus of Nazareth have been published since *The Earliest Christian Mission to 'All Nations'* appeared in 1995 as the first in the series of *University of South Florida International Studies in Formative Christianity and Judaism*.

'Sectarian Judaism', 'Jewish Proselytism', and 'Jewish-Christianity' (the three "Key Terms in Current Discussions" noted in my Introduction) became major fields of study and publication during the 1990s. The best single survey of the field of Jewish proselytism now is Louis H. Feldman's chapter on "The Success of Proselytism by Jews in the Hellenistic and Early Roman Periods" in *Jew and Gentile in the Ancient World* (1993). Also noteworthy is the conceptual analysis in Martin Goodman's *Mission and Conversion* (1994). Alan Segal's brilliant work, including *Paul the Convert,* and Shaye J. D. Cohen's important articles have examined the issue of first-century Jewish identity, including questions of 'Sectarian Judaism' and 'Jewish-Christianity'.

There would be no end to citation of arguments and analysis differing from my own, but Bruce J. Malina's 1996 essay "Jesus and Gentiles" shows how some of the data examined in *ECMAN* can be claimed for opposite conclusions. It is as though Malina sees a duck where I see a rabbit.

N. T. Wright's *Jesus and the Victory of God* (1996) relates directly to the earliest Christian mission. If I had read that book before writing mine I would have considered 'return from Exile' more seriously in relation to the mission to all nations. Richard Bauckham's 1995 essay, "For Whom Were Gospels Written?" is a much shorter work. It promises to rearrange Gospel studies, but lends support to mine.

Where my book differs from other recent publications, I hope that the differences will be judged in terms of conceptual analysis and strict attention to chronology and documentary evidence. Students finding their way among academic fashions do well to remember that the book with the most recent publication date — or the last item logged onto the web — is not necessarily the best source of information on a subject.

My own involvement in Christian mission and in the Anti-Apartheid Movement of the '70s and '80s prompted me to undertake this research into the earliest mission to all ethnics. I hope that this paperback edition will be of use to Jesus' disciples today who hear the words of the resurrected Lord, recorded in the conclusion of Matthew's Gospel, as directed to them.

James LaGrand
Beacon Light Church,
Gary Indiana
Pentecost 1999

FOREWORD

A point of critical importance in any interpretation of the Gospel of Matthew is the apparent contradiction between Jesus' missionary instructions to the twelve in chapter 10, "Do not take the road to the nations . . ." (10:5), and his missionary instructions to the eleven at the end of the Gospel: "Go therefore and make disciples of all nations . . ." (28:19). Probably the most popular approach in recent scholarship has been to suppose that Matthew has synthesized divergent traditions about the Christian mission, one reflecting a Jewish Christian restriction of the Gospel to Jews, the other emphasizing the universal mission to all nations, both ascribing to Jesus the view of mission taken by opposing groups in the early church. Both views are held to have been current in the community for which Matthew wrote his Gospel, and Matthew has succeeded in preserving both by placing them in salvation-historical progression: Jesus' own ministry and the mission of his disciples during his ministry Matthew represents as limited to Israel, while only after the resurrection does mission to all the nations become appropriate. Thus Matthew effects a skilful compromise between competing views, enabling his community, with its strongly Jewish Christian roots, to affirm the 'Gentile' mission. There are several decisive objections to this view.

First, it is now at last being seriously questioned whether the evangelists wrote their Gospels for specific Christian communities to which they belonged. I have argued elsewhere that the evidence suggests, to the contrary, that the Gospels were intended from the start to circulate generally among the Christian communities of their time. If this argument has weight, we should see whether particular features of each Gospel can be understood without resort to hypothetical reconstructions of the particular history and character of each evangelist's supposed community.

Second, it has also become reasonably clear in recent scholarship that there is no evidence for a group in the early church which opposed taking the Christian gospel to the nations. Not even the most conservative Jewish Christians are elsewhere represented as saying what Matthew 10:5-6 says, while even those in the Jerusalem church who insisted that converts be circumcised and obey the whole Torah (a crucially different policy from Matthew 10:5-6) were only briefly influential at all. We are left hypothesizing a Jewish Christian group who could plausibly have originated the saying of Jesus in Matthew 10:5-6 solely on the evidence of this text itself.

Third — and this is the approach that James LaGrand develops in detail and at length in this significant book — the idea of a tension between the two missionary commands in Matthew fails to take account of the way the particularity of Israel and the universality of the nations related both in Jewish eschatology and in the general early Christian understanding of the church's mission. Understood in the properly Jewish terms which we may suppose both Jesus and Matthew thought, the particularity of Israel was not in contradiction or even tension with the expectation of the salvation of the nations. Israel was not conceived in narrowly racial terms, but as open to the inclusion of people from all nations within the one people of God. Moreover, Israel's role in God's purpose was to be a light to the nations. In this way, as LaGrand puts it, "Matthew's bias to the nations is to be explained *in terms of his Jewishness*" (p. 169 n. 61). No more than Paul's 'bias to the nations' should it be understood as anti-Jewish or as reflecting the agenda of a 'Gentile' church. Rather, Matthew's universalism is tightly bound to his Jewish particularism. The restriction of Jesus' and his disciples' mission during his ministry to "the lost sheep of the house of Israel" reflects Jesus' own, entirely Jewish conviction that Israel must first become a light to the nations before the mission to the nations could begin: "Jesus' ministry to Israel related to Israel's indispensable role in the mission to the nations. So it is that the most 'particularistic' words and deeds of Jesus are the most promising to the nations" (pp. 205-6). If the restricted mission of Matthew 10:5-6 only makes sense as reflecting the historical circumstances of Jesus' own ministry, why should not the universal mission of 28:19-20 genuinely reflect a commission given by the risen Christ to the eleven in Galilee? It is LaGrand's argument for the authenticity of this commission that enables him to claim that Matthew reflects "the earliest Christian mission to all nations," predating the hellenists of Acts and the Paul of the Pauline letters, predating even the Pentecost event in Acts.

This is no more than a crude indication of the way James LaGrand reads the whole narrative of Matthew's Gospel as designed to set out an Israel-centred view of the universal mission of the church. He combines the view that Matthew's work has a coherent editorial design with argument that at the same time Matthew is faithful to the historical reality of Jesus and his teaching. No doubt many will judge his conclusions to be unacceptably conservative. But this is not reactionary conservatism. It is an argument, as I have suggested above, which relates very well to some current developments in study of the Gospels and earliest Christianity. There are good reasons why we should be questioning the long prevalent supposition that the early church had to break out of its Jewish particularism before it could conceive of a mission to all the nations, along with the view that it was Jewish Christians of diaspora origin (the 'hellenists' and Paul), predisposed to a more open attitude to non-Jews, who pioneered the 'Gentile' mission. One of the merits of LaGrand's work is that he explains Matthew's attitude to Israel and the nations on the basis of Old Testament and Jewish theology, rather than on the basis of a questionable reconstruction of developments in the early church.

Richard Bauckham

1

INTRODUCTION

Writing in 1971 on "The Origins of the Christian Mission", Martin Hengel observed that

> after Harnack's standard work [*The Mission and Expansion of Christianity in the First Three Centuries*], for decades the beginnings of the Christian mission ... ceased to occupy the main attention of scholars. Since Ferdinand Hahn's *Mission in the New Testament*, published in 1963, there has been a new monograph every year.[1]

The pace has continued unabated since 1971. But remarkably, Harnack's work remains a standard point of reference in the field. His profound familiarity with the relevant documentary evidence available in his time and his analytical brilliance give such weight to his judgments that virtually all subsequent scholarship in the field has been influenced both by the formulation of his questions and by his answers. Harnack's integrity as a scholar enabled him to correct himself in subsequent editions of the work first published in 1902; and even when he is wrong, he is instructive.

A. *Harnack and the Continuing Influence of the Tübingen School*

Two of Harnack's specific judgments are immediately pertinent to the present study, which attempts to clarify our understanding of the earliest Christian mission in the light of Matthew's Gospel: Jesus himself "preached only to the Jews",[2] and "the Gentile mission cannot have lain within the horizon of Jesus"[3]

---

[1] Martin Hengel, *Between Jesus and Paul: Studies in the Earliest History of Christianity* (Philadelphia: Fortress, 1983 [1971]), 48.

[2] Adolf von Harnack, *The Mission and Expansion of Christianity in the First Three Centuries* (New York: Harper, 1962 [1908], vol. I), 36.

though "one might even argue that the universal mission was an inevitable issue of the religion and spirit of Jesus."[3] As important as these specific judgments are for our present study, the broader terms of reference which Harnack incorporates into his work are much more important for an understanding of his influence in the field. In a chapter entitled "From Jewish to Gentile Mission", he concludes that "about 140 A.D. the transition of Christianity to the 'Gentiles', with its *emancipation from Judaism*, was complete."[5] Harnack himself consciously broke ranks with 'the Tübingen School' and therefore reference should also be made here to the influence of F.C. Baur and his followers. One of the strongest continuing influences of this school has been its identification of universalism in the early church, and especially "Pauline universalism as against Jewish particularism".[6]

In starkest summary, the Tübingen understanding of early church history can be expressed as a Hegelian triad: Jewish Christianity or "Petrinism" was challenged by Gentile Christianity or "Paulinism" and synthesized in the late second century as "catholicism". The direct influence of this simple formula can be discovered in S.G.F. Brandon's book *The Fall of Jerusalem* and, in modified form, in other studies as diverse as H.J. Schoeps' *Paul: The Theology of the Apostle in the Light of Jewish Religious History* and Walter Schmithals' *Paul and the Gnostics*.[7] F.C. Baur himself was able to recognize complexities in the

---

[3] *Mission and Expansion*, 38 note 1. With reference to Mt 10.23, Harnack characteristically qualifies this judgment with the words, "if the saying is genuine".

[4] *Ibid.*, 37.

[5] *Ibid.*, 70 [emphasis added]. *Um das Jahr 140 war der volle Übergang der christlichen Mission zu der <Heiden> und die Loslösung von dem Judentum perfekt. "Der Übergang von der Juden- zu Heidenmission"*, Mission und Ausbreitung (Leipzig: Hinrichs'she, 1924), 77. D.L. Baker designates Harnack "a neo-Marcion", citing Harnack's suggestion (in *Marcion*) that the Old Testament is now finally dispensable. *Two Testaments: One Bible* (Downers Grove: Inter-Varsity, 1991), 49. *Cf.* Harnack's appraisal of Marcion as Paul's best interpreter in the second century, *History of Dogma*, vol I (New York: Dover, 1961), 29.

[6] Ferdinand Christian Baur, *The Church History of the First Three Centuries*, vol.I (London: Williams and Norgate, 1878 [1853]), 68. Already in 1894 Harnack was able to refer to "the traditional contrasting of Paulinism and Jewish Christianity, in which Paulinism is made equivalent to Gentile Christianity". Harnack rightly criticizes this 'traditional view' for overlooking "the dependence of the Pauline Theology on the Old Testament or on Judaism". *History of Dogma*, vol I, 89.

[7] S.G.F. Brandon, *The Fall of Jerusalem and the Christian Church: A Study of the Effects of the Jewish Overthrow of A.D. 70 on Christianity* (London: SPCK, 1951); H.J. Schoeps, *Paul: The Theology of the Apostle in the Light of Jewish Religious History* (Philadelphia: Westminster, 1961); Walter Schmithals, *Paul and the Gnostics* (Nashville: Abingdon, 1972). *Cf.* Brandon's "Tübingen Vindicated?", *The Hibbert Journal* 49 (1950) 41-47. Re 1949 *Theologie und Geschichte des Judenchristentums*: "Prof. Schoeps freely acknowledges that his work may truly be regarded as a rehabilitation of the views of the Tübingen School." 43.

development of the Christian movement which his followers often rushed past or ignored. For example, after acknowledging that Stephen could be called "the forerunner of the apostle Paul", Baur emphasizes that "it is important ... to notice that this opposition to Judaism to which Stephen was the first to draw public attention seems to have existed in the church of Jerusalem for some time."[8] But Carl von Weizsäcker, writing years later, applied the Tübingen formula flat out:

> there can be no doubt that the marvelous extension of the faith beyond the limits of Judaism —in other words, Gentile Christianity— was due to Saul, soon now to be called Paul, and to no other.[9]

The idea of evolutionary development in religious thought was strong in the nineteenth century, and application of the Hegelian formula to the early church presupposed substantial periods of time for such development. Subsequent scholarship forced the notion of evolutionary process into narrower time frames than those proposed by Baur, but the basic notion of evolutionary development—with or without the triad formula—has continued to shape studies of the earliest mission of the church. Other influences of 'the Tübingen School' continue in the field; perhaps the most important is their radical challenge to the use of New Testament texts as historical documents.[10]

Dix, Munck, and Cullmann

Three studies of the primitive church appeared in the 1950s which have not yet received the careful attention they deserve in studies of the earliest Christian mission to 'all nations': *Jew and Greek* by Gregory Dix; *Paul and the Salvation of Mankind* by Johannes Munck; and *Peter:Disciple - Apostle - Martyr* by Oscar Cullmann. Each study was independent of the others and also clearly independent of the formative influence of "the traditional contrasting of Paulinism and Jewish Christianity".[11] The little book by Dix was published after his death in 1952 from a manuscript which he had hoped to expand. Munck's major work is polemical and even belligerently revisionist. Cullmann's book, like Munck's, is self-consciously revisionist; the influence it has had in the Ecumenical Movement seems to have satisfied the author's primary intentions in undertaking the study. But even today each of these books

---

[8] F.C. Baur, *Church History*, 45.
[9] C. von Weizsäcker, *The Apostolic Age of the Christian Church*, vol I (London: Williams and Norgate, 1894), 93.
[10] Horton Harris, *The Tübingen School* (Oxford: Clarendon, 1975), 256.
[11] Harnack's critical phrase, cited above. *History of Dogma*, vol I, 89.

challenges established patterns of understanding the earliest expansion of Christianity.[12]

One of the striking moves that Dix makes is to shift the semantic range of a number of key words in the discussion of the earliest Christian mission. His reference to Christ Jesus throughout the book as "Messiah Jesus"[13] and his designation of the faith of the primitive church as "Syriac Christianity" may have reduced the impact of his work on professional New Testament scholars. Nevertheless, this appearance of eccentricity represents a real gain in the field because the move insulates his discussion from many accumulated distortions.

Dix divides the "apostolic generation" into three decades: AD 30-40, AD 40-50, and AD 50-60. Of the first he notes that "for all its obscurity to us, this is the vital period of Christian history."[14] He emphasizes "the primacy of the personal factor of Jesus"[15] in the "hurricane process of Christian expansion across the alien Greek world in a single generation".[16] Most important for the present study are Dix's arguments regarding the "Jewish Christian mission to the Dispersion" and the resulting "ferment in Judaism".[17] According to Dix,

> It was the Jewish-Christian missions to the Jews of the Dispersion which first faced the question, not of accepting but of *seeking* Gentile converts. This step had been taken at Antioch ... somewhere between *c*.A.D. 40 and 44.[18]

Johannes Munck, like Harnack and Dix, writes with a profound knowledge of the ancient documentary sources. Unlike Dix, Munck has gained wide attention for his work so that his views are well-known in the field even by those scholars who reject them. In a characteristically polemical challenge to the continuing influence of 'the Tübingen School', Munck asserts a very different formulation from theirs:

---

[12] Gregory Dix, *Jew and Greek: A Study in the Primitive Church* (New York: Harper, 1953); Johannes Munck, *Paul and the Salvation of Mankind* (Richmond: John Knox, 1959 [1954]); Oscar Cullmann, *Peter: Disciple-Apostle-Martyr, A Historical and Theological Study* (Cleveland: World, 1958 [1952]).
Jesus' Promise to the Nations by Joachim Jeremias (ET 1967) also first appeared in the 1950s. This study, cited frequently below, significantly reformulates Harnack's judgments about Jesus' anticipation of a mission to all nations.

[13] Markus Barth sometimes makes this same move in his Anchor Bible translation of *Ephesians* (Garden City: Doubleday, 1974). The translation of χριστός as "Messiah" appears in the NEB Matthew and, with notable frequency, in the New RSV Gospels and Acts.

[14] Gregory Dix, *Jew and Greek*, 27.
[15] *Ibid.*, 5.
[16] *Ibid.*, 4.
[17] *Ibid.*, 30.
[18] *Ibid.*, 33.

> The primitive Church and Paul were universalistic as Jesus was, because they knew that the Gospel was for the Gentiles as well as Jews, whereas the later Catholic Church lost that universalism. It no longer divided the human race into Israel and the Gentiles, but turned its message to the Gentiles.[19]

By citing Bengt Sundkler's 1936 article "Jésus et les païens" with approval,[20] Munck reintroduces that study of Jesus' particularist mission into current discussions and clarifies his own use of the term 'universalism'.

Oscar Cullmann works from many well-know New Testament texts to establish a convincing picture of Peter as an 'apostle to the nations'. The parallels between Peter and Paul which he points out are striking, especially over against the modern programmatic contrast between Petrine and Pauline impulses in the earliest Christian community and mission. Peter's native village was Bethsaida, and "Hellenistic influence is attested precisely for this region."[21] It was "customary in the Dispersion" to give children two names so, like Paul (Saul) of Tarsus, "Peter had been given from the outset both the Hebrew name Symeon and the Greek name Simon of similar sound."[22]

According to Cullmann's reconstruction (based mainly on information in Acts), Peter assumed a unique position of leadership in Jerusalem, including responsibility for "the missionary field in Samaria" which Cullmann understands to be "the original field of the Christian mission".[23] While still in Jerusalem, "Peter takes the first position as a missionary to Gentiles [in addition to τὸ ἔθνος τῆς Σαμαρείας Acts 8.9] and explicitly justifies this mission" (Acts 10 - 11.18).[24] After handing over leadership of the Jerusalem church to James the Lord's brother, "Peter actually undertook extensive mission journeys" so that "he, just like Paul and Barnabas, interrupted his missionary travels to go to Jerusalem for the so-called Apostolic Council" (I Cor 9.5).[25]

A practical complication in carrying out the decree, according to Cullmann, was that "all of the local churches probably were already of mixed membership at the time of their origin,"[26] but the Council separated the areas of "two missionary organizations",[27] the one from Antioch and the other from Jerusalem. In Acts 15,

---

[19] J. Munck, *Paul and the Salvation of Mankind*, 255.
[20] *Ibid.*, 270.
[21] O. Cullmann, *Peter: Disciple-Apostle-Martyr*, 17.
[22] *Ibid.* See II Peter 1.1 (ℵ, A, 1739 *et al.*) for "Symeon" reference.
[23] *Ibid.*, 36. (Acts 8.4-25.)
[24] *Ibid.*
[25] *Ibid.*, 42.
[26] *Ibid.*, 44.
[27] *Ibid.*

Peter speaks simply as the representative of the mission dependent on Jerusalem. ... He can claim, in spite of the presence of Paul and Barnabas, that he has been elected to preach the gospel to the Gentiles ... within the Jewish Christian mission.[28]

B. Key Terms in Current Discussions

Terms used in biblical scholarship sometimes obscure rather than clarify historical understanding because the terms' semantic ranges widen and contract in response to newly discovered data, academic fashions, and ordinary language developments. 'Sectarian Judaism', 'Jewish proselytism', and 'Jewish Christianity' are three terms in current use which can serve as examples of the challenge which established terminology presents to the investigation of the earliest Christian mission.

Sometimes it is possible to cut through problems of terminology by forming clear definitions of established terms at the beginning of a study or by positing new terms, clearly defined.[29] But because historical scholarship is cumulative, such a move only rearranges the difficulties of analysis and communication. In the present study it seems best, accordingly, to follow established usage as much as possible and to assert control of problematic terms through linguistic (or conceptual) analysis.

1. 'Sectarian Judaism'

The discovery of the Dead Sea Scrolls has had a dramatic effect on biblical studies in the twentieth century. The Qumran Library has provided access to long-lost data which is of prime importance for exegesis of New Testament texts as well as texts in the Hebrew Bible. Moreover, our vivid new awareness of the community at Qumran has placed established views of 'sectarian Judaism'

---

[28] O. Cullmann, *Peter: Disciple-Apostle-Martyr*, 49-50.

[29] "I don't know what you mean by 'glory'," Alice said.
Humpty Dumpty smiled contemptuously, "Of course you don't —till I tell you. I meant 'there's a nice knock-down argument for you!'"
"But 'glory' doesn't mean 'a nice knock-down argument'," Alice objected.
"When I use a word," Humpty Dumpty said, in rather a scornful tone, "it means just what I choose it to mean — neither more nor less."
"The question is," said Alice, "whether you can make words mean so many different things."
"The question is," said Humpty Dumpty, "which is to be master —that is all."
Through the Looking Glass. The Complete Works of Lewis Carroll (New York: Random House, no date [1896]), 214.
Alice's protest has been sustained by the 'ordinary language' philosophers whom we cite below in our analysis of 'Israel' and 'the nations'. Those who follow Humpty Dumpty unwittingly (or in a conscious effort to be master in the field) frame questions in such a way that they become difficult or impossible to answer with ordinary language. Questions involving the special word "Gentile" or the special usage of the German word <Heiden> are noteworthy examples.

in a completely new perspective. This perspective also affects current attempts to locate and understand the earliest Christian mission.

Readers of the New Testament and Josephus have always been aware of various parties and sects existing in Palestine and the Diaspora at the time of Jesus' ministry in Galilee and Judea. But the discovery of the Scrolls has aroused new interest in Essenes and Zealots, Pharisees and Sadducees, *'am ha'aretz* and Samaritans, Galileans and Judeans, as well as 'Hebrews' and 'Hellenists' (Acts 6.1) and other more or less well-documented groups. This new interest has exposed as simplistic and anachronistic earlier notions of 'mainstream Judaism' and 'normative Judaism'.[30] New Testament studies are now more firmly based even if the foundations are more difficult to describe with confidence. It is within this variety of competing and sometimes overlapping theological views and corporate allegiances that the formation of the earliest Christian mission to all nations is to be discovered. The term 'sectarian Judaism' serves as a tag for this broad and 'open-textured' concept,[31] but two important strictures on the term itself should be noted.

First, although the Essenes obviously were organized in opposition to the establishment with their own self understanding and so can reasonably be called a sect, the *'am ha'aretz* just as obviously do not qualify for the term in this sense.[32] Other terms such as 'parties' or 'denominations', 'nationalisms' or 'pieties' have also been used to describe the various political movements and ideological groupings in Palestine and the Diaspora in the first century AD. But besides carrying anachronistic modern connotations, these terms, no less than 'sectarian Judaism', imply lines more sharply drawn than can be defended on the basis of our knowledge of the socio-political-theological field.

A second stricture is more fundamental: the term 'Judaism' itself is of doubtful usefulness as part of an umbrella concept, not only because of its modern identification with Rabbinism or 'normative Judaism' but especially

---

[30] The idea of 'normative Judaism' informs George Foot Moore's classic study, *Judaism in the First Centuries of the Christian Era: The Age of the Tannaim* (Cambridge, U.S.A.: Harvard, 1958 [1927-1930]). See "Preface" to vol III, vi. For a critique see J. Neusner's "Judaism after Moore: A Programmatic Statement", *JJS* 31/2 (1980).

[31] The term 'open-textured concept' is borrowed from Friedrich Waismann's essay "Verifiability", *Logic and Language*, ed. Anthony Flew (Garden City: Doubleday, 1965 [1951]), 125. See note 66 below on 'systematic ambiguity'.

[32] Ernst Troeltsch, writing in 1911, distinguished between 'church' and 'sect' as two types of religious organizations in early modern Europe, each with its own set of values. The 'church' accepts the state, the 'sect' does not. H.R. Niebuhr applied a similar typology to American history, using the categories of 'sect' and 'denomination'. Troeltsch and Niebuhr cited by P.R. Vander Meer, "Religion, Society, and Politics: A Classification of American Religious Groups", *Social Science History* 5/1 (1981), 4. If Niebuhr's formula is applied to first-century Palestine, the Sadducees and Pharisees seem to qualify as 'denominations'; the Essenes as a 'sect'. But the *'am ha'aretz* were not even a religious organization.

because the ancient variants of this word explicitly excluded Samaritans,[33] and later also Christians.[34] Refinements of the term, such as the distinction between 'early Judaism' and 'late Judaism'[35] can actually intensify the problem of anachronistic associations. Since all of the groups and movements which concern us identified themselves with the term 'Israel' and with the God of Abraham, Isaac, and Jacob, 'sectarian Israelitism' or 'Yahwism'[36] would be more logical labels than 'sectarian Judaism'. But such usage is rare among biblical scholars and ancient historians, and the concept identified by the usual term 'Judaism' is so important that the term cannot be avoided.

A grasp of Samuel Sandmel's summary statement of the historical outcome of first century 'Judaism' is perhaps the best single control of the term's use in historical reference: "There were many versions of Judaism, of which ultimately only Rabbinism and Christianity have survived to our day."[37]

---

[33] The clearest illustration of this point is provided by the cross-examination recorded in Josephus' *Antiquities* xi. 344-47: "And, when they said that they were Hebrews but were called the Sidonians of Shechem, he again asked them whether they were Jews (εἰ τυγχάνουσιν Ἰουδαῖοι). Then ... they said that they were not ... ."
R.J. Coggins acknowledges the weight of modern scholarly usage by his remarkable decision to use "Judaism" as a generic term covering the beliefs and practices of both Jews and Samaritans. *Samaritans and Jews* (Oxford: Basil Blackwell, 1975), 8.

[34] Ignatius, *Magnesians* 10.3 (K. Lake, trans.): "It is monstrous to talk of Jesus Christ and to practise Judaism." This epistle (*ca.* AD 108) is the "earliest document where Christianity and Judaism appear side by side, as two distinct and separate religions". Philippe Menoud, "The Early Church and Judaism", *Jesus Christ and the Faith* (Pittsburgh: Pickwick, 1978 [1951]), 436.

[35] See Charlotte Klein on "'Late Judaism' and 'Jewish Religious community'" in *Anti-Judaism in Christian Theology* (Philadelphia: Fortress, 1978), 15-38. Klein's observations are sobering, but when 'late Judaism' is simply relabeled 'early Judaism' —as is now customary— the moral and theological problems remain.

[36] Some scholars of earlier generations were able to sustain the use of such terms as "Israelitism" throughout a work, *e.g.* C.H.Toy, *Quotation in the New Testament*. New York: Scribner's, 1884. Now such usage is typically confined to sections bracketed, as it were, by self-conscious definition within works which employ the term "Judaism" broadly elsewhere; *e.g.* J. Neusner (extending the boundaries of acknowledged Jewish sources to take account also of *LAB, II Baruch*, and *IV Ezra*) "three other important writings which indisputably derive from Israelite hands and also inform us about Israelite thinking ...." "'Judaism' after Moore", *JJS* 31/2, 146. Experimenting with the category "biblical Yahwehism" J.A. Sanders asks, "How and when was ancient Near Eastern wisdom Israelitized and Yahwized, so to speak?" *Torah and Canon* (Philadelphia: Fortress, 1972), xviii.

[37] S. Sandmel, *Philo's Place in Judaism* (New York: Hebrew Union, 1956), 211. Others have also made this point, and Sandmel may not have been the first with this formulation.

Introduction 9

2. 'Jewish Proselytism'

The nature and extent of 'Jewish proselytism' in pre-Christian and early-Christian times has long been a matter of dispute among scholars, and contradictory assessments of this movement continue to appear in current studies.[38] At the turn of the century Harnack built on the data and arguments brought forward by Emil Schürer and concluded that "the propaganda of Judaism was extremely successful in the provinces."[39] Harnack went on to suggest that "missionary enthusiasm was inherited by Christianity from Judaism."[40] Joachim Jeremias' study *Jesus' Promise to the Nations* also begins with the assertion that "at the time of Jesus' appearance an unparalleled period of missionary activity was in progress in Israel."[41] But Johannes Munck is emphatic in his insistence that "Judaism ... had no interest in any mission to the Gentiles"[42] and he denies any "theoretical basis for supposing that Judaism had more interest in proselytizing just then [50 BC-AD 50] than before and since".[43] Kirsopp Lake's earlier statement was more narrowly defined, but no less emphatic in its claim that "there is no evidence at all that missionaries were sent out in the modern or Christian sense."[44] Arthur Darby Nock in a number of his studies also made a point of noting his view that in Judaism "missionary effort was rare (proselytes were people who had 'come in')."[45]

No one denies the existence of a proselyte movement antedating the earliest Christian mission. The question at issue, in broad terms, is whether there was any *mission* from within Judaism or whether, as A.D. Nock and others insist, the impetus for the movement came almost entirely from outside Judaism.[46] There have been some attempts to bring newly discovered data to

---

[38] F.M. Derwacter juxtaposed strikingly contradictory statements from Gibbon on the one side of the page and from G.F.Moore and J.Juster on the other following the title page of his own work, *Preparing the Way for Paul: The Proselyte Movement in Later Judaism* (New York: Macmillan, 1930). After two notable contributions to the discussion in 1939 and 1940 from Rabbinic materials by Bernard Bamberger and William Braude (see n 55 below), Bamberger was able to write in the introduction to the 1968 edition of his study that "there is not much new to report on the study of proselytizing during the Talmudic period" (xix).

[39] Harnack, *Mission and Expansion*, 8.

[40] *Ibid*. My translation from 1906 edn., 8: <*denn das Christentum hat seinen Missionseifer mindestens zum Teil von den Judentum geerbt*>.

[41] J. Jeremias, *Jesus' Promise to the Nations*, 11.

[42] J. Munck, *Paul and the Salvation of Mankind*, 255.

[43] *Ibid.*, 270.

[44] K. Lake, "Proselytes and God-Fearers", *The Beginnings of Christianity*, Part I, vol V (Grand Rapids: Baker, 1966 [1932]), 74.

[45] Arthur Darby Nock, *Early Gentile Christianity and Its Hellenistic Background* (New York: Harper, 1964), x.

[46] Whether or not Nock's literal interpretation of the Greek word is relevant to first-century Judaism, the etymology is not decisive in ordinary English usage. At least since the eighteenth century it has been possible to speak of "zeal for proselytism that ... plainly stopped not at toleration and equality", and to refer to "proselytizing bigotry". (*OED*,

bear on the subject,[47] but the dispute remains largely a matter of different judgments based on the same body of evidence.

The phenomenon of Jewish proselytism was certainly important in setting the stage for the earliest Christian mission, but the answer to the question in scholarly dispute —whether or not Jews *sought* converts from the nations— is scarcely less important for attempts to locate and describe the earliest Christian mission. If a solution to the problem is to be found, two other questions which are often neglected must be faced at the outset: the first relates to space (ideological as well as geographic), the second to time. In other words, the question 'Was there a missionary impulse from within Israel?' should not be pressed towards a generalization, but should be answered in precise terms of *where* and *when* such an impulse might have asserted itself.

Writing on the "Background to the Ministry of Jesus" in relation to the dispersion which followed the Babylonian exile, T. W. Manson observes that

> in the centuries immediately before and after the beginning of the Christian era, Judaism was pulled in two opposite directions. ... One way meant taking the religion of Israel to the Gentiles, with all the risks of contamination and assimilation to their ideas and standards. The other meant separation from all the defilements of the pagan environment, with all the perils that go with spiritual isolationism.[48]

This pull in opposite directions is obvious in the documentary sources (including the Hebrew Bible itself) and can be expected to have produced sharply different and even violently opposed responses from individuals and groups. On the one hand, it is certainly true and, indeed, an understatement to say that "for wide circles of later Judaism there was no missionary inclination."[49] On the other hand, Martin Hengel's awkward reference to "a partially very active mission"[50]

---

vol VIII, 1490). In fact, the careful distinction between 'proselytism' and 'mission' in the discussions above appear to reverse ordinary language usage where a "mission" is usually noble, and even "missionaries" are respectable, whereas "proselytizing" is used in a derogatory way and "proselytizers" are almost always persons who, in one way or another, go beyond the bounds of decency in compelling others to 'come over' to their side. No doubt this secular development has been influenced by anti-semitism in Anglo Saxon countries, but it is nevertheless a fact which must be reckoned with.

[47] See, for example, Isaac Rabinowitz "A Reconsideration of Damascus and '390 Years' in the 'Damascus'(Zadokite) Fragment", *JBL* 73 (1954) 11-35, and J. Murphy O'Connor, "An Essene Missionary Document?" *Revue Biblique* 77 (1970) 201-229.

[48] T.W. Manson, *The Bible Today* (New York: Harper, 1955), 75.

[49] F. Hahn, *Mission in the NT*, 21. Marcel Simon argues that widespread proselytizing activity continued beyond AD 135, but says that "it was very perceptibly impaired toward the end of the fourth century." *Verus Israel: A study of the relations between Christians and Jews in the Roman Empire (135-425)*(Oxford: U. Press, 1986 [1948]), 301.

[50] M. Hengel, *Judaism and Hellenism: Studies in Their Encounter in Palestine During the Early Hellenistic Period* (Philadelphia: Fortress, 1974 [1968]), vol I, 313.

Introduction

may be accurate, and evasive only with reference to the falsely generalized academic question.

The question as to *when* the missionary impulse found expression in Jewish proselytism is at least as important to remember in the examination of evidence as the question *where*. Jeremias gives little explanation for his assertion that "this development reached its climax in the lifetime of Jesus and the apostles" and then declined,[51] but this pattern does seem to be supported by the available evidence and not simply by a theological presupposition regarding 'the fullness of time' (Galatians 4.4). Marvin Pope outlines this pattern convincingly in his article on "Proselytes",[52] and Salo Baron graphically describes the last stage as "Closing the Ranks".[53]

F.M. Derwacter's careful and imaginative study, *Preparing the Way for Paul: the Proselyte Movement in Later Judaism*, can still be read with profit. But although he comes to a reasonable conclusion, with an explanation of the "Reaction and Decline of Proselytism",[54] he cites rabbinic documents throughout the study as reliable records of pre-Christian times. William Braude's *Jewish Proselytizing in the First Five Centuries of the Common Era* and Bernard Bamberger's *Proselytism in the Talmudic Period*, both written soon after Derwacter's work, provide valuable catalogues of rabbinic material relating to proselytism.[55] These two writers share the thesis that the rabbis affirmed proselytes and proselytism. This thesis has its own importance and can shed some light on pre-Christian proselytism, but both works are less immediately relevant to an understanding of the earliest Christian mission than is commonly supposed.[56]

3. 'Jewish-Christianity'

Some of the most impressive contributions of recent biblical studies to an understanding of the first Christian century have been advances made in the

---

[51] J. Jeremias, *Jesus' Promise to the Nations*, 11.

[52] M. Pope, "Proselytes", *IDB*, vol 3 (Nashville: Abingdon, 1961), 921-31.

[53] S. Baron, *A Social and Religious History of the Jews*, vol II (New York: Columbia University Press, 1952 [1937]), 131-41. *Cf.* David Rokeah's observation: "At the end of the first century C.E. and the beginning of the second ... there was no readiness on the part of the sages to relax any regulations in order to promote proselytism, and certainly no such readiness afterwards. The silence of the pagan sources for the period after 150 C.E. is telling." *Jews, Pagans and Christians in Conflict* (Jerusalem/Leiden: Magnes/ E.J.Brill, 1982), 43. *Contra* M. Simon cited above, n49.

[54] F.Derwacter, *Preparing the Way for Paul*, 138-152.

[55] W. Braude, *Jewish Proselytizing in the First Five Centuries of the Common Era* (Providence: Brown University Press, 1940); B. Bamberger, *Proselytism in the Talmudic Period* (New York: Ktav, 1968 [1939]), *passim*.

[56] The Mishnah certainly contains very old material, but the date of the written composition (*ca.* AD 200) must be taken seriously. Controversial ideas and institutions underwent radical change during the middle decades of the first century AD.

understanding and appreciation of 'Jewish Christianity'. Nevertheless, the term itself is so extraordinarily troublesome that attempts to define the notion sometimes compound the confusion associated with it. As already indicated above, with reference to 'sectarian Judaism', the term 'Jewish' alone envelopes bewildering complexities in the first century. It is not surprising that the compound term 'Jewish Christianity' becomes almost unmanageable with all its accretions up to the present time of associations which are anachronistic to the earliest Christian mission.[57] The vagaries of critical usage of the compound term do not necessarily reflect the phenomenon itself. But it is important to realize that "Jewish Christianity was a polymorphic entity."[58]

The use of *two* terms, 'Jewish Christianity' and 'Judeo-Christianity', recommended by Robert Murray is worth noting. The proposed distinction between sociological and theological phenomena, which Danielou's translator accepted as a correction, is debatable. But this distinction has refocused current discussions.[59] Moreover, the debate reminds us that the term 'Jewish Christianity' —whatever it might represent in the first century— has been a technical term for a specific area of study at least since the time of F.C. Baur.[60]

Strict attention to the dates of documents used as sources of information relevant to the earliest Christian mission is as important with respect to 'Jewish Christianity' as with respect to 'Jewish proselytism'. Whether or not F.J.A. Hort and R. Seeberg are correct in the use each made in the cut-off point of

---

[57] "Perhaps the basic difficulty with the label is that both Judaism and Christianity have led chameleon existences throughout the course of history. The changing perspectives of Judaism and/or Christianity as they appear throughout the centuries along with the changing perspectives of the observers ... provide the modern scholar with variables that cause the term 'Jewish Christianity' to reconfigurate itself much like the image of a kaleidoscope." B. Malina, "Jewish Christianity or Christian Judaism: Toward a Hypothetical Definition", *Journal of the Study of Judaism in the Persian, Hellenistic and Roman Period* 7/1 (1976), 46.

[58] G. Strecker, "On the Problem of Jewish Christianity", [1964] Appendix 1, W. Bauer, *Orthodoxy and Heresy in Earliest Christianity* (London: SCM, 1972), 285. Strecker himself often presses this 'polymorphic entity' into shapes determined by academic theories.

[59] Acknowledging a debt to Gregory Dix's 'Syriac Christianity', Jean Danielou suggests "three possible references" for the term 'Jewish Christianity'. The third, representing his own main interest, is "Christian thought expressing itself in forms borrowed from Judaism". *The Theology of Jewish Christianity*, trans. J.A. Baker (London: Darton, Longman & Todd, 1964 [1958]) 7-10. Murray recommends "'Jewish Christianity' for the sociological phenomenon of Jews who were Christian and 'Judaeo-Christianity' for Danielou's 'ideological' sense". *The Heythrop Journal* 15 (1974). 303.

[60] In a review article, Ernst Bammel blames Danielou for introducing "the watering down of the accepted style" of reference to <*Judenchristentum*>. *JTS* 28/1 (1977) 114. The best single article defining the term "Jewish Christianity" in relationship to its past use and present usefulness is A.F.J. Klijn's "The Study of Jewish Christianity", *NTS* 20 (1974) 419-431.

AD 135 for their reconstructions of 'Jewish Christianity',[61] it is clear that *only developments before Bar Kokhba's revolt have immediate bearing on the present study.* Once the classic second- and third-century documents for the study of 'Jewish Christianity' are put out of bounds, the New Testament texts themselves, along with other sources of the period, suggest the possibility that from the very beginning something like D. Georgi's "missionary Hellenistic Jewish Christianity"[62] was in force in the church. The 'particularist Jewish Christianity', for which we have later evidence, seems to have been in large measure a reactionary development.

As Malina points out, "all Christianity is Jewish in some way (although not all Judaism is Christian in some way) ..."[63] and Helmut Koester notes laconically that "everyone in the first generation of Christianity was a Jewish Christian."[64] This obvious point is frequently made in current discussion, but its implications are still being worked out. Jesus was a Jew, and Paul was a Christian Jew (or Jewish Christian) as were Peter and Matthew.[65]

Besides the vagueness and ambiguity involved in the terms of modern scholarship, there is ambiguity in the key words and concepts of the sources themselves. Much of the challenge involved in understanding 'sectarian Judaism', 'Jewish proselytism', and 'Jewish Christianity' is the basic necessity of trying to identify and understand the concepts 'Israel' and 'the nations'. Etymological studies and translations from one language to another provide clues to understanding such basic concepts. But as the many scholarly studies

---

[61] References to Hort and Seeberg in Klijn's "The Study of Jewish Christianity", *NTS* 20 (1974), 422.

[62] Dieter Georgi begins his reconstruction with an imaginative description of "The Jewish mission".*The Opponents of Paul in Second Corinthians* (Philadelphia: Fortress, 1986 [1964]), 83-150. Georgi's work has had the power to force open established definitions of earliest Jewish Christianity. For a persuasive use of the category 'Hellenistic Jewish Christianity' see Ferdinand Hahn's *Mission in the NT*; n.b. 59ff and criticism of J. Munck on 82 n1.

[63] B.J. Malina, "Jewish Christianity or Christian Judaism", *JSJ* 7/1 [1976] 46.

[64] H. Koester, "Gnomai Diaphoroi" [1965], *Trajectories Through Early Christianity* (Philadelphia: Fortress, 1971), 115.

[65] Already in the first decades after Pentecost, Paul and other Jewish Christians were developing what has come to be called 'Gentile Christianity'. The NT also indicates that there were 'Jewish Christians' who opposed this development (Acts 21.20-23). But from the very beginning (before Paul's turn-about) it seems likely that some of the leaders of this opposition were themselves 'gentiles'! —if proselyte Christians can be termed 'gentiles'. Certainly by the turn of the century 'Judaisers' cannot be assumed to have been born Jews.

of the term 'Israel' suggest, there remains a systematic ambiguity[66] which can be understood only through a wide-ranging study of *uses* of the term.

C. Aim of the Present Study

The aim of the present study is to clarify the identity and vocation of the Messianic mission to the nations in the light of Matthew's Gospel, with particular attention to the earliest stage, the three decades immediately following Jesus' death and resurrection (*ca.* AD 33 - 63).

Literature in circulation during this period must be considered, along with records actually written during the time between the crucifixion of Jesus and the destruction of Jerusalem. A great deal of interesting later literature is eliminated from consideration as source material when these criteria are applied strictly. Nevertheless, a vast amount of relevant written material remains, of which only a selection of a sample can be examined carefully here. By far the most important literature current in Jesus' time and Matthew's was the Hebrew Bible itself.

In the first part of the study, we will evaluate the terms which control our own inquiry and consider some of the *uses in fellowship and witness* of the terms and concepts 'Israel' and 'the nations' which would have been available to the followers of Jesus.

In the main section of the study, Matthew's Gospel will be examined in the context of Israel's literature, as a document written later than Paul's letters but before AD 70. Matthew's story of Jesus' words and deeds intentionally defines Jesus as the promised Messiah of Israel. Through death and resurrection, Israel's Messiah empowers the Apostolic community to be God's agent for the salvation of mankind. According to Matthew's Gospel (as in 'Paul's Gospel' Rm 16.25) *the mission to all nations is constitutive of 'the Messianic mystery'*. This mission is the definitive sign of the coming Kingdom. All who are called to be disciples of Jesus are now commissioned by the resurrected Lord to be apostles to the nations.

---

[66] Friedrich Waismann begins his essay on "Language Strata" with a consideration of "Types of Ambiguity", including the antithetical sense of primal words. "In Latin *altus* means high and deep, *sacer* both sacred and accursed." This type of ambiguity is relevant to the use of the term 'the nations' (τὰ ἔθνη) in the First Gospel and for the interpretation of Saul/Paul's response to 'the nations'. The term 'systematic ambiguity' can be used to indicate the systematic or systemic way in which the earliest Christian community retained ambiguities which were constitutive of the meaning of the terms with reference to 'Israel' and 'the nations'. *Logic and Language* (New York: Doubleday, 1965 [1946]), 227 and 234.

Part One

Israel and the Nations

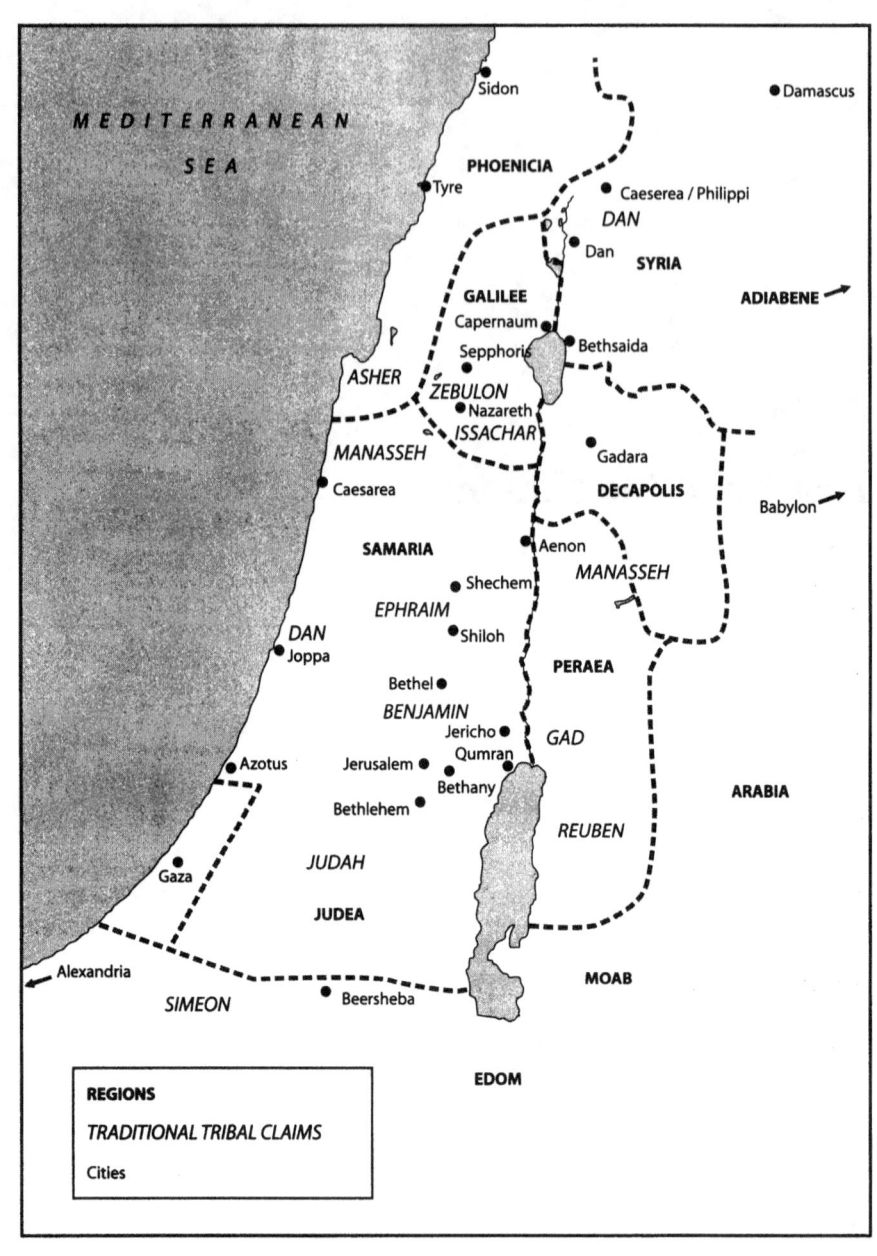

The Land of Israel *ca.* AD 30

2

MODERN TERMS AND CONCEPTS:
PROBLEMS AND CHALLENGE

Answers to questions about the earliest Christian mission are shaped very largely by the questions themselves. This is the case not only because presuppositions accompany the questions about 'sectarian Judaism', 'Jewish proselytism', and 'Jewish Christianity', but also because the questions themselves are defined by the fundamental concepts 'Israel' and 'the nations'. It might be said fairly that these two concepts are the basis for analysis in the field and so defy analysis, like the lines and points in geometry.[1] As in geometry, some axioms should be stated at the outset.

The first axiom is obvious, but often disregarded: any modern investigation of the earliest Christian mission depends upon modern concepts and the use of ordinary language (such as vernacular English, French, German, or modern Hebrew).

A second axiom is that the concepts 'Israel' and 'the nations' were defined in principle for the earliest Christians by the usage in the Hebrew Bible, which itself encompassed development and change in the concepts. The Hebrew terms were redefined by translation into Aramaic and Greek —in the targums, the Septuagint including the Apocrypha, and extra-biblical writings —and by application to new situations. These translations and situations were already old at the time of the emergence of the earliest Christian mission.

---

[1] The title of Stephen G. Wilson's study, *The Gentiles and the Gentile Mission in Luke-Acts* (Cambridge: University Press, 1973) implies established assumptions about 'Jews and Gentiles', as does the title of David Bosch's earlier study, *Die Heidenmission in der Zukunftschau Jesus* (Zürich: Zwingli, 1959).
Heinrich Kasting's book, *Die Anfänge der urchristlichen Mission*, does not declare familiar assumptions about 'Jews and Gentiles' in the title, but these assumptions define <*die Auseinandersetzung um die Heidenmission*>. In Kasting's view, moreover, <*Der universale Missionsbefel haftet nicht an den Osterereignissen (Mt 28,19; Apg 1,8), sondern gehört in ein späteres Studium urchristlicher Traditionsbildung hinein.*> (München: Chr Kaiser, 1969), 109.

A third axiom is that the Christian mission itself, as an intellectual event and social movement, radically affected the understanding of the terms 'Israel' and 'the nations'. This effect can be expected to be sharpest —but not necessarily the same— for those engaged in the movement and those actively opposing it.

A corollary of the third axiom is that the relevant word-usage in Semitic languages (as well as in Greek and Latin) might be quite different in AD 90 from usage in AD 40. Nevertheless, the possibility that some documents dated even later than AD 200 might reflect usage contemporary with the earliest Christian mission should not be ruled out of consideration. The importance of the Mishnah is so obvious that it is routinely used as a source for understanding the Jewish background of the New Testament.[2] The Mishnah certainly preserves ancient Semitic concepts and word usage. But the fact that the oldest New Testament texts antedate the written text of the Mishnah by 150 years must not be forgotten.

Now and Then

The procedure of studying biblical texts with a first aim of determining "What did it mean?" and then determining "What does it mean today?" is useful and sometimes liberating.[3] Nevertheless, this two-fold dictum is itself a dangerous simplification, suggesting that twentieth-century scholars can proceed unfettered by their own language and culture to analysis of ancient texts in their historical context. If the complexity of modern language usage and the persistent problems of conceptual analysis are not faced at the outset, the supposed 'original meanings' of the texts are likely to be defined with an illusory clarity and simplicity. Everyone knows from personal experience how difficult it can be to achieve unanimity or even a consensus of opinion on any

---

[2] The clearest and best-known illustration of this use of the Mishnah and later Rabbinic writings in defining 'the Jewish background of the NT' is the format of Gerhard Kittel's *Theological Dictionary of the New Testament* (Grand Rapids: Eerdmans, 1963-74 [1932-73]). Two other works which have been influential on modern writers' attempts to reconstruct 'the Jewish background of the NT' are Strack and Billerbeck's *Kommentar* and George Foot Moore's *Judaism*.
Str-B. persistently warn readers that their Rabbinic sources are later than the NT documents, e.g., <*R. Ammi (um 300) hat gesagt ...* > (vol I, 191). Nevertheless, the title of their three-volume work seems to encourage users to disregard questions of chronology in reconstructions of 'the Jewish background of the NT'. Hermann L. Strack und Paul Billerbeck, *Kommentar zum Neuen Testament aus Talmud und Midrash* (München: Oscar Beck, 1922-26). The influence of G.F. Moore's three-volume work on 'the Jewish background to the NT' is especially remarkable in view of the fact that Moore specified the primary sources of Judaism from "the second century of the Christian Era" as those which concerned him. He emphasized that he had "not attempted a descriptive account of Judaism in NT times". G.F. Moore, *Judaism in the First Centuries of the Christian Era: The Age of the Tannaim* (Cambridge, U.S.A.: Harvard University Press, 1930), vol III, vii, v, and vii.

[3] Krister Stendahl, "Biblical Theology, Contemporary", *IDB*, vol I (1962), 419. Stendahl's celebrated defence of this two-fold dictum has "achieved just renown", according to James Barr in his like-named article in the 1976 *Supplementary Volume*, 106.

subject today, and how it seems impossible to get even two or three people to agree on certain subjects. Yet historians are tempted to solve problems presented by ancient texts in ways that assume a range of agreement among writers and readers in antiquity such as never occurs today.

In the discussion of 'Israel' and 'the nations' which follows, the aim is to clarify 'the lines' and 'points' which must be used throughout our analysis of the Christian mission in the middle third of the first century AD. We begin with reflection on the problems and challenge of modern terms and concepts.[4] After acknowledging the beam in our own eye, we turn cautiously to the background of the New Testament usage, and the meaning of the terms in the earliest literature which used the terms 'Israel' and 'the nations'. The NT writings themselves provide the core linguistic sample for the present study and will be surveyed briefly, with reference also to other texts (in Hebrew, Aramaic or Syriac, and Greek) which were written immediately before or after the middle decades of the first century AD. Last to be considered in this preliminary survey are the early Rabbinic texts and writings of Syriac Christians.

Strict attention to the dates of written composition would separate these Semitic texts by the Rabbis and Syriac Fathers for consideration in a survey from the second century to the present. But as already suggested, there are methodological reasons for closely examining the possibility that later Semitic usage preserved concepts of 'Israel' and 'the nations' more or less intact from the middle decades of the first century AD.

Four Approaches to the Problems and Challenge

In *The Semantics of Biblical Language*, James Barr criticizes biblical theologians for their neglect of modern linguistic science.[5] But he himself disclaims competence to deal with philosophical developments in semantics and

---

[4] Our procedure reverses the order prescribed by Stendahl's two-fold dictum. Stendahl's brief comments on Bultmann and Cullmann are sound, but he dismisses Karl Barth's 'dialectic' method too quickly with the assertion that "Barth speaks as if it were a very simple thing to establish what Paul actually meant in his own terms." (In the same paragraph, Stendahl himself speaks knowingly of "the true picture of Pauline thought"!)
In relation to Karl Barth's argument (1932), it is certainly true that "historical conditioning is two-sided: the modern interpreter, no less than the text, stands in a given historical context and tradition." Anthony C. Thiselton, *The Two Horizons: New Testament Hermeneutics and Philosophical Description* (Grand Rapids: Eerdmans, 1980.) A simple analogy may serve to illustrate the importance and inescapable priority of our own 'horizon' in the interpretation of ancient texts: For the translation of English to French or Italian to German, it is a publisher's rule is to employ a translator whose first language is the target language. Analogously, the interpreters with the surest grasp of issues in their own time and culture are the most likely guides (after appropriate study) into other times and cultures.

[5] In 1961, James Barr referred to "the prevailing use of procedures which ... constantly mishandle and distort the linguistic evidence of Hebrew and Greek languages as they are used in the Bible". *The Semantics of Biblical Language* (Oxford: University Press, 1961), vii.

conceptual analysis,[6] and this disclaimer suggests a neglect on his part as serious as the theologians' neglect of which he is so sharply critical.

A. Conceptual Analysis

The terms 'philosophy' and 'philosophical' are used very many ways in ordinary language as, for example, when someone speaks of 'a philosophy of history', 'a philosophy of sport', or 'a philosophical response to failure'. But when Friedrich Waismann describes "a typically philosophical question" he uses the term in a way directly relevant to the present study: "For example, from the question whether a judge has decided justly in a particular case—that is to say, has given a judgment in accordance with the law—we can pass to the question whether the laws themselves are just."[7] Such 'philosophical questions' as well as the strictly linguistic questions approved by James Barr should be addressed to the data on 'Israel' and 'the nations', both in the ancient texts and in the studies which have informed our present understanding of the beginning of the Christian mission.[8]

The terms 'sectarian Judaism', 'Jewish proselytism', and 'Jewish Christianity' have already been cited to show the need to question established questions about the earliest Christian mission. Another term intimately related to 'Israel' and 'the nations' provides an even more striking demand for conceptual analysis: 'the Jewish Messiah'.

The difference between Ernst Jenni's perception of this concept, outlined in his article in the *Interpreter's Dictionary of the Bible*,[9] and Ellis Rivkin's perception as presented in the article in the Supplementary Volume[10] certainly is not to be explained in terms of developments in the field of biblical research between 1962 and 1976[11]. Similarly, the difference between discussions of

---

[6] In a footnote, Barr observes that "even the word 'linguistic' is perhaps not too clear, since it is used very much for certain procedures distinctly philosophical. In this book 'linguistic' always refers to the science of linguistics and the material it handles: the phonology, grammar and lexicography of various languages and the semantic value of the various forms observed and classified in these processes." *Semantics*, 2. For Barr's response to D. Hill's criticism of this exclusive definition see *Biblica* 49 (1968), 378.

[7] F. Waismann, *The Principles of Linguistic Philosophy* (London: Macmillan, 1965), 5.

[8] A. C. Thiselton's book, cited above with reference to 'What a text meant' and 'What it means' is a sustained argument for the relevance to biblical studies of "procedures distinctly philosophical", crediting Gadamer for the concept of 'The Two Horizons'.

[9] E. Jenni, "Messiah, Jewish", *IDB* vol 3 (1962), 360-365.

[10] E. Rivkin, "Messiah, Jewish", *IDB* Suppl Vol (1976) 588-591.

[11] Joseph Klausner's 1933 essay, "The Jewish and the Christian Messiah", can take the place of the articles by Jenni and Rivkin in this illustration. Klausner raises issues which are fundamental not only to an understanding of the earliest Christian mission but to any Christian theology. Restricting ourselves here to introductory 'philosophical questions', we might ask whether Klausner's conception of the 'Jewish Messiah' is a better description of Jesus of Nazareth than is his conception of the 'Christian Messiah'. Another question, anticipated by reference to Jesus, is whether the fundamental difference between the concepts 'Jewish Messiah' and 'Christian Messiah' is best explained in terms of what philosophers call 'existential import', that is to say, a difference like that between a unicorn and a lamb.

'Christology' and discussions of 'Messianism' is not well explained by the distinction between the Greek root of the term designating one area of study and the Semitic root of the other. Perhaps the simplest and clearest way to illustrate this deep ambiguity between Jenni's 'Jewish Messiah' and Rivkin's (or between 'Christology' and 'Messianism') is by use of Ludwig Wittgenstein's duck-rabbit.

"... the duck-rabbit. It can be seen as a rabbit's head or as a duck's." 194e[12]

"But what is different: my impression? my point of view? —Can I say? I describe the alteration like a perception, quite as if the object had altered before my eyes." 195e[13] The duck-rabbit illustration of the question of the relationship between two perceptions of the same data in like-named concepts is useful because it discourages answers which suggest that the problem would be solved if we could get back into another age or into another language.

In modern languages and thought, as well as in Hebrew, Aramaic, Greek, and Latin, there are problems in the relationship between words and concepts besides the various kinds of ambiguity. Augustine asks, "What then is time? If no one asks me, I know; but, if I want to explain it to a questioner, I do not know."[14] The philosophical question Augustine raises is not answered by reference to a Latin grammar or lexicon or even by reference to modern linguistic science.[15] 'Time' is an elusive concept. Even so, like Augustine, we

---

(J.Klausner, "Appendix: The Jewish and the Christian Messiah", *The Messianic Idea in Israel From Its Beginning to the Completion of the Mishnah*, New York: Macmillan, 1955.)

[12] Ludwig Wittgenstein, *Philosophical Investigations*, trans. G E.M. Anscombe (Oxford: Blackwell, 1958), 194: <*Die folgende Figur, welche ich aus Jastrow* [Fact and Fable in Psychology] *entnommen habe, wird in meinen Bemerkungen der H-E.-Kopf Heissen. Man kann ihn als Hasenkopf, oder als Entenkopf sehen.* >

[13] L. Wittgenstein, *Philosophical Investigations*, 195: <*Aber was ist anders: mein Eindruck? meine Stellungnahme? —Kann ich's sagen? Ich beschreibe die Änderung, wie eine Wahrnehmung ganz als hatte sich der Gegenstand vor meinen Augen geändert.* >

[14] Augustine, *Confessions*, xi/ 14, V.J. Bourke, trans. *The Fathers of the Church* vol 21 (Washington: Catholic University of America Press, 1953), 343.

[15] Certainly Augustine's question is not answered in James Barr's book *Biblical Words for Time* (London: SCM, 1962), even though this passage is quoted at the beginning of Barr's presentation and stands in Latin facing Barr's first "Introductory" page.
Those who understood Barr's *Semantics of Biblical Language* as an argument against 'word studies' might have been surprised at the title of this book published the next year. Barr himself seems unconscious of the irony and certainly does not seem to have written the book as a theological joke. His concluding chapter explains the book itself as an 'anti-word-study': "this study was embarked on, not with the intention of establishing the biblical view of time .... Our main purpose ... is to examine and criticize certain methods

are confident of the reality and the importance of time, and conscious of our use of the concept 'time' —not least in an analysis and evaluation of the earliest Christian mission.

Augustine's comment, slightly changed, can serve also to illustrate another kind of elusive concept: "What then is race? If no one asks me, I know; but, if I want to explain it to a questioner, I do not know." No one has trouble understanding news reports about race riots in Miami, Florida, or Colombo, Sri Lanka. But whereas 'time' is certainly a term with real meaning —however difficult or impossible analysis of the concept proves to be— it may be that the word 'race' connects with a concept which has no existential import: like the word 'unicorn', or the phrase 'the present King of France'. Certainly one concept of 'race', developed by spurious science during the past two or three hundred years, is worthless with reference to the facts which it is presumed to represent. "Race", Ashley Montagu says, "is the phlogiston of our time."[16] This analogy from the history of science is worth remembering when dealing with the term 'race' in modern studies or in translations of ancient texts.

Wittgenstein characterizes philosophy as "a battle against the bewitchment of our intelligence by means of language".[17] Waismann claims that "it is always language which leads us into the fallacy of misapplied concept and which as a matter of course uses the same words with different meanings."[18] Earlier in the same essay Waismann explains that

> philosophical questions ... disturb us only if we do not see how language functions; if we think we are discussing questions of fact, when we are merely being mislead by peculiarities of linguistic forms. The danger is that there are innumerable ways of

---

which are not uncommon." (*Biblical Words*, 153.)
Barr's acknowledged lack of competence to deal with 'procedures distinctly philosophical' (*Semantics*, 2) is evident in his criticism of Oscar Cullmann. Barr's frustration at being unable to match his refutations to Cullmann's arguments is remarkable. He concludes one argument by saying that "this point is of importance whether or not we regard it as the meaning of Cullmann's sentence at this point." Barr then glosses his sentence with an even more remarkable footnote: "Whether or not this argument is intended or implied by Cullmann at this point, it is one which has in fact been used." Barr concludes the footnote by refuting a different writer, G. Delling. (*Biblical Words*, 49.)

[16] Cited by Michael Banton and Jonathan Harwood, *The Race Concept* (London: David & Charles, 1975), 59. Like 'phlogiston' in the seventeenth century, 'race' continues to function as a powerful interpretive concept. Ashley Montagu, best-known for his part in the series of UNESCO studies on race, is a professor of anthropology at Rutgers University. Montagu's own conclusions on the subject are sharply focused in the title of his major work: *Man's Most Dangerous Myth: The Fallacy of Race* (5th edn. New York: Oxford, 1974). The existence of the *concept* 'race', and of the various concepts and sub-concepts related to the term, cannot be denied. Moreover, the term 'racial prejudice' connects to a modern reality, so that 'racial prejudice' has existential import even if 'race' does not.

[17] Ludwig Wittgenstein, *Philosophical Investigations* (Oxford: Blackwell, 1958), 47: <Die Philosophie ist ein Kampf gegen die Verhexung unsres Verstandes durch die Mittel unserer Sprache.>

[18] Friedrich Waismann, *Principles of Linguistic Philosophy*, 11.

being misled by the analogies, metaphor and similes of language and even if we are constantly on the watch we are constantly being caught in a linguistic snare.[19]

Being 'constantly on the watch' characterizes the method of these 'ordinary language' philosophers. What might appear to be an exaggerated suspicion of ordinary language (explaining also the earlier attempt by some of them to create a special language suitable for solving philosophical problems) is balanced by a deep respect for the power, complexity, and unavoidability of ordinary language for serious attempts to deal with reality.[20]

B. Linguistics

If it is necessary for our study of the earliest Christian mission to ask philosophical questions, it is well also to take warning from G.J. Warnock who observes that

> particularly in philosophy —particularly, that is, when words and expressions or the 'concepts' they represent are being, not actually used, but only thought about— there is a constant temptation to misrepresent actual cases.[21]

In conceptual analysis it is convenient to use a single word, such as 'time' or 'race', to represent a concept. When making use of this short-hand procedure, however, we should bear in mind J.L. Austin's assertion that "the phrase 'the meaning of a word' is, in general, if not always, a dangerous nonsense-phrase."[22] Austin's own philosophical studies are very closely related to linguistic science. What he writes as "a preliminary remark" on the subject "The Meaning of a Word" is worth quoting at length here as a statement of basic linguistic principle:

> Properly speaking, what alone has meaning is a sentence. Of course, we can speak quite properly of, for example, 'looking up the meaning of a word' in a dictionary. Nevertheless, it appears that the sense in which a word or a phrase 'has a meaning' is derivative from the sense in which a sentence 'has a meaning': to say a word or

---

[19] *Ibid.*, 4.

[20] Describing the historical development of this philosophy, R. Caponigri distinguishes "analytical philosophy or ordinary language analysis" from logical positivism and "the goal of constructing 'ideal' languages for the sciences". But he notes that "there is a unity between the two strands." A. R. Caponigri, *Philosophy from the Age of Positivism to the Age of Analysis. A History of Western Philosophy.* vol 5 (Notre Dame: University Press, 1971), 303.

[21] G.J. Warnock, *English Philosophy since 1900* (London: Oxford University Press, 1958), 108. "Our concepts are more complex than our linguistic forms,"(109) which explains the necessity of conceptual analysis.

[22] J.L. Austin, "The Meaning of A Word", *Philosophical Papers* (Oxford: University Press, 1961), 24. The two tables which introduce this essay have "Specimens of Sense" beginning "1.1 What-is-the-meaning-of (the word) 'rat'?" and "Specimens of Nonsense" with the first example "1.1 What-is-the-meaning-of a word?"

a phrase 'has a meaning' is to say that there are sentences in which it occurs which 'have meanings': and to know the meaning, that the word or phrase has, is to know the meanings of sentences in which it occurs. All the dictionary can do when we 'look up the meaning of a word' is to suggest aids to the understanding of sentences in which it occurs. Hence it appears correct to say that what 'has meaning' in the primary sense is the sentence.[23]

Linguists, like philosophers, make mistakes. Moreover, there are various linguistic theories and schools so that general appeals to 'linguists' or to 'modern linguistic science' are no more focused than appeals to 'philosophers' or 'the discipline of philosophy'. In his earlier work, James Barr himself sometimes lapses into such *argumentum ad verecundiam*. But Barr's overarching intention, clearly, is to expose his own work and the work of other interpreters of ancient texts to the various methods and judgments of current linguistic science. Similarly, our references to linguistics here and elsewhere in this book are an acknowledgment of the fundamental importance of 'language analysis' for interpreting ancient texts. Specific references to one or another linguist or linguistic theory should be taken as calls for criticism by linguists as well as acknowledgments of particular debts.

Four ideas developed by linguists which are used throughout the present study are 1/ the analysis of 'units of meaning' in a 'hierarchy of tagmemes', 2/ the distinction between 'synchronic' and 'diachronic' analysis, 3/ the notion of 'semantic field', and 4/ the observation of 'back-formation', not only in the history of language but also in the history of ideas.

Units of Meaning

Acceptance of the sentence as the basic unit-of-meaning implies that 'appeals to the text' normally will involve reference to complete sentences. Consequently, citations of biblical texts in the present study usually involve more than a single-number 'verse'. Obvious implications for textual criticism and translation follow from the view that the *sentence* is the basic unit of meaning. Before noting some of these implications, it may be useful to consider the place of the sentence in what Kenneth Pike calls "a hierarchy of tagmemes".[24]

Language, mapped out in tagmemic terms, includes morphemes, words, phrases, clauses, sentences, paragraphs, chapters, discourses (such as the biblical epistles and gospels), groups of closely related discourses (such as Luke-Acts and Colossians-Ephesians), larger groups of discourses (such as the Pauline

---

[23] *Ibid.*, 24. This simple point is the strongest basis for J. Barr's criticism of 'word studies' in his book which was published the same year (1961): "It is the sentence (and of course the still larger literary complex such as the complete speech or poem) which is the linguistic bearer of the usual theological statement." *Semantics of Biblical Language*, 263.

[24] K.L. Pike, *Language in Relation to a Unified Theory of the Structure of Human Behavior* (The Hague/Paris: Mouton, 1971 [1959], 6.
What follows is a simplified application of Pike's theory, adapted from his 1963 lectures in the Summer Institute of Linguistics (Norman, Oklahoma). *Cf.* W.A. Cook, *Introduction to Tagmemic Analysis* (New York: Holt, Reinhart and Winston, 1969).

corpus), and still larger units such as the New Testament, the Bible, and the whole body of Christian theological writings related in time or in a continuous, developing tradition. To say that the sentence is 'the basic unit of meaning' is not to deny the validity of analysis at other levels.

The notion of a 'hierarchy' of 'tagmemes' (meaning-units in slots, forming larger meaning-units) implies that larger units in the literary complex have a higher claim than the smaller on the interpreter. Indeed, J.P. Louw has argued plausibly that "the paragraph" should be considered "the basic unit of semantic analysis".[25] Moreover, when still larger units are used as the basis of analysis, agreement or disagreement on boundaries can be decisive for the interpretation of sentences within the larger unit. Whether an interpreter accepts a larger or smaller number of 'authentic' Pauline epistles, for example, often determines the range of concepts he or she will draw upon in translating sentences in the Epistles to the Romans and Galatians.

If the sentence is not necessarily the most important unit of meaning in a discourse, it is, in some structural way, the minimum unit of meaning. Analysis below the sentence level involves synthesis of the tagmeme-in-question with other tagmemes supplied by the interpreter to form a provisional sentence. Nevertheless, analysis below the sentence level is important and often necessary for interpretation. At the lower tagmemic levels, as well as at the sentence level and above, the notion of 'hierarchy' is useful. Accordingly, 'phrase studies' and 'clause studies' should outrank 'word studies'.[26]

Returning to the claim that sentence is 'the basic unit of meaning', we note two obvious implications, one for textual criticism and one for translation. First, although textual criticism is usually thought of in terms of the establishment of the *words* of a text, the punctuation supplied by modern editors of critical texts also defines units and grammatical relationships between units. Second, since translation is the most important step in interpretation, the persistent notion of 'literal (or verbal) fidelity' can result in serious distortion of the meaning of ancient texts.

The New Testament citations in the present study almost always carry forward the decisions of the editors of the Bible Societies' *Greek New Testament*. Nevertheless, these implicit endorsements must be considered as judgments open to re-evaluation by the critical reader.[27] After the Greek sentence has been marked off with punctuation, 'the basic unit of theological sense for translation' remains subject to interpretation.

A good illustration of this challenge to the translator is the first sentence following the opening salutation in the Epistle to the Ephesians. The Greek

---

[25] J.P. Louw, *Semantics of New Testament Greek* (Philadelphia: Fortress, 1982), vii.

[26] As already noted with reference to conceptual analysis, individual words sometimes serve as ciphers for concepts. Kenneth Pike refers to such 'meanings of words' as 'hypermeanings' *Language*, 612). It seems probable that false generalizations from this linguistic (psychological) phenomenon account for the seductive attraction of 'word studies'.

[27] In the present study the most striking example of a textual-critical judgment about punctuation which affects interpretation regards Mt 8.7. In Matthew's record of Jesus' words, the Greek sentence should be read as a rhetorical question, "Am I to come and heal him?" (*Contra* the editors of the UBS *Greek New Testament*.)

sentence runs from verse three through verse fourteen in the UBS text. The Wordsworth-White edition of Jerome's Latin translation divides this passage into nine units punctuated by colons. Both the Revised Standard Version and the New English Bible divide the passage into two paragraphs, subdivided into a total of six sentences in the RSV, eight in the NEB. Standard French and German versions translate this one Greek sentence into four paragraphs which include a total of six sentences.[28]

If we assume that the editors are correct in their punctuation of the Greek sentence and that the various translators were following the same grammatical division of the Greek text, it is clear that the translators have identified several units of theological sense within this single Greek sentence. The consensus of the translators seems reasonable, and so it appears that 'the sentence' which is "the linguistic bearer of the usual theological statement" (Barr) is typically a Greek 'clause' in Ephesians.

The analysis of the longer Greek sentence into shorter 'sentences' (as in translation) is itself a basic interpretive move. Theological judgments are often made at these points of division. Since the grammar of the Greek sentence must remain the basic court of appeal 'to the text' in any serious attempt at exegesis, shorter 'sentences' are always provisional. Indeed, sentence divisions established by translators are often valuable indications of earlier opinions and traditions in interpretation.

Emphasis on the Greek sentence (or clause) as the basic unit for translation certainly shifts the focus of attention away from what Joseph Lightfoot called "the principle of faithfulness". This doubtful principle attempts to represent the same New Testament Greek word with the same English word throughout the translation and "as far as possible" in the same word order.[29] What Bishop Lightfoot advocated as a guiding principle for the English Revised Version of 1885 has guided many other Bible translations, ancient and modern. But Frederick Grant correctly points out that even individual New Testament writers such as Paul "did not, as a matter of fact, use [specific terms] always in the same sense".[30]

The sound principle of translating 'sentence for sentence' rather than 'word for word' has been followed boldly by the translators of the New English Bible and in several other modern language translations. But F.F. Bruce points out that what he calls "the law of equivalent effect" in translation is not a modern discovery. John Purvey in his 1395 Prologue states his view "that the

---

[28] *Novum Testamentum Latine*, Secundum Editionem Sancti Hieronymi, eds. J. Wordsworth & H. White (Oxford: University Press, 1920). *Le Nouveau Testament*, Version Synodale, 7e Edition (Paris: Alliance Biblique Française, 1957). *Das Neue Testament*, Revidierter Text (Stuttgart: Privileg. Wurtt. Bibelanstalt, 1956), The revised Zwinglian translation also divides the unit into six sentences, but includes them in a single paragraph (Zürich: 1978 [1955]), as does the New RSV.

[29] Cited by F.C. Grant, *Translating the Bible* (Edinburgh: Nelson, 1961), 138 & 91. This 'principle of faithfulness' is best known from the work of the second-century Jewish proselyte Aquila, whose Greek translation of the Hebrew Bible was in reaction to the earlier (LXX) translation and its Christian interpretations.

[30] *Ibid.*, 152.

best translating out of Latin into English is to translate after the sentence and not only after the words".³¹

Before moving to other linguistic issues, we should note one warning about skillful 'sentence for sentence' translations: an interpreter's skill as a translator sometimes gives subtle and unwarranted force to his or her views and assumptions. Clumsy translations call attention to half-digested bits and pieces from the original language. This can be to the advantage of an independent interpreter, especially with regard to words which represent developed concepts and ideas —words which telescope 'meanings' into what Kenneth Pike calls 'hypermeanings'.³² 'Christ' has already been noted in this connection. Ἰσραήλ and τὰ ἔθνη also raise problems for interpretation today which are more likely to be covered-over than solved by elegant translations.

Synchronic and Diachronic Analysis

The distinction between 'synchronic' and 'diachronic' made by Ferdinand de Saussure in his 1907-1911 lectures *Cours de linguistique général* has been fundamental to the development of modern linguistic science. Saussure's celebrated comparison of language to a chess game illustrates his insistence that adequate synchronic analysis must precede any attempts at diachronic linguistic analysis: "What has gone before is quite irrelevant to the current state of play at any point."³³ For the purposes of our study of the earliest Christian mission, the acceptance of this view of language demands an attempt to understand 'the current state of play' in our own language about the earliest mission. With reference to ancient documents, the acceptance of Saussure's judgment demands strict attention to time frames in analysis of 'the current state of play at any point'. This warning is relevant to the whole continuum of language structure: morphemes, words, phrases, clauses, sentences, and larger units of discourse.

The fact of semantic change which allows the same word in the same language to signify something quite different and even opposite in a different time is well known.³⁴ The possibility that some word-usage might be quite different in AD 90 from what it had been in AD 40 has already been noted above. Ancient texts not only informed current usage but Scripture texts continued to be used and contextualized in the period of the earliest Christian mission. This fact complicates the problem of determining 'the current state of play at any point'. Moreover, the problem of archaic texts remaining in use make it impossible to isolate a pure synchronic sample of language. This is

---

[31] F.F. Bruce, *The English Bible: A History of Translation from the Earliest English Versions to the New English Bible* (London: Lutterworth,1970 [1961]), xi & 19.

[32] K. L. Pike, *Language*, 612.

[33] Cited by Geoffrey Sampson, *Schools of Linguistics* (London: Hutchinson, 1980), 37.

[34] "The phrase 'to count your beads' originally meant to count your prayers, but because the prayers were reckoned by little balls, the word beads came to be transferred to these objects, and lost its original sense." (O. Jesperson, *Language*.) Relevant to our present study is Edward Sapir's observation: "Language moves down time in a current of its own making. It has a drift.... Nothing is perfectly static." Cited by S. Ullmann, *Semantics: An Introduction to the Science of Meaning* (Oxford: Blackwell, 1962), 194 & 193.

only one of many complications. As Jonathan Culler notes, "the notion of a synchronic state is a methodological fiction."[35]

Saussure's method has been applied to anthropology by Claude Lévi-Strauss and to many fields including biblical criticism by the subsequent development of 'structuralism'.[36] The present study uses the notion of 'synchronic analysis' mainly to emphasize long-established methods of guarding against the distortions of anachronism in the treatment of written evidence. By demanding recognition of approximate dates of written composition, we can insist at least that later documents not be used without argument as 'background'for earlier ones.

'Diachronic analysis' of language and concepts within a single culture can be useful in determining continuity as well as change. Since the development of concepts is tied to both language and social experience, changes in time are sometimes less marked within one language and culture than bilingual and transcultural changes within the same time frame. The fundamental notions of 'development' and 'fulfillment' (and theological ideas such as 'progressive Revelation') imply continuity as well as change. Diachronic analysis is required for any sort of judgment in terms of these themes, which are prominent in the New Testament. Moreover, with reference to the interpreter's 'two horizons', any historical study includes an unavoidable element of diachronic analysis.

Semantic Field

The term 'semantic field' has been widely accepted by linguists since the formulation of 'field theory' by Jost Trier in 1931.[37] The wide currency of this term together with the related terms 'semantic range' and 'associative field' seem to justify explicit use of these terms in our study of the earliest Christian mission. These terms are especially useful for linguistic and conceptual analysis of 'Israel' and 'the nations'.

"Verbal symbols segment experience, even though in an essentially arbitrary way," according to Eugene Nida, so that "the fundamental principle underlying this occurrence of words" in a language can be likened to "a conceptual map of human experience".[38] Projecting this idea, Nida claims that

---

[35] Jonathan Culler, *Saussure* (Glasgow: Fontana, 1976), 38. Saussure "never deals with the problem of semantic change itself, the diachronic alterations of signifieds"(44).

[36] Culler cites Lévi-Strauss' inaugural lecture at the *College de France* in 1961 and refers to his "epoch-making article on Structural analysis in 'Linguistics and Anthropology' fifteen years earlier". *Saussure*, 93.

[37] *Der Deutsche Wortschatz im Sinnbezirk des Verstandes.* Cited by John F.A. Sawyer, *Semantics in Biblical Research* (London: SCM, 1972), 30. Many other notions discussed by semanticists, such as 'synonymy', 'antonymy', and 'paradigmatic and syntagmatic relations of sense' are relevant to determinations of meaning in ancient texts. Sometimes these terms are implied or explained in other words in the analyses below. See John Lyons, *Introduction to Theoretical Linguistics* (Cambridge: University Press, 1968), 405, 407 & 428.

[38] E.A. Nida, *Message and Mission: Communication of the Christian Faith* (New York: Harper & Row, 1960), 80. In an essay "On the Semantic Structure of Language" published in 1963, Uriel Weinreich uses the same image: "The semantic 'map' of each language is different from those of all other languages." Cited by A. W. Read in *Current Trends in*

"the semantic structure reveals more clearly than any other part of language a people's world view."³⁹ Linguists have often demonstrated that

> there are semantic distinctions made in one language which are not made in another; moreover, ... particular fields may be categorized in a totally different way by different languages.⁴⁰

These claims and observations by linguists suggest many problems in conceptual analysis, especially when the concepts to be analyzed have been relayed from quite different languages, such as Hebrew to Greek, and from different cultures, such as Judaism to Hellenism. Because the receptor language and culture have lives of their own,

> a foreign concept may be taken into a language ... by modifying the semantic range of an item of similar meaning in the native vocabulary or by expanding it so as to accommodate the new meaning alongside the original one.⁴¹

Two basic principles stated by Nida are immediately relevant to our evaluation of the various terms for 'Israel' and 'the nations' in one or another ancient-language text and cultural context, and again in ancient and modern translations: "1/ There are no exact synonyms within a language and 2/ There are no exact equivalents between languages."⁴² With reference to the modern terms, 'Israel' and 'the nations', anachronism or 'fossilization' occurs but —as these pejorative labels imply— the exact carry-over of meaning may be more apparent than real.

Back-Formation

The linguistic term 'back-formation' describes "a word formed by subtraction of a real or supposed affix (as a suffix) from an already existing longer word".⁴³ The formation of the English word "gentile" from the plural "gentiles" is such a 'back-formation'. The plural form itself was introduced into

---

Linguistics, vol 10, ed. T. A. Sebeok (The Hague/Paris: Mouton, 1973), 177. Stephen Ullmann compares details from three such 'maps' in a chart, listing the four Hungarian words and the one Malay word commonly used to translate the two English words 'brother' and 'sister'. *Semantics:Intro*, 247.

³⁹ E.A. Nida, "Linguistic and Semantic Structure" [1964], cited by A.W. Read in *Current Trends in Linguistics*, vol 10, 193.

⁴⁰ J. Lyons, "Semantics: General Principles", *Introduction*, 429. See also B.L. Whorf, "Figure 10", *Language, Thought, and Reality*, ed. John Carroll (Cambridge, USA: MIT Press, 1964 [1956]), 210.

⁴¹ Theodora Bynon, *Historical Linguistics* (Cambridge: University Press, 1977), 236.

⁴² E.A. Nida, *Learning a Foreign Language* (New York: Friendship, 1957), 187 & 188.

⁴³ *Webster's Third New International Dictionary of the English Language Unabridged*, ed. P.B. Gove (Springfield: G. & C. Merriam, 1963), 158, col 3. Note that this broad definition of 'back formation' does not imply that the process necessarily involves mistaken assumptions about the form of the Latin loan-word itself.

the English language through Bible translation at least as early as 1382.[44] The back-formation 'gentile' appears twice in the Authorized Version of 1611, translating Ἕλλνος and Ἕλληνι in Romans 2.9-10. Originally a homonym of *gentil* (modern English "gentle"), the singular adjective and substantive "gentile" facilitated the development of the modern concept 'Gentile'.

The word "gentile" seldom, if ever, occurs today in ordinary language, but its use in ecclesiastical English has grown substantially since 1611. For twentieth-century biblical scholars and Bible translators, the concept 'Gentile' and the word itself seem to have become indispensable.[45] In German and Dutch the linguistic development of <Heiden> is different (related to the English word 'heathen'), but the conceptual developments flow directly from ecclesiastical Latin; the modern French <païens> (related to the English 'pagans') maintains the same pattern of conceptual development.[46]

Before considering the concept 'gentile' /Heiden /païens further with reference to various nationalities, we should take careful note of the history of the development of the English word "gentile", which was separate from the already established English word "gentle". Neither the old loan-word "gentiles" nor the back-formation "gentile" is normally used in modern English translations of non-biblical Greek texts. In contrast to such words as ἔθνη and Ἕλληνος (which were well-established in ordinary Greek during the period of the earliest Christian mission), the English term "gentile" only functions in relation to church or synagogue. It is remarkable, therefore, that despite the strong commitment of twentieth-century philosophers and linguists to 'ordinary language' the term "gentiles" (with or without a capital 'g') continues in use in the 1970 *New English Bible*, the 1976 *Today's English Version* (Good News Bible), the 1978 *New International Version*, and the 1989 *New Revised Standard Version*. As already noted, the singular "gentile" appears in only one sentence

---

[44] *Middle English Dictionary*, ed. Sherman M. Kuhn (Ann Arbor: U of M Press, 1963), vol 4, 70. The conceptual back-formation 'gentil' from the plural 'gentiles' not only sounded the same (and was spelled the same) as the existing English word 'gentil', but also derived from the same Latin word. Remarkably, 'sense 4' in the *MED*, "Pagan, heathen (ca 1400)", is very nearly the opposite of the first three senses,
    1: Of noble rank or birth ... also used of Christ (1230),
    2: Having the character or manners prescribed by the ideals of chivalry or Christianity;
    3: Belonging to a person of rank.

[45] If 'ordinary language' is adequate for translation of biblical texts and for historical discussion, the special term 'gentile' would seem to be unnecessary in an investigation of the earliest Christian mission. Accordingly, in my translation of Greek texts and formulations of the issues, I avoid the terms 'gentiles' and 'gentile'. Nevertheless, in this book these terms appear repeatedly in quotations of modern opinions and in translations cited by others.

[46] *Petit Larousse* provides an intriguing formula which combines linguistic and conceptual analysis: "Gentiles n.m. (lat. *gentiles*, païens, empr. à l'hébreu.) Pour les anciens Hebreux, étranger. Pour les chretiens, paien." (Paris: Librarie Larousse, 1959), 472.

Also of interest is the note appended to Romans 3.29 in *Le Nouveau Testament*, Version synodale, 7e: "des païens: Litt.:nations, Le vieux mot français *Gentils*, ou le mot *Païens*, plus frequemment employe de nos jours, designe dans l'Ecriture sainte, toutes les nations en dehors du peuple d'Israël."

in the 1611 Authorized version. But this singular term is used in three other places in the 1948 RSV (six in the NRSV) and eleven times in the 1973 NIV.[47]

C. The Several Israels and Various Nationalities

'Israel' and 'nations' are lively terms today. Both words appear regularly in front-page newspaper stories and are used by reporters and commentators on radio and television. But how the words and sentences of these news reports correspond to our use of the terms "Israel" and "the nations" in translations of ancient documents is problematic. On the one hand, it is clearly possible for modern politicians and ordinary citizens who have no religious convictions and no special interest in the Hebrew Bible or the Greek New Testament to use the terms without conscious reference to any history before the twentieth century. On the other hand, even secular political scientists and anthropologists realize that the modern meanings of these terms have been shaped by biblical concepts and theological doctrines. When these terms, with all the conceptual freight they carry, are used in reflection on the elements of the first-century mission of 'Israel' to 'the nations' described in the New Testament, what appears to be clarity of expression might be simply 'bewitchment by language'.

In his 1971 survey of *The Several Israels*, Samuel Sandmel specifies "The Hebrew Israel", "The Christian Israel", "The State of Israel", and "The True Israel".[48] In each case the name 'Israel' is the same transliteration of the Hebrew name יִשְׂרָאֵל and the concepts are systematically related, perhaps even identical in their 'core meaning'. But Sandmel's emphasis on the differences between these modern concepts is extremely important. In his list, "Hebrew Israel" is roughly the 'Israel' of the Hebrew Bible, "Christian Israel" is the 'Israel' with which Presbyterians identify when they sing the Psalms, "the State of Israel" is the 'Israel' to which newspaper reporters refer, and "the True Israel" is the elect people of God.

One of these concepts, 'the state of Israel' seems easiest to eliminate from our discussion of the first-century Christian mission. But it is difficult to assess the impact of the nation-state established in Palestine in 1948 on modern language. Certainly the emergence of the modern state of Israel has captured and continues to hold the attention of news reporters. The establishment of this new nation-state also has refocused the understanding of 'Israel' documented in Jewish and Christian theological writings and in the liturgies of church and synagogue since 1948. As a separate concept, the nation-state 'Israel' will be considered below, paradoxically, as one of various nationalities.

---

[47] Robert Young, *Analytical Concordance to the Bible* (Grand Rapids: Eerdmans, no date); J.W. Ellison, *Nelson's Complete concordance of the Revised Standard Bible* (Nashville: Thomas Nelson, 1984 [1957]); E.W. Goodrick and J.R. Kohlenberger, *The NIV Complete Concordance* (Grand Rapids: Zondervan, 1981); J.R. Kohlenberger, *The NRSV Concordance* (Grand Rapids: Zondervan, 1991). *Re* this remarkable proliferation of "gentiles" in our time, see J. LaGrand, "Proliferation of the 'Gentile' in the NRSV", *Biblical Research*, XLI, 1996.

[48] Samuel Sandmel, *The Several Israels* (New York: Ktav, 1971). *Cf.* his article "Israel, conceptions of" in the 1976 *IDB* Supplementary Volume.

The Several Israels

The first of "the Several Israels" in Sandmel's list is the 'Israel' of the Hebrew Bible. This concept developed historically and in theological reflection. Documentation of this development in the *Tanak* (and in the ancient Greek translations) will be surveyed below in an attempt to evaluate implications for first-century understanding of 'Israel'. This survey is more than an extended exercise in etymology. The communities established by the Christian mission used the Hebrew Bible and, indeed, these Scriptures were claimed as the constitutional documents for the mission. We must reckon with the possibility that Hebrew meanings which lost currency in medieval and modern times still functioned powerfully in the first century.[49] But before attempting an analysis of ancient meanings, we should consider some salient points of the twentieth-century concept of 'Hebrew Israel' which are likely to affect any such analysis.

The semantic fields of the synonyms 'Hebrews', 'Israel', and 'Jews' are not exactly the same in biblical Hebrew, koine Greek, and the modern languages of biblical commentary. If we put aside the uses of the term 'Hebrew' as the name of the biblical language (revived or resuscitated in modern Palestine), 'Israel' as the name of the country, and 'Jews' as the name of the people in the state of Israel and in Dispersion, it can be said safely that the three terms 'Hebrews', 'Israel', and 'Jews' occur as synonyms in free fluctuation in modern discussions, with "Jews", "Jewry", and "Judaism" used by far the most frequently in current references to what Sandmel has designated as "Hebrew Israel".

The word "Jews" (or <*Juden*>) has a much broader semantic range in modern usage than יהוּדִים and Ἰουδαῖοι had in the Hebrew Bible or in the New Testament. The Hebrew word does not appear in the book of Exodus,[50] but in our own time the people under Moses' leadership are often designated 'Jews' in carefully prepared materials for religious education, as well as in devotional tracts: "So it was with the manna in the desert which *the Jews* could gather only enough for one day without worms appearing in it."[51] In the New Testament Ἰουδαῖοι and Σαμαρεῖται stand as antonyms or 'complementary opposites', most notably in the paradigmatic sentence οὐ γὰρ συγχρῶνται Ἰουδαῖοι Σαμαρείταις (John 4.9).[52] But the modern term 'Jews', encompassing all ancient 'Hebrews' and 'Israelites' as well as modern Jews, is so well established that even in a study entitled *Samaritans and Jews* the author notes that

---

[49] See "Israel's Origin as a Free Peasantry" by R.A. Horsley and J.S. Hanson, *Bandits, Prophets, and Messiahs: Popular Movements at the Time of Jesus* (Minneapolis: Winston, 1985), 5.

[50] The word does occur tied to 'the tribe of' (למטה יהודה), as in Exodus 31.3.

[51] Andre Pery, *The Heidelberg Catechism with Commentary* trans. A.O. Miller and M.B. Koons (Philadelphia: United Church, 1962 [1959]), 219 [emphasis added]. Such usage is also notable in modern Jewish writings, *e.g.* throughout Louis H. Feldman's "Prolegomenon" to the M.R. James edition of *The Biblical Antiquities of Philo* (New York: Ktav, 1971).

[52] *Re* "Antonymy, complementarity and converseness", see J. Lyons, *Introduction to Theoretical Linguistics*, 460-470.

Modern Terms and Concepts 33

some ambiguity will be almost inevitable, since at times the word 'Jews' will be used specifically of those to whom and by whom the Samaritans were opposed, while at other times the suggestion will be made that Samaritans must be seen *within the wider phenomenon of Judaism*.[53]

Not only is the semantic range of the modern term 'Jew' broader at certain boundaries than that of the Hebrew and Greek words from which it is formed, but the semantic range is also narrower at other boundaries. The 'conceptual map' of twentieth-century English is evidently different from that of first-century Greek. Both Jesus and Paul emphatically identified themselves as Ἰουδαῖοι (John 4.22, Romans 3.9). But in modern usage the terms 'Jews' and 'Christians' are so well established as antonyms that scholarly references to 'Jesus the Jew' or to 'the Jewishness of Paul' seem calculated to force readers to re-orient their world views.[54]

The move from Samuel Sandmel's formulation of 'Hebrew Israel' to the simple modern term 'Jews' seems unavoidable in any attempt to trace the concept through current discussions. But the two senses of 'Jew' recorded in the *Shorter Oxford English Dictionary* are remarkable both because of the authority of the *OED* in representing 'ordinary language' usage and because of the stark simplicity of the definitions:

Jew 1. A person of Hebrew race: an Israelite.
  2. transf. Applied to a grasping or extortionate usurer, or a
      trader who drives hard bargains or deals craftily 1606.

A following entry reinforces the second sense: "Jew v. colloq. 1845 transf. To cheat or overreach."[55]

These two definitions focus in the sharpest way the problem that accompanies the use of the term 'Jew' in translating ancient documents. Two powerful sub-concepts are obvious in these definitions, the notion of race as biological descent, and the horrible and persistently seductive congeries of notions conveniently identified as 'anti-Semitism'. The amount of useful literature on both subjects is vast, and useless material on both is at least equal in volume. Our present concern is simply to be "on the watch" lest we be caught "in a linguistic snare" (Waismann) using the term 'Jews', so we shall do no more here than note the extent of the development of these ideas in medieval and especially modern times.

"The term 'anti-Semitism' is not old and was apparently first used by W. Marr, who began the publication of his *Zwanglose antisemitische Hefte* in

---

[53] R.J. Coggins, *Samaritans and Jews: The Origins of Samaritanism Reconsidered* (Atlanta: John Knox, 1975), 8 [emphasis added].

[54] Geza Vermes, *Jesus the Jew: A Historian's Reading of the Gospels* (Glasgow: Collins, 1973). See also Richard Rubenstein, *My Brother Paul* (New York: Harper & Row, 1972).

[55] *The Shorter Oxford English Dictionary on Historical Principles*, C.T. Onions: W. Little, H.F. Fowler, & J. Coulson, eds. (Oxford: Clarendon, 1959 [1933]), vol I (A-M), 1063 & 1064.

1880."[56] J.N. Sevenster and many other reasonable observers of the phenomenon have noted that the term itself is inappropriate, since "Babylonians and Arabs are just as Semitic as Jews"[57] and 'anti-Semitism' relates specifically to Jews. But it is precisely the tie-in with the modern development of the concept 'race' that gives the term its special meaning and significance for our analysis. On the one hand, 'anti Semitism' is dependent on the 'race' concept; on the other hand, 'anti-Semitism' itself was formative to a remarkable extent in the development of racial theory in modern Europe, notably in Count Arthur de Gobineau's 1853 *Essai sur l'inégalité des races humaines* and in Houston Stewart Chamberlain's two-volume work, *Die Grundlagen des Neunzehnten Jahrhunderts*, published in 1899.[58]

Assuming that Sevenster is correct in his assertion that "racial distinction ... was not, or hardly, a factor of any significance in ancient times,"[59] we have good reason to be 'on the watch' against the second sense of 'Jew' recorded in the *OED* encroaching on the first sense. But even if it were possible to disentangle the persistent strand of 'anti Semitism' from the popular concept of 'race', the first *OED* definition of 'Jew' as "a person of Hebrew race; an Israelite" would still be problematic. The authority of the *OED* in recording modern English usage is not in doubt, and it is certainly possible to use the first *OED* meaning of 'Jew' to translate and interpret ancient texts. But two considerations can serve to urge caution against uncritical transfer of the modern concept of 'race' into the ancient documents.

Since the modern term 'Jew' refers immediately to modern Jews, the validity of the concept should be tested first against the modern reality. Raphael Patai, in an *Encyclopaedia Britannica* article, asserts that "the findings of physical anthropology show that, contrary to popular view, there is no Jewish race."[60] This assertion appears to contradict the popular view directly, but it is possible to synthesize these "findings of physical anthropology" into a modified

---

[56] J.N. Sevenster, *The Roots of Pagan Anti-Semitism in the Ancient World* (Leiden: Brill, 1975), 1.

[57] *Ibid.* See also Hannah Arendt, *Anti-Semitism* (New York: Harcourt, Brace & World, 1968 [1951]), vii: "Antisemitism, a secular nineteenth-century ideology —which in name, though not in argument, was unknown before the 1870's— and religious Jew-hatred...are obviously not the same." Arendt notes that relations between Jews and non-Jews in Europe were at an all-time low during the 15th and 16th centuries; Heiko Oberman has attempted to trace *The Roots of Anti-Semitism in the Age of Renaissance and Reformation* (Philadelphia: Fortress, 1984), xi.

[58] Gobineau cited by Oscar Handlin, "The Linnaen Web", *Race and Nationality in American Life* (Garden City: Doubleday, 1957), 67; H.S. Chamberlain cited (with comments by Joseph Goebbels and Adolph Hitler) in *The Nazi Years: A Documentary History*, ed. Joachim Remark (Englewood Cliffs: Prentice-Hall, 1969), 4-6.

[59] J. N. Sevenster, *Roots*, 2. See also S. Sandmel, *Anti-Semitism in the New Testament?* (Philadelphia: Fortress, 1978), xx: "Prior to 1880 whatever hostility existed toward Jews in western Europe was religious, not racial." The modern ideology of 'anti-Semitism' "emerged as a result of a mingling of notions about race and nationalisms".

[60] Raphael Patai, vol XII, 1054, cited by Arthur Koestler, "Race and Myth", *The Thirteenth Tribe* (London: Pan, 1977), 161.

Modern Terms and Concepts 35

'racial' definition. As it happens, the extant popular view has been shaped in large part by scientific and pseudo-scientific arguments which already included paradoxes if not outright contradictions. As a matter of fact, a dominant theme of the 'anti-Semitism', pioneered by Gobineau, has defined 'the Jewish race' as mixed or mongrelizing.[61] But quite apart from judgments on this synthesis, there is a still more radical challenge to the popular view of Jews as 'persons of Hebrew race'.

If it were possible to maintain some racial definition of modern 'Jews', against the assertion of Patai, this 'race' would be quite separate genetically from ancient Israel. In a popular study, *The Thirteenth Tribe: The Khazar Empire and its Heritage*, Koestler assembled a great deal of evidence and argument to prove that "the bulk of modern Jewry is not of Palestinian, but of Caucasian origin." Koestler's intriguing hypothesis, which hinges on the eighth-century conversion of the Khazars to Judaism, at least demonstrates that very many 'characteristically Jewish racial traits' are derived from Khazar-Turkish, not Semitic, stock.[62]

The conclusions of Patai and Koestler regarding the modern term 'Jew' do not relate directly to the question of the validity of using a racial definition for the interpretation of ancient documents, of course. If Koestler is right about "the dominant role played by the 'Thirteenth tribe' in the biological history of the Jews"[63] in modern times, it is nevertheless true that in the middle decades of the first century AD most Jews (and Christians) were of Palestinian, or at least Near Eastern, origin. More to the point, it is possible that those who identified themselves as 'children of Israel' and 'sons of Abraham' in the first century had notions of 'racial purity' which correspond in significant respects to popular modern assumptions.[64] But it is also possible that Linnaean

---

[61] "In particular, the Semites had time and again injected Negro strains into the dominant race and thus enfeebled it beyond the power of recovery." (Summary of Gobineau by Oscar Handlin, *Race and Nationality*, 67.)

[62] A. Koestler, *Thirteenth Tribe*, 159, 175 & 176. In "A Note on Sources" Koestler includes Abraham N. Poliak, Professor of Medieval Jewish History at Tel Aviv University, whose book *Khazaria* was published in Hebrew in 1944; and D.M. Dunlop, Professor of Middle Eastern History at Columbia University, whose book *The History of the Jewish Khazars* was published by the Princeton University Press in 1954.

[63] A. Koestler, *Thirteenth Tribe*, 176.

[64] Joachim Jeremias is confident of modern insight into ancient documents in this respect:

> Up to the present, it has not been sufficiently recognized that from a social point of view the whole community of Judaism at the time of Jesus was dominated by the fundamental idea of the maintenance of racial purity.

Again, with respect to civil rights in early first-century Jerusalem, he writes, "Only those families who had preserved the divinely ordained purity of the race, which Ezra restored through his reforms, belonged to the true Israel." *Jerusalem in the Time of Jesus* (London: SCM, 1969 [1962 3rd edn.]), 270 & 297. These sentences remain unchanged from the 1937 first edition of this section <*Die Reinerhaltung des Volkstums*> published in Göttingen. It is certainly remarkable that in modern times 'sufficient recognition' of this 'fundamental idea' first dawned in Nazi Germany.

categories and modern genetic theory block easy access of modern understanding to such things as the New Testament genealogies.

Before turning from 'Hebrew Israel' to modern language usage and concepts regarding various nationalities, two other 'Israels' in Sandmel's list should be considered briefly in current terms.

'Christian Israel' and 'the True Israel'

Writers in our time are modest, at least, in their explicit use of the concept *'Christian Israel'*. Their infrequent use of the term might be explained simply with reference to the pervasive force of the nation-state concept in current affairs and the frequent everyday use of the term 'Israel' as the name of the State of Israel. In any case, this reticence seems to extend also to current Christian interpretation of first-century documents.

Peter Richardson, a Presbyterian minister familiar with the ancient and modern liturgical practice of singing the Psalms, writes of "the Christian take-over of the name 'Israel'" as though this began after a hiatus in the use of the term. Richardson's full-length study, *Israel in the Apostolic Church*, begins with the claim that "the Church is not called Israel in the New Testament."[65] But Jacob Neusner is an a better position to interpret the New Testament texts at issue, because he realizes that "both the apostles and the rabbis ... re-shaped the antecedent religion of Israel, and both claimed to be Israel."[66] Sandmel, making the same point, correctly notes that "early Christianity was a Jewish movement, addressed to a Jewish purpose, and its adherents were Jews."[67]

Some of the terrible and ironic consequences of the Christian claim to be Israel, which are outlined in Sandmel's analysis, may go some way towards explaining Richardson's inability to see (or his reluctance to acknowledge) the concept 'Christian Israel' in the New Testament itself. Determination to avoid the terrible distortions which so often have accompanied confessional interpretation of historical data also may have influenced the terms of F.F. Bruce's popular study, *Israel and the Nations from the Exodus to the Fall of the Second Temple*. Nevertheless, it is remarkable that an evangelical Christian scholar could trace the history of Israel from its beginnings to AD 70 and omit reference to the birth and death (and resurrection) of Israel's Messiah. In one of the incidental references to Christianity in the book, Bruce does imply awareness of the concept 'Christian Israel' when he notes "the extraordinary

---

[65] P. Richardson, *Israel in the Apostolic Church* (Cambridge: University Press, 1969), ix, 7. Contrast Eduard Schweizer's observation, that "in the first three Gospels ... 'Israel' denotes simply all Israel, *not just the obedient remnant* that listens to Jesus' call." *Church Order in the New Testament*, (London: SCM, 1961), 22 [emphasis added].

[66] J. Neusner, *Judaism in the Beginning of Christianity* (Philadelphia: Fortress, 1984), 12. *Cf.* Herbert Danby's comment: "While Judaism and Christianity alike venerate the Old Testament as canonical Scripture, the Mishnah marks the passage to Judaism as definitely as the New Testament marks the passage to Christianity." *The Mishnah: Translated from the Hebrew with Introduction and Brief Explanatory Notes* (Oxford: University Press, 1933), xiii.

[67] S. Sandmel, *Several Israels*, 30.

way in which the names Zion and Jerusalem have entered into the religious terminology of Christianity".[68]

The last of 'the several Israels' which Sandmel lists in his 1971 survey is *the True Israel*', clearly the most important concept for our analysis and also the most threatening. Clarification of this concept demands at least an understanding of the grammatical relationships of the terms 'Israel' and 'the nations'.

The *phrase* 'Israel and the nations' stands as a paradigm of 'complementary opposites' in the Hebrew Bible. Whether the eschatological grammar of the Christian mission itself makes it possible *either* to number 'Israel' among 'the nations' *or* to include 'the nations' in 'Israel' is a question which the present study attempts to answer through analysis of Matthean texts. Let the reader beware that grammatical developments in the languages of translators, interpreters, and commentators sometimes provide false clues for this quest.[69]

Various Nations, Nationalities, and Nationalisms

"Nation" is an old word in English, but "nationality" is a fairly new word which was added to the language in what E.J. Hobsbawn calls "the Age of Revolution".[70] In English, and perhaps even more emphatically in German and French, the term 'nation' is most often tied to nineteenth- and twentieth- century notions of 'nationalism' and the idea of the 'nation state'. As we consider the term, we should heed Nils Dahl's warning that "to speak about nations in the New Testament may be an anachronism."[71]

Intense debates about the significance of 'nations' have attended the various wars and nationalistic movements from the French Revolution to the present. These debates can serve to advance current understanding of ancient 'nations' so long as the modern interpreter of ancient documents is on guard against anachronism. When we come to consider the interpretive claim that "Paul thinks in nations",[72] for example, we must not imagine Paul of Tarsus

---

[68] F.F. Bruce, *Israel and the Nations* (Grand Rapids: Eerdmans, 1969 [1963]), 31. The name "Jeshua" appears twice in this book and the name "Jesus" four times, but none of these references is to Jesus of Nazareth. ("Index", 249.)

[69] Grammatical changes, such as the addition of the adjective 'Gentile' to the translation 'nations' for the new form 'Gentile nations', warrant careful scrutiny.

[70] E. J. Hobsbawm, *The Age of Revolution: Europe 1789-1848* (London; Weidenfeld and Nicolson, 1962), 1.

[71] Nils A. Dahl, "Nations in the New Testament", *New Testament Christianity for Africa and the World: Essays in Honour of Harry Sawyerr*, eds. M. Glasswell and E. Fashole-Luke (London: SPCK, 1974), 54.

[72] Johannes Munck emphasizes this as a key to understanding Paul's writings and actions: "He thinks in nations." *Paul and the Salvation of Mankind* (Richmond: John Knox, 1959), 52. Munck cites Wrede, Lietzmann, and Althaus. Ferdinand Hahn quotes the same phrase from Gottlob Schrenk's <*Der Römerbrief als Missionsdokument*> (1954): "He thinks universally —in nations." *Mission in the New Testament*, (London: SCM, 1965), 95 [80].

to be a first-century Bolivar or Mazzini.[73] Before attempting to salvage elements from the modern conceptual development of 'nations' which can be useful for a grasp of τὰ ἔθνη in the first century AD, we should note once again the paradox of the modern Israeli state.

According to Amos Elon, "Zionism was part of the final wave of liberal European nationalism."[74] Distinguishing between 'people' and 'nation' in a way which will be considered repeatedly in our analysis of the earliest Christian mission, Elon says with self-identification, "It is true, we are an ancient people. But at the same time, we are a new nation." He describes "the national ethos of Zionism" in terms of "its main strength ... derived from European sources." Elon insists that even

> the social vision of Zionism was not inspired by the prophets, as is often erroneously thought, but by the humanist principles of Western European liberalism and by revolutionaries....[75]

If, upon examination, 'the humanist principles of Western European liberalism' prove to have been 'inspired by the Prophets', Elon's evidence can be interpreted differently. But his insistent reference to the nineteenth century is a clear warning against simply identifying ancient and modern 'Israel'.

The attempt to understand πάντα τὰ ἔθνη of the first century AD through reference to modern nations and nationalism is largely a *via negativa*. Nevertheless, the sometimes heated discussions about the role of religion, geographical homeland, language, patterns of social culture, shared myths and legends, claims to common ancestors, and other elements in the definition of a 'nation' have contributed something to human understanding. Together with the secondary discussions about different types of 'nationalisms', the issues raised offer some positive direction for the analysis of the first-century mission to 'all nations'.[76] Perhaps Anthony D. Smith is correct in isolating "the classic Fascist movements" as a unique current within the broader modern development of

---

[73] Commentators on 19th-century nationalism use the concept of a 'messiah' in a way distinctly different from the concept in Paul's 'Messianism' or 'Christianity'. Nevertheless, there is a tantalizing suggestion of relationship across the centuries between the concepts of 'nations' and 'messiah':

> Each [19th-century nationalist movement] now tended to justify its primary concern with its own nation by adopting the role of a Messiah for all. Through Italy (according to Mazzini), through Poland (according to Mickiewicz) the suffering peoples of the world were to be led to freedom.
>
> E.J. Hobsbawm, "Nationalism", *Age of Revolution*, 132-3.

[74] A. Elon, *The Israelis: Founders and Sons* (Jerusalem: Adam, 1981), 40.

[75] *Ibid.*, 10-11.

[76] For a survey, which includes a distinction between two types of nationalism "which emerged in Europe in the early part of the 19th century —territorial-political and romantic-ethnic nationalism" see the article by Hans Kohn, "Nationalism", *Dictionary of the History of Ideas*, ed. P. Wiener, vol III (New York: Scribner's, 1973), 328.

nationalism.⁷⁷ But in any case, today's interpreter of ancient documents who accepts Nazis as guides should take special warning.

Plurality and Particularity
A new focus in current discussions directs our attention to 'peoplehood' and 'ethnicity' or 'ethnic groups'.⁷⁸ As the adaptation of the ancient term ἔθνος suggests, much of this line of analysis aims at a new understanding of "the various primordial ties of religion, language, ethnicity and race".⁷⁹ Before World War II arguments from studies of ancient and contemporary 'primitive' nations were already part of discussions about 'emerging nations', but interest in 'ethnic groups' has shifted from a subsidiary to a dominant position in current reflection on 'nationalism'.

> Now the important thing about an ethnic, as opposed to other kinds of social groupings, is the rationale that sustains the sense of group belonging and group uniqueness, and which links successive generations of its members. That rationale is to be found in the specific history of the group, and, above all, it its myths of group origins and group liberation.⁸⁰

Accordingly, Amos 9.7 might be proposed as a paradigm of a biblical writer's focus on 'ethnic awareness' among τὰ ἔθνη:

> Are you not like the children of the Cushites to me,
>   O Children of Israel? says Yahweh.
> Have I not brought up Israel out of the land of Egypt?
>   The Philistines from Captor.
>   And Aram from Kir?

The 'ethnic solidarity' or 'corporate personality'⁸¹ of first-century ἔθνη is only indirectly relevant to a study of the Christian mission. But if we can gain some reliable understanding of τὰ ἔθνη in these terms, we will be in a position to consider whether Paul and Matthew (and Jesus) themselves considered πάντα τὰ ἔθνη sympathetically, in the plurality and particularity of

---

⁷⁷ "In the case of Nazism, the biological principle replaced the cultural, and the ethnic was transformed into the race." A.D. Smith, "Nationalism: A Trend Report and Bibliography", *Current Sociology*, vol XXI/3 (1973), 8.

⁷⁸ See M. Marty and D. Peerman, *Theology in the Context of the New Particularisms: Nation, tribe, race, clan, ethnic group, gender and generation* (New York: Macmillan, 1972). "Ethnicity is common descent, either real or putative, but, even when putative, the myth has to be validated by several generations of common historical experience." Pierre van den Berghe, *The Ethnic Phenomenon* (New York/Oxford: Elsevier, 1981), 16.

⁷⁹ Anthony D. Smith, *The Ethnic Revival* (Cambridge: University Press, 1981), 2.

⁸⁰ A.D. Smith, *Ethnic Revival*, 65.

⁸¹ H. Wheeler Robinson's essays, published in Germany before WW II and recently reprinted, describe *Corporate Personality in Ancient Israel* (Philadelphia: Fortress, 1980 [1935 & 1937]). *Cf.* "Ethnic Consciousness in Pre-Modern Times", *Ethnic Revival*, 63.

their 'nationality', or whether they thought of them only as 'gentiles' /Heiden/païens.⁸²

In a short article which attempts to apply some of the "developed analytical perspective... of recent historiography of European nationalism' to what we sometimes disparagingly call "tribalism" in West Africa, Paul Jenkins explores "the nature of Ewe nationalism" in ways suggestive of application to τὰ ἔθνη of our first-century sources. One of his conclusions is that "any nationalism, European or African, is only one of many different levels of group consciousness."⁸³

Jenkins' article is programmatic rather than definitive and raises more questions than it answers. For most of τὰ ἔθνη of our sources, such as the Scythians, we have even fewer answers. But we can take instruction from some of the questions Jenkins poses: "What were the terms used in Ewe to describe another Ewe individual?" and "What term did Ewe people use when they referred to non-Ewes?" For the very important question of transferring national identity, Jenkins discovered that this occurred "at some stage of its [Ewe] history" not only with former slaves but also with a sub-group that became a ruling aristocracy.⁸⁴

Returning to "Nations in the New Testament", we find a very interesting reflection added to Nils Dahl's warning:

> The world of the New Testament was not a world of nations....
> But within this world, nationality had once been more important than it was at the time of the Roman Empire. Not only ancient Israel, but also neighbouring countries such as Edom, Moab and Ammon, the Aramean kingdom in Damascus, and even Egypt were more like nation states than what later existed in these same areas.⁸⁵

The Ewes in the British Empire, the Basques in Spain and France, the Kurds in Turkey, Iran, Iraq and Syria, 'the Navajo nation' in the USA, and the Armenians and Latvians in the former USSR are a few examples of the very many 'ethnic groups' that can be cited as analogies in our own time to the 'nations' within the first-century Roman Empire.

---

⁸² Nils Dahl and many others have argued or assumed that "in the New Testament, the term τὰ ἔθνη in most of its occurrences refers to the Gentile world as a whole. Only occasionally the notion that this world is made up of ethnic groups has any significance." Dahl concedes, however, that "when the term πάντα τὰ ἔθνη, 'all nations', is used, ethnic connotations are often somewhat more prominent." Moreover, Dahl acknowledges one clear exception to his generalization:
> in the Book of Revelation we find what we may miss elsewhere, the image of people from all nations gathered into the Church of Christ. [Indeed,] even when it stands by itself, the term τὰ ἔθνη in the Apocalypse designates a plurality of nations, not the Gentiles as a collective unit. (Sawyerr Fs., 57 & 66.)

⁸³ Paul Jenkins, "Exploring the Historic Nationalism of the Ewes", *Transactions of the Historical Society of Ghana*, vol 12 (Accra, 1971), 95 & 96.

⁸⁴ Ibid., 98-99.

⁸⁵ N. Dahl, "Nations in NT", Sawyerr Fs., 56.

The Ethnocentric Attitude

We can assume that many, if not all, of τὰ ἔθνη within the purview of the earliest Christian mission generated what Claude Lévi-Strauss terms 'the ethnocentric attitude'. This attitude is evident in the way "many so-called primitive peoples describe themselves as 'the men' (or sometimes —though hardly more discreetly— as 'the good', 'the excellent', 'the well-achievers')."[86] The Greeks and the Romans amply documented their versions of this attitude. Comparing the phrase "Israel and the nations" to "Greeks and barbarians", K.L. Schmidt asks, "Is it not possible that we simply have the same exclusivism of Israel and Judah as is found also among the Greeks?"[87] If so, it seems likely that the Apostle Paul in his mission to τὰ ἔθνη was aware of a multiplicity of such analogies —including the polarity 'Greeks and barbarians' which he actually cited (Rm 1.14). But even K.L. Schmidt seems not to have stretched his imagination far enough in considering "the true significance of particularity of the ἔθνη statements in the OT"[88] and the transformation of this significance in the earliest Christian mission.

The modern terms 'gentiles' and 'ethnic groups', as alternate translations of τὰ ἔθνη, outline two different perceptions as sharply as Wittgenstein's Duck-Rabbit. For most of τὰ ἔθνη documentary evidence is slight, and recorded 'national literatures' non-existent. But the ancient Greeks, Romans, and Jews each passed on a very substantial literature. Perhaps these three literate 'nations' and their three "different types of nationality"[89] can be compared to the tip of an iceberg, representing a vastly larger number of unlettered (and undocumented) 'nations' and 'nationalisms'. Whether or not it is appropriate to extrapolate from these three to the many, the three themselves were recipients of the gospel. Accordingly, first-century Greek, Latin, Aramaic (or Syriac) and Hebrew documents are the extant primary sources for our inquiry.[90] But the world-views of these 'nations' (and combinations of two or all three, such as 'Graeco-Roman' and 'Hellenistic-Jew') and their languages continued to change and develop during almost 2,000 years of reflection on the Christian mission.

Even if Greek, Latin, and Aramaic/Hebrew were not the languages of our primary sources, these languages would be important for our analysis of the earliest Christian mission because of the significance of each in the development of our own modern European thought and languages. Detailed consideration of interpretive problems related to developments in each of the three languages would take us too far afield, but one example relevant to our understanding of the earliest Christian mission can be cited: Mishnaic Hebrew developed what

---

[86] Claude Levi-Strauss, *Race and History* (Paris: UNESCO, 1958), 12-13.

[87] K.L. Schmidt, "ἔθνος in the NT", *TDNT* vol II, 371-72. Schmidt gives a nuanced answer to his own question with the claim that "even at its greatest what we find in Greece is only analogous to what is seen in Israel in its relation to all other people."

[88] K. L. Schmidt, *Ibid.*, 372.

[89] N. Dahl, Sawyerr *Fs.*, 61.

[90] No Jewish or Christian Latin texts from before AD 90 are known to modern scholars. (This was confirmed for me by Prof Eric Segelberg in a 1987 interview in Halifax.) Non-Christian Latin texts and later Christian texts make it plausible to plot trajectories.

Nils Dahl describes as "a secondary singular [of the old word] *goy*, meaning an individual Gentile, with the feminine form *goyah*, a Gentile woman".[91]

Since lineage seems basic to the concept of 'ethnicity', some new light on the idea of common descent and kinship should be considered before we pause to reflect on the threat of expert opinion regarding τὰ ἔθνη. In ancient Greece, according to Moses Finley's reconstruction, "common descent was a stereotype, and it is doubtful that many Greeks took it seriously."[92] In forming this judgment, Finley was well aware that the theme is explicit and frequent in Greek literature. Similarly, F.W. Walbank in his essay "the Problem of Greek Nationality" refers to "ties of real or pretended kinship".[93] Current social studies, such as John Ngusha Orkar's *Pre-colonial History of the Tiv*, provide models for the kind of detailed argument which seems to be implied in these summary statements.

Orkar begins his chapter on "Patterns of Assimilation" by observing that

> All Tiv today claim direct origin from one ancestor. The myth of unitary origins is preached everywhere .... Everyone in Tivland vociferously proclaims that they always were what they are now.[94]

He concludes that this emphasis actually represents a very strong and continuing Tiv pattern of assimilating formerly alien peoples: "Aliens were assimilated totally, in the pristine meaning of that term. There was no cultural fusion."[95] Orkar's detailed work with genealogies, which include adoption, suggests an interpretation of biblical genealogies for defining ethnicity in Israel which is startlingly different from modern interpretations tied to notions of European biological science.[96] 'Adoption', which is strongly emphasized in the New Testament, involves a concept which is at once more radical and more flexible than assimilation.

---

[91] N. Dahl, Sawyerr *Fs.*, 57.
Latin held imperial sway over reflection on the Christian mission for 1,500 years, and continues as a strong influence even today. Bede's *Ecclesiastical History of the English People*, written in the early eighth century, provides a useful control for analysis related to our field because of its subject matter and its simple textual history. *Bede's EHEP*, eds. B. Colgrave and R.A.B. Mynors. Oxford: Clarendon, 1969 and *A Concordance to the Historia Ecclesiastica of Bede* by P.F. Jones. Cambridge, U.S.A.: Medieval Academy, 1929.

[92] M.I. Finley "The Ancient Greeks and Their Nation", *The Use and Abuse of History* (New York: Viking, 1975), 124.

[93] F.W. Walbank, "The Problem of Greek Nationality", *The Phoenix: The Journal of the Classical Association of Canada*, 5/1 (Spring 1951), 54.

[94] John Ngusha Orkar, *A Pre-Colonial History of the Tiv of Central Nigeria C.1500-1850* (Halifax, Canada: Dalhousie University Ph.D. dissertation, 1979), 101.

[95] J. Orkar, *Pre-colonial Tiv*, 157.

[96] *Cf.* R.R. Wilson's *Genealogy and History in the Biblical World* (New Haven: Yale University Press, 1977) and M.D. Johnson's *The Purpose of the Biblical Genealogies with Special Reference to the Setting of the Genealogies of Jesus* (Cambridge: University Press, 1988 [1969]).

D. The Threat of Expert Opinion

The theme of forbidden knowledge, well-known from Scripture (Gen 2.17, Deut. 29.29), folk lore, and proverbial wisdom, might be applied to attempts at clarifying and controlling the concepts 'Israel' and 'the nations'. No doubt there are twisted geniuses in every field of human endeavor. But there seems to be an unusual supply of candidates for a rogues' gallery of experts prominent in the discussion of 'Israel' and 'the nations', even if Gobineau and H.S. Chamberlain are dismissed from consideration. Gerhard Kittel is most notable in this list, but Hendrik Verwoerd, J. Enoch Powell, and C. Peter Wagner are others who seem genuinely capable of advancing human understanding while promulgating ideologies and doctrines which are morally repulsive.

The essay "Gerhard Kittel and the Jewish Question in Antiquity", published in 1951 by William Foxwell Albright, is a cautionary tale to all in the field.[97] Any decent scholar who peruses even the one outrageous book *Das antike Weltjudentum*, published by Kittel in 1941, must return to articles bearing G. Kittel's name with grave suspicion. Indeed, an impulse to boycott the *Theological Dictionary of the New Testament* would be understandable since the whole work bears his name as editor.[98] How so many great and good biblical scholars agreed to publish under his editorship is amazing. Students particularly interested in τὰ ἔθνη should not be surprised that the article "People and Peoples in the LXX", under the heading ἔθνος was written by another Nazi, G. Bertram of Giessen.[99] What is surprising and disconcerting is that this article and those by Kittel himself—many of which are linked to the ethnic theme— are valuable. In fact, when Kittel was not producing poisonous rubbish for his own specialist magazines, *Forschungen zur Judenfrage, Mitteilungen über die Judenfrage*, and *Archiv für Judenfragen*, he made valuable contributions to respectable periodicals.[100]

Two characteristics of Kittel's work are specifically threatening. First, as Albright notes, "his early work was distinguished from that of other New Testament students of his generation mainly by his emphasis on the importance of Rabbinic studies."[101] Serious attention to Jewish sources might seem to be a guarantee against infection by anti-Semitism, but it certainly did not inoculate or cure Kittel. Second, the distinction between 'ancient Israel' and 'the Jews of the first century', which is basic for our analysis and often neglected in

---

[97] W.F. Albright, *History Archaeology, and Christian Humanism* (New York: McGraw-Hill, 1964 [1951]), 229-240. See also R.P. Ericksen's *Theologians Under Hitler: Gerhard Kittel, Paul Althaus and Emanuel Hirsch* (New Haven/London: Yale University Press, 1985).

[98] The logic of Sartre's persuasive argument, based on what he describes as the "syncretic totality" of anti-Semitism in the anti-Semite, implies the validity of such a boycott. Jean-Paul Sartre, *Anti-Semite and Jew* (New York: Schocken Books, 1965 [1946]), 17 and *passim*.

[99] *TDNT*, vol II, 364-69. *Re* Bertram as a Nazi see W.F. Albright, "Gerhard Kittel", 232.

[100] W. F. Albright, *Ibid.*, 230. For an ambiguous example see Kittel's earlier article, <*Die* γενεαλογία *der Pastoralbriefe*>, *ZNW*, vol xx (1921).

[101] W.F. Albright, "Gerhard Kittel", 230.

current studies, was the factual basis for the invidious distinction between 'Jewish' and 'Israelite' which came to dominate Kittel's work.[102]

Hendrik Verwoerd was not a biblical scholar, but he developed ways of thinking about and organizing ethnic groups in 'national' terms which are noteworthy here. Verwoerd's analysis and awesome, regrettable power to put his theory of 'separate development' (Apartheid) into practice seem even to have helped spread the Christian gospel to 'all the nations' in South Africa through the missions of the Afrikaner churches (NGK and GKSA).[103] But what has been promoted by Afrikaner church and state as a positive ideology of 'plural development' for ethnic groups or 'nations' is certainly not an attractive model for our reflection on the earliest Christian mission. Desmond Tutu's observation exposes a cruel inconsistency in Verwoerd's thought and practice:

> Blacks find it hard to understand why the Whites are said to form one nation when they are made up of Greeks, Italians, Portuguese, Afrikaners, French, Germans, English, *et c. et c.* and then by some *tour de force* Blacks are said to form several nations—Xhosas, Zulus, Tswanas, *et c*. The Xhosas and Zulus, for example, are much closer to one another ethnically than, say, the Italians and the Germans in the White community.[104]

Nevertheless, there seems to be some truth, twisted by Verwoerd's evil genius, which is overlooked by the established view that Christianity "presupposes the abolition in principle of all national distinctions (in terms of Gl. 3:28; Col. 3:11ff.)".[105]

It may seem inappropriate to place J. Enoch Powell and C. Peter Wagner in the rogues' gallery along with Nazi and Apartheid propagandists. But each in his way represents the continuing threat of expert opinion on current discussions of the earliest Christian mission to all nations.

In the late 1960s Enoch Powell, MP, gained an international reputation in the British Press as a 'racialist'. Since he had graduated with distinctions

---

[102] W.F. Albright, "Gerhard Kittel", 232. See Charlotte Klein's argument, noted above, regarding 'Late Judaism' (*Spätjudentum*): "The very terminology adopted makes this historical background appear from the outset in the worst light." *Anti-Judaism in Christian Theology* (Philadelphia: Fortress, 1978), 15. When 'Christianity' and 'Judaism' are viewed as parallel first-century developments (following the analysis of Sandmel, Neusner and others) earlier developments in the preceding century become 'proto-Judaism' or 'Early Judaism'.

[103] Whether Verwoerd's Afrikaner Christianity shaped his ideology or the reverse, and whether the Afrikaner churches set state policy or only moved within the range allowed them by the government are important questions which cannot be answered simply, and often are not answered honestly. Two non-White 'Dutch Reformed' denominations, the *Sendingkerk* and the *NGKA*, certainly have gained through 'separate development'. Ironically, the greatest gain is that both were quarantined from the Afrikaner *Apartheid* teaching itself. They might say to the NGK 'mother church' what Joseph said to his brothers: "As for you, you meant evil against me, but God meant it for good" (Gen 50.20).

[104] Desmond Mpilo Tutu, "Open Letter to Mr. John Vorster", *Hope and Suffering* (Grand Rapids: Eerdmans, 1984 [1976]), 30.

[105] Representative statement from Hans Windisch's Ἕλλην article, *TDNT*, vol II, 516.

from Cambridge and began his career as a Professor of Greek in Australia, it is not surprising that he published *A Lexicon to Herodotus*.[106] Powell also published English poetry, as well as articles and reviews in theological journals. It seems strange, nevertheless, to discover that one of the guides to basic information about ancient Greek ideas of 'nation' and 'race' is the most notorious racist in post-colonial Britain.

The subtitle of Peter Wagner's book *Our Kind of People*, indicates moral sensitivity to the issues he raises: "The Ethical Dimension of Church Growth in America". Neither Peter Wagner nor Donald MacGavran, his mentor in 'church growth' theory, give evidence of anti-semitism or racism in their personal lives or publications. But Peter Wagner, while canvassing biblical texts which are basic to the present study, advocates mission and church fellowship centered in 'homogeneous units'.[107] Moving from descriptions of numerical success to prescription, Wagner rationalizes his moves with interpretations of ancient texts. These interpretations seem to be shaped precisely by what the Belhar Confession terms 'the heresy of Apartheid'.[108]

---

[106] J. Enoch Powell, *A Lexicon to Herodotus* (Cambridge: University Press, 1938). *Cf.* B. Smithies and P. Fiddick, *Enoch Powell on Immigration* (London: Sphere, 1969).
[107] C.P. Wagner, *Our Kind of People* (Atlanta: John Knox, 1979), 8-33 and *passim*.
[108] See *A Moment of Truth: The Confession of the Dutch Reformed Mission Church 1982*, eds. G.D. Cloete and D.J. Smit (Grand Rapids: Eerdmans, 1984), *passim*.

3

IDENTIFICATION IN ANCIENT SOURCES:
THE HEBREW BIBLE AND THE SEPTUAGINT

The earliest Christian mission claimed the Hebrew Bible as its basis, its constitutional document.[1] But these Scriptures were formed over a very long period of time, so this written record also provides the modern interpreter with evidence for centuries of change and development in the use of the terms 'Israel' and 'the nations'.[2] Accordingly, the Hebrew Bible is a background source of information on the historical meaning of the concepts represented by these terms as well as a primary source of information about the function of 'Israel' and 'the nations' in the Christian mission.

A. *The Hebrew Bible*

Within the framework of the biblical narrative from Genesis to Malachi (including 'the Writings') more than one model or paradigm of 'Israel and the nations' occurs. The representation of Israel as a *family* persists throughout the Hebrew Bible[3] and recurs in the New Testament. In Genesis and Exodus this

---

[1] Ways in which this claim shaped Matthew's Gospel will be considered in "Part Two" along with questions about the validity of the claim.

[2] The usefulness of biblical texts as evidence for the reconstruction of historical events and cultural patterns (including thought forms and language usage) is the subject of a continuing debate. According to Julius Wellhausen, "We attain to no historical knowledge of the patriarchs [from the narrative in Genesis] but only of the time when the stories about them arose in the Israelite people." This formulation is sharpened by Wellhausen's argument that the "Hexateuch" was written later than the prophetic writings. *Prolegomena to the History of Ancient Israel* (Cleveland: World, 1957 [1878]), 319, "Introduction" & *passim*.

[3] The *Tanak* (Torah, Nevi'im, and Kethuvim) is called "the Hebrew Bible" in the present work to emphasize the original language (although it includes Aramaic) and the extent of the Scriptures (or 'canon'). The term should not be transposed to 'the Bible of the Hebrews' —this would imply a misleading answer to another important question. Perhaps the best-known term for these Scriptures, 'the Old Testament', has its own advantages and disadvantages. Worst of the disadvantages is the implication of obsolescence.

model of 'the children of Israel' is put forward as an explanation of their pre-history: the elect people of God were called out of Egypt as heirs of the promises declared to Abraham.

The earliest form of Israel as a people (עם) or nation (גוי) is the *confederation* of 'Twelve Tribes'. The paradigm of 'Israel and the nations' shifted decisively with the establishment of monarchy in Israel. But Israel's organization as a *kingdom* (or kingdoms) did not banish the earlier models of 'Tribal Confederacy' and "Children of Israel" from their self-identification. Finally, within the boundaries of the Hebrew Bible, *post-Exilic Israel* developed "a unique form of common life without any real analogy among the communities of the ancient world".[4] The Messianic idea, which was anticipated already by pre-Exilic prophets, projected a *model Israel* (or a congeries of models) which encompassed and transcended the earlier paradigms.

1. The Children of Israel in Covenant with Yahweh

Throughout the Hebrew Bible, 'Israel' is a theological concept: 'the people of God'.[5] The plurality of models which represents this people reflects socio-political changes in their history. But the biblical reality represented by the different models can be understood only in relation to Yahweh, the God who elected Israel in love. He established his covenant with them, called them out of Egypt, gave them the Torah, spoke by the prophets, symbolized his presence in the Ark and in the Temple, and finally directed their path through Exile to Messianic hope. Christians declare that the final revelation of God's love for his people is expressed in a Son, Jesus the Messiah.

History, as the story of God's mighty acts and as the revelation of Yahweh's steadfast love for his people, is supremely important for biblical faith.[6] Nevertheless, attempts to define 'Israel' historically without primary reference to the theological concepts of 'election' and 'covenant' move outside the usage of the Bible and become dependant on meager sources of information which themselves are quite alien to the biblical narrative. The apparently chronological sequence 'Hebrews', 'Israel', 'Jews' in the Hebrew Bible might seem to be a clue for historical reconstruction. But this sequence does not adequately indicate the separate uses of the terms in the Bible.

---

[4] R.C. Dentan, *The Knowledge of God in Ancient Israel* (New York: Seabury, 1968), 24.

[5] "In biblical thought, God and Israel are interdependent." R.C. Dentan, *ibid.*, ix. In basic linguistic terms, "God" is a recurrent and persistent part of the associative field of the name "Israel" in biblical texts relating to each stage of Israel's history.

[6] According to George Mendenhall, "The Bible represents a radical transition in the foundation of religious faith from ancient myth to historical event." *The Tenth Generation: The Origin of the Biblical Tradition* (Baltimore: Johns Hopkins University Press, 1974), x, note 5. Roland de Vaux declares, "If the historical faith of Israel is not in a certain way founded in *history*, this faith is erroneous and cannot command my assent." *The Bible and Modern Scholarship*, ed. J.P. Hyatt (London: Kingsgate, 1966), 16.

The fact that the term 'Hebrews' appears infrequently in the biblical narrative is noteworthy. Even so, the term occurs often enough to indicate some clear patterns of usage.[7] Since the term 'Israel' has priority over 'Hebrews' and 'Jews' in every stage of Biblical usage, we turn first to a preliminary identification of Israel.

Israel's story begins with their salvation by God from Egypt in the Exodus. As the prophet Hosea later characterized this beginning, Israel was God's own child: "When Israel was a child, I loved him,/ and out of Egypt called my son."[8] God, who called Israel into being, existed himself in earlier times, of course. He revealed himself as the God of their fathers,"the God of Abraham, the God of Isaac, and the God of Jacob" (Ex 3.6 &.15). Moreover, God's name, Yahweh, identified him as the Creator of all things.[9] The name 'Israel' itself can be understood as a patronymic, an identification of this people as 'children of the God who rules'.[10]

---

[7] See brief discussion below and J. LaGrand, "'Hebrews' in the TANAK", *Proceedings of the Eastern Great Lakes & Midwest Biblical Society*, 1991. *Cf.* N.P. Lemche, "'Hebrew' as a National Name for Israel", *Studia Theologica* 33 (1979) 1-23. Later uses of the term in the Apocrypha, Pseudepigrapha, and New Testament are clearly derivative from the biblical usage, but "the current state of play" (Saussure) is decisive in post-biblical usage. Since the sixteenth century, the term 'Hebrews' has been used as a synonym for both 'Israel' and 'Jews' and as a name specifying the earliest period of Israel's history, as well as a name encompassing all periods. *N.b.* C.H.J. de Geus's complaint, *The Tribes of Israel* (Amsterdam: van Gorcum, 1976), 186 n259. *Cf.* the change in Rudolf Kittel's title *Geschichte des Hebräers* (1874) to *Geschichte des Volkes Israel* (Gotha: Perthes, 1922).

[8] This expression of divine paternity also was declared to Pharaoh in the revealed words: "Thus says Yahweh, Israel is my first-born son. So I say to you, 'Let my son go that he may serve me'" (Ex 4.22-23). Matthew's idea, that this beginning was recapitulated or 'fulfilled' by Jesus, is considered in **Part Two**. *Cf.* Paul's citation of Hos 1.10 in Rm 9.26.

[9] W.F. Albright argues that the tetragrammaton יהוה is derived from the causative (*hiphil*) form. *From Stone Age to Christianity* (Garden City: Doubleday, 1957), 16. D.N. Freedman presses this argument by translating Ex 3.14 as "I will bring into being" and יהוה in Ex 34.6 as "God creates what he creates." Cited by Brevard Childs, *The Book of Exodus: A Critical Theological Commentary* (Philadelphia: Westminster, 1974), 62. G. von Rad notes "the belief —already latent in principle in the earliest Jahwehism— that Jahweh is the cause of all things". *Old Testament Theology* vol I (Philadelphia: Westminster, 1961 [1957]), 53. In the immediate context of Ex 3.14, Yahweh is the God who creates Israel as a people.

[10] "The term Israel, as a name binding together the confederation of tribes and meaning 'God rules', would also have had a predominately sacral-religious and not political connotation." W. Eichrodt, *Theology of the Old Testament* vol I (Philadelphia: Westminster, 1961 [1933]), 40.
The scientific etymology of the name 'Israel' is not immediately relevant to the use of the term in the Hebrew Bible or, in turn, in the earliest Christian mission. (W.F. Albright concludes that "the name is pre-Mosaic and ... the tribal chief *Yisrael* replaced the tribal chief *Ya'quob* during the Patriarchal Age." "The Names 'Israel' and 'Judah'", *JBL* 46 [1927], 161. Similarly, G.A. Danell concludes that "behind the identification of Israel and Jacob there lies a union of two tribes." *Studies in the Name Israel in the Old Testament* <Upsala: Appelbergs, 1946>, 37.) The explanation in the Bible of the name [Gen 32.23 & 35.9] is

God's deliverance of Israel from Egypt was a demonstration of his love for the downtrodden and of his power over against the foolish arrogance of human tyranny. But his adoption of this slave people as his own children, so that they could come out and serve him (Ex 4.23), was an act of election with deeper meaning and broader significance than the immediate political liberation. Israel was chosen to live in covenant with Yahweh. The covenant made at Sinai declares Israel's identity in relation to Yahweh and over against the nations.[11] This covenant also confirms Israel as heir to the covenant which God made with Abraham (Gen 15 & 17; Ex 2.24). The link to Abraham is important —not least in Matthew's Gospel —but mysterious.

Whoever the Israelites (or proto-Israelites) were in Egypt, at the Exodus "a crowd of mixed ancestry escaped with them" (ערב וגם / καὶ ἐπίμικτος πολὺς συνανέβη αὐτοῖς Ex 12.38). Whether or not the "rabble" (האספסף) in Numbers 11.4 are still identifiable as groups inadequately assimilated into Israel, the division here as elsewhere in the biblical narrative is marked only by obedience and disobedience. Moses does not make a distinction between those who complained (or began the lament) and the heirs of God's promise (Nu 11.12). "The whole congregation of the children of Israel" (כל־עדת בני ישראל) lusted after the flesh pots of Egypt soon after their escape (Ex 16.2), in any case. The first Passover regulations, which are part of the canonical account of the escape itself, emphasize the identification of the "mixed multitude" (ערב) with Israel by specifically relating the regulations to new-comers as well as those born into the community (בני ובאזרח הארץ Ex 12.19).[12]

Yahweh's election distinguished sharply between the Israelites and the Egyptians in the Exodus (Ex 12.27). This distinction is re-emphasized at Sinai where Yahweh reminds the Israelites that

> You have seen for yourselves how I treated the Egyptians and how I bore you up on eagle wings and brought you here to myself (Ex 19.4).

---

relevant, however, as Danell recognizes (17). The biblical story explains how "Israel" came to be the patronymic for the descendants of Jacob. The mysterious encounter also explains how those called "Israel" —like Jacob himself— are heirs to this encounter with God (*El*). Without this second explanation it is not easy to see how Jacob/ Israel rather than Abraham emerges as the eponym of God's people in the biblical narrative.

[11] "The first obligation of the covenant was to reject all foreign relations — *i.e.* with other gods, and by implication, with other political groups. It meant that they could not make covenants with their neighbors either in the desert or later in Palestine for to do so would be to recognize the pagan deities as witnesses and guarantors of the covenant." G. Mendenhall, *Law and Covenant in Israel and the Ancient Near East* (Pittsburgh: Biblical Colloquium, 1955), 38.

[12] "It is a serious error to assume that the 'Israelites' of the period immediately preceding the conquest were a homogenous body." W.F. Albright, citing Ex 12.38 and Num 11.4, *Archeology and the Religion of Israel* (Baltimore: JH University Press, 1946), 99. Brown-Driver-Briggs cites Ex 12.38 for its definition of ערב as "mixture, mixed company, heterogeneous body attached to a people". *A Hebrew and English Lexicon* (Oxford: Clarendon, 1959), 786/1. *Cf.* G. Beer, *Exodus* (Tübingen: Mohr, 1939), 69.

If Yahweh's covenant with Israel can be compared to an ancient suzerainty treaty, it is a lopsided contract based on his sovereign power of electing love.[13] Israel's complete dependence on Yahweh's love and mercy for their existence is emphasized by Yahweh's response to Moses' intercession after the incident of the golden calf:

> Here then is the covenant I will make (said Yahweh). Before the eyes of all your people, I will work such marvels as have never been wrought in any nation anywhere on earth (Ex 34.10).

The Ten Words of the Covenant not only emphasize the singularity of Yahweh (Ex 20.2), but also clarify Israel's singularity among the nations.[14] Within the larger context of the Covenant Code (Ex 21-23), the prohibition against boiling a kid in its mother's milk anticipates the necessary abstinence from the ritual acts performed to the Canaan (Ex 23.19b).[15] The promise of "hornets to drive the Hivites, Canaanites, and Hittites out of your way" (Ex 23.28) indicates the continuing protection of the Creator, whose miraculous control of his creatures already marked Israel's escape from Egypt. It will be unnecessary for Yahweh's people to make a covenant with any of the nations or their gods (Ex 23.32). Yahweh, the jealous God (אל קנא / θεὸς ζηλωτής) expressly prohibits calling other gods as witnesses "besides me" in any covenant (Ex 20.4-5). The biblical account of the conquest of the Promised Land by Yahweh's covenant people has obvious implications for all subsequent statements and reflections on 'Israel and the nations'.

The Hebrews

Even in the pre-history of God's people the name 'Israel' takes precedence over the designation 'Hebrews', but the references to 'Hebrews' in Genesis and Exodus are the most significant of this term's infrequent appearances in the Bible. So we now turn to an examination of these early occurrences, and continue with a survey of the term in the Tanak, before considering the definition given to Israel by the Conquest.

There is a very old tradition of considering the biblical 'Hebrews' as an ethnic group, but the earliest occurrences of the term in the Bible itself imply no more than negative reference to individuals or groups distinguishable from

---

[13] M.G. Kline, *Treaty of the Great King: The Covenant Structure of Deuteronomy* (Grand Rapids: Eerdmans, 1963), 14. "The covenant relationship itself may very well be regarded as a guarantee of freedom from every other political suzerainty." G.E. Mendenhall, *Law and Covenant*, 7.

[14] "Yahweh ... entered into covenant only with Israel." G.E. Mendenhall, "Covenant", *IDB* 1, 719. Cf. C.J. Labuschangne, *The Incomparability of Yahweh in the Old Testament* (Leiden: E.J. Brill, 1966).

[15] Brevard Childs and others conclude from Ugaritic evidence that "the biblical prohibition was directed specifically against a Canaanite ceremony, which was probably connected with its fertility cult." *Exodus*, 486.

dominant ethnic groups.¹⁶ In other words, in its earliest biblical usage 'Hebrews' appears to be analogous to the modern terms 'non-European' and *'Gastarbeiter'* or, more crudely, 'foreigners', 'aliens' and even 'savages', 'vagabonds', 'fugitives', 'outsiders', 'riff-raff', or 'lesser breeds without the law'.

Certainly some such translation is plausible for each of the occurrences of 'Hebrew' in the Joseph stories: Genesis 39.14 ("Look, he has brought an alien [עברי] into the house to mock us"); Genesis 39.17 ("That foreign [העברי] houseboy"); Genesis 41.12 ("A young man, a displaced-person [עברי], servant to the captain of the guard"); and Genesis 43.32 ("Egyptians would not eat with savages [העברים], because that was unthinkable for an Egyptian.") This last example is especially significant because it indicates that Joseph had been assimilated and was no longer an 'outsider' or 'savage' himself. To be sure, the earlier reference to מארץ העברים (Gen 40.15) could be taken to be an ethnic or national designation. But the larger context makes a generalized reference beyond the pale of civilization at least as plausible. ("I was kidnapped out of the land of the vagabonds" or —from the context of Egyptian order— "... snatched from chaos".)

In the book of Exodus the first references to "Hebrews" are to pregnant women and midwives of "the children of Israel". When Pharaoh summons the midwives they are called "Hebrews" and when they answer Pharaoh they themselves refer to "Hebrew women" (Ex 1.15, 16 & 19). Likewise, the apparently abandoned baby who is rescued by Pharaoh's daughter is recognized as a 'Hebrew' (Ex 2.6). The dramatic context of this scene is Pharaoh's plan to reduce the population of resident aliens by means of infanticide, for reasons of state security.

By the time Moses has grown up, he identifies with the oppressed foreign workers because of the clandestine education he has received from the "Hebrew nurse" (Ex 2.7), his natural mother. If the oppressed non-Egyptian workers were not a coherent group previously, they no doubt gained some sense of unity and corporate solidarity in their common suffering.¹⁷ Their sense of common cause and 'brotherhood', which Moses claimed, did not keep them from fighting

---

¹⁶ Church historian Eusebius Pamphilus carried forward and firmly established the then-current Christian usage of this and other technical terms of his time (fourth century AD). (*E.g.* "Flavius Josephus, the distinguished historian among the Hebrews, ..." and "at that time the whole church under them consisted of faithful Hebrews." *Eccles. History* I.5 and IV.5.) Synchronic evidence is more immediately relevant, such as the *Amarna Letters* to which we turn next. (For interpretation of the biblical evidence itself, the 'tagmemic hierarchy' is fundamental: consider the specific sentences in which the word occurs, the larger immediate contexts, Exodus-Genesis taken together, the *Torah*, and finally the whole *Tanak*.)

¹⁷ The biblical narrative indicates that this corporate solidarity was decisively shaped by the Exodus when the term 'Israel' becomes definitive. But at least some of the 'Hebrews' in Egypt claimed common descent and spoke a common language. Already at this time, their 'putative common descent' had been 'validated by several generations of common historical experience'. (Pierre van den Berghe, *The Ethnic Phenomenon*, 16, cited above, 39/ n 78).

amongst themselves, however, and they certainly were not ready to follow Moses as their leader (Ex 2.11 & 13).

After Yahweh had "heard the cry of the children of Israel" (Ex 3.9) and chosen Moses as his agent for their liberation from Pharaoh's bondage, he instructs Moses to say specifically:

> Yahweh, the God of the Hebrews, has met with us. Permit us, accordingly, to go a three-day journey into the wilderness to sacrifice to Yahweh our God. (Ex 3.18)

This designation of Yahweh as "the God of the Hebrews" is repeated five times in dialogue with Pharaoh (Ex 5.3; 7.16; 9.1 & 13; 10.3). The theological theme, "Let my people go, that they may serve me" (7.16), is fundamental and so is Yahweh's self designation as "the God of the Hebrews". The translation "Yahweh, the God of the oppressed" does not evade but clarifies the theological sense. The revelation was put into Pharaoh's terms of reference, and that is how he would have heard it.

In these stories in Genesis and Exodus, the term 'Hebrews' refers to Israelites as outsiders or marginal people in Egyptian society. But after the Israelites have been defined by the Exodus, the Conquest, and settlement in the Promised Land, 'Hebrews' reappear in the biblical narrative of I Samuel. The first two occurrences of the term are easily understood in the same sense, this time from the perspective of the powerful Philistines who are at once contemptuous and suspicious of an unruly mob of stateless people: "What does this great shouting in the vagabond camp [במחנה העברים] mean?" (I Sam 4.6), and "Fight like men, Philistines, or you shall become slaves of runaways [חעברן לעברים]!" (4.9). This same perspective explains Philistine policy of eliminating local blacksmiths "lest the vagabonds make swords and spears for themselves" (13.19); as well as their descriptive exclamation in the next chapter: "Look! The riff-raff are coming out of the holes where they have been hiding!" (14.11). Earlier, when Saul had broadcast news of a provocative victory and called his troops to arms by blowing a horn, his announcement began, העברים לאמר ישמעו, with the LXX reading οι δοῦλι for the noun (I Sam 13.3). The MT narrative continues, "Thus all Israel learned..." (13.4).

Saul's apparent self-identification as a 'Hebrew' is different from previously recorded usage in the Bible. In any case, with this term he challenges those who lack the conventional means of waging war (13.19) to mobilize for battle.[18] Not surprisingly, "some Israelites, aware of the dangerous and difficult situation," went into hiding, and "other Hebrews" fled across the Jordan (13.6-7). Only after Saul's success was obvious did some "Hebrews who had previously

---

[18] The description of the Israelites armed with digging tools, ploughshares, sickles, and axes coming to battle with the Philistine army is a classic picture of a peasant revolt. This picture does not always come clear in the modern retelling of the biblical story. When the picture is put in proper focus, Saul's rallying call might remind the modern reader of Spartacus' Roman slave revolt (73-71 BC) or of the more recent challenge by Karl Marx and Friedrich Engels in the *Communist Manifesto* (1848), "Workers of the world unite!"

sided with the Philistines" come over to join Saul and Jonathan (14.21).Israelites who had been hiding also now join the fray. "Thus Yahweh saved Israel that day" (14.22-23).

The story gets complicated, and it is not clear that Saul and his forces continue to identify themselves as 'Hebrews' after their success. But David certainly is a 'Hebrew'. Nabal, in answer to his own question —"Who is David?"— remarks sarcastically, "These days there are many servants who run away from their masters" (I Sam 25.10). The subsequent question of the Philistine chiefs characterizes David and his men as a renegade regiment: "What are these Hebrews doing here?" (29.3).

Each of these references to 'Hebrews' (in Gen, Ex, & I Sam) fits the pattern of extra-biblical *'Apiru* usage. Ever since the modern discovery of the Amarna letters (1887), there has been scholarly debate about if and how the biblical 'Hebrews' relate to the *'Apiru*. There is now wide agreement that the 'Hebrews' were *'Apiru*.[19] But, of course, there were more *'Apiru* than the number joined together as 'Israel' in covenant with Yahweh. This conclusion has fundamental significance for understanding Israel's history and theology. Saul's rallying cry to his people as 'Hebrews' is not surprising in the context of Israel's covenant. They celebrated their deliverance from slavery every year at Passover. The Ten Words of the Covenant are introduced with a reminder of their corporate beginning in slavery, and one form of the Sabbath commandment includes the injunction to "remember that you too were once slaves in Egypt" (Deut 5.15). Variations on this theme are repeated insistently in the Covenant Code: "You shall not molest or oppress an alien, for you were once aliens yourselves in Egypt" (Ex 22.20); ... you know how it feels to be an alien, since you were once aliens yourselves in Egypt (Ex 23.9). Memory of such 'Hebrew' origins would sharpen the focus of the poetic idea of 'no people' or 'not my people' being transformed into "Sons of the living God" (Hosea 1.10, *cf.* NT citations).

Finally, the few texts which seem to have influenced Christian and Jewish readers of the Bible to give an ethnic definition to 'Hebrew' should be noted

---

[19] John Bimson and others still insist that "the Habiru were nothing to do with the movement of any Hebrew group; nor should the 'Apiru of the Egyptian records be linked with the biblical Hebrews." *Redating the Exodus and Conquest* (Sheffield: JSOT, 1978), 24. The evidence and arguments about the relationship of 'Hebrews' and *'Apiru* are too complicated to summarize here, but M. Greenberg's *The Hab/piru* (New Haven, 1955/1961) surveys most of the questions and is cited by scholars on both sides of the debate. For a classic statement of the relationship see G.E. Mendenhall's "The *'Apiru* Movements in the Late Bronze Age", *The Tenth Generation*, 122-141. *Cf.* N.P. Lemche's conclusion: "There must have been in the later Israel a historical remembrance that their own society, during the first days of its existence, was interpreted by its neighbours and opponents as a society of habiru." *Studia Theologica* 33 (1979) 21.

(The name 'Hebrew' for the *language* of Israel may have originated as a contemptuous designation of the Aramaic these people spoke, just as some people's French is called *"Patois"*. But I have seen no published argument supporting this suggestion.)

here,[20] both for completeness of this survey and to show that these texts too can be interpreted in terms of the sociological definition of *'Apiru*.[21] 'Abram the Hebrew' (Gen 14.13), very simply, was 'a wandering Aramean' (Deut 26.5 —this text might apply as well to his grandson Jacob/Israel). Abram described himself as 'a resident alien' in Canaan (or 'stranger and sojourner' גר ותשב Gen 23.4). The reappearance of 'Hebrews' in Deuteronomy and the Later Prophets is more problematic.

The regulations regarding 'Hebrew slaves' in Deuteronomy 15.12 and especially Jeremiah 34.9 & 14 are judged by most scholars to involve archaic language derived from the very similar regulations in Exodus 21.2. But even the older text is extremely troublesome because it involves the whole complicated question about whether slavery is, or ever could have been, divinely sanctioned.[22] In any case, it is not easy to see why a 'refugee' or 'Hebrew' should have rights not guaranteed to other human beings. But in the Exodus passage and also in Deuteronomy 15.12 and Jeremiah 34.9 & 15 the 'kinship' claimed for the 'Hebrew' —even identifying him as ביהודי (Jer 34.9)— is explained in terms of the flight from Egypt.

Jonah's testimony, "I am a Hebrew" (Jonah 1.9), would be the latest example of such usage in biblical speech if dated to the eighth century BC, and the book was written much later than that. Nevertheless, modern interpreters who cite this verse as an early example of the use of the term 'Hebrew' for ethnic identification should note that Jonah is identifying himself as a fugitive. His use of the term fits the oldest pattern of biblical usage exactly.

2. Conquest of the Promised Land by the Tribes of Israel

The formation of the Confederation of Twelve Tribes has become the focus of attention in the current *Quest for the Historical Israel*.[23] Three quite different models have been proposed for an understanding of the emergence of Israel in Canaan: Conquest, Immigration, and Social Revolution.[24] At first glace these alternatives seem mutually exclusive. Certainly some of the arguments put forward in support of reconstructions conforming to one or another of these models contradict basic interpretations of historical and textual

---

[20] The persistence of this idea in post-biblical times has been noted above and will be noted again below. With reference to the biblical 'Hebrews', "there can be no doubt that they do not constitute an ethnic unity." G. von Rad, *TDNT* 3, 358; *contra* A.F. Rainey, "Hebrews", *Harper's Bible Dictionary* (San Francisco: Harper & Row, 1985).

[21] G.E. Mendenhall interprets "the late confession in Deuteronomy 26:5" as referring to Jacob, who was "neither 'a wandering Aramean' nor a 'Syrian ready to perish'. He was in fact a 'fugitive Aramean' who by flight and stealth cut himself off from the community of which he had been a member, and according to biblical tradition, was rescued from extermination only by the direct intervention of Yahweh." *Tenth Generation*, 137.

[22] This question is refocused in the New Testament, notably in Paul's letter to Philemon.

[23] G.W. Ramsey, *The Quest for the Historical Israel* (Atlanta: John Knox, 1981).

[24] N.K. Gottwald, *The Hebrew Bible: A Socio-Literary Introduction* (Philadelphia: Fortress, 1985), 261-76.

evidence used by scholars working with an alternate model. Since few, if any, biblical scholars limit their concerns to antiquarian interest, almost all argument about Israel's origins can be seen to have significance also for interpretations of Israel's later self-understanding and the self-understanding of the scholars who identify with Israel, as Christians or Jews.

In the present study, our immediate concern is to grasp the first-century understanding (or understandings) of Israel. If we can clarify our own understanding of the biblical accounts of the Conquest which occurred more than 3,000 years ago, we can hope to improve our grasp also of the views of these events which informed the earliest Christian mission. On the one hand, it would be naive to suppose that first-century views of the Conquest approximated the best reconstructions of modern scholarship. No doubt some medieval and modern misconceptions originated in the first century AD or earlier. On the other hand, it seems likely that *some authentic theological, political, and cultural memories* of the Conquest surviving into the first century would have been lost (and occasionally rediscovered) during the subsequent 1,900 years.

Of the three models cited, 'conquest' has the advantage of relating immediately to the biblical interpretation of the establishment of the Twelve Tribes in the Promised Land. We can safely assume that first-century reflections on these events interpreted them in terms of Divine guidance of Israel from Egypt to Canaan, including violent conquest directed by Yahweh. But it is *not* safe to assume that first-century views were identical with the 'conquest theories' of nineteenth- and early twentieth-century biblical scholarship.

Today, as Norman Gottwald observes, "the conquest theory is highly problematical"[25] not only in relation to modern archeological findings but also in the light of accounts in the Hebrew Bible itself. Even where 'conquest' is spoken of explicitly, as in Deuteronomy 6.1 ("These then are the commandments, the statutes, and the ordinances which Yahweh your God commanded that you be taught to observe in the land which you are entering for conquest ..."), 'conquest' (לרשתה) can be translated "to possess" or "to inherit", as in the LXX translation κληρονομῆσαι. (*Cf.* Deut 2.12 in relation to Jer 32.8.)

George Mendenhall's proposed view of the Conquest as "a peasants' revolt against the network of interlocking Canaanite city states"[26] has been perceived by some scholars as a challenge to established opinion not only, but a contradiction of the biblical accounts themselves.[27] It is true that even modifications of Mendenhall's proposal amount to "a fundamentally new conception of Israel's rise to power"[28] when compared to earlier modern formulations of 'conquest' or 'immigration'. But this "new conception" enables

---

[25] *Ibid.*, 261.

[26] G.E. Mendenhall, "The Hebrew Conquest of Palestine", *BA* 25 (1962), 73.

[27] Peter Craigie protests that Mendenhall's view depends on "a very different picture from that conveyed by the biblical writers". *The Problem of War in the Old Testament* (Grand Rapids: Eerdmans, 1978). 50. *Cf.* John Bimson, *Redating Exodus*, 31.

[28] *Ibid.*, 272.

the modern reader most "adequately [to] account for what the Bible tells us of Israel's emergence in Canaan".[29] While allowing for "an important dimension of armed conflict in Israel's emergence from the start" and recognizing "the exodus Israelites – as the final catalyst that clinched a long-brewing social revolution among depressed and marginated Canaanites",[30] this model sharply focuses the meaning of God's covenant with Israel.

To be sure, this model does not eliminate 'the problem of war in the Old Testament',[31] but when the terms at issue encompass social revolution the problem appears in a new light.

> Not only did the early Israelites, under the leadership of Yahweh (and Moses, Joshua, Deborah, *etc.*), establish their independence as a peasantry free from any ruling class, they also formed a covenant with Yahweh and each other to maintain that freedom. ... God himself was their ruler and object of exclusive loyalty: 'You shall have no other gods ....' Because God was the true king, there could be no human institution of kingship, no state in early Israel.[32]

This statement of "Israel's origins as a free peasantry in Covenant with God" by Horsley and Hanson includes the graphic illustration of Joshua's literal instructions to the people to "put your feet upon the necks of these kings" (Joshua 10.24-25).

עַם and גּוֹי

"The question is whether Israel was an *'am* or a *goy*. The answer is plainly that Israel was both." So E.A. Speiser concludes his essay, "'People' and 'Nation' of Israel". But before arriving at this conclusion he demonstrates "a clear and manifold distinction between the two nouns".[33] We have referred to the Greek and English translations of these two words, and we shall refer to them again in the present study. But we should note here that Speiser resists the temptation to define Israel as an עַם over against the גּוֹים, even though "unlike *'am*, *goy* is never possessively construed with *YHWH*; there is no such construction as *goy-YHWH*."[34] This and other of Speiser's observations are instructive, as is his rough definition of the two terms:

---

[29] *Ibid.*

[30] *Ibid.*

[31] *Ibid.*, 9; *cf.* 33-43, "God as Warrior"; & 45-63, "The Problem of Holy War".

[32] Richard A. Horsley and John S. Hanson, *Bandits, Prophets, and Messiahs: Popular Movements in the Time of Jesus* (Minneapolis: Winston, 1985), 5.

[33] E.A. Speiser, *Oriental and Biblical Studies*, ed. J.J. Finkelstein and Moshe Greenberg (Philadelphia: University of Pennsylvania Press, 1967 [1959]), 169.

[34] *Ibid., loc. cit.*

People tends to emphasize common cultural and social characteristics, while *nation* is mainly a political designation associated as a rule with state and government. In neither instance is there any explicit stress on racial origins.[35]

Speiser's sober conclusion that Israel was both a 'people' and a 'nation' (or 'state') is unavoidable, even though Israel's singularity over against 'the nations' is stressed repeatedly in the Bible (*e.g.* Ex 34.10 & Nu 23.9). In the Exodus and Conquest this contrast between 'Israel' and 'the nations' is easy to grasp even if difficult to express grammatically.[36] According to Gottwald, "the Israelite confederacy was a consciously contrived 'substitute state' opposed to surrounding city-state organization, indeed a veritable 'anti-state'."[37] If it is reasonable to suggest that Israel, as עם קדוש אתה ליהוה (Deut 7.6), was in some sense also a 'substitute people',[38] it becomes possible to reformulate Speiser's conclusion paradoxically: ancient Israel was neither a *goy* nor an *'am*.

It is always hazardous to transpose claims of divine election and miraculous community into secular categories for historical analysis. But in such transposition, the terms 'family' and 'people' seem more appropriate than 'voluntary association' for modern expression of the ancient covenant relationships because these simple terms follow biblical usage. Moreover, as C.E. L'Heureux observes,

> The regular and very frequent means of expressing ethnic identity in Hebrew consists of *bene* followed by the name of the people or its eponymous ancestor (*bene yisrael, bene 'ammon*, et c.)[39]

Nevertheless, even if it is correct to insist that "common descent ... constituted the prime criterion of affiliation in preconquest Israel",[40] we should heed

---

[35] Speiser makes an observation about the different semantic ranges of the Hebrew words and their translation-equivalents in English (and Greek) which is also instructive: "The gap between Hebrew *'am* and *goy* is greater than between our 'people' and 'nation'." *Ibid.*, 164.

[36] As noted in chapter 2 above, the addition of the adjective "other" in contrasting "Israel and the [other] nations" is a major interpretive move; the introduction of "Gentile" into this formulation ("Israel and the [gentile] nations") involves ideological reconstruction.

[37] N.K Gottwald, *Hebrew Bible*, 282.

[38] See N. Gottwald's reference to "that remarkably ancient sociologically mutant people who called themselves Israel". *The Tribes of Yahweh: A Sociology of the Religion of the Liberated Israel, 1250-1050 B.C.E.* (Maryknoll: Orbis, 1979), xxii. This idea is best expressed in the biblical phrase עם קדוש אתה ליהוה (Deut 7.6; 14.2; 26.18; *cf.* Ex 19.5; Mal 3.17 & Ps 136.4b). R.G. Boling thinks that the distinction between *goy* and *'am* is even sharper than Speiser allows; he notes that Israel as an *'am* "resists ethnic or nationalistic definition". *Joshua: A New Translation with Notes and Commentary* (Garden City: Doubleday, 1982), 121. 'Anti-family' implications of 'the new covenant' are explicitly stated many times in the NT, most sharply by Jesus' words recorded in Luke 14.26.

[39] C.E. L'Heureux, "The *yelide hapera*", *BASOR* 221 (1976), 83.

[40] *Ibid.*

Isaac Rabinowitz' warning that such terms as 'household', 'clan', 'family', 'tribe' and 'people'

> go beyond a mechanically applied notion of consanguinity; even the narrowest in point of kinship, the 'house' could be used to designate the Rechabites, meaning all who chose to follow the nomadic ideal as promulgated by Jonadab son of Rechab (Jer 35.18) and not merely the latter's own offspring. ... Just as 'son of a prophet' did not necessarily mean a person whose father was a prophet, so a 'son of Israel' did not necessarily mean one whose father was literally a carrier of the genes of the patriarchs, but one who shared the characteristics —history, way of life, and destiny— that constituted the 'people' of Israel.[41]

'Adoption' is not a prominent term in the Hebrew Bible, and the concept of legal adoption of a child into a nuclear family seems foreign to Israel,[42] but the term 'covenant' itself seems always to imply divine adoption and, in turn, assimilation into the family of God. If this is so, modern arguments about whether the ethnic origins of Israel are to be discovered in Mesopotamia or Canaan are part of a misplaced debate.

Caleb and Ruth

The stories of Caleb and the book of Ruth are two of very many vivid descriptions in the Hebrew Bible of *adoption* and *assimilation* into the Tribes of Israel. It would not be an exaggeration to call these explicit references. Although neither the term 'adoption' nor a definition of the process of 'assimilation' is spelled out, both Caleb and Ruth are presented in the Bible itself as *model* 'children of Israel'.

Whether the reader is to understand that Caleb's ancestors joined Jacob and his sons before they entered Egypt (Gen 18) or that Caleb's father Jephunneh (or he himself) joined Israel after the Exodus (Judges 1.16), Caleb is identified *both* as a leader among the Israelites "of the Tribe of Judah" (Numbers 13.3/6) *and* as a Kenizzite (Josh 14.6 *cf.* Gen 15.19). The biblical text, so far from suggesting that Caleb was a 'proselyte', presents him not only as a true Israelite but the truest Israelite of them all. Caleb's own recollection, to Joshua, of his "complete loyalty to Yahweh" (Josh 14.8) is a modest summary of his words and

---

[41] I. Rabinowitz, "Government", *IDB* 2, 452.

[42] With reference to Gen 15.1-3, W.F. Albright argues that Abraham accepted adoption (which is well-attested at Nuzi). *Yahweh and the Gods of Canaan: A Historical Analysis of Two Conflicting Faiths* (Garden City: Doubleday, 1968 [1965]), 66. Relevant to our larger theme is W. Eichrodt's comparison of "adoption in the sense of a fictitious consanguinity" to "the unification of the tribes into the people of Yahweh [which] brought about an enlargement of the circle of those linked by solidarity, creating a new physical and psychical whole within which an inward bond of a higher sort held the members of the covenant together with the firmness of a clan community". *Theology of the Old Testament* vol 2 (Philadelphia: Westminster, 1967 [1964]), 238.

deeds when he stood alone (Nu 13.30/ 14.24) and with Joshua (Nu 14.6 & 30) as the remnant of Israel, faithful to the Covenant with Yahweh.

Ruth's previous identification as a Moabite is more obviously significant to the biblical account than is Caleb's Kenizzite lineage. And Ruth is not only a model of Covenant faithfulness but also, as an ancestor of David, a matriarch in Israel.[43] The Book of Ruth claims to represent "the time of the Judges" (Ruth 1.1) and this claim seems to have been acknowledged by first-century Jews.[44] Whatever the date of written composition, Ruth's paradigmatic oath of allegiance to Yahweh (1.16-17) is an authentic representation of the ancient faith of Israel. The later statement of embattled separatism in Nehemiah 13.1 ("no Ammonite or Moabite may ever be admitted into the assembly of God") is easy enough to explain in its own context. But this prohibition in Nehemiah reiterates Deuteronomy 13.1-3, which has its setting in pre-Conquest Israel.

The text in Deuteronomy, and others relating to the nations in the Conquest, juxtaposed with the Book of Ruth (and very many other indications of 'adoption' and 'assimilation' in the Hebrew Bible) presents a challenge to our understanding of the Conquest which also must have confronted those engaged in the first-century Christian mission to the nations. To conclude our survey of the issues raised by the biblical text itself in identification of 'Israel' and 'the nations' among the people in the Promised Land, *three simple points* should be emphasized.

First, Abram himself was cut off from the land of the Chaldeans and from his ethnic heritage (Gen 12.1). Without pursuing any theological explanations, we can say that the biblical narrative indicates this immigrant's extraordinary commitment to 'the promised land'. His son Isaac and grandson Jacob were born in Canaan (Gen 21 & 25), and his great-grandchildren lived there before the sojourn in Egypt. If the language of these foreigners in Egypt was the language of Canaan it was because they were —in a peculiar way— 'Canaanites'.

Second, the biblical injunctions to Israel to annihilate the Canaanites or to be absolutely separate from them can be understood best as representing the demands of the jealous God for radical allegiance to Him in the covenant. Canaanites who became Israelites could no longer be Canaanites in any ordinary sense: political, social, or religious. As the biblical accounts insist, and as modern archaeologists and historians have demonstrated in surprising ways, Israelites were the opposite of Canaanites.[45]

---

[43] This is implied in the elders' benediction with its reference to Rachel and Leah (Ruth 4.11) and is stated explicitly in the book's concluding verses. Matthew follows established tradition when he emphasizes this point in presenting the Messiah's genealogy (Mt 1.5).

[44] This claim is supported by the LXX arrangement "where Ruth is placed immediately after the book of Judges" and by "an older arrangement of the biblical books" described in *Baba Bathra* 14b BT "in which Ruth preceded Psalms at the beginning of the writings". D.R.G. Beattie, *Jewish Exegesis of the Book of Ruth* (Sheffield: JSOT, 1977), 2 & 1.

[45] "The conflict was certainly not merely one of 'ethnic groups'. There could have been no important ethnic or linguistic contrast between the 'Canaanites' and the 'Israelites' in 1200 BC. There was, however, an enormous contrast of value systems." G.E. Mendenhall,

Third, as already noted, a large "mixed multitude" of Israelites escaped from slavery in Egypt (Ex 12.38). Later Moses reminds them, "Your ancestors went down to Egypt seventy strong, and now Yahweh your God has made you as numerous as the stars of the sky" (Deut 10.22). Whatever explanation is given for the various numbers recorded elsewhere in the narrative, it is obvious that the population of Israel which came to occupy the Promised Land was many times greater than can be explained in terms of ordinary generation from the original Patriarchs.[46] Arguing against the idea of an *ethnic* conquest, Mendenhall insists that "there was no statistically important invasion of Palestine at the beginning of the twelve tribe system of Israel."[47] But, as Mendenhall and others have developed the argument for social revolution, the importance of 'the Exodus component' is all the more amazing because of its 'statistical insignificance'. With reference to the "first obligation of the covenant to reject all foreign relations", Mendenhall explains that

> of course, outside groups could enter the community by acknowledging the suzerainty of Yahweh ... in which case they simply became a part of Israel. Thus it is not at all unreasonable to speak of early Israel as a missionary religion, particularly when the Amarna Letters are full of references to various ways in which the leaders of a coalition attempted to gain adherents.[48]

The anachronism of the designation "missionary religion" is problematic but, if used with care, the term can serve as a useful summary explanation for the aggressive, radical assimilation which Mendenhall describes:

> The Decalogue constitutes a revolutionary movement .... Perhaps for the first time in human history, a real elevation to a new and unfamiliar ground in the formation of a community took place —a formation based on common obligations rather than common interest —on ethic, rather than on covetousness.[49]

Working earlier with a different 'conquest' model, W.F. Albright made the same point about this missionary religion:

> It is a serious error to assume that the 'Israelites' of the period immediately preceding the Conquest were a homogeneous body .... Their remarkable history and their religious zeal were undoubtedly the principle cohesive forces in their organization. Under no circumstances must we underestimate the power of the religious factor.

"Social Organization in Early Israel", *Magnalia Dei*, *Fs*. G.E. Wright (Garden City: Doubleday, 1976), 146.

[46] "The biblical traditions themselves certainly hint that the Israel that came into existence in Canaan contained elements which were not descended from the eponymous Jacob." J. Bimson, *Redating the Exodus*, 16.

[47] G.E. Mendenhall, "The Hebrew Conquest of Palestine", *BA* 25 (1962), 73.

[48] G.E. Mendenhall, *Law and Covenant in Israel*, 38.

[49] G.E. Mendenhall, *Tenth Generation*, 21-22.

Mosaic Yahwehism was a missionary religion, still in its first and most active phase.[50]

3. Israel as the Kingdom of God

"Yahweh is never called *Melek* prior to the monarchy" in Israel,[51] but he certainly occupied the place of earthly sovereign as well as Deity in Israel's Covenant.[52] Early Israel was a 'theocracy' in a way which was not only different from 'theocracies' where the human king was divinized but even opposite to the Egyptian 'theocracy' with its Pharaoh-god, for example. Certainly there could be no sovereign alongside Yahweh in the covenant community, and Israel's egalitarian constitution would seem to have precluded the possibility of any human 'king' or 'ruler'.

The idea that ancient Israel was formed on 'charismatic leadership' has had strong support in modern scholarship, at least since the early contribution to the current discussions by Max Weber.[53] The cultural anthropologists' term 'acephalous' is seldom used by biblical scholars, but the biblical narratives suggest that 'all Israel' (Judges 2.4) had no constitutional head.[54] Special leaders, such as Moses and Joshua, were called for specific assignments. So Yahweh raised up Othniel, Caleb's nephew, to rescue Israel from its apostasy and to serve as judge (Judges 3.9). Likewise Ehud, Deborah, and the others. "The idea of monarchy was consciously rejected," as John Bright notes,[55] citing Gideon's response to Israel's petition in Judges 8.23. ("I will not rule over you, nor shall my son rule over you. Yahweh must rule over you." *Cf.* Jothan's parable, Judges 9.7-21.)

"In Israel", according to Gerhard von Rad, "the monarchy arose under Philistine pressure."[56] Whatever prompted it, the request from "all the elders

---

[50] W.F. Albright, *Archeology and the Religion of Israel* (Baltimore: Johns Hopkins University Press, 1953 [1942]), 99.

[51] G. von Rad, " מלך and מלכות in the OT", *TDNT* 1, 570.

[52] "Early Israel was the dominion of Yahweh, consisting of all those diverse lineages, clans, individuals, and other social segments that, under the covenant, had accepted the rule of Yahweh and simultaneously had rejected the domination of the various local kings and their tutelary deities —the *baalim*. As a necessary corollary, Yahweh was the one who exclusively exercised the classic functions of the king, as described in the prologue to the Code of Hammurabi and in other early codes as well." Mendenhall, *Tenth Generation*, 29.

[53] M. Weber, *Ancient Judaism* (Glencoe: The Free Press, 1952 [1917-19]), 11, 17-18.

[54] In West Africa, the Tiv and Igbos provide example of acephalous government in modern times. "The Song of Deborah" (Judges 5) is one of the oldest documentary sources of information about early forms of leadership in Israel. Unfortunately, the LXX seems to be translating a different test from the MT in verse 2. But if the LXX is a translation of an old text (or a legitimate translation of the puzzling MT), the Greek is informative about "revelation" and "the willing people".

[55] J. Bright, *The Kingdom of God: The Biblical Concept and Its Meaning for the Church* (New York: Abingdon, 1953), 32.

[56] G. von Rad, *ibid.*, *TDNT* 1, 565.

of Israel" that Samuel appoint a *king* to judge them ככל הגוים (I Sam 8.5) is presented as a move to blur the distinction between 'Israel and the nations'. Whether the elders themselves *reluctantly* accepted the necessity of being 'like the others' or eagerly anticipated becoming 'a real nation', the narrative emphasizes Samuel's distress and Yahweh's judgment: "They have not rejected you, but they have rejected me, that I should not be king over them." (I Sam 8.7b; *cf.* 11.12.) The die is cast. But even so, Samuel does not use the word מלכ but rather נגיד ('leader') when he anoints Saul (I Sam 10.1).

Such emphatic biblical judgments, as well as the narrative description of the development of monarchy in Israel, support Mendenhall's view that the decision to appoint kings was counter-revolutionary and a move towards the 'paganization' of Israel:

> the transition from a religious community to a political power structure had eroded away the old religious ethic in favor of 'being like the rest of the nations', obsessed with power, concentration of wealth, and competition in the insane world of power politics.[57]

Walter Brueggemann agrees with the thrust of Mendenhall's argument but insists that "the critical perversion came not with David but with Solomon."[58] As for David, and 'David's Truth', Brueggemann points to the obvious when he notes that "David is the dominant figure in Israel's narrative. ... Israel is fascinated by David."[59] Nevertheless, the importance of the time before the monarchy for Israel's self-identification is focused by the persistent idea that only the first five books of the Bible are 'normative'.[60]

It is certainly true that "Israel's faith had already assumed its normative form long before David was born."[61] Under David, "all the tribes of Israel" were united (II Sam 5.1) and Israel's covenant relationship with Yahweh was reaffirmed —and necessarily redefined. Perhaps already under David, and certainly in memory of David, the royal or 'messianic' theology took shape. (Ps 2.7; 89.27 *et al.*) But it is David the faithful shepherd, the courageous

---

[57] G.E. Mendenhall, *Tenth Generation*, 28; with special note on Isaiah.

[58] W. Brueggemann, "Trajectories in Old Testament Literature and the Sociology of Ancient Israel", *JBL* 98 (1979), 169.

[59] W. Breuggeman, *David's Truth in Israel's Imagination and Memory* (Philadelphia: Fortress, 1986), 13.

[60] The function of the Torah as an early canon is easier to assume than to prove. There is evidence of "the subordination of the Prophets to the Law" in some developments of Judaism which continued on in Rabbinic Judaism. W. Zimmerli, *The Law and the Prophets* (London: SCM, 1971 [1968]), 14. *Cf.* emphasis on the Torah in ancient synagogue liturgies, in the LXX translation, and in the doctrine of the Sadducees and Samaritans.
The Jesus Movement gave at least equal weight to the Prophets. Modern Christian and Jewish focus on Israel's monarchy probably owes its shape to medieval European history.

[61] J. Bright, *Kingdom of God*, 19.

warrior, the fugitive and wanderer, the forgiven sinner, and above all the psalmist who was remembered as the ideal king.[62]

God's emphatic promise to David's descendants (II Sam 7.16) is traced in its fulfillment by the biblical writers with evident embarrassment. There is support in the Hebrew Bible for what can be surmised of the Rechabites views and the later Samaritan insistence that apostasy followed Eli. Certainly Solomon conspicuously violated the prohibitions listed in Deuteronomy 17.14-17, even though he had been promised (and later is praised for) unmatched wisdom (I Kg 3.12). If it is argued that David and the Davidic ideal symbolize Israel's unity, it must be admitted that *Israel's disunity* could hardly have been more graphically displayed than in the divided kingdoms of 'Israel' and 'Judah'. Oddly, the biblical material is "far richer and more diversified" for the Northern Kingdom than for David's dynasty,[63] notably with the stories of Elijah and Elisha. It is true that the name 'Israel' is used in a restricted and pejorative sense for the Northern Kingdom over against 'Judah' in the narratives of this period. But the term 'Israel' also retains its fundamental use as designation of the people of God: in the books of Chronicles, for example, "even reckoning with the division, both alike are Israel."[64]

The later prophets claimed the term 'Israel' as the designation of the people of God. Long after the Northern Kingdom has been destroyed and its subjects lost in exile, the survivors of Judah's exile are designated 'Israelites'. The terms 'Judah' and 'Jews' also appear in the biblical text, but far less frequently and with a narrower significance.[65]

The New Israel

The concept 'New Israel' is not explicitly stated either in the Hebrew Bible or in the New Testament, and the use of the term by Christian theologians from the second century onwards has been rightly criticized as implying 'a different Israel'. Nevertheless, a biblical concept of 'new Israel' is clearly and significantly implied in the prophetic writings —notably in Isaiah 42, Jeremiah 31, and Ezekiel 37 —as well as in the New Testament.

In order to represent biblical thought in our use of the term 'new Israel' we must heed Brevard Childs' insistence that "the new reality of which the Bible speaks has taken shape within historical Israel."[66] This new reality could emerge "only when there was an obedient response" to God's redemptive action.[67] As a Christian theologian, Childs sees this new reality or 'new

---

[62] Philo refers to David "as the psalmist, never as the king". S. Sandmel, *Philo of Alexandria* (New York: Oxford University Press, 1979), 103.

[63] Herbert Donner, "The Separate States of Israel and Judah", *Israelite and Judean History*, eds. J.J. Hayes and J. M. Miller (Philadelphia: Westminster, 1977), 397.

[64] H.G.M. Williamson, *Israel in the Books of Chronicles* (Cambridge: University Press, 1977), 110 citing M. Gill.

[65] G. von Rad, "Israel, Judah and Hebrews in the Old Testament", *TDNT* 3, 357.

[66] B. Childs, *Myth and Reality in the Old Testament* (London: SCM, 1957), 96.

[67] *Ibid.*, 97.

Israel' as pointing to fulfillment in Christ. But within the Hebrew Bible itself the concept of a 'new Israel' is persistent. This concept develops a special shape and focus in the post-Exilic writings.

The idea of Israel as "a people dwelling alone, and not reckoning itself among the nations" (Nu 23.9) persisted even during the monarchies, so that the term 'nation' requires an adjective when applied to Israel: 'a holy nation' or 'a peculiar nation'. Likewise the term 'nationalism' demands an adjective— 'theological nationalism'— when it is applied to the fundamental issues of Israel's history. But the idea of Israel constituted at Sinai as a 'congregation' [עדה] and the term 'covenant theology' are more appropriate at every period of Israel's history than 'holy nation' and 'theological nationalism'. Certainly after the Exile the term 'nation' seems hardly applicable in any sense.

In the biblical narrative, the idea of 'a holy remnant' is related to the idea of 'a holy nation'. Already before the story of Israel's emergence in the Exodus, the 'remnant' idea is graphically presented with the story of Noah (Gen 6.5-8); the account of Caleb and Joshua can also be interpreted in terms of 'a faithful remnant', as already noted. During the period of kings, the concept is dramatically presented in the story of Elijah where the remnant of seven thousand are true to Yahweh and the covenant (I Kg 19.18). But it is especially in relation to the Exile that terms for 'remnant' (שְׁרִיר שְׁאֵרִת שְׁאָר) become prominent.

The prophet Zephaniah saw hope for Israel in the remnant of the poor and humble (Zeph 2.3/.7;3.12-13), and Isaiah prophesied that a remnant of Israel would repent and return to God. (See his son's name, *Shearjashub*, Is 7.3.) The biblical applications of the concept vary, and it should be noted here that Jeremiah and Ezekiel disallow even the hope of a remnant's escape from the total judgment against Israel (Jer 44.14, Ez 5.10). But the idea of 'a remnant' continued to define the later reflection on the trauma of Exile, as can be seen in the apocalyptic literature. "The remnant, as a spiritual Israel, is clearly differentiated from the political Israel."[68] This characterization of Zephaniah's usage of the term identifies a clear line in Israel's post-exilic self-understanding.

B. *The Septuagint and Apocrypha*

The translation of the Hebrew Bible into Greek was an event with profound implications for Israel's self-identification and for Israel's mission to the nations. Assessment of the Septuagint as a source of information on the earliest Christian mission is complicated by the snarled complexity of Septuagintal studies, but some main lines are clear. The argument that the term 'Septuagint' should be applied only to the authorized translation of the Torah has its own importance

---

[68] Ernst Jenni, "Remnant", *IDB* 4, 33.

for our concerns,[69] but we follow current usage in identifying early translations of Isaiah, Jeremiah, Joshua, Judges, Ruth, the other books of the *Tanak*, and even deutero-canonical books as included in 'the Septuagint'. These writings, in different ways, all claim our attention as scriptures related to the earliest Christian mission.

For our present purposes we shall consider first some of the broad implications of the Greek translation of the Hebrew Bible. Secondly we shall consider those additions to the *Tanak* which may have served as Scripture also for the earliest Christian mission. These Greek translations of the *Apocrypha* (and some Greek compositions, such as II Maccabees) bridge gaps in our documentary information about post-Exilic Israel before the New Testament period.

1. The Law and the Prophets

That 'the Law and the Prophets' were translated at all is an important fact to consider in attempting to understand 'Israel and the nations'. On the one hand, if the translation was intended for the benefit of non-Jews, such intentions would have had obvious significance for Jewish proselytism and, by analogy and projection, for the earliest Christian mission.[70] On the other hand, if the translation of the Torah was undertaken for the benefit of Greek-speaking Jews and, indeed, if the 'Later Prophets' were translated for *haphtarah* ('the explanation' or 'the second lesson') in the synagogue liturgy,[71] the implications for our consideration of 'Israel' and 'the nations' are more subtle but no less profound. This second, more likely, possibility would indicate that ability to understand Hebrew in the third century BC was a negotiable element in an individual's identity with Israel and the God of Israel. This point might seem hardly worth mentioning because of the well-known history of Alexandrian Judaism, which includes Philo's vast literary production. But language is one of the fundamental elements of what we now call 'ethnicity'. In one basic sense of the term, then, third-century Israel was not 'ethnic'.[72]

---

[69] "This title, though originally applied only to the translation of the Pentateuch, was eventually transferred to the whole of the Old Testament." Alfred Rahlfs, *Septuaginta*, vol 1 (Stuttgart: Würtembergische Bibelanstalt, 1935), xxii.

[70] The pseudepigraphal *Letter of Aristeas* is an important document in the background of the earliest Christian mission to the nations, whether or not it includes any genuine information about the origins of the LXX. According to this text (which probably was written by a Jew in the second-century BC, but claims to have been written by a non-Jew a century earlier), the LXX was translated for non-Jews at their request, specifically at the request of the King of Egypt to the Jewish High Priest. *Aristeas* 11.

[71] "The translation most likely came about through the needs of the Alexandrian Jews themselves." Schürer-Vermes, *The History of the Jewish People in the Age of Jesus*, III/1 (Edinburgh: T. & T. Clark, 1986 [1891]), 475.

[72] Language disputes have been prominent in modern definitions of nationalism and in ethnic rivalries in Canada, Belgium, Palestine, and various parts of Africa. The earliest recorded dispute in the Christian community between "the Hellenists" and "the Hebrews"

The flexibility of the Covenant community in the third-century BC with regard to language can be appreciated by contrast to two later times and situations. From our vantage point, it is not obvious that at the time of 'the closing of the ranks' among the Jews after AD 135,[73] translation of the Bible into Aramaic, much less Greek, would have been allowed —if the deed had not already been done. Projecting still further ahead in history to another Semitic religion, we should note that Muslim self definition, from the seventh-century AD onward, specifically prohibits the translation of the Koran from Arabic to any other language. 'Submission' (*islam*) of the faithful to the will of God (*Allah*) simply demands learning the language of 'the Word of God'.[74]

The primacy of Israel's early history in post-exilic Jewish self-identification is emphasized by the appearance of the *Torah* first in Greek translation. If H. St. John Thackeray and others are correct in calculating that the 'Later Prophets' were the next books to appear, beginning with Isaiah, this *priority of translation* is closely related to the *priority of citation* in the New Testament. The many New Testament citations of biblical Psalms can be related also to the fact that the Psalter was translated into Greek long before the other 'Writings'.[75] Whether such correspondence indicates "a special mode of thought in the LXX and ... a characteristic piety" shared and developed by the New Testament writers, as H.J. Schoeps has argued,[76] is not certain. In some texts, at least, the Septuagint stands as an early witness to a mainstream which was narrowed and diverted by the Rabbis after AD 135.[77]

(Acts 6) is commonly supposed to have been defined in large part by 'mother tongue'. (C.F.D. Moule, "Once More, Who Were the Hellenists?" *Expository Times*, lxx [1958-59].) But Douglas Hare is probably right in *not* listing language among the four aspects or "ethnic solidarity" which figured in "the Conflict between Jews and Christians" in the first-century Christian mission. *The Theme of Jewish Persecution of Christians in the Gospel According to Matthew* (Cambridge: University Press, 1967), 3-18.

[73] Salo Baron, *A Social and Religious History of the Jews*, II (New York: Columbia University Press, 1952 [1937]), 131-41; cited above, 11/ n 53.

[74] "The Koran cannot be translated. That is the belief of old-fashioned Sheyks and the view of the present writer." Marmaduke Pickthall, *The Meaning of the Glorious Koran* (London: Allen & Unwin, 1930), vii. "While Philo and his Alexandrian co-religionists looked upon the translation of the Seventy as a work of inspired men, the Palestinian Rabbis subsequently considered the day on which the Septuagint was completed as one of the most unfortunate in Israel's history, seeing that the Torah could never be adequately translated." Max Margolis, "Preface to the First Edition of the Translation", *The Holy Scriptures according to the Massoretic Text* (Philadelphia: Jewish Publication Society, 1955 [1916]), vi.

[75] S. Jellicoe, *The Septuagint and Modern Study* (Oxford: Clarendon, 1968), 65-68.

[76] H.J. Schoeps, *Paul: The Theology of the Apostle in the Light of Jewish Religious History* (Philadelphia: Westminster, 1961 [1959]), 28.

[77] It is difficult to prove a tendentious line in any of the decisions by the Masoretes or in the choice of available texts and the translation by the Seventy. Some books of the LXX were badly translated (notably the important book of Isaiah), but Qumran texts seem to indicate that for Joshua, I&II Samuel and I&II Kings the LXX is based on a better Hebrew text than the MT. Frank Moore Cross, Jr. *The Ancient Library of Qumran*

Whatever the intentions and purposes of the original translators of the Septuagint, the result of their labors served as an authorized translation which was considered to be the inspired Word of God.[78] The Greek Bible certainly was a fundamental factor in the formation of the New Testament and of the earliest Christian mission to the nations. Moreover, for the modern student of Christian origins it provides bilingual controls for the interpretation of such biblical concepts as עם / λαός, גוים / ἔθνη, כל / πᾶς, ישראל / Ἰσραήλ, and יהודים / Ἰουδαῖοι. Equally important is the evidence which this ancient translation provides for pre-Christian, Jewish interpretations of 'messianic' and 'universalistic' texts of Scripture.

2. Canonical and Deutero-canonical 'Writings'

Referring to Jewish writings in the inter-Testamental period, Schürer-Vermes observe that "these works are so diverse that it is difficult to unite all the individual features into a comprehensive picture."[79] Even 'Writings' which have been part of Jewish and Christian 'canons' since the second century are difficult to evaluate when we attempt to view them in a first-century perspective. On the one hand, Ezra, Nehemiah, I and II Chronicles, and Esther represent strong currents of thought up to the time of the earliest Christian mission to the nations. But we should note that Chronicles, Ezra, and Nehemiah never made it into the Syrian Church canon, and Esther apparently was not included in the Qumran Library, was never quoted in the New Testament, and was thought doubtfully canonical by some Rabbis.[80] On the other hand, Tobit, Sirach, Judith, and I Maccabees, although not judged canonical by Jews and Protestant Christians, are important background documents on the origins of Christianity.

'Judaeans', 'Jews' and 'Israel'

Writing about "Ezra and the Origins of Judaism", Klaus Koch notes that "the term *yehudim* first appeared in the Old Testament writings during the exile, obviously replacing the older term *bene yehuda*."[81] This semantic change is important and often overlooked or confused by modern scholars. Followers of Julius Wellhausen consider the priest Ezra "as the 'father' of Judaism".[82] But using evidence from the book of Ezra to good effect, Koch argues that "if there was ... a change from ancient Israel to Judaism, then it occurred later than Ezra,

---

(Garden City: Doubleday, 1961) 178-80. In any case, it is important to note that the LXX is a pre-Christian Jewish translation: "Even in Palestine it achieved considerable prestige, being freely used by Josephus." Schürer-Vermes, *History of the Jewish People*, III/1, 480.

[78] Philo certainly regarded the LXX as a sacred text and he is probably representative of the whole Greek-speaking Diaspora in this respect. Shürer-Vermes, *Ibid.*, 480 & 142.

[79] Schürer-Vermes, *History of the Jewish People*, III/1, 177.

[80] D.J. Clines, *Ezra, Nehemiah, Esther* (Grand Rapids: Eerdmans, 1984), 2 & 254 citing BT *Megillah* 7a and *Sanhedrin* 100a. It is likely that "Esther was rejected by the sectaries" at Qumran, according to F.M. Cross, *Ancient Library*, 165 citing H.L. Ginsberg.

[81] K. Koch, "Ezra and the Origins of Judaism", *JSS* 19 (1974). 174.

[82] *Ibid., loc. cit.*

and presumably much later."⁸³ What is most important in Ezra for our consideration is that 'Israel' appears to be the deliberately chosen theological designation of the Covenant people. With few exceptions, this remains true in the writings which follow.

H.G.M. Williamson has shown how significant the term 'Israel' was in the Chronicler's retelling of the story of the divided monarchy. The term demonstrates "that a faithful nucleus does not exclude others, but is a representative centre to which all the children of Israel may be welcomed if they will return".⁸⁴ In Nehemiah היהודים are much more prominent than in Ezra, with the terms 'Jews' and 'Israel' apparently in linguistic free fluctuation. But close examination of the few occurrences of the term 'Israel' even in this book reveals a special theological emphasis in each text, as in Nehemiah 1.6 (refocusing היהודים /LXX ἄνδρες Ἰούδα of 1.2), and notably in 13.3: ויבדילו כל־ערב מישראל/ καὶ ἐχωρίσθησαν πᾶς ἐπίμικτος ἐν Ἰσραήλ. ⁸⁵ Before surveying the use of the term Israel in later Writings, we note a few more specific points relating to Ezra.

It is somewhat surprising that the book of Ezra, with its theme of return to the Land of Israel, was translated and read by Jews who had become thoroughly settled in Egypt and elsewhere.⁸⁶ Surely Ezra raises the question, which has reappeared in modern Zionism,⁸⁷ whether readiness to return to the Promised Land is an obligation for all who identify with Israel. It seems that while embracing Ezra-Nehemiah as instructive (and later 'canonical'), neither Palestinian nor Diaspora Jews accepted an 'ethnic' territorial definition of their self-identity as Israel.

As it happened, the book of Ezra proved remarkably susceptible to divergent interpretations in Israel's self-definition. On the critical question of the place of Samaritans within or over against 'Israel', the text of Ezra indicates that Ezra's aim was "to establish one Israel out of all 12 tribes"; in Ezra's view Samaritans are "only members of the northern tribes of Israel".⁸⁸ When we trace traditions about Ezra as a leader of Israel up to and beyond the time of the

---

⁸³ *Ibid.*, 197.

⁸⁴ H.G.M. Williamson, *Israel in the Books of Chronicles* (Cambridge: University Press, 1977). 140.

⁸⁵ With reference to Neh 13.3, D.J. Clines notes that this verse by the redactor (not from Nehemiah's memoirs) "reflects an interpretation of Dt. 23:3-6 ... but it is contrary to the intention of Dt. 23 itself (*cf.* vv.7f.), and conflicts with the inclusion of non-Jews among those who bound themselves to the pledge in Neh. 10". *Ezra, Nehemiah, Esther*, 237-8.

⁸⁶ Translations of the 'Writings' were later, less careful, and often the result of individual initiative, according to S. Jellicoe, *Septuagint and Modern Study*, 66.

⁸⁷ Modern Zionism dates from the 1897 World Zionist Congress in Basel, convened by Theodor Herzl. The movement has been divided internally (and strongly opposed by some Jews who remain outside the movement) precisely on definitions of the territorial question.

⁸⁸ K. Koch, "Ezra and the Origins of Judaism", *JSS* 19 (1974), 193. *N.b.* Ezra 6.17, 21.

earliest Christian mission, we discover that "Ezra became a symbolic figure in apocalyptic writings as well as in rabbinic literature."[89]

Esther
Although no evidence of an *Esther* scroll has been discovered at Qumran, the vast number of ancient copies and translations which have survived to modern times —including expanded versions as well as targums and *midrashim*— indicates the widespread popularity of this book.[90] Among the linguistic peculiarities of Esther which are noteworthy for our purposes is the absence of any explicit naming of God —or of God's people Israel. That God is in the author's mind not only at 4.14 but throughout the Hebrew text has been argued convincingly by the books defenders. That היהודים refers to 'Israel' is assumed.[91] The Greek translators did not add "God" and "Israel" to the text in front of them, but the Greek Additions supply these terms in abundance and so bring Esther into line with other biblical texts.

The Greek Additions, taken alone, are extremely interesting in linguistic terms relating to 'nations' (τὰ ἔθνη) and 'people' (ὁ λαός). The story is introduced by Mordecai's dream in which the Covenant people are identified as 'the righteous nation' or 'the nation of the just' (δικαίων ἔθνος 1.1f). The *Additions* conclude the book with Mordecai's thanks to God and the identification of "my nation, that is Israel" as "those who cried to God and were delivered" (τὸ δὲ ἔθνος τὸ ἐμόν, οὗτος ἐστιν Ισραηλ, οἱ βοήσαντες πρὸς τὸν θεὸν, καὶ σωθέντες 10.3f). Despite this use of ἔθνος referring to Israel, the plural form with 'all' a few lines further on clearly refers to 'those beyond the pale', in paradigmatic contrast with Israel as God's 'people': διὰ τοῦτο ἐποίησεν κλήρους δύο, ἕνα τῷ λαῷ τοῦ θεοῦ, καὶ ἕνα πᾶσι τοῖς ἔθνεσιν (10.3g). Earlier, Mordecai prayed for "the salvation of Israel" (σωτηρίαν Ισραηλ 4.17e) in a section integrated into the translated text in such a way that 'Israel' and 'Jews' occur as synonyms in free fluctuation.

Most notable for analysis of 'Israel and the nations' is Haman's hateful letter with its description of Israel as "a certain hostile people" or "one people of bad will" (δυσμενῆ λαόν τινα 3.13d) which, by its very constitution, "stands in opposition to every other society in the world" (ἐν ἀντιπαραγωγῇ παντὶ διὰ παντὸς ἀνθρώπῳ κείμενον 3.13e). This and other descriptions in the letter sound remarkably like the complaints we might imagine, earlier, from Canaanite

---

[89] *Ibid.*, 197.

[90] W.J. Fuerst, "The Rest of the Chapters of the Book of Esther", *The Shorter Books of the Apocrypha*, ed. J.C. Dancy (Cambridge: University Press, 1972), 132.

[91] "The absence of the name of God from the book of Esther can hardly be accidental.... But the story of the institution of a festival of rejoicing must be, for Israel, a story of a mighty deed of its God." D.J. Clines, *Ezra, Nehemiah, Esther*, 268-69. Clines and others use both "God" and "Israel" in commentary on the Hebrew text.

leaders against the Covenant community entering the Promised Land or, later, from conservative Romans protesting the earliest Christian mission.[92]

In the basic Esther text the climax of the story includes notice of many in the land committing themselves to the covenant (מתיהדים / καὶ πολλοὶ τῶν ἐθνῶν περιετέμοντο, καὶ ιουδάιζον 8.17). Their conversion is attributed to 'fear of the Jews', but we might give them the benefit of the doubt and interpret this as 'fear of Yahweh' since the reader must supply the name of the LORD elsewhere in the text as well. In any case, the 'binding' (קימו) on the community of the festival of thanksgiving[93] refers specifically to "whoever joined with them" (ἐπὶ τοῖς προστεθειμένοις ἐπ' αὐτῶν Esther 9.27. cf. Lev 18.26).

Tobit

Tobit is a fantastic story whose setting is the Assyrian Captivity of the northern Tribes of Israel. The book contains very old material, and even in its present form should probably not be dated later than 200 BC.[94] The two Greek versions in the ancient Codices of Sinaiticus (א) and Vaticanus (*B*) as well as the fragments discovered in the Qumran Caves testify to its continuing popularity and influence into the Christian era. The term 'Jews' does not appear in the text —although it is often supplied by modern translators and commentators—[95] and the author is consistent in his use of the term 'Israel' as the designation of the Covenant people.

Tobit "of the Tribe of Naphtali" (Tobit 1.1) is committed not only to the unity of all the Tribes of Israel, realized through worship in the Jerusalem Temple and the memory of King David, but also to "the converts who had attached themselves to Israel" (1.8, cf. Deut 14.28-29 & 26.12). In the Greek text, Tobit expresses his loyalty to his 'nation' (τῷ ἔθνει) in captivity in Assyria, and his 'country' (τῇ χώρα μου), the Land of Israel (1.3-4).

Tobit's prayer of thanksgiving to God acknowledges Israel's duty to "confess God in the presence of the nations" (ἐξομολογεῖσθε αὐτῷ, οἱ υἱοὶ Ισραηλ, ἐνώπιον τῶν ἐθνῶν 13.3) which held them captive. Tobit expresses his confidence that God will again gather his people "from all the nations among whom he has scattered us" (ἐκ πάντων τῶν ἐθνῶν, οὗ ἐαν σκορπισθῆτε ἐν αὐτοῖς 13.5). The book concludes with Tobit's vision of the new Jerusalem and a statement of his hope for the conversion of all the nations to

---

[92] Extant writings from the second-century provide an indication of conservative Greco-Roman reaction to the mission from the beginning. Celsus, *On the True Doctrine: A Discourse against the Christians*, trans. R.J. Hoffmann (New York: Oxford, 1987).

[93] "The piel of *qûm* in vv. 21, 27, 29, 31, 32 [and its] cultic significance" is noteworthy with reference to the perpetuity and comprehensiveness of the festival. Brevard Child, *Introduction to the Old Testament as Scripture* (Philadelphia: Fortress, 1979), 603.

[94] J. Dancy, *Shorter Books*, 10. *Cf.* 5th cent. BC Aramaic mss. of the related "Story of Ahikar" discovered in the ruins of Elephantiné. R.H. Charles, *APOT* vol II, 777-84.

[95] J. Darcy summarizes the story of "related Jewish families living in exile" (*op.cit.*, 1). O. Eissfeldt likewise refers to "the Jewess Sarah" in *The Old Testament, An Introduction*, trans. P.R. Ackroyd (New York: Harper, 1965 [1934]), 583.

truly fear and worship God (καὶ πάντα τὰ ἔθνη ἐπιστρέψουσιν ἀληθινῶς φοβεῖσθαι κύριον τὸν θεὸν 14.6-7).

Ecclesiasticus

Sirach (*Ecclesiasticus*) extols the universal sway of Wisdom (ἐν παντὶ λαῷ καὶ ἔθνει 24.6), but singles out Israel as Wisdom's true home, specifically because of "the book of the Covenant of the most high God" (24.8 &.23). Israel is identified as "the people called by Your name" (κεκλημένον ἐπ' ὀνόματί σου 36.11). In the same prayer, the plea for mercy towards Israel is balanced by reference to "all the nations" (πάντα τὰ ἔθνη) and "the other nations" (ἔθνη ἀλλότρια), that they too may 'fear the Lord' (36.1-2). But the force of the verbs hardly allows an interpretation which focuses on positive concern for the nations themselves.

References to Noah and Abraham carry forward the ambiguities of the older biblical texts with regard to 'mankind' (πᾶσα σάρξ 44.18) and 'the nations' (πλήθους ἐθνῶν 44.19). But most significant for the future developments between 'Israel' and 'the nations' are the references to the 'zeal' of Phinehas (ἐν τῷ ζηλῶσαι αὐτὸν ἐν φόβῳ κυρίου 45.23) and of Elijah (τῷ ζήλῳ αὐτοῦ ὠλιγοποίησεν 48.2). Following these references to 'zeal', Sirach's special mention of Nehemiah is a reminder that besides being a rebuilder of ruined walls (Sir 49.13), Nehemiah was a determined reformer (Neh 13.1-3 &.23-25/ LXX 23.1-3 &.23-25).

Sirach 50.25-26 expresses contempt for the Samaritans, perhaps building on a line drawn from the book of Nehemiah. Assuming that the original Hebrew text read לא גוי and עם נבל, it is difficult to see what meaning was intended in reversing the לא עם and גוי נבל of Deuteronomy 32.21. In any case, this distorted echo of Scripture, itself devoid of value as prophecy or wisdom, seems to have become influential in later relations between Jews and Samaritans.[96]

Judith

Although written in Hebrew, the book of Judith may have been fashioned in conscious imitation of Greek models of historiography.[97] Beginning as it

---

[96] Early references comparable to Sirach's "stupid people living in Shechem" (50.26) can be found in *Jubilees* 30.17 ("see how the Shechemites fared and their sons") and in the *Testament of Levi* 6 ("the sentence of God was for evil upon Schechem").
A scrap of the Hebrew text of Sirach in Qumran Cave 2 and the more substantial section discovered earlier in the Cairo Genizah indicate that the book was popular early as well as later with the Rabbis. (Schürer-Vermes, *History of the Jewish People*, 3/1 203 & 205.) The ancient translator's preface not only provides valuable information about the document itself and about the LXX, but also provides an early three-fold analysis of the Bible: "the law and the prophets and the other books of our fathers" (verse 24).

[97] Although originally written in Hebrew, "Judith displays in its compelling narrative structure a remarkable acquaintance with Greek historiography, Herodotus above all, and an appreciation of the Herodotean narrative's force." Mark S. Caponigro, "Judith as a Hellenistic Jewish Text", *Abstracts AAR/JBL Annual Meeting 1988*, 283.

does with Nebuchadnezzar as the king of the Assyrians (1.1), the narrative can hardly serve as a straight-forward source of historical information. Nevertheless, this delightful stew of fact and fiction maintains a disciplined use of the term 'Israel' throughout, and the "woe to the nations!" (οὐαὶ ἔθνεσιν 16.17) at the end of the story conforms to a clear pattern of biblical usage. Other bits and pieces in the text provide some clues for later developments in the relations of 'Israel' to 'the nations'.

The name 'Judith' itself is the feminine 'Jew' (יהודית / Ἰουδίθ). Her self-identification as "a daughter of the Hebrews" (καὶ εἶπεν Θυγάτηρ εἰμὶ τῶν Ἑβραίων 10.12) surprisingly fits the older biblical usage, both in the sense that she is explaining herself to foreigners and, according to her story, is a fugitive. (*Cf.* Jonah 1.9.) Nevertheless, it is difficult to escape the impression that a new sense of the term's meaning is emerging, with a secular, ethnic identification of 'the children of Israel' intended here. This impression is reinforced by the more elaborate explanation by Achior of these people as "descendants of the Chaldeans" (εἰσιν ἀπόγονοι Χαλδαίων 5.6ff).

Achior himself plays an important role in defining Israel's relationship to the nations. Deuteronomy 23.3 (and related texts in Ezra and Nehemiah) allows interpretations which unconditionally bar Ammorites from becoming Israelites. But in Judith, "all that the God of Israel had done" (14.10) and was able to do in response to individual faith is not limited by such interpretations. Achior, the Ammonite, was circumcised and "admitted as a member of the community of Israel, as his descendants still are" (προσετέθη εἰς τὸν οἶδον Ισραηλ ἕως τῆς ἡμέρας ταύτης 14.10).[98]

With reference to subsequent developments of the ideology of zeal in Israel, Judith's single emphatic reference to 'zeal' (ἐζήλωσαν τὸν ζῆλόν σου 9.4) with its reminder of Simeon's act of programmatic violence in Genesis 32 (Judith 9.2) stands in tension with the celebration of Achior's reception into Israel. But whatever the author's intentions, the elements of Judith's story provide explosive material for later developments of the 'zeal' motif.

I Maccabees

First Maccabees would be an important source of information about the background of the earliest Christian mission even if the book itself had not been widely circulated and influential in the first century AD.[99] Like Esther (and unlike other Scriptures), I Maccabees does not refer to God by name. But unlike the Hebrew *Esther*, this book does include prayers. In prayer, Judas Maccabeus refers to God as "the Savior of Israel" (ὁ σωτὴρ Ισραηλ 4.30). References to 'Israel' and 'the nations' throughout the book carefully follow biblical patterns of usage. "The wicked men" who seduced their fellow Israelites "to make a

---

[98] Like Caleb, Achior is completely assimilated and a model of faith for other Israelites.

[99] "The purpose of First Maccabees [is] Hasmonean propaganda", according to Jonathan Goldstein, *I Maccabees: A New Translation with Introduction and Commentary* (Garden City: Doubleday, 1976), 381. Jason of Cyrene wrote an anti-Hasmonean reply which was abridged to appear in LXX Codices ℵ & A as "II Maccabees" (*Ibid.*, 4).

covenant with the heathen" (διαθώμεθα διαθήκην μετὰ τῶν ἐθνῶν 1.11) introduce the narrative. The idolatry which results inexorably from the apostasy of uniting Israel with the nations εἶναι πάντας εἰς λαὸν ἕνα (1.41-43) is the setting for the reaction of the faithful which follows.

Mattathias' individual act of disciplinary violence against the "man of Judah" (ἀνὴρ Ἰουδαῖος 2.23) who deliberately engaged in an act of idolatry follows the pattern set by Phinehas (2.26 and Nu 25.6-9). The deed was done in the sight of the congregation of Israel (πολλοὶ ἀπο Ισραηλ 2.15) and Mattathias immediately rallied "everyone zealous for the law and the maintenance of the covenant" (2.27). Mattathias and his sons then fled into the desert, like David of old. In his last will and testament, Mattathias lists exemplars from Israel's history and singles out Phinehas and Elijah as models of 'zeal' (2.54 &.58).[100]

The use of the terms ἔθνος and ἔθνη throughout the Greek translation of I Maccabees is characteristically pejorative (*e.g.* 2.10 &12) with the paradigm of "the nations gathered ... to fight against Israel" (συνήγαγεν Ἀπολλώνιος ἔθνη ... πολεμῆσαι πρὸς τὸν Ισραηλ 3.10 *cf.* 5.9) balancing the paradigm of apostasy already noted (1.11 &.41-3). Nevertheless, the author is able (apparently with no sense of irony) to designate Israel itself a 'nation' when entering into a treaty with Rome which he approves (τῷ ἔθνει Ιουδαίων 8.23 & 25; *cf.* 6.58).

---

[100] "From the first, the Hasmonaeans were ready to kill apostate Jews'." J. Goldstein, *I Maccabees*, 64.

4

USAGE IN NEAR-CONTEMPORARY LITERATURE

Post-biblical writings in Hebrew, Aramaic, and Greek which relate to 'Israel' and 'the nations', and which were in circulation at the time of the earliest Christian mission, include texts now usually designated as the 'Pseudepigrapha', the Qumran literature, and the writings of Philo of Alexandria and Flavius Josephus. The mission itself soon produced writings, which include documents which came to be included in the New Testament. Most of this literature just cited can be dated confidently before AD 70. All of it must be dated before AD 135.[1]

No post-biblical writings had an influence on the earliest Christian mission equal to that of the Hebrew Bible. Whether or not the Pseudepigrapha, the Qumran writings, or the various writings of Philo and Josephus had any direct influence at all on the earliest Christian mission is a question which can be answered responsibly (and tentatively) only by means of detailed reference to specific texts. Even exact coincidences of wording in the Pseudepigrapha and documents of the Christian mission can be traced to the Hebrew Bible sometimes, as we shall see when examining Matthew's Scripture citations. Similarly, after the first rush of 'parallelomania' in response to the modern discovery of the Qumran library,[2] careful scholars have made the point that

---

[1] James Charlesworth has expanded the designation "Pseudepigrapha" with reference to date-of-composition. His edition of *The Old Testament Pseudepigrapha*: Vol 1, *Apocalyptic Literature and Testaments* (Garden City: Doubleday, 1983) includes the "Vision of Ezra (Fourth to Seventh Century A.D.)" 581-585, and even "Apocalypse of Daniel (Ninth Century A.D.)" 755-770.

[2] See S. Sandmel's article, "Parallelomania", *JBL* 81 (1962) 1-13.

New Testament duplication of the exact wording attested at Qumran indicates a relationship, but not necessarily paternity.[3]

A. Pseudepigrapha and Qumran Library

The term 'Pseudepigrapha' has come to designate a large, amorphous category of ancient writings rather than to describe a unifying characteristic of these writings. In a similar way, 'the Qumran Literature' refers to any of the various writings which have been discovered in modern times in the vicinity of the Essene Community near the Dead Sea. This library includes scrolls of the Hebrew Bible, some Greek translations of parts of the Bible, Aramaic targums, representative samples of literature we now call the 'Apocrypha' and 'Pseudepigrapha', and compositions by members of the Community intended for use in their liturgy as well as writings relating to the administration, the history, and the distinctive teachings of the Community.

1. Pseudepigrapha

The most obvious and important characteristic of the writings which are awkwardly termed 'Apocrypha' and 'Pseudepigrapha' is their dependence on the Hebrew Bible, especially on the *Torah* but also on Isaiah, Jeremiah, Daniel, other prophets, and the Psalms. A second characteristic of the collection relates not to origins but to survival: these writings were preserved not by the Rabbis but by Christian communities.

This literature expresses the continuing and changing division between 'Israel' and 'the nations' in ontological and biological terms, so the undoubted Christian use of this material makes paradoxical what modern scholars have sometimes described as an early 'triumph of Gentile Christianity'. Extant manuscripts are quite late (*e.g.* the fourth- and fifth-century codices of the Septuagint), so questions about use of this literature in the *earliest* Christian mission can be answered only speculatively. But Christian interpolations in many of the documents indicate appropriation early in the Christian era.

Because the *Wisdom of Solomon*, the *Additions to Daniel*, and *II, III,* and *IV Maccabees* —and even the *Psalms of Solomon*— are represented in the ancient codices of the Septuagint, these texts might be considered *biblical* writings. At the very least, it seems reasonable to give these books priority in our assessment of literature expected to have influenced the earliest Christian mission. It is outside the scope of the present work, however, to weigh all the evidence for first-century influence, or to explain the meaning in the first century of the various 'canons' that emerged later.

---

[3] Pierre Benoit warns against "an imprudent tendency to accept as immediate contacts arising from direct influence what in fact may be no more than an independent manifestation of a common trend of the time". *Paul and Qumran: Studies in New Testament Exegesis*, ed. J. Murphy-O'Connor (London: Chapman, 1968), 1.

The Wisdom of Solomon
The opening chapters of *Wisdom* give a focus to the prophecy of Isaiah which relate this book in an important way to the earliest Christian mission.[4] Questions outside the range of the present study are whether the author can claim originality for these patterns of interpretation (and, in turn, claim direct influence on the Christian mission) or whether these patterns were already well-established before *Wisdom* was written. But this book's linguistic usage regarding 'Israel' and 'the nations' is relevant to our study.

The author does not name "Israel" or "the Jews", but there is no doubt about the focus of *Wisdom* on Israel (*n.b.* chapters 11-19). Although not named, Israel is designated "the holy nation" (ἔθνος ἅγιον 17.2 *cf.* Mt 21.43). In Wisdom 3.8 'nations' (ἔθνη) and 'peoples' (λαῶν) in parallel are used as terms of wide reference; but the universal reference in 10.5 is to "the nations' unanimity in wickedness" (ἐν ὁμονοίᾳ πονηρίας ἐθνῶν συγχυθέντων). By contrast, Israel is "the devout people and blameless race" (λαὸν ὅσιον καὶ σπέρμα ἄμεμπτον 10.15). Whatever the author's intentions, the emotive metaphor of 'blameless race', or 'untainted seed' is susceptible to various interpretations and ideological applications. In the *Additions to Daniel* the reprimand of the Jewish elders taps the same metaphor (σπέρμα Χαναὰν, καὶ οὐκ Ιουδα Susanna 56 Θ), but in that story the actual physical descent of the wicked elders is not in question.

II Maccabees
Second Maccabees is unrelated to I Maccabees except, perhaps, as a partisan reaction to the earlier book.[5] *III* and *IV Maccabees*, in turn, are independent from each other and from II Maccabees. The ideology of 'zeal', which is directed against all things Greek in I Maccabees, is necessarily tempered in these three Greek-language compositions. Nevertheless, II Maccabees does include the phrase "zealous for the laws" (ζηλωτὴς τῶν νόμων 4.2), III Maccabees concludes with a ritual slaughter of about 300 men who had brought pollution into the Covenant community (οὕτως τε ἐμπεσόντα τῶν μεμιασμμένων ὁμοεθνῆ 7. 1-15, *n.b.* verses 14-15), and IV Maccabees concludes with a reference to 'the zealous Phinehas' (τὸν ζηλωτὴν Φινεές 18.12).

Of these three Greek texts, II Maccabees is by far the most interesting in its varied word usage regarding 'Israel' and 'the nations'. The term 'Israel' itself appears infrequently, but the term οἱ Ἰουδαῖοι also carries theological significance (*e.g.* 1.1, 7, 10; *cf.* III Macc 2.28 *et al.*) Most characteristically, the Covenant people are designated τὸ γένος or τὸ γένος ἡμῶν (II Macc 5.22; 6.12; 7.16 & 38; *cf.* ὁμοεθῆ III Macc 8.14). An individual's place in the Covenant

---

[4] "Isaiah, and interestingly enough, the Wisdom of Solomon, seem to have exercised the greatest influence upon the way he [Matthew] formed his Gospel." W.R. Farmer, *Jesus and the Gospel* (Philadelphia: Fortress, 1982), 11. Whether or not Farmer's claim of literary dependence is admitted, the parallel lines of theological development are impressive.

[5] "These two books present sharply different accounts indeed, ... their authors were bitter opponents." J. A. Goldstein, *I Maccabees*, 4.

community is not guaranteed by privilege of birth, however, as indicated most clearly by the example of the renegade Jew (τὸ γένος Ἰουδαῖος, ὕστερον δὲ μεταβαλὼν τὰ νόμιμα) in III Maccabees 1.3.

The appearance of the new term 'Judaism' (Ἰουδαϊσμός) with reference to 'the religion of Israel' is noteworthy. (*E.g.* II Macc 2.21; 8.1; 14.38 & III Macc 4.26; *cf.* Gal 1.13-14.) Also worth noting is the reappearance of the old term 'Hebrews' (οἱ Ἑβραῖοι, *e.g.* II Macc 7.31; 11.13; 15.37; IV Macc 4.26; 8.1; & 17.9). But this old name seems to be used simply as an archaic synonym for 'Israel' or 'the Jews' without any claim to a special understanding of the biblical usage and without any indication of intent to express a new, technical meaning.

The Psalms of Solomon

The *Psalms of Solomon* press the biblical usage of the terms 'Israel' and 'the nations' hard.   References to 'zeal' (*e.g.* 2.24 & 4.3) imply both endorsement of the ideology and strong disapproval of the programmatic violence which accompanied that ideology.   However the pious authors' quietism is explained, their intensity of emotion against 'the nations' achieves a sublime absoluteness seldom matched by affirmative commentary on violent action:

> And he shall gather together a holy people,
>   whom he shall lead in righteousness,
> And he shall the judge the tribes of the people
>   that has been sanctified by the Lord his God.
> ...   .
> And neither sojourner nor alien
>   shall sojourn with them any more. (*Psalms Sol* 17.26, & 28b)

This extravagant hope in God's action is ambiguous, since "particularistic tendencies run side by side with universalistic ones."[6] Modern readers familiar with the concept of pluralism might suggest that one way to eliminate sojourners and aliens is to break down the barriers which define them as outsiders. There is no indication in the text, however, that this idea was intended or even imagined by the original writer and readers.

Enoch, Twelve Patriarchs and Jubilees

Enoch, the *Testaments of the Twelve Patriarchs*, and the *Book of Jubilees* (attributed to Moses) are pseudepigraphal in the strict sense. The astonishing originality of themes and forms in this literature together with the strong ties to the Hebrew Bible stand as warnings against any academic insistence on simple evolutionary development of thought and piety in the post-biblical period.

---

[6] Paul Winter, "Psalms of Solomon", *IDB* 3, 959/2. Winter explains the psalmist's "aversion to alien residents in the land of Israel" in terms of a yearning for "the liberation from entanglement in non-Jewish affairs"(960/1).   Gray's trans in *APOT* is quoted above.

The apocalyptic perspective of *Enoch* is universal and, indeed, cosmic. The relevance of a vantage point in primordial history for a vision of 'Israel' and 'the nations' which transcends mundane categories is illustrated also in the related *Testaments of the Twelve Patriarchs*. Assuming the unity of mankind and humanity's original communion with their creator, Naphtali tells his sons that

> the nations wandered and abandoned the Lord, changing their good order to obey logs and stones, spirits of deceit.   (*Test Naphtali* 3.3)

The *Book of Jubilees*, which is dependant in part on Enoch, moves in quite the opposite direction to give the division between 'Israel' and 'the nations' a new twist in the rewriting of biblical history. The metaphor of 'seed' dominates the author's concern for Israel, "a righteous generation and a holy seed" (25.4) kept separate from "the seed of Canaan" (25.10). Jubilees' account of Simeon and Levi's slaughter of the Shechemites focuses on the urgent need to avoid any mixing with "the seed of the nations" (30.7).[7]

The Qumran Library
The fact that Enoch, some of the Testaments of the Patriarchs, and the Book of Jubilees were found among the Dead Sea Scrolls along with the *Damascus Document* is evidence of the widespread influence of these writings in Israel. The religious, social, and political beliefs and zealous commitments of the Essenes themselves are best understood from analysis of their own compositions and from their vast holdings of books of the Bible and commentaries. But the community's use and, probably in some cases, adaptation of very many earlier 'sectarian' writings forces a new perspective on modern attempts to assess the currents and cross currents of partisan piety and ideology in Israel and the Diaspora before AD 70.[8] If the barb in Jesus'

---

[7] In *Jubilees* and in later currents of thought and social action, the idea of 'mixing seed' seems to have focused Jewish antipathy against Samaritans. "From the beginning of the first century AD they [Samaritans] were regarded as being on a level with the Gentiles in all things ritual and cultic." J. Jeremias, *Jerusalem in the Time of Jesus* (Philadelphia: Fortress, 1975 [1937]), 356. In the complicated triple formula of Mishnah *Demai* 5.9 the Samaritans seem worse, or at least more immediately threatening, than other non-Jews.

[8] Three striking examples of extrabiblical teachings to which Jesus alludes in Mt's Gospel can be documented from the Qumran Library: a/ " ...that they may love all that He has chosen and hate all that He has rejected", *1QS 1.4*: "You have heard it said that 'You shall love your neighbor and hate your enemy'." (Mt 5.43 *cf.* Lk 6.27.)
b/ "No man shall assist a beast to give birth on the Sabbath day. And if it should fall into a cistern or pit, he shall not lift it out on the Sabbath." *CD* 11.13-14. Before healing a man's withered hand on the Sabbath, Jesus asks, "who among you, if he has one sheep and it falls into a pit on the Sabbath, will not extend his hand to lift it out?" (Mt 12.11-12.) Besides the *qal wahomer* force of the argument ('If a sheep, how much the more a human being?') this seems also to have been a partisan challenge to the Pharisees ('If you are really zealous for the law, answer like an Essene!')

argument with the Pharisees about healing a lame man on the Sabbath (Mt 12.9-14) is directed at the Essenes, the Pharisees who felt snagged might be expected to join forces with the Essenes to get back at him. But what is surprising in terms of modern attempts to reconstruct partisan relations and ideological alignments in Jesus' time is that the sect conspiring with the Pharisees are called "Herodians" in the parallel account in Mark 3.6.[9]

The biblical usage relating to 'Israel' and 'the nations' was preserved and maintained at Qumran through the community's use of the biblical texts. Many extra-biblical 'psalms' or hymns have been uncovered also where the words of God are directed "to all the sons of Israel" (לכל בני ישראל), as in 4Q380.[10] The Covenant community is explicitly designated "Israel" in "The Manual of Discipline" (1QS) and "The War Scroll" (1QM), but many other designations clearly indicate a narrower reference to a faithful 'remnant'. In "The Damascus Document" (CD & 4QD), which seems to be older than the community but adopted (and possibly adapted) by it, the list of "priests, Levites, Israelites, and proselytes" (CD 17.3) raises the very important question whether 'Israel' in the sense of 'remnant' was open to transformed individuals from 'the nations'.

LAB, Joseph and Aseneth, II Baruch, and IV Ezra

Pseudo-Philo (*Liber Antiquitatum Biblicarum*), which re-writes the biblical history from Adam to David, is not strictly pseudepigraphal but was mistakenly ascribed to Philo in ancient times. Its absence from the Qumran Library is noteworthy if it was composed in Hebrew before AD 68.[11] It is very like the Genesis Apocryphon (*1QapGen*) in form, but its partisan teaching is less consistent with Qumran than with what later emerged as Rabbinic Judaism. Physical descent is an important focus of *LAB*'s strong, positive emphasis on Israel as the Covenant people of God. Moses' father Amran, for example, testifies that

> It will sooner come to pass that ... the immeasurable world fall ... than that the race of the children of Israel should be diminished ... therefore I will ... go in and take my wife and beget sons. (*LAB* 9.3 & 4)

---

c/ Celibacy was rare in Israel's history, but it was a norm among the Essenes. In accord with Essene piety but in sharp contrast to later Rabbinic teaching and practice, Jesus says, "There are eunuchs who have made themselves eunuchs for the sake of the Kingdom of heaven. Whoever is able to receive this, receive it." Mt 19.12b.
G. Vermes, *The Dead Sea Scrolls in English* (Baltimore: Penguin, 1965), 72 & 213.

[9] W.R. Farmer, "Essenes", *IDB* 2, 145. *Cf.* Josephus, *Antiq* xv.372 and C. Daniel, *Revue de Qumran* 6 (1967), 31-53.

[10] E.M. Schuller, *Non-Canonical Psalms from Qumran: A Pseudepigraphic Collection* (Atlanta: Scholars Press, 1986), 248.

[11] Daniel Harrington proposes "a date prior to AD 70". *Outside the Old Testament*, ed. M. de Jonge (Cambridge: University Press, 1985), 8. More plausibly, L.H. Feldman has argued for a date between AD 70 and 135. "Prolegomenon", *The Biblical Antiquities of Philo*, trans. M.R. James (New York: Ktav, 1971), xxviii.

Even if composed earlier than the beginning of the Christian mission, or at exactly the same time, this work seems unlikely to have influenced early Christian reflection on 'Israel' and 'the Covenant' in any positive way. Rather, Pseudo-Philo marks off an alternative to the Christian mission.[12]

Joseph and Aseneth is a creative *midrash* on Genesis 41.45, 50-52 and 46.20 which exposes any physical definition of Israel as 'the pure seed of Jacob' to be inconsistent with biblical history and Covenant theology. In polar opposition to the line followed in LAB, the Book of Jubilees, and the Psalms of Solomon, this book seems designed "to reassure Jews about the desirability of mixed marriage with converts".[13]

Although the term 'Hebrews' occurs in 1.5 with 'ethnic' or 'racial' connotations, the word seems simply to have been carried over from the Moses story in the first chapters of Exodus. More important for our concern is Joseph's prayer to

> Lord God of my father Israel ... who gave life to all and called them from the darkness to light, and from error to truth, and from death to life. (*JosAsen* 8.9)

Joseph implores his Creator to "bless this virgin and renew her by your spirit and form her anew" so that she may indeed *become* a member of Israel (1.9).

The "Judaism as depicted in JosAsen is not mission minded", as Chr. Burchard rightly observes,[14] but the Covenant faith of Israel which is represented in this romance is consistent with the faith presented in the biblical account of Israel's *creation* in the Exodus and with the subsequent development of the Christian mission to the nations. The book itself may have had a positive influence on the Christian mission, as suggested by its early acceptance "in the Eastern Church as a book of devotion",[15] even if this *midrash* fell out of favor with non-Christian Jews after 'the closing of the ranks' early in the second century AD.

The parallels between Aseneth and Abraham in the biblical accounts (and in targums and *midrashim*) are remarkable. Aseneth is renamed "City of Refuge" and promised by the Lord's messenger that

> in you many nations will take refuge with the Lord God, the Most High, and under your wings many peoples trusting in the Lord God will be sheltered. (*JosAsen* 15.7
> *cf.* LXX Zech 12.15).

---

[12] M.R. James translation from Old Latin, *op. cit.*, 100. F.H. Feldman characterizes the work as "early Talmudic" and "one of the most significant links between early haggadah and rabbinic midrash". *Ibid.*, ix.

[13] Schürer-Vermes, "Jewish Literature Composed in Greek", *HJP* III/1, 548.

[14] Chr. Burchard, "Joseph and Aseneth", *Outside the OT*, 94. Quotation of text is Burchard's translation.

[15] *Ibid.*

Moreover, the fact that it is Simeon and Levi who plot violence against Joseph and Aseneth, before being restrained by Levi's own prophetic insight (23.1-13), suggests that this passage was constructed by the author in conscious opposition to the current Jewish ideology of separation which celebrated Simeon and Levi as exemplars of 'zeal' for their violent action in the Dinah affair (Gen 34).

II Baruch and *IV Ezra* were written before AD 135,[16] but after AD 70. This means that these books appeared soon after the beginnings of the Christian mission and, according to our calculations, after the appearance of the First Gospel. One of the characteristic features of both of these non-Christian, Jewish apocalyptic writings is their explicit response to the destruction of Jerusalem. Both books are universal in reference, but neither envisions such a radical program of accepting the nations into Israel as was undertaken in the Christian mission.

Second Baruch begins by describing the scattering of Israel "that they may do good to the nations" (1.5) and follows this up with a reference to individuals from the nations "who left vanity behind and have fled under your wings" (41.4). Proselytes "who mingled with the seed of the people who have separated themselves" (42.5) seem assured of judgment which focuses on their life in Israel.[17] *Fourth Ezra* demonstrates genuine sympathy for all the children of Adam (7.46 *et al.*), but the focus of the author's concern is very specifically with Israel, for whom God created the world (6.56 *cf.* 4.23).

B. Philo and Josephus

As important as the two vast collections of writings from Philo of Alexandria and from Flavius Josephus are to students of the Hebrew Bible and the New Testament, there seems to be no evidence that the earliest Christian missionaries or the New Testament writers themselves read anything that either man wrote. For our present purposes, however, it is important to note that both men self-consciously identified with Israel and both wrote in Greek, the language of the Septuagint and the New Testament.

---

[16] "According to most scholars, the original Jewish document known today as 4 Ezra was composed about A.D. 100." B. Metzger, *OT Pseud*, 520. "The Apocalypse of Baruch seems to come from the first or second decade of the second century." A. Klijn, *Ibid.*, 617. Dating 'the age of the Tannaim' from "somewhat before ... 70 and concluding ... about 200", J. Neusner designates IV Ezra and II Baruch as "the major writings in the Pseudepigrapha" in this period. *Method and Meaning in Ancient Judaism* (Chico: Scholars Press, 1981), 24.

[17] "The expression *wrmt' mthsb* ... is unknown and cannot be satisfactorily emended. The author wants to say that the periods before the conversion no longer have significance." A.F.J. Klijn, *OT Pseud*, 634. This matches R.H. Charles' interpretation in *APOT* II, 502. Nevertheless, the immediately preceding verse (42.4) condemns those who separated themselves from Israel and "mixed with the nations". Interpreted by itself 42.4 might suggest Israel's complete segregation, but such an interpretation is impossible in tandem with 42.5.

Philo (ca. 20 BC - AD 50) was an older contemporary of Jesus and the Apostles. He survived the pogrom in Alexandria under Emperor Gaius (Caligula), but died before the destruction of the Temple. Josephus (ca. AD 37-100) was a younger contemporary of the Apostles. He was involved, by his own accounts, on many sides of the great issues and events of his day —but not with the Messianism identified with Jesus of Nazareth. The beginnings of the Christian mission only appear in a few hints in his writings.

Philo's knowledge of Hebrew and Aramaic seems to have been slight, at best,[18] and in his own writings he "neither quotes nor even mentions any of the books found in the Apocrypha or Pseudepigrapha".[19] But it is his treatment of history that separates his work most clearly from that of Josephus. Philo's allegorical hermeneutic makes Scripture so contemporary that, as Sandmel observes, the effect is "to dissolve the history in Scripture".[20] Josephus, in an altogether different way, introduces the biblical notion of "God's role in the historical process into a conventional history".[21]

Information about various Jewish sects, which both Philo and Josephus provide, has been re-examined profitably since the modern discovery of the Qumran Caves. Josephus, amoeba like, seems to have been able to absorb everything Jewish into himself, including what has come to be called 'mainstream' or 'normative'. In a quite different way, Philo defines his own Judaism so broadly that it seems to defy practical application. Nevertheless, Philo was certainly a leading representative of Jewry in his own time, and "Philo never forgot or abandoned the literal type of Judaism", according to E.R. Goodenough.[22] Even if he seems to us to be very unlike the later Rabbis, "no Jew in history ever surpassed Philo in loyalty to Judaism."[23] His writing is complicated (and not always consistent), but his loyalty was simpler and more consistent than that of Josephus.[24] When we consider how Philo or Josephus —or both— attempt to define 'Israel' and 'the nations' we do well to remember that it was early Christians, not the Rabbis, who valued and preserved the writings of both Philo and Josephus.[25]

---

[18] Samuel Sandmel raises the question, "Did Philo know Hebrew-Aramaic?" and demonstrates that the answer must be a qualified 'yes'. *Philo of Alexandria: An Introduction* (Oxford: University Press, 1979), 131; *cf.* 15 & 27. Schürer-Vermes conclude that "his knowledge of Hebrew seems to have been superficial at best." *HJP* III/2, 873.

[19] S. Sandmel, *op.cit.*, 132.

[20] *Ibid.*, 25.

[21] T. Rajak, *Josephus: The Historian and His Society* (Philadelphia: Fortress, 1983), 9.

[22] E.R. Goodenough, "Philo Judeus", *IDB* 3, 797.

[23] "What cannot be denied Philo ... is his thoroughgoing Jewish loyalty." S. Sandmel, *Philo Introduction*, 134; *cf.* 13:

[24] "From the time of his surrender [in AD 67] to the end of his life Josephus remained a client of the Flavian emperors (hence the adoption of the name Flavius)." J. Goldin, "Josephus, Flavius", *IDB* 2, 987.

[25] "Philo's writings were preserved and transmitted by Christians, not by Jews. His legacy of writings was lost to Jews (who have preserved from that age only materials in

Philo and Josephus routinely use the term 'Israel' as a synonym for 'Jews'.[26] As already noted, both men identify with 'the Jewish nation' emphatically and use phrases such as "our nation" and "our whole nation" (τοῦ σύμπαντος ἡμῶν ἔθνους Jos *Life* 24). This shared emphasis on the term and concept 'nation' relates to special interests and concerns of both authors. But their positive use of the term 'nation' contrasts with some contemporary Greek usage, where Ἕλλην is opposed to τὰ ἔθνη in a way reminiscent of the biblical contrast between 'Israel' and 'the nations'.[27] Still more striking, by way of contrast with the positive use of this term 'nation' by Philo and Josephus, is the characteristic use of גוי in the later writings of the Rabbis.

In the writings of Josephus even the term ἐθνικός occurs in non-pejorative use (χαρακτῆρσιν γὰρ Ἑβραϊκοῖς γεγραμμένα καὶ φωνῇ τῇ ἐθνικῇ *Antiq* xii. 36), providing a synchronic control for interpretation of the few occurrences of this term in the New Testament (notably Mt 5.47 & 6.7).

'Hebrews'

Both Philo and Josephus use the term 'Hebrews' with reference to Israel before the Exodus (*n.b.* Jos *Antiq* i.46). Philo demonstrates special awareness of the biblical usage when he links the term to 'pilgrimage' —περάτης γὰρ ὁ Ἑβραῖος ἑρμηνεύεται (*Migration Abraham* 20). But both Philo and Josephus seem to use the term 'Hebrews' also in a specialized 'ethnic' sense when referring to Jews (and perhaps Samaritans) in Palestine.[28] A striking variation of this specialized usage in *Antiquities* xi.344 may accurately represent contemporary Samaritan self-identification: after requesting remission of taxes for the seventh year when they did not sow, the delegates were asked by the official who they were. Answering, "Hebrews" (Ἑβραῖοι), they admitted under cross-examination that they were *not* "Jews" (Ἰουδαῖοι ... οὐκ).

Josephus is our main source of historical information about Israel during his lifetime, so all of his references to Samaritans are important for our assessment the first-century concept 'Israel'. Most notable are his record of a retaliatory massacre of Samaritans under Eleazar ben Dinai (*ca.* AD 52, *War* ii.232), and his account of an earlier desecration of the Temple by Samaritans (*ca.* AD 6, *Antiq* xviii.30). If, as is generally agreed, Josephus

---

Hebrew or Aramaic and none at all in Greek)." S. Sandmel, *Philo Introduction*, 14.

[26] But *n.b.* Josephus' precise definition of the term Ἰουδαῖοι in *Antiq* xi/173: "This name, by which they have been called from the time when they went up from Babylon, is derived from the tribe of Judah."

[27] J.H. Moulton & G. Milligan, *The Vocabulary of the Greek Testament Illustrated from the Papyri and Other Non-Literary Sources* (Grand Rapids: Eerdmans, 1980 [1930]), 181.

[28] Josephus uses the term 'Hebrews' for Hebrew-Aramaic language and script and also "for measures, coins, names of the months, or national characteristics of the Palestinian Jews in General", according to K.G. Kuhn, *TDNT* III, 367. Similarly, Philo uses the term in contemporary reference "for that which, though Jewish, is not common to all Jews, especially the Hebrew or Aramaic language", according to W. Gutbrod, *TDNT* III, 373.

designates sects or parties in Israel as 'philosophies', why did he not include Samaritans ('Observers' שמרים) in his lists?

"In the first century AD ... we are in one of the periods of embittered relationship between Jews and Samaritans", according to Joachim Jeremias.[29] If this is so, Josephus's failure to list 'Observers' as a 'philosophy' may indicate that he considered them beneath contempt. But we should not assume that Josephus intended his lists to be complete catalogues of the available options. Accordingly, each should be understood in terms of the author's immediate purpose. In *Antiquities* xviii, for example, Josephus is calling for disapproval of the 'Zealots', the new "fourth philosophy".

As a man of action, and even a man of war, Josephus is more easily associated with 'zeal' by modern readers than is Philo. But in fact it was Philo who wrote approvingly of the

> thousands of men keeping watch, zealots of the laws [ζηλωτά νόμων] strictest guardians of the institutions of their fathers, merciless to those who would do anything to subvert these.   (*On the Special Laws* ii.253)[30]

Josephus had his own reasons for insisting that the party of 'zealots' represented a wholly new and shocking way of thinking and acting.

Finally, it can be said that both Philo and Josephus were positively interested in the proselyte movement. Both men apparently had non-Jewish readers in mind when they wrote. With reference to the "single proselyte" in Matthew 23.15, we shall return to Josephus for his account of the conversions at Adiabene (*Antiq.* xx). We began the comparison of Philo and Josephus by noting that both use the words "Israel" and "Jews" as synonyms. But it should be noted in concluding this brief survey that Philo understands that "Israel means seeing God" (*On the Preliminary Studies* 51). This specific use of the term 'Israel' is different but no less theological than the persistently theological reference of the term in the Hebrew Bible. Moreover, Philo's 'Israel' was founded by Abraham who himself came away from superstition and is a model for proselytes.[31] In many passages Philo insists that proselytes must be honored (e.g. *On Special Laws* i.51-52 & *On Virtues* 181-182).

---

[29] J. Jeremias, *Jerusalem in the Time of Jesus* (Philadelphia: Fortress, 1975[1937]), 354.

[30] W.R. Farmer's translation, "Zealot", *IDB* 4, 936.

[31] *On Abraham* 273-76. Philo begins this section declaring that "faith in God (ἡ πρὸς θεὸν πίστις) is the one sure and infallible good" (268), anticipating in a striking way the Apostle Paul's argument about 'salvation by faith' which also uses Abraham as the exemplar. In *On the Virtues*, Philo again cites Abraham, as "a Chaldaean by birth, the son of an astrologer ... the standard of nobility for all proselytes". Sandmel's trans., *Philo: Intro*, 71-2.

If E.R. Goodenough is correct in his interpretation of *Questions and Answers on Exodus* ii. 2, Philo even allowed uncircumcised proselytes equality in the Israel of those who shared the vision of the true God.[32]

C. Paul in his own account and Luke's

The Church's judgment about Paul's importance in the early mission to the nations is obvious, both from the number of his letters to young churches which have been included in the canonical New Testament and from the attention given to Paul's work in Luke's account of the life and mission of the Church from the beginning until AD 62. But neither Paul himself, in his epistles, nor Luke in *Acts* claims that this great apostle was involved in *the earliest Christian mission*.

Both Paul and Luke indicate that Saul of Tarsus was violently opposed to those in 'the Way' because of their mission to the nations.[33] In other words, in the sense of 'being turned around', Paul was *converted* from being a deadly opponent of the Church's mission to becoming its most famous leader. The terms of Saul's conversion (and the opposition which he drew to himself, in turn, from 'zealous Jews') are fundamentally related to his identification of 'Israel' and 'the nations'.

Saul did not abandon his Covenant identity with Israel and Israel's God when he became an apostle to the nations. Rather, the revelation of "the mystery of the Messiah" to him (Col 4.3) made his Covenant identity secure beyond any threat (Rm 8.37-39). Paul's former commitment to programmatic violence (in attempts to cut out of Israel the cancer of pollution from the nations) was exposed by this revelation to be blasphemous, not simply excessive. Paul never forgot his own former partisan activity, nor the logic which continued to goad pious Jews into desperate attempts to maintain or re-establish Israel's purity (Rm 10.2-4; *cf.* Acts 13.45; 21.20-21; 22.1-4). He was willing and able to defend his position of leadership in the church and mission, but Paul's memory of his own acts of murder against God's elect compelled him to designate himself "the least of all saints" (Eph 3.8-13; *cf.* I Cor 15.9-10 over against Gal 1.19 & 2.9).

Saul (now Paul) himself writes about his youth and his early years as a Christian (Phil 3.4b-6; *cf.* Rm 11.1 & Acts 22.3). These accounts, together with his

---

[32] E.R. Goodenough, "Philo's Exposition of the Law and his *De vita Mosis*" [1933], *Goodenough*, eds. E.S. Frerichs & J. Neusner (Atlanta: Scholars Press, 1986), 75.

[33] "In order to understand Paul, it is necessary to recognize that he came into the church out of a background in Judaism in which the current of zeal for the law ran strong. His doctrine of justification should be studied against the background of a theology in which zeal for the law was regarded as redemptive." W.R. Farmer, "Zealot", *IDB* 4, 938. Note especially Gal 1.13-14, Phil 3.4b-6 and Acts 8.1, 9.1-2, 22.3-4.

Alan Segal demonstrates the relevance of 'metamorphosis' in Paul's thought and experience of conversion, but stops short of identifying Paul's 'turning point' precisely on the question of admitting 'the nations' into 'Israel'. "The Costs of Proselytism and Conversion", *SBL Annual Meeting Seminar Papers* (Atlanta: Scholars Press, 1988), 360-362.

references to three years in Arabia and fourteen years in Syria and Cilicia (Gal 1.17-21), form a significant part of our documentary evidence on the earliest Christian mission.

The detailed accounts in *Acts* of some of Paul's later work explain the immediate context for his letters. But any reconstruction of the *earliest* Christian mission must view this later period as a trajectory. Modern scholars, when comparing Paul's own records of work in this later period with Luke's account, rightly insist that the Pauline epistles be given priority of consideration. By the same token, we should remember that Paul himself is clearly aware of missionary colleagues and predecessors. In writing to the church in Rome before his first visit there, for example, he emphasizes his awareness of that congregation's foundations in faith apart from any work by him. It is Luke's account of Paul's missionary activity which tempts the modern reader to view Paul as 'the Apostle to the nations' —a phrase which Paul himself never uses.

Luke's focus on Paul is notable, but *Acts* (which was written later than Paul's earliest epistles)[34] also provides some important information about the activity of the Twelve, the Seven, and other named and unnamed missionaries who were active before Paul's turn-about. We shall consider very briefly the preaching of Peter and John, Stephen and Philip (Acts 2.7 & 8), and the conflict between the 'Hebrews' and 'Hellenists' (Acts 6). But first we survey references to 'Israel' and 'the nations' in terms of τὸ μυστήριον, the phrase Paul himself uses to describe and explain his call to be an 'apostle to the nations'.

'The Mystery'

The biblical idea of a heavenly council or assembly (סוד) in which God reveals his will to the prophets (Is 6, I Kg 22, Jer 23.18 *et al.*) is developed in Daniel (2.18, 19 and 4.6[9]) as an eschatological mystery (רז) known to God alone and those to whom he reveals it.[35] Paul brings this Semitic usage of the term τὸ μυστήριον to definitive focus on 'Israel' and 'the nations'.

Following Charles Masson, Raymond Brown and others, we can speak of a *definition* of the term in Ephesians, but τὸ μυστήριον remains a mystery or,

---

[34] All of the canonical epistles which bear Paul's name are accepted as 'Pauline' in the present study. Even the Pastoral Epistles are considered part of the basic Pauline corpus in our 'tagmemic analysis', with *Acts* and the other canonical NT writings forming the appropriate larger literary context for determining meanings in Paul's writings.
We shall not try here to determine whether J.N.D. Kelly is right in his argument that Paul himself actually wrote the epistles to Timothy and Titus (*A Commentary on the Pastoral Epistles*. London: A & C Black, 1963) or whether Clement of Rome had better information than recent Pauline scholars about Paul's trip to Spain (ἐπὶ τὸ τέρμα τῆς δύσεως I Cl 5.7). For AD 62 as the date of composition for Acts see below (Chapter 6).

[35] R.E. Brown, *The Semitic Background of the Term "Mystery" in the New Testament* (Philadelphia: Fortress, 1968 [1958-9]), 5, 58 & *passim*. *Cf.* G. Bornkamm, *TDNT* IV, 814-15 & 820; J. LaGrand ΤΟ ΜΥΣΤΗΡΙΟΝ: *The New Testament Development of the Semitic Usage* (Grand Rapids: Calvin Th.M. diss., 1976), 21-25; and Charles Masson, *L'Epitre de Saint Paul aux Ephesiens* (Paris: Delachaux & Niestle, 1952), 177-179.

more precisely, *the* mystery. Ephesians 3.1-7 begins with reference to the fact that Paul is in prison because of his work to bring the nations into "the commonwealth of Israel" (Eph 2.12). The theme of suffering is concrete and obvious, though less explicit than in the 'mystery' sentences in Colossians (1.24-29; 2.1-3; 4.2-4). The stewardship of the mystery (ἡ οἰκονομία τοῦ μυστηρίου Eph 3.9) is being worked out through Paul's identification with the body of Christ.[36]

Colossians 1.24-29 is a very long sentence which includes more than one profound theological idea. When the sentence is broken up in translation, the brilliant conclusion, "Christ in you, the hope of glory", is too often isolated by interpreters from its immediate referent (τί τὸ πλοῦτος τῆς δόξης τοῦ μυστηρίου τούτου ἐν τοῖς ἔθνεσιν) and the immediate life-context marked by the first word in the sentence, νῦν. Paul had undergone various sufferings in his mission to the nations and was now in prison specifically because the zealous Jews opposed his program of bringing the nations into Israel (Acts 21.27-22.25). It is noteworthy that Paul himself had not yet visited Colossae (see 2.1) but was confident that 'his Gospel' (Rm 16.25) had been preached there, with the result that old patterns and relationships were consciously and visibly transformed.[37]

The focus of Romans 11.25-27 is first of all on 'Israel' and only secondarily on 'the nations'. But Paul now understands that the salvation of "all Israel" (πᾶς Ἰσραήλ) itself is to be accomplished through the entry of "the complete number of nationals" (τὸ πλήρωμα τῶν ἐθνῶν 11. 25). So the mission to the nations is the strategic center also of the formulation here of what is called 'the stewardship of the mystery' in Ephesians 3.8-12. The doxology which concludes the Epistle to the Romans (16.25-27) is important precisely as a summary of everything written in the letter.[38]

---

[36] Paul's Christ-mysticism presses his readers to understand the Elect as 'one body' (I Cor 10.17) and even 'one person in the Messiah Jesus' (Gal 3.28). "They, with one another and Christ, form a joint personality" directed and empowered by the Spirit of God. Albert Schweitzer. *The Mysticism of Paul the Apostle*(New York: Seabury, 1968[1931]), 118.

[37] The widely-held interpretation of Col 1.3-8 which explains Epaphras as Paul's deputy is not the only view compatible with Col 1.3-8 and 4.12 (and Philem 23), although Eduard Lohse has given strong support to this interpretation with detailed and interrelated arguments. (*Colossians and Philemon*, trans. W. Poehlmann & R. Karris (Philadelphia: Fortress, 1971 [1968]), 2, 22-23, 173-174 & 176.) "On our behalf" is surely the correct reading in 1.7, so Paul meant at least that his own identification with Epaphras' teaching was as complete as if Paul himself had sent him out and told him what to say. But it is not certain that this fellow-servant (τοῦ ἀγαπητοῦ συνδούλου ἡμῶν) was actually deployed by Paul. It is conceivable that Epaphras was commissioned even before Paul's turn-about.

[38] *N.b.* Romans 9-11; J. LaGrand, ΤΟ ΜΥΣΤΗΡΙΟΝ, 41-45. J. Munck argues that P46 provides the solution to the textual critical problem: Paul himself sent the letter out in two forms (both concluding with the doxology). "After writing and sending Romans 1-15 as a letter to Rome [he] added chapter 16 to a copy of it and sent this to Ephesus." *Christ and Israel: An Interpretation of Romans 9-11* (Philadelphia: Fortress, 1967 [1956]), 16. K. Donfried marshals some compelling arguments for the acceptance of this last chapter as an integral part of the original letter. "A Short Note on Romans 16", *JBL* 89 (1970), 441.

After this cursory view of Paul's references to the fundamental concepts 'Israel' and 'the nations' it is disproportionate to record his incidental uses of the terms 'Judaism' (Ἰουδαϊσμός) and 'Hebrew' (Ἑβραῖος) except to note that Pauline usage can be compared instructively to usage in Acts. On the one hand, Paul's use of the term 'Judaism' is suggestive in relation to strains of 'formative Judaism' reported in Acts and again by later Christian writers such as Ignatius. On the other hand, it seems possible that Paul's use of the term 'Hebrews' may relate specifically to the 'Hebrews' in Acts 6 *in contrast* to usage which became standard for later Jewish and Christian writers.

'Judaism' and 'Hebrews'
Paul's positive self-identification with Israel is not in doubt. But his reference to his former life "in Judaism" (ἐν τῷ Ἰουδαϊσμῷ Gal 2.13-14) is ambiguous, indicating both individual achievement and culpable 'zeal' which led him to persecute the Church of God in an attempt to destroy it. Certainly his was "an unenlightened zeal for God" (Rm 10.2) and it may be that Paul saw this 'Judaism' itself as the πώρωσις ἀπο μέρους τῷ Ἰσραήλ (Rm 11.25). In any case, it seems likely that Ignatius of Antioch, a half-century later, would have understood Galatians 2.13-14 in this way. Using the same term, Ἰουδαϊσμός, Ignatius declares, "It is inconsistent (ἄτοπον) to talk of Jesus Christ and to practice Judaism" (*Magnesians* 10.3).

Paul's uses of the term 'Hebrews' in *Philippians* 3.5 (Ἑβραῖος ἐξ Ἑβραιῶν) and especially in *II Corinthians* 11.22 (Ἑβραῖοί εἰσιν; κἀγω.) seem aimed at countering the claims of a sect within Israel which used the term for self-designation. If this is so, Paul's responses may shed light on the dispute recorded in Acts 6 between 'Hellenists' and 'Hebrews' in the earliest Christian community. The usual critical assumption is that there were only two parties, a minority complaining against the majority. But this may be a mistaken simplification. It often happens that one minority complains about what they see as *preferential treatment given to another minority* in coalitions of the sort described in Acts.

Already in his 1932 article "The Hellenists", H.J. Cadbury noted the difficulty of identifying the 'Hellenists' of Acts 6, since "Ἑλληνιστής is not a common word in the Greek of the age that we call Hellenistic."[39] Much of what Cadbury wrote in this article has formed the basis for subsequent discussions about 'Hellenists' and 'Hebrews'. But without accepting Cadbury's identification of Hellenists as non-Jews in Luke's narrative, we can take warning that if this odd word designates 'returned diaspora Jews who spoke Greek' it may have had other specific denotations as well. (*N.b.* Acts 9.29; in 11.20 read "Greeks" with P74, A *et al.*) The second term Ἑβραῖοι is at least as strange and

---

[39] *Beginnings of Christianity*, vol V, eds. Foakes Jackson & Lake, 59.

difficult to define with confidence, but Abram Spiro may be right in his assertion that "the 'Hebrews' of vi 1 are Samaritan Christians."[40]

Jewish and Christian writers seldom consider seriously the positive claims of the Samaritans as 'observers' (שמרים), but it is not hard to imagine that the Christian leaders in Jerusalem were engaged in 'affirmative action' in favor of 'the Hebrews' until the protest from another minority group ('the Hellenists') forced a reform. The pattern of Jesus' ministry makes affirmative action by his followers in favor of those prejudiced against by the larger society possible and even likely (Mt 25.40). Luke, in his Gospel, makes a point of Jesus' special attention to Samaritans (Lk 9.51-53; 10.25-37, 17.15-19). If, by the time of the 'grumbling' in Acts 6.1, 'Observers' were integrated into the Christian community, the narrator may have been careful to use one of their own terms of self-identification rather than "Samaritans".[41] As we have seen, Josephus records an instance of Samaritans identifying themselves as 'Hebrews' and some inscriptional evidence referring to 'Hebrews' might also be interpreted as the self-designations of Samaritans.[42]

---

[40] *The Acts of the Apostles: Introduction, Translation and Notes* by Johannes Munck revised by W.F. Albright and C.S Mann (Garden City: Doubleday, 1967), 301. C.S. Mann was wrong in his assumption that all in the field would concur: "Dr.Spiro's material [Appendix V] has put beyond question the interpretation of *Hebraioi* as 'Samaritans' or 'Samaritan Christians'." (294) Johannes Munck himself did not identify the "Hebrews" as Samaritans, even though Spiro's material and Mann's note appear in his posthumously edited commentary. Munck had suggested that "Stephen may well have been a Hebrew." *Paul and Salvation of Mankind*, 227; *cf.* 135-167.
As the record stands in Acts, Stephen's speech represents "a fiercely Samaritan viewpoint", according to C.H.H. Scobie, "The Origins and Development of Samaritan Christianity", *NTS* 19 (1972-73), 398. M. Scharlemann acknowledges "the likelihood of Samaritan influences at work on Stephen", *Stephen: A Singular Saint* (Rome: Pontifical Institute, 1968), 57.
We propose an interpretation of Acts 6 picturing a church *not split in two*, but including returned diaspora Jews exposed to special economic problems ("Hellenists"), Samaritans in Jerusalem ("Hebrews"), and others (including the Twelve) belonging to identifiable sub-groups —Galileans, *'am ha'aretz*, Pharisees, Essenes *et al*. This complicated reconstruction conforms to the evidence we have of the earliest Jesus Movement: "apostolic Christianity was ecumenical in the strict etymological sense of the term, with Pharisees, Essenes, Baptists, and Samaritans included among its adherents. All these sects were then widely scattered over the civilized world (*oikoumene*)." W.F. Albright, *Acts*, 263.

[41] "The author of Acts is elsewhere sensitive to the matter of language." H. Cadbury, *op.cit.*, 61.

[42] *Antiq* xi.344. Later evidence for Samaritan synagogues in Egypt, Thessalonica and elsewhere is cited by Schürer-Vermes (*HJP* III/1, 60,66-67).
Modern designation of (Israelite) synagogues as 'Jewish' ordinarily precludes the question of which were Judean and which Samaritan in origin. But the inscriptions found in Corinth (συνα] γωγη Ἐβρ [αίων) and Rome (συναγωγη Αιβέων) together with Paul's use of the term in II Cor 11.22 is a reminder that among the many synagogues in these cities, at least one in each city might have been 'Samaritan'. *Vocabulary from Non-Literary Sources*, Moulton and Milligen, 178, citing Diessmann, who does not think the designation means 'Hebrew-speaking Jews'. According to John Bowman, "in the time of the New Testament

The determination that the "Hebrews" in Acts 6 were 'Samaritans in the Jerusalem church' does not imply that the term in its contemporary use always designated Samaritans. Nevertheless, Earl Ellis' identification of the 'Hebrews' with 'those of the circumcision'[43] raises the interesting possibility (not considered by Ellis) that some 'Observers' continued to insist on careful (Samaritan) observance of the Law as the starting point for Christian faith. Biblical scholars easily overlook this possibility when they assume a Judean perspective which casts Samaritans as second-class citizens of Israel (or outsiders) rather than as Israelite 'Observers' unswayed by Judean deviations.

Jerusalem, Judea and Samaria

Just before his Ascension, Jesus instructed the Eleven to be his witnesses "in Jerusalem, throughout Judea and Samaria, and to the ends of the earth" (Acts 1.9). According to Luke's account of the miraculous events of Pentecost which followed, the Eleven were able to testify of the mighty acts of God in different languages to Jews, ἄνδρες εὐλαβεῖς ἀπὸ παντὸς ἔθνους (Acts 2.5). The appointment of the Seven, although designated for welfare work within the community, seems to have increased the outreach in Jerusalem dramatically. But whatever the immediate results of Stephen's preaching in Jerusalem, his martyrdom resulted in a dispersion of believers throughout Judea and Samaria (8.1) in which every member functioned as a missionary (8.4).[44]

---

there were still many Samaritans in Palestine, probably even more Samaritans than Jews." *The Samaritan Problem* (Pittsburgh: Pickwick, 1975 [1959]), 57.

[43] E. Ellis *Studia Evangelica* IV, (Berlin: Akademie-Verlag, 1968), 390-399.

[44] Acts 8.1 is a puzzling text, but its correct interpretation is very important for reconstructions of the earliest Christian mission. ("All except the Apostles were scattered throughout Judea and Samaria.") Three quite different interpretations are possible:

1/ Secure in their position in a polarized community at the opposite end from Stephen, the Twelve remained in Jerusalem unthreatened and personally unaffected by the persecution;
2/ Although the most obvious targets of the persecution, the Twelve stood firm in their new spiritual maturity (following Pentecost);
3/ The Twelve were already beyond Judea and Samaria in their missions.

Although "1/" is perhaps the most common interpretation, "2/" or "3/" (or a combination of both) seems preferable. E. Haenchen chooses "2/": "By remaining, these preserve the continuity of the community." *The Acts of the Apostles: A Commentary* (Philadelphia: Westminster, 1971 [1968]), 293. J. Munck similarly attributes the steadfastness of the Apostles to courage in the face of persecution, linking this to his unusual interpretation of the command to "stay in Jerusalem" as extending beyond Pentecost (*Acts*, 4 & 71.)

The choice of "3/" demands recognition of Jerusalem as a staging station, with one or more of the Twelve there resisting the impulse to flee for cover in the hinterland. Such deployment-in-mission is likely to have developed, in any case, by the time Paul returned to Jerusalem and met only Peter (Gal 1.18). "Where were the others? The most likely explanation is that they were travelling through the country, on a mission of preaching and healing." G. Theissen, *Sociology of Early Palestinian Christianity* (Philadelphia: Fortress, 1978 [1977]), 9. *Cf.* Kirsopp Lake, "The Twelve and the Apostles", on the subsequent position of leadership in Jerusalem of James, the brother of Jesus:

Philip's experience in Samaria (Acts 8.5-8), with the Ethiopian government official on the road to Gaza (8.26-40), and finally in the Philistine city of Azotus (Ashdod) were extraordinary, but Luke pointedly uses Philip's ministry as an illustration of the activity of the whole company of anonymous missionaries.

D. Other New Testament Writings and The Didache

Luke's *Acts* is an indispensable source of information about the earliest Christian mission to all nations.[45] But other New Testament writings, besides the Pauline Epistles and the Gospels, also provide information which should be considered independently.

Simon Peter, almost alone of the Twelve, is the focus of some of the important narrative in Acts. But Luke does not inform his readers that Peter was actively engaged in missionary journeys to "Pontus, Galatia, Cappadocia, Asia, and Bithynia". Nevertheless, such activity is clearly implied in the opening of *I Peter*. Moreover, the recipients of this letter "once were no people, but now are the people of God"

> a chosen race, a royal priesthood, a holy nation, a people God claims for his own to proclaim the glorious works of the One who called you from darkness into his marvelous light (I Pe 2.9 & 10).

This 'Petrinism' is strongly committed to and engaged in the Christian mission to all nations. It is compatible with the narrative accounts of Peter's activity in Acts, but not with some scholarly reconstructions based on Acts.

The epistle of *James* is addressed "to the twelve tribes in the dispersion" (Ja 1.1) and tells us that James, the brother of Jesus, was engaged in the Jewish Christian mission to the Diaspora, even if he was strongly tied to Jerusalem as we learn from *Acts* and Paul's letters. Gregory Dix notes that "Acts passes very lightly over" this mission, but it "caused a ferment in Judaism".[46]

The book of *Revelation* addresses itself to 'Israel' and 'the nations' in ways at least as striking as the formulations in Paul's letters. The book's introductory reference to "the seven churches in the province of Asia" implies

---

> If, as may be the case, all the original apostles except James [*sic.*] left Jerusalem and became missionaries, the 'Seven' would be the natural persons to be the *zeqenim* of the community. It is by no means improbable that the disturbance in the Church described in chapter vi. produced a more complete reorganization than Luke has thought fit to describe.
>
> (K. Lake, *Beginnings of Christianity*, V, 56.)

[45] "From the Ascension to AD 48 we are virtually tied to Acts for our information. If we reject it, then we know almost nothing at all of these vitally formative twenty years of Christian history. ... Although not 'church history' in the modern sense, the Gospels and Acts "are 'proclamations' (κηρύγματα) of the Messiahship of Jesus, revealed, so to speak, by the historical facts about Him." G. Dix, *Jew and Greek*, 38.

[46] G. Dix, *Jew and Greek*, 30.

long and serious engagement in mission to that area by the Apostle John.⁴⁷ The positive uses of the terms 'Israel' (*e.g.* 2.14; 7.4-8; 21.12) and 'Jews' (by implication, contrasted to fraudulent Jews 3.9), and to 'a royal nation of priests' and 'God's holy people' (1.6; 5.8 *et al.*) are complemented by very many positive references also to τὰ ἔθνη and people ἐκ πάσας φυλῆς καὶ γλώσσης καὶ λαοῦ καὶ ἔθνους (5.9; *cf.* 7.9; 14.6 *et al.*) culminating in the vision of the New Jerusalem where

> the nations shall walk by the Light of the Lamb and the kings of the earth shall bring their treasures ... the glory and honor of the nations shall be brought into it
> (Rev 21.24 & 26).

This most eloquent celebration of the redemption of the nations, like earlier apocalyptic literature in Israel, includes ambiguous and even sharply negative references to 'the nations' (11.2; 12.18; 19.15; & 20.3) and to 'the kings of the earth' (18.9). Incidentally, the term 'Hebrew' appears once in the book, designating the language of the place-name Armageddon (17.16).

In addition to accounts of the activity of Peter, John, and James the son of Zebedee⁴⁸ in the narrative of Acts there is no early documentary evidence for leadership from the Twelve among the earliest, anonymous missionaries to the nations. Such leadership is assumed in the concluding words of Matthew's Gospel, but even here the 'leadership' can be expected to replace itself immediately. As we shall see, the mandate from the risen Lord implies that each disciple becomes an apostle to the nations. There is one document which can be dated before AD 70, however, which is specifically titled "The Teaching of the Lord through the Twelve Apostles to the Nations" (Διδαχὴ κυρίου διὰ τῶν δώδεκα ἀποστόλων τοῖς ἔθνεσιν). ⁴⁹

---

⁴⁷ Whether John is the son of Zebedee or another apostle, he is independent from Paul.

⁴⁸ Of the disciples in Jesus' inner circle, James may have been the first to become visibly active in bringing the nations into the Christian community. This would explain why Herod singled him out, and why his execution seemed appropriate to the [zealous] Jews (Acts 12.1-4). Luke's report of the martyrdom of James, immediately following Peter's open defence of active recruitment from the nations, supports such an interpretation. James the brother of Jesus, who almost seems to take James' place in the narrative, was quite a different character from this 'son of thunder' (Mk 3.17).

⁴⁹ Jean-Paul Audet's *La Didache Instruction des Apotres* (Paris: J. Gabalda, 1958) established him as the leading authority on this document, but Audet's judgment (187-206) that the *Didache* achieved virtually its present form before AD 70 remains highly controversial. *Cf.* J.A.T. Robinson who suggests *ca.* AD 60, *Redating the New Testament* (London: SCM, 1976), 326 citing C.H. Turner.
Most scholars agree that at least the 'Two Ways' material was in written form during the Apostolic Age. But since precisely the title and sections of disputed early date are important in our argument, our claim that it "can be dated before AD 70" must be tentative. At the very least, the *Didache* is an important trajectory from the earliest mission.

The Teaching of the Twelve Apostles

The *Didache* speaks of the Church as being gathered into the Kingdom "from the ends of the earth" (9.4). Moreover, Christian eucharistic worship "in every place and time" fulfills the prophecy of Malachi 1.11 so that "my name is revered among the nations" (14.3). Of equal relevance to our interest are the repeated references to travelling missionaries, with the 'apostles' (πᾶς δὲ ἀπόστολος 11.4, *cf.* verse 3) clearly including more than the original Twelve designated in the title.[50]

---

[50] G. Theissen (who dates this document to "the first half of the second century") observes that "wandering prophets and teachers were still the decisive authorities at the time of the Didache...; they would settle for a period in a particular community (*Didache* 13.1f)." *Sociology of Early Palestinian Christianity*, 9.

5

LATER TRAJECTORIES OF THE CONCEPTS 'ISRAEL' AND 'NATIONS'

The New Testament writings, especially the written Gospels, represent 'Syriac Christianity', according to Gregory Dix's useful characterization.[1] The formation of Rabbinic Judaism is also reflected in the New Testament writings. The *Mishnah* explicitly claims events before AD 70 for its foundations,[2] but as *documentary* sources the tractates of the Mishnah cannot be dated before the beginning of the third century; the classic expressions of Syriac Christianity by Aphrahat appear at the beginning of the fourth century.

The traumatic events of AD 70 and, most emphatically, those of AD 135 revolutionized attitudes and understandings of 'Israel' and 'the nations' so that later sources of information about the beginnings of the Christian mission must be considered secondary sources. Nevertheless, Hebrew, Aramaic, and Syriac documents written as late as the third and fourth centuries claim diachronic consideration in a review of the earliest Christian mission to the nations because of their use of Semitic linguistic forms. Even where the documents were

---

[1] The written Gospels are "the most substantially and obviously 'Syriac' documents of the New Testament", according to Gregory Dix, *Jew and Greek*, 4.

[2] "The Mishnah, which was the first document in the canon of formative Judaism, *ca.* AD 200, presented a system of Judaism aimed at the sanctification of Israel and bore a teleology lacking an eschatological dimension." J. Neusner, *Messiah in Context: Israel's History and Destiny in Formative Judaism* (Philadelphia: Fortress, 1984), ix. Detailed prescriptions for Temple worship carried forward in the Mishnah (e.g. *Kodashim*: *"Zebahim"* ('Animal Offerings'), Danby, 468ff.) imply a radical transformation of meaning in context. (Only Samaritans continued animal sacrifice after AD 135 and into our own time.) "When the actual Temple was destroyed, the Pharisees were prepared for that tremendous change in the sacred economy. They continued to live *as if* —as if the Temple stood, as if there were a new Temple composed of the Jewish people." Neusner, *Ibid.*, 13.

originally written in Greek (or possibly Latin or Coptic), Syriac-Christian or Jewish documents can be judged 'Semitic' if the community that produced them was bilingual or trilingual, with a Semitic language as its mother tongue and medium of worship.

A. Syriac Christianity

The unified, coherent body of Syriac Christian literature which appears early in the fourth century, with the writings of Aphrahat and Ephrem, is very different in form from the Mishnah. In sharp contrast to the procedure of the Rabbis, Aphrahat and Ephrem do not attribute anything to earlier authorities by name. (When Ephrem quotes Bardaisan, Marcion and Mani, it is to refute them.)[3] The earliest Syriac-language Christian document extant is the Odes of Solomon, if indeed it was composed in Syriac in the early second century.[4] The fact that questions about the original language of the *Odes* remain open for discussion is instructive. Just as pre-Christian Jewish writings composed in Greek should be considered in the background of the Christian mission, so 'Syriac Christian' documents written in Greek —following in line with the New Testament writings themselves and the *Didache*— should also be considered along this 'trajectory'. Accordingly, such early Greek-language Christian writings as *I Clement*, the epistles of Ignatius of Antioch, Justin Martyr's *Dialogue with Trypho the Jew*, and the anonymous *Epistle to Diognetus* will be noted occasionally in the present study.

Aphrahat's *Demonstration XVI*, "On the Peoples Which Are in the Place of the People",[5] explicitly addresses the theme of 'Israel' and 'the nations'. Aphrahat demonstrates the divine 'vocation of the nations' from Hebrew Bible texts. Next he similarly demonstrates 'the rejection of Israel',[6] despite what Jacob Neusner and others describe as the "striking ... absence of anti-Semitism

---

[3] Walter Bauer, "Edessa", *Orthodoxy and Heresy in Earliest Christianity* (London: SCM, 1972 [1934]), 25. *Cf.* Robert Murray, *Symbols of Church and Kingdom: A Study in Early Syriac Tradition* (Cambridge: University Press, 1975), 337.

[4] Since no very early quotation is extant, *The Odes of Solomon* cannot be dated with confidence. After their modern discovery in 1905, J.R. Harris suggested that most of the odes had been written by the end of the first century (*editio princeps*, Cambridge, 1909), and a date before AD 135 is now widely accepted. (J.H. Charlesworth, "Odes of Solomon", *IDB Suppl.* [1976], 637.) *Re* original language *vide* J.A. Emerton, "Some Problems of Text and Language in the Odes of Solomon", *Journal of Theological Studies* 18 (1967), 376.
Especially noteworthy for our present purposes are the negative or ambiguous references to *'amma* ('nations' or 'peoples') in *Odes* 19.5, 23.15 (*Codex Nitriensis*), & 29.8, in contrast to the later usage of Aphrahat and Ephrem.

[5] J. Neusner trans., *Aphrahat and Judaism: The Christian-Jewish Argument in Fourth-Century Iran* (Leiden: E.J.Brill, 1971), 60-67. *Cf.* alt. trans. "On the nations which are in the place of the nation", R. Murray, *Church and Kingdom*, 41.

[6] J. Neusner, *op. cit.*, 60.

from Aphrahat's thought",[7] and the strong covenant-consciousness which Arthur Vööbus notes in Syriac Christianity.[8]

Referring to the language Aphrahat uses to formulate his ideas, Robert Murray notes that

> We do not normally use the same word for God's people and for the Gentiles, but Syriac does, with 'amma in singular and plural: the Church of the Gentiles is 'amma d-men 'amme.[9]

Accordingly, Murray translates this phrase as "the nation from the nations".

Aphrahat seems not to have considered that Israel itself was 'the nation from the nations' at the Exodus (Ex 12.38) in such a way that the new Covenant and the new Exodus recapitulate and confirm Israel's divine vocation.

I Clement was written in Greek from Rome, certainly before AD 135 (probably in AD 96) and was frequently quoted a century later by Clement of Alexandria.[10] In this letter, "the house of Israel" (7.3) seems naturally to apply also to the Christian readers. But these readers are clearly 'a nation from among the nations" (ἔθνος ἐκ μέσου ἐθνῶν 29.3). This echo of Deuteronomy 4.34 and 14.2 is a striking anticipation of Aphrahat's formulation.

Most significant for modern reflections on the earliest Christian mission to the nations is Clement's deliberate contrast between persons who are filled with the Holy Spirit and those motivated by 'zeal'. Those filled with the Holy Spirit are inspired to serve as God's agents in bringing into the brotherhood the whole number of the elect (2. 2-3). Those motivated by 'zeal' (ζῆλος) oppose God's will. Clement lists cautionary examples of 'zealots' from the time of Cain (4.7), Joseph's brothers (4.9), and Moses' sister Miriam (4.11); more recent examples are the opponents of Peter and Paul (5.4-5) and those who precipitated the destruction of Jerusalem in AD 70 (6.4).

Justin Martyr (d. AD 165) was born in Flavia Neapolis (ancient Shechem) and so could claim to be a Samaritan, but he was not a 'Hebrew' or one of the שמרים.[11] Justin's surviving writings by themselves form a significant trajectory from the earliest Christian mission, with frequent and explicit references to 'the nations', 'Jews and Samaritans', 'proselytes', and 'Israel'. Self-consciously indebted to Greek philosophy as he was, Justin can hardly be designated a representative of Syriac Christianity without qualification. But he certainly

---

[7] *Ibid.*, 61.

[8] "We are first impressed with the covenant-consciousness in the primitive Syrian Christianity. ... The covenant ... assumes the structural position of molding all its theology, ethics, and organizations." A. Vööbus, *History of Asceticism in the Syrian Orient*, vol IV, quoted by Neusner, *Aphrahat*, 4.

[9] R. Murray, *Church and Kingdom*, 41 n 1.

[10] Kirsopp Lake, *Apostolic Fathers*, vol I, (London: Heinemann, 1965 [1912]), 5&6.

[11] Justin refers to himself as a "Samaritan" (*Dialogue with Trypho the Jew* 120), but also notes that he is not circumcised (*ibid.*, 29).

influenced the later development of Syriac Christianity through his pupil Tatian, the compiler of the *Diatessaron*.

The anonymous *Epistle to Diognetus* is akin to Justin's writings and can be dated, plausibly, to the middle of the second century.[12] If it was written before AD 70 (as implied by the reference to Jewish sacrifice in 3.5) it would have special claims on our attention.[13] But even if it was composed in the third century, Diognetus marks off an interesting trajectory from the earliest Christian mission to the nations. The author refers to Christians "warred upon by the Jews as foreigners" (5.17) and formulates a brilliant definition of Christians as a peculiar people among the nations:

> For the distinction between Christians and other men is neither in country nor language nor customs. For they do not dwell in cities in some place of their own, nor do they use any strange variety of dialect, nor practise an extraordinary kind of life. ... They dwell in their own fatherlands, but as sojourners in them; they share all things as citizens, and suffer all things as strangers. Every foreign country is their fatherland, and every fatherland is a foreign country. (5. 1,2&5)[14]

B. Rabbinic Judaism

The fact that the Mishnah was not written until *ca.* AD 200 has been noted and emphasized repeatedly in the present study precisely because so much of what is recorded in the Mishnah seems relevant to an understanding of the earliest Christian mission to the nations. The main point of repeated warnings about anachronism is that *any later documents*, whether Jewish or Christian, can be used as evidence for the earliest Christian mission only indirectly, by means of hypothetical retracing of their trajectories. Besides the diachronic factor involved in use of Rabbinic data for reconstruction of developments in the first-century Christian mission, two or three other considerations should also be kept in mind.

After AD 135, the major emerging claimants to the religion of Israel were Christianity and Rabbinic Judaism. By the time the Mishnah was written these claimants were rivals, defining themselves to some extant by opposition to each other. In retracing the Rabbinic trajectory for information about the first-century Christian mission, therefore, allowance must be made for the possibility that the codification of the Mishnah itself may have filtered out the very

---

[12] J.J. Thierry's edition (Leiden: E.J.Brill, 1964) cites C. Richardson dating the epistle *ca.* AD 150. J. Quasten opts for Harnack's third century date. *Patrology*, vol I (Utrecht: Spectrum, 1966 [1950]), 248.

[13] This dating (cited by Thierry, *loc. cit.*) has not been endorsed by modern scholars. The author specifically refers to 'Jews' (3. 1&2), but he may have had the continuing practice of Samaritans in mind. Most likely, he was referring to the continuing preoccupation of the Jews with the details of physical sacrifice, as recorded in the *Mishnah* long after the actual practice was suspended (and superseded).

[14] K. Lake trans., *Apostolic Fathers*, vol I, 359-61.

elements that would be of most value for reconstruction of Israel's first-century responses to the nations.

Rabbinic targums and *midrashim* are now supplemented by modern discoveries in the Qumran Caves (and elsewhere) of similar writings from the first century and earlier. These materials can help scholars plot the trajectory of Judaism more accurately.[15] Long before the modern discovery of Qumran, R.H. Charles argued that pre-Christian apocalyptic writings[16] can be plotted in alternative trajectories which open up perspectives quite different from those of later Rabbinic Judaism.[17]

The emergence of the Pharisees from the catastrophe of AD 70 as 'the sole significant force' does not mean that their influence was immediately dominant among non-Christian Jews, as Jacob Neusner points out. "The very fact of the war of 132-5 CE suggests that others, not Pharisees, held predominance in the life of the Jewish people."[18] There may be advantages in reserving the technical designation 'zealots' for only those 'zealous Jews' who actively pressed for the war against Rome. But references to 'zeal' in literature

---

[15] The use of *Rabbinic* Targums for reconstruction of 'the Jewish background' of the earliest Christian mission involves a serious problem: "Christians tended to base their arguments on verses of Scripture, and the Targum-interpretation of those verses was often deliberately designed to exclude the Christian argument." John Bowker, *The Targums and Rabbinic Literature* (Cambridge: University Press, 1969), xi.

[16] R.H. Charles, in his 1913 "Introduction to Volume II" of *APOT*, declares "the apocalyptic and legalistic sides of pre-Christian Pharisaism —starting originally from the same source— developed ultimately into Christianity and Talmudic Judaism" (vii).
Charles himself identified with the apocalyptic writings and was an enthusiastic advocate of this literature as the continuation of ancient prophecy, foundational to Christian faith. In his (jarring) reconstruction, "legalistic Pharisaism in time drove out almost wholly the apocalyptic element as an active factor (though it accepted some of its developments)". (*Ibid.*)

[17] J.M. Robinson and Helmut Koester introduced the metaphor of 'trajectory', into current discussions of Christian origins. (*Trajectories through Early Christianity* (Philadelphia: Fortress, 1971.) In "Gnomai Diaphoroi", Koester declares that it is not enough to read the known sources and scrutinize the newly discovered texts in order to redefine their appropriate place within the conventional picture of early Christian history (114). His point —akin to a main point in the introduction to the present study— is that "the conventional picture itself" must be set aside. But to reject the limitations of the sources is to produce artistic reconstructions (like the free-forming new patterns of a kaleidoscope, set off by intellect and imagination as by a flick of the wrist) rather than sober projections from known facts.
Even within the prosaic limitations of the known sources the differences in pictures can be as startling as between two in a kaleidoscope series, or as between a *duck* and a *rabbit* (Wittgenstein). Relevant to the present study is the sharp contrast between 'the meaning of righteousness in Matthew' defined by a linguistic sample chosen from closely related Christian writings before AD 70 (including the Hebrew Bible and the Pauline Epistles) *or* by a linguistic sample including Rabbinic documents dated after AD 200 with Pauline writings excluded, as by Benno Przybylski, *Righteousness in Matthew and His World of Thought* (Cambridge: University Press, 1980).

[18] J. Neusner, "Judaism after the Destruction of the Temple", *Israelite and Judaean History*, eds. John H. Hayes & J. Maxwell Miller (Philadelphia: Westminster, 1977), 673.

circulating at the time of the earliest Christian mission (as well as the references in Paul's letters, Acts, and *I Clement*) suggest that various factions and coalitions of 'zealous Jews' were prominent before AD 70, and even until 135.

Finally, two important facts of linguistic usage in the Mishnah regarding 'Israel' and 'the nations' should be noted. As in almost all the biblical and post-biblical writings which we have surveyed, 'Israel' is the name of the covenant people of God. There are hardly any references at all to 'Jews' or 'Judaism' in the Mishnah.[19]

The Semitic terms גוי and גוים in the Mishnah, for 'nation' and 'nations', are relevant to our consideration for many reasons related to definitions of 'Jews', 'Samaritans' and other nations after 'the closing of the ranks' (Salo Baron). Most important for modern discussion of the earliest Christian mission is the conceptual development marked by the grammatical development in Mishnaic usage of the singular גוי for an *individual* national or 'gentile'.[20]

---

[19] Two unimportant exceptions are *Nadarim* 11.12 (a wife's declaration "I will remove me from all Jews" as a ground for divorce) and *Ketuboth* 7.6 (similarly, "a wife that transgresses the Law of Moses and Jewish custom"). Danby trans., 280 and 255. Even less relevant to our argument are the frequent references to Judea.

[20] N. Dahl, "Nations in the New Testament", *New Testament Christianity for Africa and the World* (London: SPCK, 1974), 57 (cited above, 41-42). For a short history of the English "Gentile" see J. LaGrand, "Proliferation of the 'Gentile' in the NRSV", *Biblical Research*, XLI, (1996) 77-87.

Part Two

Jesus and the Nations

The World of the Messianic Mission *ca.* AD 35

The move from the Pauline epistles to Matthew's Gospel leads us alternatively forward and backward in time for information about the earliest Christian mission to all nations. The Greek story attributed to Matthew was written later than Paul's letters.[1] But Jesus' ministry in the land of Israel, the subject of the narration, preceded Paul's ministry. In this sense, Matthew's Gospel itself is diachronic.

Like Matthew's first readers, Christians and inquirers through the centuries have read the Gospel for information about Jesus' words and deeds which they could apply to their own life of faith. Most often even the critical efforts of scholars to understand Matthew have been part of a conscious effort to see through the screen of Matthean formulation (or Marcan, Lucan, or Johannine) to the authentic, original teaching and activity of Jesus.[2] But the recent development of 'redaction criticism' and 'composition criticism' has given a new, positive focus to questions about the evangelists' socio-theological involvements and ideas.

Redaction criticism has added to, rather than displaced, the earlier methods of source criticism and form criticism. Positive interest in the evangelists' lives and ideas has encouraged, in turn, a new focus of scholarly opinion on the mission and teaching of Jesus.[3] Two technical explanations for this new industry are worth noting. First, some of the Gospel material which had been stripped away from Jesus and attributed to the evangelists by earlier source- and form- critics is now being re-evaluated. This re-evaluation of 'the teaching of Matthew' (or of John,

---

[1] The dating of the four Gospels relative to the Pauline corpus is hardly a matter of debate. Those who assign a late date to some Pauline letters assign a still later date to Mt's Gospel.

[2] "The real theological motive during this period in gospel study [19th and early 20th century] was without doubt the quest of the historical Jesus." Georg Strecker, "The Concept of History in Matthew" [1968], *The Interpretation of Matthew*, ed. G. Stanton (London: SPCK, 1983), 67.

[3] It is more than a coincidence that Günther Bornkamm, a pioneer in modern redaction criticism (*Tradition and Interpretation in Matthew*, Philadelphia: Westminster, 1963 [1960]), is also acknowledged as a pioneer in the renewed research into the life of Jesus (*Jesus of Nazareth*, New York: Harper & Row, 1959 [1956]). Deep theological concerns motivate the 'new quest of the historical Jesus'. Ernst Käsemann, in an argument against his teacher Rudolf Bultmann, summarizes his own quest as "aimed at finding out whether the earthly Jesus is to be taken as the criterion of the Kerygma". "Blind Alleys in the 'Jesus of History' Controversy" [1965], *New Testament Questions of Today* (Philadelphia: Fortress, 1969), 47.

'Q', Luke, and Mark) demands methods equivalent to those used to determine 'the teaching of Jesus'. Second, there is a growing awareness that we are dependent on the narrative forms themselves for our understanding of what Jesus taught and accomplished.[4]

The question of Matthew's originality, of his Jewishness, and of his attitude towards foreigners are three perennial questions in Matthean scholarship which have been re-focused by redaction criticism. These questions are related, and all bear directly on the use of the First Gospel as a source of information about the earliest Christian mission to all nations.

Proper assessment of Matthew's *originality* in the composition of his Gospel must be grounded in awareness of two important rival claims to originality. Both Jesus himself, whose words and deeds Matthew reports, and the earliest Christian fellowship, whose communal formulations Matthew incorporates in his work, had life and energy which are attested also outside of Matthew's story.

Any answer to the question of Matthew's *Jewishness*, similarly, must take account of Jesus' Jewishness and the Jewishness of Matthew's traditional sources. These background issues will be addressed in our survey of the multiple tradition about Jesus and of the Scripture quotations which form part of the foundation for Matthew's narrative.

Relating to *foreigners*, two texts which appear only in Matthew's Gospel are included in our preliminary assessment of the context of Jesus' ministry: according to Matthew 10.5-6 Jesus prohibits evangelization of non-Jews; in Matthew 23.15 Jesus condemns the Pharisees' proselytizing. These same texts will be reviewed again in relation to the overall structure of the Gospel. But as testimonies to Jesus' own words these texts are first considered in terms of the Gospel's trajectory through first-century Messianic expectations and Jewish proselytism.

The *structure and design* of the First Gospel clearly demonstrate Matthew's own perspective on world mission. Our division "Signals of Things to Come" and "The Establishment of the Kingdom" relates to the evangelist's fundamental theme of 'promise' and 'fulfillment' to bring our study to its conclusion.

---

[4] Narrative form may be a necessary part of 'the grammar of faith' for Christians (Romans 1.16-17). Käsemann's argument (*op. cit.*, 57) which speaks of "the theological relevance of written Gospels' history in the controversy with the enthusiasts" supports such a claim. The same logic answers John Dominic Crossan's rhetorical question: "Is the narrativity of Jesus' parables a formal and stylistic warrant for Catholic Christianity's choice of narrative gospels as against Gnostic Christianity's preference for discourse gospels?" *Four other Gospels: Shadows on the Contours of the Canon* (Minneapolis: Winston Press, 1985), 186.

6

LIVING TRADITIONS IN THE BACKGROUND OF THE GOSPEL

A. *The Multiple Tradition about Jesus*

A significant amount of time elapsed between the occurrence of the last events reported in the Gospels and the publication of the written accounts. According to Bo Reicke's calculations, this time-gap amounted to about thirty years, AD 33-62.[1] Not surprisingly, Matthew's Gospel incorporated material which is also attested in one, two, or three of the other canonical Gospels. We can be confident, therefore, that some of the references to 'the nations' in the Gospel did not originate with Matthew himself. Considered in series with references in the shared tradition, even single references in Matthew to 'the nations' can be evaluated as possibly originating in the Jesus movement during the years AD 33-66, or originating with Jesus himself during his three-year ministry.[2]

---

[1] Bo Reicke concludes that it is "advisable to give the Synoptic gospels a date around AD 60 without ... ascribing different ages to them". "The New Testament Era and the Date of the Gospels", *Die Nuwe Testamentiese Wetenskap Vandag* (Pretoria: University Press, 1980), 76. *Cf. The Roots of the Synoptic Gospels* (Philadelphia: Fortress, 1986), 180.
Following Reicke's dating of Jesus' crucifixion and the Jewish revolt, our usual reference to 'the apostolic age' will be "AD 33-66". *New Testament Era* (Philadelphia: Fortress, 1968 [1964]), 2 and 183. Gregory Dix brackets this period "between the crucifixion of Jesus in Jerusalem and the crucifixion of Peter in Rome". *Jew and Greek*, 4.

[2] Only a theory of Matthean priority which made the other evangelists utterly dependant on Matthew for these references would allow speculation that his formulation of them all is original. The Two-Document Hypothesis of Marcan priority continues to dominate working assumptions in the field, but today few NT scholars would insist that triple attestation is simply Mark's material copied by Matthew and Luke or that 'non-Q' material in Matthew and Luke is simply imaginative reconstruction or editorial comment.

J.A.T. Robinson suggests that

> whereas epistles were written for specific occasions (though they might be added to or adapted later), gospels were essentially for continuous use in the preaching, teaching, apologetic and liturgical life of the Christian communities. They grew out of and with the needs.[3]

Following the same idea with reference to baptism and eucharist, Bo Reicke notes that "there is a heavy concentration of context-parallel triple traditions upon or around the text units that deal with Christ's baptism and passion."[4] As an explanation for the close harmony in the passion narratives, Reicke suggests that "the development of the traditions has gone backwards. First there was the passion story, and it was memorized in a relatively uniform way particularly at the eucharist."[5]

Birger Gerhardsson, like Reicke, asserts that "the Gospels build upon a common oral tradition" but he concedes that "there must also be some kind of literary connection between them, in any case between the synoptics."[6] He accepts Marcan priority, but not exactly in the terms of the still-dominant Two Document Hypothesis. Somewhat provocatively, Gerhardsson suggests that

> The first one who wrote a Gospel (I think it was Mark) certainly was a pioneer; yet, *his achievement was hardly very creative*. He had good text material, he did not need to re-interpret it very much, nor change its form very much.[7]

The real achievement, Gerhardsson claims, was writing up the material in a way that was acknowledged to be faithful. Each of the writers of canonical Gospels shared this achievement.

The questions of synoptic relations and the date of Matthew's Gospel will be reviewed when we consider the author's design and the structure of the written Gospel. For the moment, our concern is with what Gerd Theissen calls

---

Our survey is limited to the four canonical Gospels. Regarding 'other gospels':
a/ Formal relationships could be explored.
 (For example, *Gospel of Thomas* Logion 39 and Mt 23.15 *re* 'entering'.)
b/ There is no explicit reference to 'the nations' in the *Gospel of Thomas*. (Logia 65 & 66 relate the parables of the wicked tenants and rejected stone; 53 relates to circumcision.)

[3] J.A.T. Robinson, *Redating the New Testament* (London: SCM, 1976), 94.

[4] Bo Reicke, *The Roots of the Synoptic Gospels*, 65.

[5] Reicke, "The New Testament Era and the Date of the Gospels", *NT Wetenskap*, 74.

[6] B. Gerhardsson, *The Gospel Tradition* (Malmo: Gleerup, 1986), 28.

[7] *Ibid.*, 49.

"the time of the Jesus movement"[8] and the witness of the multiple tradition to "a continuity between Jesus and the Jesus movement".[9]

Whether or not all four canonical Gospels actually attained their present form during the period AD 33-66, it is widely agreed that they are faithful witnesses to the Jesus movement of this time.[10] Gregory Dix describes the four Gospels as "the most substantially and obviously 'Syriac' documents of the New Testament".[11] The noteworthy differences between the four (and between the Synoptics and John) make their common witness the more remarkable. Each presents Jesus as the promised Messiah who fulfilled prophecy and the will of God decisively through his death and resurrection. Each Gospel in its own way also testifies to the presence of the victorious Messiah in the life and mission of the faithful community.[12] Specifically to the point of our present study is the agreement of the four Gospels on Jesus' promise to the nations.[13] Indeed, it can be argued that *each* of the four evangelists has constructed his Gospel in terms of the Messianic mission to all nations.

Variations of a Theme

Certainly the conclusion of the First Gospel is a clear, explicit statement of endorsement for the mission to the nations. When we consider Matthew's

---

[8] "The Jesus movement is the renewal movement within Judaism brought into being through Jesus and existing in the area of Syria and Palestine between about AD 30 and AD 70." G. Theissen, *Sociology of Early Palestinian Christianity* [*Soziologie der Jesusbewegung*] (Philadelphia: Fortress, 1978 [1977]), 21.

[9] *Ibid.*, 4. Commentators often define this issue in terms of the 'Jewishness' of Matthew and of his first readers. Ernst von Dobschütz points out that "Strack-Billerbeck dedicate their whole first volume of 1,055 pages to it [Mt], in contrast to only 867 pages for the other three Gospels and Acts altogether in volume 2." "Matthew as Rabbi and Catechist" [1928] *Interpretation of Matthew*, 24. Theissen also cites Mt more often than the other three together in *Sociology of Early Palestinian Christianity*, 126-128.

[10] This wide agreement is not unanimity. G. Bornkamm judges that the Fourth Gospel is of such a different character from the Synoptics as to be only a secondary source ("*nur als sekundäre Quelle*") for his study *Jesus of Nazareth* (quotation from 1956, 12). Similarly, E. Käsemann insists that "nothing in this Gospel is historical in the sense of being authentic" (*NT Questions*, 49).
C.H. Dodd's *Historical Tradition in the Fourth Gospel* (Cambridge: University Press, 1963) marks the beginning of a new seriousness in considering the Fourth Gospel as a primary source of information on Jesus' life and ministry. In the present study, acceptance of John 4 as an authentic representation of Jesus' attitude to Samaritans and Jews ("salvation is from the Jews", 4.22) affects our exegesis of Matthew 10. 5b-6.

[11] G.Dix, *Jew and Greek*, 4; "at all events the Gospel is a product of the Hellenistic Church." R. Bultmann, *The History of the Synoptic Tradition* (Oxford, 1963), 369.

[12] Despite the official assurance by the young men at the empty tomb in Mark 16.6-7, the abrupt ending at Mark 16.8 ("...for they were afraid.") did not satisfy some early readers, hence the additional (longer and shorter) endings.

[13] This phrase is the title of J. Jeremias' study which will be cited frequently below, *Jesus' Promise to the Nations* (London: SCM, 1967 [1959]).

design we shall demonstrate, what has often been claimed, that this 'Great Commission' can be traced back through the whole book. Similarly, Mark's report of Jesus' teaching from Isaiah in relation to the Temple might be taken as a clue to Mark's design: "Is it not written that 'My house shall be a house of prayer for all the nations'?"[14] At least, "it is generally recognized that a major concern of Mark is the Gentile mission."[15]

In the beginning of the Third Gospel, Simeon's prophecy identifies Jesus as "a light for revelation to the nations"[16] and the second volume of Luke-Acts leaves no doubt about Luke's understanding of the outcome of Jesus' ministry. The Fourth Gospel also projects the Messianic mission to all mankind: "I —once I am lifted up from the earth— will draw everyone to me" (Jn 12.32). John's special interest in mission to Samaritans may be a clue to the origin and purpose of the Fourth Gospel.[17] Among the many intriguing texts in this Gospel is the evangelist's report of the high priest's prophecy (Jn 11.49-50) and the interpretation "that Jesus would die for the Jews (ὑπὲρ τοῦ ἔθνους) and not for them only but in order to bring together all the dispersed children of God as one people" (Jn 11.51-2).[18]

The united witness of the four Gospels to the emergent mission to all nations is important documentary evidence. Together with Paul's epistles (written somewhat earlier), the canonical Gospels testify to what E.P. Sanders describes as "the overwhelming impression ... that Jesus started a movement which *came to see the Gentile mission as a logical extension of itself*".[19]

---

[14] According to E.P. Sanders, "The quotation of Isa. 56.7 in Mark 11.17 is not likely to be an authentic saying [of Jesus]." *Jesus and Judaism* (Philadelphia: Fortress, 1985), 221. Sanders' argument, if accepted, could add weight to our own at this point, assuming either: a/ Mark selected the Isaiah quotation, or b/ Mark added the words "to all the nations" to a Jesus-traditional quotation (or filled out the text of Mt-Lk).

[15] C.H.H. Scobie, "Jesus or Paul? The Origin of the Universal Mission of the Christian Church", *From Jesus to Paul* (Waterloo: Wilfred Laurier University Press, 1984), 54.
F. Hahn considers it "a peculiar and significant fact that the oldest of our Gospels [*Mark*] comes from Gentile Christianity". *Mission in the NT* (London: SCM, 1965 [1963]), 111.

[16] With reference to Lk 2.23, S.G. Wilson concludes that "it is significant that Luke picks up this prophecy only at the end of the Gospel and in Acts; he does not anachronistically place its fulfillment in Jesus' earthly ministry." *The Gentiles and Gentile Mission in Luke-Acts* (Cambridge: University Press, 1973), 38.

[17] H. Odeberg, *The Fourth Gospel* (Uppsala, 1929) cited by C.H.H. Scobie in "The Origins and Development of Samaritan Christianity", *NTS* 19 (1972-73), 401. *Cf.* John Bowman, "Samaritan Studies", *BJRL* 40 (1957-58) 298-315; W.A. Meeks, *The Prophet-King: Moses Traditions and the Johannine Christology* (Leiden: E.J. Brill, 1967), 256- 257; H.G. Kippenberg, *Garizim und Synagogue* (Berlin: W. de Gruyter, 1971), 324-327; and O. Cullmann, *The Johannine Circle* (Philadelphia: Westminster, 1976 [1975]) 46-49.

[18] It is noteworthy that John uses ἔθνος especially of the Jewish nation. See also Luke's usage in 7.5 and 23.2 and the implicit parallelism in Mt 21.43.

[19] When Paul was writing his early letters in the 50s "no Christian group objected to the Gentile mission." Moreover, according to E.P. Sanders, "the majority of Jews" were united with the earliest Christians "in thinking that, at the end, some Gentiles would be admitted to

Attempts to get behind the documentary evidence to the earliest Jesus traditions and the sayings of Jesus, through source- and form-criticism, necessarily remain subject to debate and revision.[20]

Multiple Attestations of Jesus' Deeds and Words
The Third Gospel in the canon reports that "many have already undertaken to compile a narrative of the events which have been fulfilled among us" (Lk 1.1-4). This suggests that Luke knew other accounts in addition to some or all the other canonical Gospels. The evangelist himself no doubt had specific examples in mind, but the modern reader cannot be certain whether Luke's words refer to written or oral accounts (or both) and whether these compilations included collections of relevant Scripture texts, sayings of Jesus, and acts of apostles, as well as narrative accounts of Jesus' ministry.

With the exception of our four written Gospels, all such earlier accounts are now lost,[21] but in each of our four Gospels there is evidence of earlier, traditional formulation. As already noted, the canonical Gospels are *narrative* accounts which record Jesus' teaching and action, words and deeds. Whether or not 'saying sources' (such as the hypothetical "Q" and the second-century *Gospel of Thomas*) were already written down, accounts of Jesus' actions must also have existed (as Luke's word διήγησιν implies) in writing or in set memorized forms.[22]

Two twice-attested stories of Jesus' *action* which are important to our subject are the healing of the centurion's servant (Mt 8.5-13, par Lk 7.1-10) and the healing of the Canaanite woman's daughter (Mt 15.21-28, par Mk 7.24-30). These will be considered below in relation to the structure and purpose of Matthew's Gospel. But the stories themselves should not be thought to be

---

the people of God", *Jesus and Judaism*, 220 & 221.

[20] External and internal evidence for the date of Matthew's Gospel will be considered briefly below in relation to the purpose and design of the Gospel.

[21] Even if we assign very late dates to Matthew's Gospel and Luke-Acts (early second century), the earliest other 'gospel' writings extant —the *Gospel of Thomas* and "Edgerton Papyrus 2" —appear to be later, probably mid- second century. "Extant Christian manuscripts (or fragments thereof) dating to the second century and preserved in Egypt" include seven from the OT, the Gospel of Jn, Mt, and Titus. *The Roots of Egyptian Christianity*, eds. Birger Pearson & J. Goehring (Philadelphia: Fortress, 1986), 133.
Without attempting to assess Morton Smith's "Secret Gospel of Mark" (accepted in J.D. Crossan's "working hypothesis", *Four other Gospels*, 108f), we maintain Helmut Koester's earlier position that "the canonical gospels are ... the most primitive and original literature that could be called 'gospel'" and that "the often different forms and outlines of the apocryphal gospels appear by comparison as secondary alterations, if not tendentious falsifications." H. Koester, "One Jesus and Four Primitive Gospels" (1968), *Trajectories*, 158.

[22] See John J. Vincent, "Did Jesus Teach His Disciples to Learn by Heart?" *Studia Evangelium*, III/ii, ed. F.L. Cross (Berlin: Akademie-Verlag, 1964) 104-118, and W.D. Davies' summary assessment of the work of H. Riesenfeld and B. Gerhardsson, *The Setting of the Sermon on the Mount* (Cambridge: University Press, 1977) Appendix XV.

products of Matthew's originality, however appropriate they may appear to be in the development of his narrative.[23]

Specific References to 'Nations' in the Triple Tradition

Jesus taught in Aramaic, presumably, and there is some variation in the Greek word-usage among the four evangelists. Nevertheless, a cluster of ἔθνη 'sayings of Jesus' which appear to be characteristic of Matthew's own thinking appear also in the other synoptic Gospels and should be considered part of 'the triple tradition'.[24]

According to Matthew 20.17-19 and parallels (Mk 10. 32-34 and Lk 18.31-33) Jesus predicted his passion as he and his disciples were travelling up to Jerusalem. All three synoptic Gospels attest the prediction that the Son of Man would be "handed over to the nations to be mocked and scourged and crucified". As contrast to the new order of human relations in the Kingdom of heaven, Matthew 20.25 (par Mk 10.42 and Lk 22.25) records Jesus' disparaging reference to "the rulers of the nations" who "lord it over" their fellows; "their great men exercise power over them." Mark's formulation of rulers as "those who seem to rule" and Luke's note on the self-aggrandizing names which dictators affect are distinctive, but congruent with the thrust of this saying in each of the synoptic Gospels. In a prophetic saying about the Temple, Matthew 24.7-8 (par Mk 13.8 and Lk 21.10-11) represents Jesus anticipating the time when "nation will rise against nation" and "kingdom against kingdom" prior to "the End of the world".

These triple attestations of Jesus' references to ἔθνη are prominent, even obtrusive, in each of the three written formulation. If these negative uses of the term presented challenges to each editor-writer, the strength of the tradition apparently allowed little flexibility for creative integration into the text. In each, the juxtaposition of 'the nations' to the End is obvious. The first in the series signals the catastrophic end of Jesus' earthly ministry, the second projects a model for eschatological politics, and the third marks the ultimate end of the age. All seem to be tied to a traditional account of the days leading up to Jesus' trial and crucifixion. The meaning of the term is related to institutional and organizational structure, just as ἔθνη / גוים often is in the Hebrew Bible.

Double Traditions

In the saying of Jesus about concern for food and clothing, "that people of every nation seek after" (Mt 6.32/ Lk 12.30), the term ἔθνη is used in a way similar to the organizational-institutional usage in the triple-attested sayings

---

[23] It is most reasonable to assume that Matthew and Mark, in the one case, and Matthew and Luke in the other, got the story from the same source.

[24] The characteristic use of ἔθνος for the Jews in the Fourth Gospel was noted above. In the synoptic Gospels the terms 'kingdom', 'people', 'Son of Man' (and even terms which appear infrequently, or only once, such as 'foreigner', 'Samaritan', 'Magi', 'Canaanite', and 'Centurion') are important for an assessment of the theme of 'the nations' in the Triple Tradition, and in Jesus' own outlook.

already considered. But here the focus has shifted within the semantic range from the political to the cultural sense of 'nation' (ἔθνος). There is no explicit reference to the End, but the saying is best understood in terms of 'eschatological ethics'.

One last example of a saying of Jesus which might seem peculiarly Matthean if it were not attested elsewhere in the multiple tradition is Matthew 24.4/ Mark 13.10 which explicitly envisions a mission to all nations *before* the End:

> And this good news of the Kingdom will be proclaimed throughout the whole world as a witness to all the nations, and then the End will come. (Mt 24.4)

The variation in Mark's wording only emphasizes the identity of the idea when compared with Matthew's text:

> First it is necessary that the good news be proclaimed to all the nations. (Mk 13.10)

This saying is the most challenging of the "straightforward prophecies of a Gentile mission", according to Stephen Wilson who rightly considers its critical assessment as a crux in the debate about Jesus' expectations and intentions for the nations.[25] Our point here is that the basic formation of this Jesus-saying antedates *Matthew's* use of it in his written Gospel.

These examples of triple and double attestations of the term ἔθνη in the written Gospels do not exhaust the evidence for the motif in the multiple tradition about Jesus. In the characteristic usage of the Fourth Gospel, outsiders opposed to the followers of Jesus are called 'the world': "If the world hates you, understand that it hated me before it hated you" (Jn 15.18). But κόσμος, like ἔθνη in the synoptic Gospels, is systematically ambiguous: God's *love* for 'the world' is an emphatic over-arching theme of the Fourth Gospel (Jn 3.16). Even terms which emphasize alienation most emphatically, such as 'Samaritans', 'foreigner' (Lk 17.19) and the uniquely Matthean ἐθνικοί (Mt 5.47 and 6.7), are also ambiguous in their Gospel contexts.

Urgency and Significance in Time

The texts just cited as evidence of the multiple tradition of Jesus' verbal references to the nations form an unwieldy list. But even when taken out of their contexts in the individual Gospels, these disparate *'nations'-sayings* are linked by the co-ordinate theme of strategic time. Our reference to the prominence of the End in the 'nations'-sayings from the triple tradition already implied recognition of shared elements of eschatology in the synoptic Gospels. Jesus' insistence on the urgency of human decision combined with a no less emphatic call for confidence in God's providence is clearly portrayed by each of the Gospel writers. As a constitutive element of the Gospels this mysterious

---

[25] S.G. Wilson, *Gentiles and Gentile Mission*, 18-28; 30-31.

projection must be acknowledged as emerging from the multiple tradition about Jesus.

"Salvation history" seems an appropriate rubric under which to collect the traditional elements which gave shape to views of human history and teleology in the four Gospels. But *'Heilsgeschichte'* has become the hallmark of a school of biblical interpreters and theologians, so the term must be used carefully. Hans Conzelmann's 1954 analysis of the Third Gospel in terms of *"Die Mitte der Zeit"* at once sharpened the focus on *heilsgeschictliche* lines in the Gospels and supplied a basis for arguing that only Luke's understanding of time should be characterized in such terms.[26] An example of the arguments implying that Luke alone among the Gospel writers has *heilsgeschichtliche* views appears in Kenzo Tagawa's important article "People and Community in the Gospel of Matthew". Tagawa protests against any interpretation of the First Gospel which "presupposes a Lukan view of the history of salvation as the framework also of Matthew's theology".[27]

When we consider the structure and design of Matthew's Gospel, we will have occasion to emphasize the importance of Matthew's own characteristic representation of the meaning of Jesus' death and resurrection in the history of salvation. But Tagawa's warning and our knowledge of the hazards of harmonization should not distract us from grasping the clear, strong, shared tradition about Jesus' words and deeds which provides the basis for statements in all four Gospels about Messianic time.

Sayings of the Risen Jesus

'Sayings of the risen Jesus' cannot be considered simply in series with the other traditions about Jesus' teaching and actions during his earthly ministry.[28] But neither can these sayings and the witness of angels recorded in the Gospels be disregarded. Faith in the resurrection of Jesus is basic to the Gospel accounts and to the mission to the nations. Accordingly, two or three formal connections should be noted in the now somewhat disjointed common tradition witnessing to the Resurrection.

---

[26] H. Conzelmann, *Die Mitte der Zeit. Studia zur Theologie des Lukas* (Tübingen: J.C.B. Mohr, 1954); ET *The Theology of St. Luke* (London: 1960).

[27] Kenzo Tagawa,"People and Community in Matthew", *NTS* 16 (1969-70), 157.

[28] M. Eugene Boring's use of this phrase is defined by the subtitle of his book, *Sayings of the Risen Jesus: Christian Prophecy in the Synoptic Tradition* (Cambridge: University Press, 1982). Boring's nuanced definition of the ambiguity between "a 'historical' saying" and "the post-Easter address of the exalted Lord to his community"(1) does not give much consideration to the meaning of Jesus' resurrection appearances.
The resurrection of the Messiah, in NT perspective, is "a unique event in which God in his own way embraced the totality of nature and history, and by which he is bringing his good will concerning man and all creation to fulfillment". *Acquittal by Resurrection*, Markus Barth and Verne H. Fletcher (New York: Holt, Reinhart & Winston, 1964), vi. Acceptance of such a claim to uniqueness puts all historical methods in suspension.

"A messenger of the Lord" on Easter morning instructs Mary Magdalene and the other Mary to tell the disciples that Jesus has been raised from the dead "and, indeed, goes before you to Galilee, where you will see him" (Mt 28.7). Mark's Gospel attests this same saying, adding a special reference to Peter (Mk 16.7). In Luke's Gospel "two men" speak somewhat differently to unnamed women, but their reminder is cast in terms of what Jesus had said "when he was still with you in Galilee" (Lk 24.6). In the last chapter of the Fourth Gospel Jesus meets the disciples in Galilee (Jn 21.1f), but no explicit instructions for the mission are recorded.

According to John 20.19f, Jesus appeared to the disciples in Jerusalem already on the first Easter Sunday and commissioned them: "Just as the Father sent me, so I send you" (verse 21). Luke's account, at the end of his Gospel, of a commissioning in Jerusalem just before the Ascension (anticipating Pentecost) is a complex formula indicating that proclamation is to be "to all nations, beginning at Jerusalem". This formula is restated at the Ascension (Lk 24.46-49/ Acts 1.7-8).

Jesus' commissioning statement in Galilee, recording in Matthew's Gospel (Mt 28.16-20), is carefully formulated. But as a conclusion to the Gospel it is abrupt. If the ending of Mark's Gospel at 16.8 is deliberate this abruptness itself might be seen as a parallel in the witness of Matthew and Mark to the Resurrection.

B. Scriptures as Background and Directives

Paradoxically, it is the Scripture quotations in the First Gospel which are most strikingly original. But Matthew did not compose these texts.[29] He simply showed how Jesus fulfilled "what had been said through the prophet Isaiah", for example, that the chosen servant of Yahweh "will proclaim justice to the nations ...in his name the nations will find hope" (Mt 12.18/21; Is 42.1&4).

Besides their use as foundational building blocks in Matthew's narrative (where they are controlled by Matthew's selection and application), these texts have a life of their own in the Hebrew Bible and in Israel's self understanding at the time of Jesus' ministry. Accordingly, these Scripture quotations which serve as clues to the background of Jesus' ministry can also be traced as trajectories through Jesus' time and Matthew's. The Gospel according to Matthew proclaims the climax of God's continuing relationship with his people, in the words and action of Jesus the Messiah. What is recorded in this book not only reflects but also 'fulfills' earlier Scripture.

Some of the Scripture quotations in the First Gospel are attributed to Jesus, some are deeply enmeshed in the narrative, and some are added as

---

[29] S.V. McCasland's claim that "Matthew Twists the Scriptures", *JBL* 80 (1961) 143-8, goes well beyond the questions of text and translation quoted by Matthew. Information from Qumran on pre-Massoretic text-types current in Palestine in Jesus' time and Matthew's, however, make it difficult to prove any twisting of Scripture texts by Mt. (When more than one text or translation was available, Mt no doubt chose the one that seemed most apt.)

commentary by the evangelist himself. This multiformity suggests that in considering biblical quotations, as with analysis of other elements in the text, we should consider not just one *Sitz im Leben* but three.

According to Richard Edwards, "the third *Sitz* is the theological *Sitz im Leben* because redaction criticism assumes that the theological stance of the redactor will make itself known in all aspects of his work."[30] It is certainly true that the third *Sitz* is theologically oriented, but theology was also a normative element in the *Sitz im Leben Jesu* and in the formation of the very earliest Christian community after the Resurrection. Consequently, some of Matthew's selection and application of biblical quotations had already been determined by earlier theological reflection. We can ask whether Matthew's additions and changes develop and refine or substantially alter those earlier reflections,[31] but there can be no doubt that the use of biblical quotations in all three stages was theologically determined.

The designation of *three* stages of development related to three clearly defined life-situations is a simplification of the complex process of growth in the Gospel material. Source criticism, form criticism, and redaction criticism represent various attempts to describe and analyze the complexities of the process of growth. But identification of three clearly marked life-situations is a useful simplification. The years of Jesus' teaching and healing ministry, the early response of believers to the Resurrection, and the literary formation of Matthew's Gospel seem to have been three definitive phases of theological reflection.

1. *Sitz im Leben Jesu*

A melancholy observation by G.B. Caird is worth noting before any new attempt is made to determine some main lines of Jesus' thought or to claim any *ipsissima verba Jesu*:

> It is the paradox of synoptic studies that the most sceptical and devastating results have been achieved by those who set out to provide a firm historical foundation on which the superstructure of faith might with confidence be reared.[32]

But the claims and counterclaims of old dogmas and new methodologies should not weaken our grasp of the fact that Jesus' teaching ministry can be dated with confidence in the first third of the first century AD and located firmly in the Land of Israel. We can also be sure that Jesus quoted Scriptures. Many of his specific citations would have been remembered after the Resurrection. Moreover, something of the pattern and thrust of his use of Scripture would

---

[30] R. Edwards, *The Sign of Jonah in the Theology of the Evangelists and Q* (London: SCM, 1971), 19.

[31] In the same way we can ask whether the earliest Christian community preserved and developed Jesus' own pattern of biblical interpretation or whether the Resurrection marks a radical change in their Messianic understanding of the Hebrew Bible.

[32] G.B. Caird, *Jesus and the Jewish Nation* (London: Athlone Press, 1965), 4.

have been remembered. C.H. Dodd, in his oft-quoted statement about the earliest development in the Church's use of the Hebrew Bible, notes that "to account for the beginning of this most original and fruitful process of rethinking of the Old Testament we found the need to postulate a creative mind." [33] This creative mind, Dodd claims, was Jesus himself.

J. Duncan Derrett's suggestion that "Jesus used biblical material as his 'blue print'" is plausible.[34] The 'blue-print' image exaggerates, but Joachim Jeremias and others have followed this same line of explanation: "from the time of his baptism he was conscious of being God's servant promised in Isaiah."[35]

The narrative of Matthew's Gospel does not attribute each Scripture quotation to Jesus himself, but it is reasonable to assume that Jesus did cite many or all of these texts —and many more— during the course of his teaching ministry.[36] Any such assumption presupposes a remarkable shared interest and knowledge among many of his hearers if such citations were to grip the minds and imaginations of his audience.

Jesus' Audience and Bible Knowledge

First-century Jews in the land of Israel —and no less the Samaritans ("Observers")— can be designated appropriately as "the People of the Book".[37] Public reading in synagogue and Temple, family reading, synagogue instruction based on the Scriptures, memorization of selected passages and private reading of popular scrolls were all deeply ingrained in Israel's life before AD 70.

Substantial sections of the Law (*Torah*) and Prophets (*Haphtarah*) were read each Sabbath and festival day in the synagogues.[38] This much is certain, whatever the historical reasons were for the development of the Synagogue[39] and whether or not the evidence available today allows confidence in

---

[33] C.H. Dodd, *According to the Scriptures: The Sub-Structure of New Testament Theology* (London: Collins, 1952), 110.

[34] J.D.M. Derrett, "Jesus' Fishermen and the Parable of the Net", *NovT* 22 (1980), 108.

[35] J. Jeremias, *New Testament Theology: The Proclamation of Jesus* (New York: Scribner's Sons, 1971), 55.

[36] Like others in his time, Jesus accepted "the Old Testament as containing a divine revelation". C.H. Dodd, *The Founder of Christianity* (London: Macmillan, 1970), 53.

[37] This phrase, which seems to have originated in the Koran (*Sura* II), is a just summary of Josephus' first-century description of his people: "We have given practical proof of our reverence for our own Scriptures. ... It is an instinct with every Jew, from the day of his birth, to regard them as the decrees of God, to abide by them, and, if need be, cheerfully to die for them." (*Against Apion* I.8, Thackery trans.)

[38] See the instructions in the Mishnah; *Megillah* 4.4: "He that reads in the Law may not read less than three verses...." *The Mishnah*, trans. H. Danby (Oxford: UP, 1933), 206.

[39] See J. Weingreen, "The Origin of the Synagogue", *From Bible to Mishna* (Manchester: University Press, 1976) 115-131; and J.W. Bowker, "Speeches in Acts: A Study in Proem and Yelammedenu Form", *NTS* 14 (1967) 96-111.

reconstructions of a triennial lectionary cycle.[40] So we can assume that many in the crowds who listened to Jesus were informed by attention to systematic selection of long readings, translation, and explanation of Scripture in synagogue services. This assumption is supported in part by the emphasis in all four Gospels on Jesus' own involvement in synagogue activity.[41]

The Palestinian Targum (*Neofiti*) and the Babylonian Targums (*Onkelos* and *Jonathan*) are later examples of Scripture interpretation directly related to the synagogue pattern of long, connected readings. Some of the biblical interpretations in the First Gospel fit this same pattern of direct relationship to synagogue reading, and all of Matthew's citations and allusions are likely to have been influenced in some way by the synagogue.[42]

The use of Scripture in connection with Temple worship in Jerusalem not only related to the synagogue usage but also continued as an independently significant pattern of use until *ca*. AD 70. The use of the Psalms is especially noteworthy in connection with the Temple.[43]

Questions about the Resurrection community's relationship to the Temple in Jerusalem are historically and theologically significant, and the right answers to these questions are almost certainly not simple. The history of Temple worship in Israel following the construction of Solomon's Temple was more complicated than is commonly supposed. On the one hand, the Hebrew Bible mentions the establishment of rival sanctuaries at Bethel and Dan (I Kg 12.30).[44] On the other hand, the Qumran community had developed very considerable, if not complete, independence from the Jerusalem Temple. In different ways, both Pharisaic Judaism and Christianity were essentially independent from

---

[40] Arguments based on such speculative reconstructions are of doubtful value, but J.W. Bowker's broader argument deserves serious attention: "In view of the very precise purposes for which the synagogue was established, completely distinct as it was from general prayer and worship, it would be most surprising if the choices of passages to be read was left to chance." "Speeches in Acts", *ibid.*, 98.

[41] Luke states explicitly that Jesus attended services regularly ("and he went to the synagogue, as his custom was, on the Sabbath day" Lk 4.16). Moreover, "Acts emphasized that early Christian evangelists preached in synagogues, and that was a reflection of what was believed to have been the practice of Jesus." "Speeches in Acts", *ibid.*, 96.

[42] Although written in the seventh or eighth century AD, the Palestinian Targum preserves ancient and even pre-Christian material. (See Martin McNamara, *Targum and Testament, Aramaic Paraphrases of the Hebrew Bible: A Light on the New Testament*. Shannon: Irish University Press, 1968, 13 & *passim*.) So too the First Gospel must be assumed to preserve pre-Christian synagogue traditions of interpretation.

[43] J. Weingreen, *From Bible to Mishna*, 123.

[44] According to Y. Aharoni, another "unquestionably Israelite temple discovered by archaeologists is at Arad" in Judea. "Temples, Semitic", *IDB* Suppl, 875. This temple was destroyed, probably in the reforms of Hezekiah and Josiah, but a similar one was established at Lachish in post-exilic times (*ibid*). In the seventh century BC yet another temple was built for Israelites (or "Jews") in Elephantine on the Upper Nile. The use of the temple in Leontopolis from the second century BC and the temple on Mt. Gerazim (destroyed by John Hyrcanus in 108 BC) further complicate the picture of one Temple for all Israel.

Temple rituals before the Destruction in AD 70.⁴⁵ Jesus' own relationship to the Temple establishment was ambiguous at least. Teaching in the Temple was a normal part of Jesus' ministry (Jn 7.14; Mt 26.56=Mk 14.49=Lk 22.53=Jn 18.20) and a strong positive identification with the Temple is presupposed in the stories of the "Cleansing of the Temple" (Mk. 11.15ff & par). Moreover, in his conversation with the Samaritan woman, Jesus seems to validate the historical claims of the Temple in Jerusalem over against Mount Gerizim with the remarkable statement, "salvation is from the Jews" (Jn 4.22). Nevertheless, his words against the Temple establishment were so strong and varied (*e.g.* in Mt 12.6; 23.35; 24.2) that some of his audience, at least, failed to notice any positive identification with the institution itself. All four Gospels record this as a fundamental issue in Jesus' trial. In any case, the earliest Resurrection community, which waited in Jerusalem for the Holy Spirit according to Luke (ἐπὶ τὸ αὐτό Acts 2.1, *cf.* 1.12-14 & Lk 24.52-53), was certainly informed by earlier involvement in Temple worship.⁴⁶

Family devotions, early education in the home, and study in the synagogue schools complemented the use of the scrolls for public readings in the synagogues and Temple. Literacy was taught from Scripture texts and the goal of education was ability to read the scrolls with understanding. "The basic curriculum of Jewish education was the Bible itself."⁴⁷ Trades were learned in apprenticeship, and Greek was also learned outside of school.⁴⁸ Translations were used where necessary, so that some of the first Christians who congregated in Jerusalem (for example, Barnabas Acts 4.36) probably had their elementary

---

⁴⁵ For a summary of the development of the idea of 'the church as the new temple' in the NT, see R. McKelvey, *The New Temple: The Church in the New Testament* (Oxford: University Press, 1969), 74,

⁴⁶ Mt, Mk (if we project the abrupt ending), and Jn (chapter 21) all end their Gospels in Galilee. The ending of Lk and the beginning of Acts, however, give no indication that some or most of the "forty days" (Acts 1.3) were spent in Galilee.
In Lk's accounts, the angels' address to the "men of Galilee" (Acts 1.11) may indicate that Lk knew the sequence of events described in the other Gospels but was secure enough in his knowledge not to harmonize his report with the other accounts. See chapter 10 below.

⁴⁷ S.V. McCasland, *IDB* 2, 35. Literacy in the Scriptures seems to have been intended for everyone identified with Israel: "At five years old (one is fit) for the Scripture...." Mishnah, *Aboth* 5.21 (Danby trans., 458), attributed to Judah b. Tema, second century AD.

⁴⁸ Josephus' comment on his own Greek style implies this distinction between *education* and the acquisition of mundane knowledge and skills:
> For our people do not favour those persons who have mastered the speech of many nations, or who adorn their style with smoothness of diction, because they consider that not only is such skill common to ordinary freemen but that even slaves who so choose may acquire it. But they give credit for wisdom to those alone who have an exact knowledge of the law and who are capable of interpreting the meaning of the Holy Scriptures. *Antiq.* xx. 264.

The extent of Aramiac-Greek bilingualism in Palestine in the first century AD is a separate question, discussed by J.N. Sevenster, *Do You Know Greek?* (Leiden: E.J. Brill, 1968), 968. *Cf.* M. Hengel, *Judaism and Hellenism* (Philadelphia: Fortress, 1974), 58-65 and S.E. Porter, "Did Jesus Ever Teach in Greek?" *Tyndale Bulletin* 44.2 (1993) 199-235.

education in the Greek Old Testament. But the majority would have first learned the Scriptures in Aramaic translations (targums). In Palestine some set pieces in Hebrew, such as Psalms and passages from the Torah, might have been included early.[49]

Memorized passages of Scripture, and especially Psalms, may have been the mainstay of family devotions, but Harnack and others have cited I Maccabees 1.56 as evidence of "a considerable circulation of the Law in private houses".[50] Before and after the persecution by Antiochus Epiphanes, it may have been common for families to have access to scrolls for use in their daily prayers. In any case, we know from the story about the Ethiopian statesman (Acts 8.27-28) and from the reference in the Mishnah to the belongings of a Levite who died in an inn (*Yebamoth* 16.7) that some individuals owned scrolls which they carried with them for study while not engaged in other business.[51]

2. The Second Stage: Continuity in Bible Study

The second *Sitz im Leben* of the biblical quotations in Matthew's Gospel is the life of the community which responded in faith to the Resurrection. This community was probably as mixed as the crowds who first heard and responded to Jesus' teaching and healing. Like those crowds, the earliest Resurrection community was still located in the land of Israel in the first half of the first century AD. There is no reason to suppose that this community neglected any of the normal patterns of Scripture use which were established in the larger community of biblical faith. The New Testament writings, which began to emerge early in the second half of the first century, almost all include biblical allusions and quotations. The range of texts from the Hebrew Bible cited in these writings is significant and offers support for the idea that "all the Scriptures" (Lk 24.27) were the earliest 'testimony book' of the believing community.[52]

---

[49] See Jean-Paul Audet's comment on the Hebrew form of the title of the book of Psalms in "A Hebrew-Aramaic List of Books of the Old Testament in Greek transcription", *JTS* ns I (1950), 149: "this is intelligible if we bear in mind the place which this collection of traditional prayers occupied in the public and private devotions of the Jews. Repetition would have been enough to make them familiar in the original language for Jews whose daily idiom was Aramaic." *Cf.* J. Jeremias, "Die Muttersprache des Evangelisten Matthäus", *ZNW* 50 (1959), 274.

[50] "Any scrolls of the law which they found they tore up and burned. Whoever was found with a scroll of the covenant ... was condemned to death by royal decree. So, they used their power against Israel, against those who were caught each month in the cities." A. Harnack, *Bible Reading in the Early Church* (London: Putnam's Sons, 1912), 30.

[51] "The mistress of the inn brought out to them his staff and his bag and the scroll of the Law that had belonged to him." *Mishnah* (Danby trans., 245).

[52] Not even exact quotations can be assumed to have been transmitted *in writing* from the second *Sitz*: "The early Church was not such a bookish community." C.H. Dodd, *Scriptures*, 29. The later Rabbinic rule "that the sacred books must be read, not recited after being learnt by heart" was unknown in the Church. C.H. Roberts, *Cambridge History of the*

The four Gospels and the *Acts of the Apostles* supply evidence for the broad and deep patterns of Scripture use in first century Palestine from which the special Messianic (or 'Christian') uses developed. Chiding the scribes in Jerusalem (διἸουδαῖαι), Jesus says, "You search the Scriptures, because you think that in them you have eternal life; and it is they that bear witness to me" (John 5.39). So also he challenges "the chief priests and elders of the people" in Matthew 21.42: "Have you never read in the Scriptures... (Psalm 118.22-23)?" It is to be expected that these men would have been biblical scholars. But the disciples on the way to Emmaus are also assumed to know "all that the prophets have spoken" (Luke 24.25). They too are chided for their lack of faith —slowness of heart to believe— not for lack of Bible knowledge.

The pattern of daily bible study (καθ' ἡμέραν ἀνακρίνοντες Acts 17.11) in the synagogue in Beroea (Macedonia) would have been the ideal base for the program of "biblical research" in the early Church, which C.H. Dodd reconstructs.[53] This text in Acts suggests that every day (before or after work) adults joined together to read and discuss passages from the (translated) Hebrew Bible —perhaps bringing personal and family scrolls or codexes with them to add to those held communally in the synagogue. If this interpretation is correct (and if the report is accurate), it is reasonable to suppose that an older pattern of meeting, perhaps once or twice a week, had been forced into an "every day" schedule by the excitement of the *kerygma*.

Messianic discussion related to biblical texts (and the emergent NT apologetic) was only one of many significant uses of the Scriptures in first-century Palestine. Before turning to an examination of the influence on Matthew's biblical quotations of this one special use, therefore, we should summarize a few points from the survey above. *The main point is that the Bible was not an esoteric book in Israel.* Copies of the scrolls were widely circulated, and regular public readings of large sections from the scrolls provided a basic framework within which various kinds of private study and small-group discussions were carried on.

Another point to remember in considering later developments of biblical quotations is that different immediate purposes were served on the different occasions when Scripture was read in public, in family gatherings, and in study groups. Such different occasions within the same communities in part explain the different types of exegesis which emerged later in the written targums, *midrashim*, and *pesher* interpretations. Another side of this same point is that different scrolls were the focus of attention on different occasions and some scrolls were more popular than others. The frequency of early Christian reference to the *Psalms* and *Isaiah*, for example, seems to have been determined largely by the popular availability of these scrolls. At the same time the

---

Bible (Cambridge: University Press, 1970), 50. Even if isolated texts were collected in written form, such 'testimony books' may not have been of any significant use to Mt. The testimony book discovered at Qumran (*4QTestim*) was among very many complete scrolls of Bible books and commentaries.

[53] C.H. Dodd, *Scriptures*, 14.

possibility should not be overlooked that already before the years of Jesus' ministry such scrolls as the Psalms, Isaiah, and especially *Daniel* were widely circulated precisely because of their susceptibility to Messianic interpretation.[54]

A summary point, which has broad implications for the interpretation of biblical citations and allusions in the First Gospel, is that the earliest Resurrection community was saturated with Scripture. The unified system of education and the pervasive socio-religious uses of the Bible in first-century Palestine make this point inescapable. Modern scholars remark on this fact, but they frequently short-circuit any significant theological connections by referring to a supposed "atomistic use of Scripture" in the early Christian communities.[55]

3. *The Range and Focus of Scriptures Cited by Matthew*

Since the three stages of Scripture quotations reflected in the First Gospel are all theologically oriented, what Barnabas Lindars terms "the New Testament apologetic" can be discerned in all three.[56] When we attempt to describe Matthew's special interests and purpose, therefore, it is important to consider what *shared* interests and purpose can be traced through two or all three stages, to avoid distortion in interpretation of the evidence. We shall return to a brief summary and adaptation of Lindars' schematization of 'messianic interpretation in the light of Easter' before turning to the larger question of messianism in Jesus' time. But even the *range* and *focus* of biblical quotations in the First Gospel are significant.

The range of Old Testament books represented by quotations and allusions in Matthew's Gospel is noted conveniently in the *"Loci Citati Vel Allegati"* of the twenty-sixth edition of the Nestle-Aland Greek New Testament. The range indicated includes 143 references to the *Law*, 266 to the *Prophets*, and 123 to the *Writings*.[57] This broad pattern contrasts sharply with the pattern

---

[54] Of all the books subsequently included in the Canon, Daniel was the most accessible to persons who read only Aramaic fluently. This is one of several important reasons for this book's popularity. D. Wenham, "Kingdom of God and Daniel", *ExpT* 98/5, 132-33.

[55] H.J. Cadbury seems to have been the first to develop the notion of 'an atomistic use of Scripture' as a critical tool for interpreting NT Scripture quotations. "The Titles of Jesus in Acts", *Beginnings of Christianity* vol 5, [1932], 369. For a sustained argument against the application of this notion to the interpretation of Mt see R.H. Gundry, *The Use of the Old Testament in St. Matthew's Gospel* (Leiden: E.J. Brill, 1967), 5 & *passim*.

[56] B. Lindars, *The New Testament Apologetic: The Doctrinal Significance of the Old Testament Quotations* (London: SCM, 1961). Lindars defines the term in relation to the resurrection experience (33).

[57] *Novum Testamentum Graece*, Nestle-Aland; list complied by Kurt Aland and Barbara Aland (Stuttgart: Deutsche Bibelstiftung, 1979), 739-775. Daniel is numbered among the prophets in our count. The tally in the "Index of Quotations" of the United Bible Societies *Greek New Testament* is 98 from the Law, 157 from the Prophets, and 65 from the Writings; K. Aland, M. Black, B. Metzger and A. Wikgren, eds. (New York: American Bible Society, 1966). For a shorter list which is limited mainly to direct quotations and unmistakable allusions see the *Third Edition* of Aland, Black *et al.* (1975).

in Philo's writings which include approximately 2,000 quotations from the Law and only 50 from the other books.[58] W.L. Knox has suggested that "the rarity of quotations from outside the Pentateuch in Philo's writings" may be explained in terms of "an Alexandrine tradition of exegesis which was established when the Pentateuch alone had been translated into Greek".[59] In criticism of Knox —who concludes that this pattern of accessibility is the only explanation for Philo's choices —F.H. Colson reasonably suggests that "Philo's personal predilections and studies will account for much if not for all" of his selection of Scripture texts. "His scriptural work is the interpretation of the Pentateuch."[60] Moreover, Philo ascribes a "superior sanctity" to Moses: "The authors of the post-Pentateuchal books are regularly called disciples of Moses."[61] Turning from Philo to Matthew, we can profitably consider both the question of the accessibility of the various Scripture scrolls and the question of Matthew's personal interests in an attempt to understand his selection of quotations.

The simple answer to the question of accessibility seems to be that scrolls of most, if not all, of the books of the Hebrew Bible were available to Matthew. Using modern chapter divisions for convenience, A.C. Sundberg's tabulation of texts cited in the New Testament shows that 30 of the 40 chapters of Exodus, 28 of the 35 chapters of Deuteronomy, 56 of the 66 chapters of Isaiah, all 12 chapters of Daniel, and 101 of the 150 Psalms are represented in the New Testament by citation.[62] These figures make it very difficult to argue that New Testament writers —including Matthew— did not have access to a wide range of complete scrolls of Scripture. Since some of Matthew's individual texts were already established in traditional quotations, questions remain about how specific texts were carried forward. But the assumption that virtually all scrolls of the Hebrew Bible were available to Matthew strongly affects judgments about the significance of the evangelist's selection of quotations, and also our judgments about how —if at all— he related the texts quoted to other words, ideas, and themes in the specific scrolls cited.[63]

The answer to the more difficult question of the full extent of Israel's literature which informed Matthew's writing is less certain, but also important. Besides defining the linguistic and conceptual field of Matthew's Gospel, a reliable full list would provide important information about the relationship of Matthew and his predecessors to the various denominations or parties in Israel before AD 70.

---

[58] W.L. Knox, "A Note on Philo's Use of the Old Testament", *JTS* 41 (1941), 34.

[59] *Ibid.*

[60] F.H. Colson, "Philo's Quotations from the Old Testament", *JTS* 41 (1941), 239.

[61] *Ibid.*

[62] Albert C. Sundberg, "On Testimonies", *NovT* 3 (1959), 272.

[63] The evangelist would have had his own perceptions of what we now refer to as "the theology of Second Isaiah", "the theology of the book of Jonah", *et c.*

Robert Gundry has argued emphatically for serious consideration of *"allusive* quotations" in forming judgments about Matthew's use of Scripture.[64] Gundry does not explain, however, why he restricts his own study almost entirely to Matthew's quotation of those texts later included in the Palestinian (or 'Jewish' and 'Protestant Christian') canon. In the tally of Nestle-Aland's citations above, the 124 for 'Writings' (*Ketubim*) is also limited to books later judged canonical (although Daniel is listed with 'Prophets'). If all of Aland's citations of allusive quotations outside the Torah and the *Nebi'im* are added, the citation of 'Writings' would total 201, including 25 references to *Sirach*, 8 to *Enoch*, and 5 to the *Psalms of Solomon*.[65]

The problems of anachronism and anomaly involved with the use of the later Christian and Rabbinic notions of 'canon' and 'canonization' are easy to see but not so easy to solve. James Sanders refers to the first century AD as a period of *"intense canonical process"*, but he does not consider the Samaritans ("Observers") at all in his 1984 essay on *Canon and Community*.[66] With reference to the Samaritans, A.C. Sundberg argues that the first century BC was their period of 'intense canonical process'.[67] It is a commonplace to speak of 'the Samaritan canon' as containing only the Torah, but the northern (or 'Samaritan') prophets Elijah, Elisha, and Hosea and also Amos, Isaiah, Jeremiah, and Ezekiel bring 'Samaritan content' into the 'Jewish canon'. In a similar anomalous way, important Jewish writings later are included only in the Christian 'Alexandrian canon'.[68]

The modern discovery of the eclectic library at Nag Hammadi has shown the folly of any assumption that a collection of books necessarily implies a

---

[64] "Recent researches in the Qumran scrolls have shown that in the NT period the interweaving of scriptural phraseology and one's own word was a conscious literary method" and "allusive quotations ... reflect the language and phrase-forms with which the writer is most familiar and in which he habitually thinks." R. Gundry, *Use of the OT in Mt,* 3.

[65] Such lists raise questions which are answered by one compiler's choices against another's. K. & B. Aland's list includes the full range of what later became the Christian OT of the 'Alexandrian canon' as well as relevant extra-Biblical literature. When allusions to allusions are included from such a wide field Mt 24.15 can be cited as an allusion to I Macc (even though the redactor himself says he is citing Daniel [11.31]).

[66] "The periods of intense canonical process were the sixth century BCE and the first CE with the periods of early Judaism and early Christianity contributing to the process." J. Sanders, *Canon and Community: A Guide to Canonical Criticism* (Philadelphia: Fortress, 1984), 30.

[67] In Sundberg's terms, the Samaritan restricted Scriptural authority to the Torah as an 'archaizing' move to counter the Hasmonian 'modernizing'. A. Sundburg, *The Old Testament of the Early Church* (Cambridge, U.S.A.: Harvard University Press, 1964), 112.

[68] In his bold hypothesis on "the Samaritan Origins of the Gospel of John", G.W. Buchanan claims that "the Gospel of John shows more interest in prophets than any of the Synoptic Gospels." Without confronting 'the canonical problem', Buchanan points to John's emphasis on northern prophets Elijah and Elisha. *Religion in Antiquity, Fs.* E.R. Goodenough, ed. J. Neusner (Leiden: E.J. Brill, 1968), 166.

community's acceptance of all the books' teachings.[69] The earlier discovery of the Qumran scrolls demonstrates that even a list of approved and authoritative literature can include more than foundational Scriptures. In terms of negative findings, however, the *absence* of evidence of an Esther scroll at Qumran —and in Matthew's citations— is noteworthy. On the one hand, Matthew's omission might mirror Qumran's. On the other hand, an individual (or 'school') omission of Esther by Matthew might reflect his judgment on this scroll's usefulness for the Gospel to all nations.[70] Without pursuing the matter further here, we can adopt Sundberg's reconstruction of "pre-Jamnia canonical practice in Palestine" as a summary description of the range of Matthew's Scripture. This range included "closed collections of Law and Prophets, and also a large, undefined group of religious writings including the books later designated as Writings in the Jewish canon, the books of the Apocrypha and Pseudepigrapha and, perhaps, other writings now lost".[71]

The *focus* of Scripture references in the First Gospel is clearly on "the Law and the Prophets" (Mt 7.12 and 22.40).[72] Matthew's selection of texts from among the scrolls available to him indicates a special interest in the Prophets. He was, perhaps, a specialist in the Prophets just as Philo had been a specialist in the Pentateuch. The eleven 'formula quotations' (1.22-23; 2.14-15; 2.17-18; 2.22-23; 3.3; 4.13-16; 8.16-17; 12.15-21; 13.34-35; 21.4-5; 27.9-10), which are marked as his explanation from Scripture of the significance of certain points in the narrative, are all taken from the Prophets. (The citation of Psalm 78 in 13.35 might count as the single exception, but the Psalmist himself was a prophet —at least when writing this Psalm.)[73]

This emphasis on the Prophets throughout the First Gospel indicates more than Matthew's specialization in his study of Israel's literature, just as the preponderance of Pentateuchal quotations in Philo implies more than a personal vocational assignment. For Matthew, 'prophecy' is the unifying principle of

---

[69] "The library cannot reflect the dogmas of one sect, however broad-minded and syncretistic." T. Säve-Söderbergh, "Holy Scripture or Apologetic Documentation? The <Sitz im Leben> of the Nag Hammadi Library", *Lex Textes de Nag Hammadi*, ed. J.-E. Ménard (Leiden: E.J. Brill, 1975), 3.

[70] The book of Esther "breathes a fierce hostility to Gentiles", which H.H. Rowley contrasts with "the missionary spirit of Deutero-Isaiah" reflected in Jonah and shared by Ruth. "Literature of the OT", *Peake's Commentary on the Bible* (London: Nelson, 162), 89. An interesting modern parallel to the Qumran evidence is Christiana Baxter's discovery that "every canonical book is cited" in Karl Barth's *Church Dogmatics* "except Esther". "Barth —A Truly Biblical Theologian?" *Tyndale Bulletin* 38 (1987), 3.

[71] A. Sundberg, "The Old Testament of the Early Church", *HTR* 51 (1958), 214.

[72] ""Not until the nineteenth century did the unified conception of the law and the prophets begin to break up" among Christian theologians. W. Zimmerli, *The Law and the Prophets: A Study of the Meaning of the Old Testament* (Oxford; Blackwell, 1065), 18.

[73] S.E. Johnson observes that these texts "are all drawn from the prophets or the Psalms" and that "the quotations themselves are Matthew's own editorial work." "The Biblical Quotations in Matthew", *HTR* 36 (1943), 137.

Scripture. "The scriptures of the prophets" (αἱ γραφαὶ τῶν προφητῶν Mt 26.56) is a remarkable way of saying "inspired Scripture".[74] Another saying of Jesus, according to Matthew, declares that until the coming of John the Baptist "all the prophets and the law prophesied" (πάντες γὰρ οἱ προφῆται καὶ ὁ νόμος ἕως Ἰωάννου ἐπροφήτευσαν Mt 11.13). For Philo, the Prophets were Moses' disciples; for Matthew, Moses was the first of the Prophets.

The idea of the Scriptures as *promise* and the Messiah as *fulfillment* is fundamental in the First Gospel. This idea is expressed categorically in the words of Jesus: "Do not suppose that I have come to abolish the law and the prophets; I have come not to abolish them but to fulfill them" (οὐκ ἦλθον καταλῦσαι ἀλλὰ πληρῶσαι Mt 5.17). This text itself is a programmatic statement of the design of the First Gospel, as John Meier has argued and as we will attempt to demonstrate below. Already as a child Jesus recapitulates and gives new meaning to the history of the salvation of God's people, as citation of the prophecy of Hosea indicates (Mt 3.13-15). From the time of his baptism, Jesus fulfills "all the prophets and the law" (Mt 11.13/ 3.15f). Matthew's use of the term 'fulfill' (πληρόω) sometimes seems to imply only "prediction over against verification". But for Matthew, as C.F.D. Moule points out, "even details in the life of Jesus are significant ...in virtue of the relation to the will of God."[75]

Earlier fulfillments of prophecy reveal the pattern of God's covenant faithfulness. But the deepest meaning of ancient prophecy and typical fulfillment is revealed in the messianic consummation of God's will.[76] "Therefore every scribe who has been discipled for the Kingdom is like the head of a household who brings out of his treasure what is new and what is old" (Mt.13.52). The Hebrew Bible is Matthew's *thesaurus*, but his own selection of "what is old" emphasizes the Latter Prophets as particularly relevant to the covenant people who have entered the Messianic Age.

Messianic Interpretation in the Light of Easter

Just as Matthew inherited the Scripture texts he cites, so the original context of messianic expectations surrounding Jesus ministry in prerevolutionary Palestine supplied the foundation and material from which Matthew developed his messianism. Not even the decisive interpretive move was Matthew's. What Barnabas Lindars identifies as the starting point for the development of the "New Testament apologetic" was the first Christian community's experience of the Resurrection. "The Resurrection amounted to

---

[74] In Luke's Gospel, the risen Lord's explanation from "Moses ... all the prophets ... all the scriptures" (Lk 24.27 *cf.* v.4) anticipates a three-part canon. But "all that the prophets have spoken" (24.25) implies a unified, prophetic literature.

[75] C.F.D. Moule, "Fulfillment Words in the New Testament: Use and Abuse", *NTS* 14 (1967-68), 311.

[76] In form, this belief is not unlike the modern idea that 'the original meaning of the text' can be retrieved through scientific research, perhaps for the first time in the 2,800 years since the prophecy was spoken.

a divine declaration of the messiahship of Jesus." What followed immediately was "the earliest period of the Church's constructive theology".[77]

Lindars' schematization of the *stages* of development of the New Testament apologetic is subtle and complicated. According to his reconstruction, specific New Testament texts cannot be dated simply on the basis of their incorporation of 'earlier' or 'later' arguments.[78] Even 'pre-apologetic' arguments from Scripture texts are carried forward in later writings.[79] Lindars does not emphasize the continuation of earlier traditions of use and interpretation of the Hebrew Bible, but this continuation is an important presupposition of his study. Lindars' analysis is useful for clarification of the earliest post-Resurrection *Sitz im Leben* of biblical quotations in the New Testament, and there is good reason to suppose that the Easter experience was decisively important in the development of the community's distinctive messianic interpretation of the Scriptures.[80] But the Resurrection is more precisely understood as the *catalyst* than the *starting point* for the New Testament apologetic.

Jesus was reticent with regard to messianic claims, according to accounts in the synoptic Gospels, but this reticence characterized neither the crowds which followed him, nor his disciples. Their acclamation (which might be designated as the earliest stage of NT apologetic) and Jesus' disciplined response was considered by the Gospel writers to be an authentication of his calling.[81] Already during the time of Jesus' teaching and healing ministry his followers would have been engaged in messianic apologetic. Already then, but especially after the Resurrection, the Scriptures provided the conceptual framework within which Jesus' disciples worked out their convictions about messianic redemption for Israel and the nations.[82]

'Resurrection' was the organizing center of the New Testament apologetic after Easter and, in Matthew's Gospel, the decisive proof of the establishment of the Kingdom. But there is substantial evidence that 'resurrection' was

---

[77] B. Lindars, *New Testament Apologetic*, 32 & 33.

[78] *Ibid.*, 72-3.

[79] *Ibid.*, 41.

[80] "The Church was committed, by the very terms of its *Kerygma*, to a formidable task of biblical research, primarily for the purpose of clarifying its own understanding of the momentous events out of which it had emerged, and also for the purpose of making its Gospel intelligible to the outside public." C.H. Dodd, *According to the Scriptures*, 14. The Resurrection gave them the confidence to get on with the task.

[81] "A self-proclaimed Messiah was, *ipso facto*, a false Messiah" in the contemporary concept held by the Pharisees. E. Rivkin, "The Meaning of Messiah in Jewish Thought", *USQR* 26 [1971], 397. This position, as well as political considerations, may have influenced Jesus' statements reported in the Gospels. *Cf.* J.C. O'Neill, "The Silence of Jesus", *NTS* 15 (1968-69) references to W. Wrede's 'Messianic Secret' and R. Bultmann, 153-154.

[82] It is *not possible* to point to "a single conceptual framework apart from the Scriptures, governing early Christianity". W.D. Davies, "From Schweitzer to Scholem: Reflection on Sabbatai Svi", *JBL* 95/4 (1976), 555.

established as a messianic theme already before Easter[83] —even if this theme was easily confused and quickly forgotten by the disciples. Other messianic themes which seem to have been stronger and more immediately relevant to the crowds that followed John the Baptist and Jesus were 'atonement' and 'judgment on the nations'.[84]

C. Messianic Expectations in Pre-Revolutionary Palestine

The Scripture texts which Matthew claims for authority are all included in 'the Jewish Canon' associated with the later deliberations in Jamnia. For our present purposes it is not necessary to speculate as to whether Matthew also considered the *Psalms of Solomon* and *Enoch* as authoritative Scripture. But the multiple allusions to these writings in the First Gospel, which Aland notes, indicate a very important correspondence of Gospel material to messianic writings already in circulation at the time of Jesus' ministry.[85] Such writings, along with the Hebrew Bible, represent the Jewish matrix of Jesus' ministry and Matthew's.[86]

"Jewish messianic thought and sentiment...had a firm hold on the bulk of the Jewish people, particularly in Palestine" in the pre-revolutionary period.[87] "Disaster was in the air and many an hour suggested that a great turning point

---

[83] All Synoptic accounts insist that Jesus predicted his own resurrection, *e.g.* Mt 28.6: "He is risen, as he said." J. Neusner and others note "the prevalent notion that the Messiah would raise the dead". *Messiah in Context* (Philadelphia: Fortress, 1984), 86. Quotations from Daniel attributed to Jesus in Matthew's Gospel support the assumption that a doctrine of resurrection was part of his teaching. Later (non-Christian) Jewish messianism also emphasized Daniel "together with the other prophets" and taught that "necessarily connected with that [Messianic] age is also Resurrection". Erwin Rosenthal, *Studia Semitica*, vol I (Cambridge: UP, 1971), 46 citing Isaac Abravanel, a 15th-century Spanish rabbi.

[84] In post-biblical times [post-OT] "the conception of Atonement underwent a great change" and "the whole idea of sin was, in fact, deepened." Kaufmann Kohler, *Jewish Encyclopedia*, vol I (New York: Funk & Wagnalls, 1902), 278.
Evidence for growing interest in the nations can be seen in "the universalizing tendency of the Septuagint version" of Isaiah. B. Lindars, *NT Apologetic*, 38. H.J. Schoeps even speaks of "the missionary purpose of the LXX". *Paul*, 28. Abravanel's 15th-century argument against the Christian claim that Jesus was the Davidic Messiah is interesting whether or not it can be traced back in an unbroken line of tradition to the first-century expectations: "nor has he fulfilled the prophecy that after the Redemption most of the nations will turn to the one true God, acknowledge and worship Him and study His Law." E. Rosenthal, *ibid.*, 47.

[85] *N.b.* allusions to *Ps Sol* 17 & 18 (Mt 13.6; 19.28; and 21.12) cited below.

[86] There is a fundamental contrast between these writings, on the one hand, and Mishnah and the later Talmuds, on the other hand. *IV Ezra* and *II Baruch* (and probably also "The Similitudes of Enoch") were written after AD 90, too late to have influenced Matthew's composition. But they were written long before AD 200 and are closer to Mt in many ways than is the *Mishnah*. See J.H. Charlesworth's note cited by J. Neusner, *Method and Meaning in Ancient Judaism* (Chicago: Scholars Press, 1981), 24.

[87] Leo Baeck, *Judaism and Christianity* (Philadelphia: JPS, 1961 [1952]), 145.

was ahead."⁸⁸ So Leo Baeck explains the motivating force behind the post-biblical writings which reflected and in turn nourished this thought and sentiment in the times leading up to Jesus' ministry.

T.W. Manson characterizes the Messianic hope as "a burning conviction held with fanatical zeal, shaped under pressure of tyranny and persecution, and inspired by deep religious faith."⁸⁹ According to Manson, the period of just over *three centuries* from 176 BC (the rise to power of Antiochus IV, Epiphanes) to AD 135 (the bloody end of the Bar Kokhba revolt) should considered "the period of the Jewish fight for freedom".⁹⁰ Manson points out that

> the ministry of Jesus falls at the end of the second of these centuries, when the Jews of Palestine had still the memory of the Maccabean triumph and no foreknowledge of the siege under Titus.⁹¹

Diverse Evidence and Distorting Caution

It goes beyond our present purposes to attempt a positive contribution to the twentieth-century understanding of messianism in pre-revolutionary Palestine, but it seems necessary to emphasize the existence of these various streams of thought, sentiment, and activity which inevitably related to the question of 'Israel and the nations'. Such emphasis is needed to compensate for the diffidence in much of the recent European and American writing on the subject. Three reasons for scholarly caution in reconstructing first-century Messianism should be noted briefly in order to see how this caution itself distorts the reality which concerns us. The first is a *reaction to* naive and sometimes triumphalist *Christian apologetic*. The second is a *response to the silence of the Mishnah*. The third is *methodological restraint* in synthesizing evidence from widely divergent sources.

The puzzling relationship between Jewish and Christian Messianism was explored briefly in the first part of the present study. Gersholm Scholem observes that "the essential conflict between Judaism and Christianity has developed and continues to exist" precisely in problems relating to Messianism.⁹² The sobering lessons of medieval and modern conflicts between Christians and Jews, therefore, must stand as warnings against careless reconstructions.

In any case, modern Old Testament scholarship has developed a certain modesty of its own. Sigmund Mowinckel begins his major study, *He That Cometh*, by declaring that "not all the Old Testament passages which in the past have been regarded as 'Messianic' deal in fact with the Messiah and the

---

[88] L. Baeck, "The Gospel as a Document of the History of the Jewish People", *ibid.*, 57.

[89] T.W. Manson, *The Servant-Messiah: A Study of the Public Ministry of Jesus* (Cambridge: University Press, 1953), 3.

[90] *Ibid.*

[91] *Ibid.*, 4.

[92] G. Scholem, *The Messianic Idea in Judaism* (London: Allen & Unwin, 1971), 1.

Messianic faith."⁹³ Even Helmer Ringgren in his positive study of *The Messiah in the Old Testament* is cautious in expressing his conclusions. With reference to the Royal Psalms, for example, he says, "The Christian theological interpretation of the so-called Messianic texts in the Old Testament is to a certain extent justified" because of "the development of eschatological messianism from ancient kingship ideology."⁹⁴ Joachim Becker, despite the title of his book *Messianic Expectation in the Old Testament*, argues insistently that Messianic expectations were formulated from Scripture long after the texts themselves were written.⁹⁵ For our present purposes it is important to note that none of the arguments about original meanings of texts in the Hebrew Bible denies the existence of a strong impulse to Messianic interpretation in post-Exilic Israel.⁹⁶

A second warning to twentieth-century scholars to pull back from emphasizing the force and pervasiveness of Messianism in first-century Palestine is the silence of the Mishnah. Josephus also avoids the subject in most of his writings and does not note any messianic significance in John the Baptist's ministry (*Antiq*. xviii.116-119). Josephus' record of AD 66-70 does note, with disapproval, the Jews' prophetic hope that "a man from their own country would become ruler of the known world" (*War* vi.312), but "messianism does not appear to figure very largely in the Jewish rebellion as a whole."⁹⁷ Although the Mishnah was not written until after the final collapse of the revolution in AD 135, this foundational document of Rabbinic Judaism is a standard source for reconstruction of the 'Jewish background' of the first-century New Testament.

"[From] the first generation of Tannaim ... not a single messianic saying remains," according to Joseph Klausner who considers this silence to be very significant.⁹⁸ The subtle explanation which he provides in his classic study, *The Messianic Idea In Israel from Its Beginning to the Completion of the Mishnah*, involves his own conviction that "it was not because these earliest Tannaim rejected the Messianic idea".⁹⁹ Jacob Neusner's explanation is simpler. In *Messiah in Context* he notes that "when we reach the first century AD, we come to a turning point in the messianic hope" marked by "the intense, vividly prevailing expectation that the Messiah was coming soon". But after AD 70 "we witness the beginning, among the Mishnah's sagas in particular, of an

---

⁹³ S. Mowinckel, *He That Cometh* (Oxford: Blackwell, 1956), 10.

⁹⁴ H.Ringgren, *The Messiah in the Old Testament* (London: SCM Press, 1956), 24.

⁹⁵ J. Becker, *Messianic Expectations in the Old Testament* (Philadelphia: Fortress, 1980 [1977]), *passim*.

⁹⁶ See Mowinckel's discussion of "The Place of the King in the Future Hope: Messiah", "The Eschatology of Later Judaism", and "The National Messiah", *op. cit*.

⁹⁷ Tessa Rajak, *Josephus: The Historian and His Society* (Philadelphia: Fortress, 1983), 141. *Cf.* T.W. Manson's *Servant-Messiah*, 34.

⁹⁸ J. Klausner, *The Messianic Idea in Israel* (New York: Macmillan, 1955), 342.

⁹⁹ *Ibid*.

active construction of a new mode of being."¹⁰⁰ The final shock leading to the transmutation came in AD 135 when "Bar Kokhba's armies ... suffered total defeat, turning the earlier destruction, in retrospect, into a crisis".¹⁰¹ The Mishnah, written in this context, is characterized by "the absence of sustained attention to events or to a doctrine of history", which explains why the Messiah as an eschatological figure makes no appearance in the system of the Mishnah".¹⁰² Much later, in the composition of the Talmud, once again "the Messiah enters. But he does so only on the rabbis' terms."¹⁰³

Heightened realization of the many forms and expressions of first-century Messianism is a third warning which has persuaded many scholars to refer only to the messianism of specific documents and to generalize with great caution and tentativeness. In part, this is the response of embarrassment in riches as new documentary evidence from the Qumran caves continues to be published. In an influential article published in 1966, M. de Jonge urges that "the use of the term 'messianic expectation' should be restricted to the expectation of a redeemer who is actually called Messiah." ¹⁰⁴ Proceeding in quite different terms, Neusner declares that "just as there was no single 'Judaism', so ... shall we look in vain for 'the Messiah myth'". ¹⁰⁵ But Neusner's further declaration that "'the Messiah' is an all but blank screen onto which a given community would project its concerns"¹⁰⁶ presses his point beyond usefulness in interpreting related texts.

The scholarly debate about the taxonomy of messiahs and end-expectations in the first century is instructive so long as the discussion does not define the realities away. On the one hand, the *wide variety* of expectations and ideals in the inter-testamentary and New Testament times has been demonstrated beyond doubt, so it is appropriate to use the plurals "messianisms" and "eschatologies" except when referring to evidence from closely related documents.¹⁰⁷ On the other hand, the different expressions of Messianic hope from Hasmonean times to the last Jewish revolt can *hardly* be described as so many *systematic developments in theology*. It is important to remember that

---

¹⁰⁰ J. Neusner, *Messiah in Context: Israel's History and Destiny in Formative Judaism* (Philadelphia: Fortress, 1984), 12.

¹⁰¹ *Ibid.*, 15.

¹⁰² *Ibid.*, 19.

¹⁰³ *Ibid.*, 228.

¹⁰⁴ M. de Jonge, "The Use of the Word 'Anointed' in the Time of Jesus", *NovT* 8 (1966), 132.

¹⁰⁵ J. Neusner, *Messiah in Context*, xi.

¹⁰⁶ *Ibid.*

¹⁰⁷ See Michael Stone's treatment of the "The Concept of the Messiah in IV Ezra" (*Religions in Antiquity*, E.R. Goodenough *Fs.* [Leiden: E.J. Brill, 1968] 295-312) which focuses on "a single document, a single problem" in a way which Neusner considers "exemplary" (*Messiah in Context*, xx). *Cf.* discussion and survey of recent literature on "Messianism/Messianic Hope", Schürer/Vermes, *HJP* II (1979), 488-554.

these expectations and ideals were not intellectually worked out or consistently held by many individuals in the crowds that followed Jesus.[108]

It is appropriate to view the corpus of New Testament writings as a single theological achievement. But even within the New Testament—Epistles, Gospels, Acts, and Revelation— it is possible and profitable to analyze *various messianisms* and *eschatologies*. Moreover, even such explicitly and systematically Messianic documents as the Pauline Epistles and Matthew's Gospel provide evidence of current disputes and conflicting expectations about the Messiah. The New Testament presents a unified and coherent witness relative to the whole range of messianic writings in circulation at the time.

Before analyzing Matthew's Gospel as a Messianic document, some attempt should be made to assess the *existing projections* of Messianism, *Jesus' role* as catalyst, and the *commitments of his disciples*. It is in this socio-political and theological grid that Jesus' mission instructions to his disciples should be understood.

The Bible and subsequent Apocalyptic

The basic documentary sources for the study of Messianic expectations in pre-revolutionary Palestine are Scripture texts, written long ago but read prophetically and applied to current events. Isaiah, the Psalms, and Daniel seemed especially relevant. What the ancient psalmist and prophets meant by the references to Israel's God as the God of all nations, and by the suggestions that Israel's happiness would be shared by mankind in the End are questions with their own importance. But the question for our consideration here is how Jesus' disciples would have interpreted these texts.[109] The selection of Scriptures by Matthew is a later stage in the process begun by Jesus' with his first disciples.

Surviving written citations of Biblical texts relating to the nations such as Psalm 117 ("Praise Yahweh, all nations! /Extol him, all peoples!") and Isaiah 60 ("Arise, shine; for your light has come/ ...And nations shall come to your light, /and kings to the brightness of your rising") are proof that such texts were read and applied messianically to the times and unfolding events in the first century.[110] Joseph Klausner is one of many ancient and modern readers who have shown the susceptibility of Hebrew Bible texts to messianic interpretation. With reference to Isaiah 56.7 ("...a house of prayer for all peoples"), Klausner

---

[108] *Constructions* of 'eschatologies' from beliefs and hopes expressed in ancient documents are not necessarily *reconstructions*. Regarding current use of the term 'eschatology', I. H. Marshall shrewdly observes that "the '-ology' ending has virtually lost its significance and the whole word simply means 'the last things'." *ExpT* 89/9 (1978), 265.

[109] Jesus' preaching must be understood in relation to the views and involvements of his contemporaries. But the uniqueness of Jesus' preaching is "not ... in this relation as such, but in the entirely new way in which this preaching was done". Herman Ridderbos, *The Coming Kingdom* (St. Catherines, Canada: Paideia, 1978 [1962]), 14.

[110] Paul's use of Ps 117 (Rm 15.11) and the Johannine use of Is 60.3 (Rev 21.24) refer these texts to Jesus as Messiah. Such citations in the NT are a sample of first-century usage.

notes "the *reception of proselytes* as one of the signs of redemption" that "in later times had such an important place in Messianic expectation".[111] Klausner's comment does not specify "later times", but some of Jesus' disciples might well have connected Isaiah 56 with the proselyte movement of their own day.

Over against the wealth of texts in the Hebrew Bible which proved susceptible to messianic interpretation, the medley of other voices might be considered marginal. As already noted, a coherent Messianic idea cannot be pieced together from the various extra-Biblical messianic writings without contradicting some of the witnesses. Moreover, the New Testament record indicates that "in dealing with his contemporaries, Jesus nowhere appeals to these Jewish apocalypses but always to the whole Old Testament."[112] Nevertheless, writings composed in the period have their own importance as evidence for the immediacy of messianic expectations in pre- revolutionary Palestine and the *persistent* —if ambiguous— *interest in the nations*.

Reference to *I Maccabees*, the *Psalms of Solomon*, the *War Scroll* and *Damascus Document* from Qumran, and the *Carmina Samaritana* can serve to illustrate something of the diversity of messianic ideology relating to the nations. The relevance of some or all of these ideologies to the disciples' individual anticipations becomes apparent if the list of the Twelve and Jesus' prohibition in Matthew 10.5b-6 are accepted as historical.

Sadducees & Pharisees

As the ruling elite, the Sadducees lost more in AD 70 than any other party. Well before AD 135 they dropped out of sight and out of mind. But in Jesus' time they were a force to be reckoned with. Such messianic claims as were identified with the Hasmonean Simon and celebrated in Maccabees 14.4ff. were already in the distant past. Nevertheless, for the crowds that followed Jesus that political model was still alive in memory.[113] Under the Hasmoneans "the reproach of the nations was removed" (I Macc 4.58b), and "Galilee of the Goyim" was restored to Israel (5.23). Even the Samaritans and the Idumeans were "brought in".[114] Moreover, from "Rome, and as far away as Sparta" the nations sued for "friendship and alliance" (I Macc 14.16/.18).

The *Psalms of Solomon* are anti-Hasmonean and usually associated with the Pharisees. In any case, the Davidic and explicitly messianic ideology of these psalms seems certain to have influenced the thought and action of some of Jesus' disciples. A vindictive xenophobic bias runs through these psalms, but

---

[111] J. Klausner. *The Messianic Idea in Israel*, 172.

[112] H. Ridderbos, *Coming Kingdom*, 15.

[113] "Were the Maccabees Remembered?" W.F. Farmer, *Maccabees, Zealots, and Josephus: An Inquiry into Jewish Nationalism in the Greco-Roman Period* (New York: Columbia University Press, 1956), 125-158.

[114] See the summary of John Hyrcanus' campaigns (128 BC) by Frank Moore Cross, "Aspects of Samaritan and Jewish History in the Late Persian and Hellenistic Times", *HTR* 59 (1966), 210.

there is also a striking ambivalence to the nations. This ambivalence is so persistent that even theories of multiple authorship seem unlikely to explain it.[115] In *Psalm* 17.30b-31 it is said of the Son of David:

> And he shall divide them according to their tribes upon the land.
> And neither sojourner nor alien shall sojourn with them any more.

Nevertheless, this is followed immediately with the line, "He shall judge peoples and nations in the wisdom of his righteousness." Similarly in the next verse: "And he shall have the heathen nations to serve him under his yoke", in turn, is "So that nations shall come from the ends of the earth to see his glory".[116]

Essenes & Samaritans

The striking ambivalence towards the nations in the *Psalms of Solomon* has its counterpart in some of the Qumran documents. The battle hymn in the "War Scroll" (*1QM*) includes the characteristic prayer:

> Smite the nations, Thine adversaries,
>   and devour the flesh of the sinner with Thy sword!

Nevertheless, the victory is celebrated with the response

> Rejoice, all you cities of Judah;
> keep your gates ever open
>   that the hosts of the nations may be brought in!

The purpose of this eschatological proselytism, however, is that

> Their kings shall serve you
>   and all your oppressors shall bow down before you;
>   [they shall lick] the dust [off your feet].[117]

---

[115] These psalms were written in Palestine *ca.*50 BC by several authors closely united in perspective and allegiances. Identification of this group as 'Pharisees' has been challenged by Robert Wright, "The Psalms of Solomon, the Pharisees, and the Essenes", *1972 Proceedings, International Organization for Septuagint and Cognate Studies*, 146.

[116] 17.34, G.B. Gray's trans., *The Apocrypha and Pseudepigrapha of the Old Testament in English*, ed. R.H. Charles, vol II (Oxford: University Press, 1913), 650.

[117] Geza Vermes trans., *The Dead Sea Scrolls in English* (Hamondsworth, Penguin, 1962), 140 & 142. The battle hymn, with its ambiguous and relatively positive view of the nations, appears in *1QM* xii and again in xix. There is no such ambiguity in Hymn xiv:

"He has called them that staggered to [marvelous deeds],
    and has gathered in the assembly of the nations to destruction without remnant."

It is important to note the fact that contradictory views of the nations occur even in the most negative sources. Some differences in the "War Scroll" might be explained by composite authorship and different historical references. P.R. Davies, *1QM, the War Scroll from Qumran: Its Structure and History* (Rome: Biblical Institute Press, 1977).

Even if we put aside the intriguing possibility that one or more of the Twelve apostles might have been directly influenced by the eschatology and peculiar messianism of the Qumran sect, we cannot dismiss the likelihood of indirect Essene influence on the disciples and on the crowds following Jesus. The main body at Qumran did not marry and depended for its life on propaganda and recruitment.

Some scholars have inferred that Essene recruitment extended to the nations. Taking his cue from the directive 'to join oneself to the House of Judah' (*Damascus Document* IV, 11), D.R. Schwartz concludes that the ancient community in view here "can reckon with true proselytes, whether from Israel or from among the Gentiles, who may come 'to join themselves' to the sectarian community."[118] If this reconstruction is correct, it seems that not only the Essene view that 'nationals' could become 'Israelites' but also that their practice of Israel's mission would have influenced the Twelve's anticipation of Jesus' mission to the nations.

The Samaritans are objects of the prohibition of Matthew 10.5b-6, so we can assume that none of the Twelve were themselves Samaritan 'Observers'. Nevertheless, from reconstructed evidence it seems likely that the Samaritans developed distinctive views of the Messiah (or *Ta'eb*) and that these views also would have claimed the attention of some of the Twelve. Aside from the record in the Fourth Gospel of the Samaritan woman's testimony ("I know that Messiah is coming...; when he comes, he will show us all things" Jn 4.25), the documentary evidence is very late and therefore of doubtful validity for our consideration. But "traditions about the Taheb's conquest of the world resulting in the nations believing in the Taheb's mission and in God" are apparently ancient.[119]

> The Thaheb is one who will restore spiritually the people of Israel to the covenant relation to JHWH... and politically give them dominion over the nations. As a preliminary to this, he will reunite Judah to Ephraim.[120]

The Setting of Jesus' Prohibition

Survival of ancient documents is subject to chance, as the discovery of the Qumran scrolls illustrates, and Messianic literature has also been subject to various kinds of suppression through the ages.[121] Even if we were convinced

---

[118] D.R. Schwartz, "'To Join Oneself to the House of Judah' (Damascus Document IV, 11)", *Revue de Qumran* 39, 10/3 (1981), 445. *Cf.* I. Rabinowitz, "A Reconsideration of 'Damascus' and '390 Years' in the 'Damascus'/('Zadokite') Fragments" *JBL* 73(1954)18-19. The document itself refers to "converts of Israel" (*CD* vi) and mandates enrollment "by name: first the priest, second the Levites, third the Israelites, and fourth the proselytes" (*CD* xiv).

[119] John MacDonald, *The Theology of the Samaritans* (London: SCM, 1964), 387.

[120] J.E.H. Thomson, *The Samaritans: Their Testimony to the Religion of Israel* (Edinburgh: Oliver and Boyd, 1919), 193-4 citing the *Carmina Samaritana*.

[121] The exclusion of almost all apocalyptic writings from the 'canon' *ca.* AD 90, and the exclusion of virtually all messianic references from the Mishnah *ca.* AD 200 are examples

that we had a representative sample of the full literature of the time, it is doubtful that what was written down ever adequately expressed the contemporary messianic ideologies and movements. As Ellis Rivkin observes, "the emergence of the messianic idea as viable was not evolutionary and developmental. It was mutational."[122] The strongest influences on Jesus' followers may have been the unrecorded messianism which was springing up exactly at his time among the *'am ha'aretz*,[123] and the eschatology which was blowing in the wind.

Whatever his self-conscious intentions, Jesus was obviously a catalyst. Some of his acts certainly encouraged messianic interpretation. His choice of twelve disciples, which is attested by each of the four Gospels, was one such act. His early deployment of the Twelve in mission was another.

Matthew's list of the Twelve and his use of the term 'apostles' in chapter 10 are problematic. Nevertheless, there are good reasons to consider as historical the selection and sending of twelve with the prohibition recorded in Matthew 10.5b-6. Since the narrative and sayings in Matthew 10 have significance in the structure and design of the Gospel we shall consider them again in terms of Matthew's theological and literary art. But if historical, the mission of the Twelve should also be considered as background and substructure for the written Gospel.

It is "reasonably certain", according to Morton Enslin, that "among the many who were eager in their acceptance of Jesus' proclamation were some who became increasingly intimate and became, so to speak, full-time followers." Moreover,

> the word which now stands in the Matthean version of Jesus' instruction to them, 'Go not into any way of the Gentiles, and enter not into any city of the Samaritans: but go rather to the lost sheep of the house of Israel'... reflects the outlook, if not the precise phraseology of Jesus himself.[124]

The disciples, and some in the crowds, could not have missed the eschatological symbolism in Jesus' choice of twelve apostles. The immediate implications related to the re-unification of an Israel divided, North and South. If the Twelve themselves brought a variety of notions about the Messiah and the End with them in following Jesus, it seems likely that the intensity with which they held these views induced them to follow Jesus. When they came together

---

of the kind of censorship which all coherent societies exercise.

[122] E. Rivkin, "The Meaning of Messiah in Jewish Thought", *USQR* 26 (1971), 384.

[123] "Many Judeaens still hoped that ultimately the Judeaen state would be ruled by a descendant of the Family of David. This hope was cherished especially among the lower classes." Solomon Zeitlin, "The Origin of the Idea of the Messiah", *In the Time of Harvest, Fs.* A. Silver (New York: Macmillan, 1963), 453. *Cf.* S. Mowinkel, *He That Cometh*, 282. Our only way of assessing the importance of new elements and new combinations is from surviving documents, including the NT writings.

[124] M. Enslin, *The Prophet from Nazareth* (New York: McGraw-Hill, 1961), 160.

the mix of their expectations and convictions must have been unstable if not explosive. The list, which include informative notes, certainly contains two names which suggest opposite poles of current messianic ideology: "Matthew the tax collector" (Mt 10.3) and "Simon the Cananaean [Zealot]".[125]

Renunciation was a clear demand in Jesus' recorded teaching. The disciple called from 'the tax office' (Mt 9.9) may have given up all thoughts of Sadducean compromise when he joined Jesus' band. The zealot would have been under constant pressure to modify his views in response to Jesus' teaching of non-violence. What they were *called to* was compelling, but not altogether obvious or clear even at the time of their first assignment to proclaim it.

Εἰς ὁδὸν ἐθνῶν μὴ ἀπέλθητε,   Matthew 10.5b-6
καὶ εἰς πόλιν Σαμαρειτῶν μὴ εἰσέλθητε·
πορεύεσθε δὲ μᾶλλον πρὸς τὰ πρόβατα τὰ ἀπολωλότα οἴκου Ἰσραήλ.

As instruction to the Twelve, for their mission during the time of Jesus' ministry, this saying recorded in the First Gospel contains both a positive command and a prohibition. The prohibition comes first and is emphatic. But the positive command necessarily carries the main point.

If the mission can be considered historical, and specifically directed to "the scattered sheep of the house of Israel", the prohibition should be understood as defining the focus of the assignment. But the prohibition is emphatic, so we should ask *why Jesus considered such a prohibition necessary*.[126] Before attempting an answer to this question in terms of the Messianic expectations in pre-revolutionary Palestine, we should consider the value of "the precise phraseology" (Enslin) of the saying as recorded in the First Gospel.

Some scholars who accept as fact Jesus' selection of twelve disciples insist that the designation of them as "apostles" in the Gospels (Mt 10.2, Lk 6.13) represents later reflection.[127] But *that* the Twelve were sent out on at least

---

[125] The Greek term Καναναῖος (Mt 10.4) has caused confusion in the past, but it is now understood to represent the Aramaic קנאן 'enthusiast, zealot'. Bauer-Arndt-Gingrich, *Greek-English Lexicon* (Chicago University Press, 1957), citing Schürer and J. Klausner. Here it indicates a (former) party affiliation. O. Cullmann, *The State in the New Testament* (New York: Scribners, 1956), 15; *cf.* G. Theissen, *Sociology*, 64: "Both a tax-collector and a zealot, a resistance fighter, are included in the most intimate group of disciples."

[126] According to J. Munck, "It is clear ... that the Jewish Christian churches in Palestine [*ca.* AD 50], like Jesus and his first disciples, were greatly concerned about the place that the Gentiles were to have in the plan of salvation." *Paul and the Salvation of Mankind*, 260.

[127] "That Jesus gathered twelve disciples round him, besides a much bigger circle that followed him, at least temporarily, is probably historical," according to Eduard Schweizer, "but they were not 'apostles'." *Church Order in the New Testament* (London: SCM, 1961 [1959], 28 [2k].

one mission before Jesus' crucifixion is generally agreed.[128] Since the prohibition is attested only in the First Gospel, however, our acceptance of it as representing Jesus' own outlook and expression demands some explanation.

It easy to explain why Mark and Luke failed to include this prohibition in their Gospels (if indeed they knew the saying) because of their commitment to the Messianic mission to all nations. With particular reference to this prohibition in the First Gospel, Geza Vermes argues that

> the authenticity of these sayings must be well-nigh impregnable, taking into account their shocking inappropriateness in an internationally open Church.[129]

Ferdinand Hahn, more cautiously says that this prohibition preserves "a particularist tendency" which can be "traced to Palestinian tradition" which, in turn, "is very old, and might well stand at the beginning".[130] Adolf Harnack, who accepts the prohibition as an accurate representation of Jesus' words, nevertheless goes on to observe that

> Matthew must have been fully conscious of the disparity between ... the words of the risen Jesus in Matt. xxviii 19f. ... and the earlier words of Jesus; nay, more, he must have deliberately chosen to give expression to that disparity.[131]

If we follow Harnack here and anticipate the discussion below regarding the purpose and design of Matthew's Gospel, we cannot claim a simple, compelling argument based on 'the criterion of dissimilarity' for attributing this saying to Jesus.[132] Our basic argument goes in the opposite direction: the saying makes sense *not only* in the design of the First Gospel *but also* in the time and ministry of Jesus.[133]

---

[128] "The mission of the disciples is one of the best-attested facts in the life of Jesus", according to T.W. Manson, *The Sayings of Jesus* (London: SCM, 1949 [1937]). 73.

[129] G. Vermes, *Jesus the Jew* (Glasgow: Collins, 1973), 49.

[130] F. Hahn, *Mission in the NT*, 544-55.

[131] A. von Harnack, *The Mission and Expansion of Christianity* (New York: Harper, 1961 [1906]), 40.

[132] Chapter **8** (*Signals of Things to Come*) represents Matthew as integrating the prohibition into his view of the Messianic mission to all nations. Obviously, this argument undercuts any use of 'the criterion of dissimilarity' which is the basis upon which Vermes and many other scholars accept these words as an authentic expression of the outlook of Jesus of Nazareth. For a review of the 'criterion of dissimilarity' see S. Goetz and C. Blomberg, "Burden of Proof", *JSNT* 2 (1981), 43.

[133] Another use of this saying, to oppose the mission to all nations, may have emerged late in the first century in reaction to the interpretation and practice represented in the First Gospel. Evidence of such use is not a clue to the origin of the statement.

Joachim Jeremias' claim that antithetic parallelism "characterizes our Lord's teaching in all the Gospel sources"[134] adds some weight to the attribution of the prohibition to Jesus himself. Moreover, since the Greek saying is the only source we have, Jeremias' observation encourages us to press "the precise phraseology" (Enslin) of the text, even if we are not prepared to push on in an attempt to discover the *ipsissima verba Jesu*.

In positive terms, the prohibition gives geographical boundaries to the disciples' assignment. They are to follow up Jesus' work in Galilee. Adolf Schlatter's summary is apt:

> *Der Zweck der Aussendung der Jünger ist, die Erwartung der kommenden Gottestat in den galiläischen Dörfern noch stärker zu machen, als es durch die Wanderpredict Jesu geschah.*[135] [The aim of the Disciples' mission in the Galilean villages is to strengthen the anticipation of the Coming Kingdom, which had already been nourished by the itinerate ministry of Jesus.]

Geographic boundaries West, North and East ('the road to the nations') and South ('the province of Samaria')[136] are clearly drawn by the prohibition and hardly require comment, except to note that Jesus himself had chosen to concentrate his work in Galilee up to this time.

Israel-centric

"Jesus' mission was Israel-centric."[137] This characterization by Peter Richardson is confirmed by Jeremias' comment on the first commission to the Twelve: "Jesus forbade his disciples during his lifetime to preach to non-Jews."[138] Jeremias also argues, from other evidence, that "Jesus limited his own activity to Israel."[139] Likewise Ferdinand Hahn declares that "there is no doubt that Jesus directed his work in the first place to Israel."[140] Bengt Sundkler focuses this point with his formulation of Jesus' understanding of the "centripetal mission of Israel".[141]

---

[134] J. Jeremias, *New Testament Theology*, vol 1, *The Proclamation of Jesus* (New York: Scribner's Sons, 1971), 14 quoting C. Burney.

[135] A. Schlatter, *Der Evangelist Matthäus: Seine Sprache, sein Ziel, seine Selbständigkeit* (Stuttgart: Calwer, 1929), 330.

[136] J. Jeremias interprets the Samaritan reference as a prohibition against travelling south. "The command not to go to the Gentiles cuts them off from the other three points on the compass: hence they are limited to Galilee." *Jesus' Promise*, 20. *Cf.* C.G. Montefiore, *The Synoptic Gospels*, vol II (New York: Ktav, 1968 [1927]), 146.

[137] P. Richardson, *Israel in the Apostolic Church* (Cambridge: UP, 1969), 66.

[138] J. Jeremias, *Jesus' Promise*, 19.

[139] *Ibid.*, 25.

[140] F. Hahn, *Mission in the NT*, 29.

[141] B. Sunkler, "Jésus et les païens", *Revue d'Histoire de Philosophie Religieuses* 6 (1936), 485 & 499. Sundkler's argument does not account for *the Galilean center*.

The words and deeds which Jesus sent the Twelve out to declare and perform were certainly intended for the people's good, but the only message recorded with the commission is "The Kingdom of heaven is at hand!" (Mt 10.7 cf. Lk 10.9). As a summary of Jesus' own teaching, this can be interpreted at least to mean that the people addressed "stood in a dangerous situation in which decision was urgent and delay dangerous".[142]

"We must take account of the eschatological perspective in Jesus' idea of mission."[143] This reminder by Sundkler is relevant to the definition of the Twelve's assignment, but before attempting to say more about their message in terms of political and theological eschatology, we should re-emphasize Adolf Schlatter's description of the disciples' mission as a follow-up of Jesus' own words and deeds. Along these same lines, T.W. Manson insists that Jesus' words and deeds clearly indicated the corporate nature of the Kingdom which challenged decision.[144] Although some critics routinely discount (as late) any hint in the Gospel of community, Manson is surely right in pointing to an authentic theme of strategic gathering here.[145] The disciples are commissioned to begin organizing the mission which would enable *Israel* to be "a light to the nations" (Is 49.6).

The notion 'Israel-centric' requires some clarification for interpretation of this commission, specifically with reference to 'the scattered sheep of the House of Israel'. Everything we know of Jesus' own ministry corroborates this specification of the *center*.[146] The phrase itself echoes Ezekiel 34 as well as Jeremiah 23.1-8 and 50.4-7. Taking Jeremiah 23 as the key to interpretation of the phrase in Matthew, T.W. Manson notes that 'scattered sheep' refer to "the people of Israel under the misrule of their kings and leaders". Manson further notes that this reference to Jeremiah 23.1-4 "is immediately followed by a prophecy of the coming of the Messiah" in verses 5-6.[147] Seen in the light of this Scripture, Jesus' directions counter both prejudicial dismissal of the Galilean *'am ha'arez*[148] and the violent nationalism advocated by the upper-class Galileans. ("From Galilee stemmed all the revolutionary movements which so disturbed the Romans.")[149]

---

[142] C.H. Dodd, *The Founder of Christianity* (London: Macmillan, 1970), 41.

[143] *Ibid.*, 499 #3.

[144] "There is nothing to suggest that Jesus himself ever abandoned the idea of finding in Israel those who would receive the kingdom themselves and then help to carry it to others." T.W. Manson, *Only to the House of Israel?* (Philadelphia: Fortress, 1964 [1955]), 21. Cf. O. Cullmann, *Peter*, 190.

[145] T.W. Manson, *Only Israel?*, 20.

[146] See discussion of "tax collectors, sinners, prostitutes, beggars, the poor, and cripples" by Luise Schottroff, *Jesus and the Hope of the Poor* (Maryknoll: Orbis, 1986 [1978]), 6-17.

[147] T.W. Manson, *Only Israel?*, 8.

[148] S.E. Johnson, *Jesus in His Own Times* (London: A&C Black, 1957), 19 citing L. Finkelstein.

[149] S. Dubnov, *History of the Jews* cited by Geza Vermes, *Jesus the Jew*, 46.

The Twelve accepted the assignment. Perhaps not every one of them would have asked to be restricted to Israel, or to be directed specifically to 'the scattered sheep'. But Oscar Cullmann argues that

> this very limitation to the *lost* sheep finally breaks through every national restriction and likewise excludes every Pharisaic-sectarian separation.... The very reduction to this fellowship within Israel creates the presupposition for the realization of the people of God that is to include all mankind.[150]

Double Prohibition as Geographic Designation

"The Kingdom of Heaven is at hand!" This summary message itself would have raised questions about the nations in the minds of the messengers. The apostles were being sent out as heralds of the End.[151] But some time was left. Their message had to fit into this remaining time (Mt 10.23b) and make sense of it. *How* and *when* the nations would be welcomed into the Kingdom did not need to be discussed at the beginning of the End, but answers to some questions needed to be given as directives for action. As such a directive, the double prohibition is explicit and unambiguous.

Adolf Schlatter, Joachim Jeremias, Albright-Mann, and others have recognized that the geographic context is basic for an historical interpretation of the prohibition. But none of these commentators has interpreted 'the road to the nations' in such a narrowly geographical way as to suggest that the Twelve would have felt free to focus on non-Jews within 'Galilee of the *Goyim*'. Such an interpretation is ruled out by the statement in the "final line in antithetic parallelism".[152] Moreover, the connotations of the term ὁδὸν ἐθνῶν would have covered τὰ ἔθνη within the target area also.[153]

The second part of the prohibition (καὶ εἰς πόλιν Σαμαριτῶν μὴ εἰσέλθητε) raises two challenges to interpretation which are especially pointed

---

[150] O. Cullmann, *Peter*, 190; foundation for 'other sheep' (Jn 10.16), 64.

[151] "There is no lack of evidence that the period [50 BC - AD 50] was one in which the prospect of an imminent eschaton was widely held." P.R. Davies, *IQM Structure and History*, 127. Of course, not all reflections on the End involved a messiah, and not all messianic views imply the same sequence and duration of events leading to the End.
Some 'messianic' texts suggest that Yahweh himself will intervene as King before the End. Christian developments of messianism (or 'Christology') and Trinitarian doctrine were able to appropriate this messianic strain in a way which diverged radically from simultaneous developments in Rabbinic Judaism. According to the Rabbinic tradition, "the Days of Messiah should not be confused with the World to Come .... The hope of the resurrection and the idea of the Messianic age were closely bound up together at a much earlier time (according to Dan. 12:2). But in the Mishnah and the earlier Baraithas these two conceptions are, more or less consciously, kept distinct." J. Klausner, *The Messianic Idea in Israel*, 413.

[152] J. Jeremias, *Jesus' Promise*, 20 n3.

[153] Albright-Mann's interpretation of "the route of the Gentiles" as referring specifically to "the route along the coastal plain" focuses on some of these connotations: "there were few Jewish settlements" on this route and so "*Kosher* food could not be obtained". *Matthew: A New Translation with Introduction and Commentary* (Garden City: Doubleday, 1971), 119.

if we keep in mind the geographical setting of Jesus' early ministry in Galilee. First, this directive cuts off any travel south to Samaria *and Judea*, whether πόλιν Σαμαριτῶν is translated 'the province of Samaria' or, more literally, 'a Samaritan town'.[154] Second, although the strategic command not to cross Galilee's southern border is simple and clear, the Samaritan reference (like the immediately preceding use of the term ὁδὸν ἐθνῶν) has strong connotations to modern readers which seem continuous with emotional connotations which would have impressed the original disciples.

It may be that twentieth-century readers react more strongly to the connotations of the term 'Samaritan' than Jesus' disciples would have. Certainly the focus of interpretation used in most modern studies is changed considerably when the simple terms of geography are accepted as denoting the basic meaning of the prohibition: Judea as well as Samaria was out of bounds for the first mission. Such a prohibition is completely plausible *early* in Jesus' ministry. But, with this reading, one or more subsequent missions (such as the mission of the seventy-two recorded in Luke 10) also seem probable. In an early response to Harnack's argument that Jesus' own ministry was restricted to Israel, Friedrich Spitta emphasized this second mission.

In Spitta's reconstruction, the mission of the seventy-two was important because it included no nationalistic limitations.[155] It is not necessary to revive Spitta's case against the idea of Jesus' Israel-centric mission to acknowledge the validity of some of his reasoning: the prohibition against work in Samaria and Judea applied only to the disciples' first mission. The idea that subsequent missions lacked nationalistic or provincial restrictions can be instructive in nuanced ways. As recorded in Luke's Gospel, Jesus sent the seventy-two "to every town and place he intended to visit" on his way to Jerusalem (Lk 10.1). At this later stage in his ministry, according to Luke, Jesus had already sent an advance-team into a Samaritan town which he expected to pass through. But he was not welcomed "because he was headed for Jerusalem" (Lk 9.53). This rebuff shifted most of their planned activity to Perea. But some Samaritan territory would still have been included, as well as the Judean territory between Jericho and Jerusalem.[156]

If Jesus put Samaria and Judea off limits for the first mission and included them in subsequent missions, the intractable problems involving the connotations of the term 'Samaritan' remain unsolved. The fundamental question is, How do Samaritans relate to Israel? If natives of Samaria count as Israelites (like

---

[154] The interpretation of πόλιν as 'province' following the meaning of the Aramaic מרינה has gained wide acceptance. J. Jeremias, *Jesus' Promise*, 19. *Cf.* Matthew Black, *An Aramaic Approach to the Gospels and Acts* (Oxford: Clarendon, 1967), 13. But 'a town' in the sense of 'any town' would have the same meaning here. Albright-Mann's proposed textual emendation of *polin* to *palin* (*op. cit., 119*) seems unjustified and unnecessary.

[155] F. Spitta, *Jesus und die Heidenmission* (1909) cited by B. Sundkler "Jésus et les païen", *Revue d'histoire et de philosophie Religieuses* 16 (1936), 467.

[156] See Jesus' story about "a Samaritan" on the way from Jericho to Jerusalem in the Third Gospel (Lk 10.15-11) and Jesus' ministry in Shechem (Jn 4.4-42) in the Fourth.

those in Judea) the next question is, Why could Samaritans not claim priority of attention as 'scattered sheep'?

Part of the difficulty in answering these questions relates to the puzzling change and continuity in the use of the terms 'Samaritan' and 'Jew' after the time of Jesus' ministry and Matthew's.[157] Modern biblical scholars, rightly consider 'the Samaritan question' as a key to understanding the Christian mission to the nations and often refer to Samaritans as 'non-Jews'. Such a designation is obviously correct, but 'non-Jew' typically is understood to mean 'non-Israelite' —as Max Meinertz explicitly labels Samaritans.[158] Recent scholarship attempts to correct this error by identifying Samaritans as a 'Jewish sect' following usage put forward by J.A. Montgomery in 1907.[159] The status of Samaritans as Israelites is thus guaranteed, by labelling them 'Jews'. But this terminology sharply contradicts first-century patterns of word-usage.

Jesus and his disciples probably would *not* have called persons from the province of Samaria Ἰουδαῖοι, but it seems clear that they would have considered them 'Israelites'[160] The prohibition itself can be seen to distinguish Σαμαρῖται from τὰ ἔθνη. But why, then, are 'Samaritans' avoided (like ἔθνη) in this first mission to the 'scattered sheep of the House of Israel'?

"Salvation is from the Jews," according to Jesus' words in the Fourth Gospel (Jn 4.22). In context this appears to be a Messianic claim, relating specifically to Jesus himself as a member of the tribe of Judah (*cf.* Heb 7.14). This statement might also imply Judea and Jerusalem as the starting point for the Messianic mission, followed by an initiative to reunite "Judah to Ephraim" preliminary to conquest of the nations.[161] But the First Gospel emphasizes the Galilean starting point for Jesus' ministry and his disciples' first mission (*cf.*

---

[157] The evidence of positive responses to Samaritans by the earliest Jewish-Christian community (recorded in Acts and anticipated by Jesus' ministry according to Lk and Jn) in contrast to the increasingly negative responses by non-Christian Jews (recorded in Lk and Jn, by Josephus, and in the Mishnah) must be taken seriously.

[158] M. Meinertz, *Jesus und die Heidenmission* (Münster, 1925), cited by Sundkler, *op. cit.*, 468.

[159] James Alan Montgomery, *The Samaritans: The Earliest Jewish Sect, Their History, Theology, and Literature* (Philadelphia: Winston, 1907), 46.

[160] Josephus refers to Jews and Samaritans as ὁμογενής (Josephus *Antiq* xi.322). But he was capable of taking quite the opposite position in the same work, labelling Samaritans "Cuthians" (*Antiq* ix.227-91 w. ref. to II Kg 17). See Ferdinand Dexinger's critique of this characterization in "Limits of Tolerance in Judaism: The Samaritans", *Jewish and Christian Self-Definition* vol 2, *Aspects of Judaism in the Graeco-Roman Period*, ed. E.P. Sanders (Philadelphia: Fortress, 1981), 106.
In the Third Gospel Jesus refers to the Samaritan cured of leprosy as a 'foreigner' (ἀλλογενής Lk 17.18), but the narrative context shows Jesus accepting him as an Israelite surpassing his Jewish companions in faithfulness. Jesus' words may be ironic, implying judgment against Jews who treated Samaritans as foreigners.

[161] See Ez 37.19, 22-3 & 28; *re* this vision J.E.H. Thomson, *Samaritans*, 194.

Mt 4.13-16). Not only the orthodox Samaritan 'Observers' (סמרים), [162] but also the Judean scribes and Pharisees (and Essenes) were off-center in Israel at the start of the Messianic Age. The Galilean *'am ha'aretz* were at the strategic center.[163]

John the Baptist's Expectations

John the Baptist's message is integrated into the explicit Messianism of the canonical Gospels, with each of the four evangelists introducing Jesus' public activity in relation to the John's preparatory ministry (Mt 3.11 and par). Jesus himself submitted to John's baptism (Mt 3.13-17, par and Jn 1.32). The Fourth Gospel pointedly notes that two, at least, of Jesus' twelve disciples had been disciples of John (Jn 1.35-37). It is possible to reconstruct accounts of John's activity and self-understanding which do not assume his radical subordination to Jesus,[164] but there is no reason to doubt that the Baptizer's message was Messianic and eschatological.[165] John's impact on the crowds and on the religious and political rulers testify to the power of his interpretation of Israel's traditions in relation to current hopes and fears.

The Messianic expectations expressed in the Baptizer's words and deeds had significance for the mission to all nations which is now obvious. John pointedly challenged the Israelite understanding of themselves as the exclusive people of God. The very act of baptism, which characterized John's ministry, implied radical, positive responses from individuals to this challenge.

Emphatically denying that physical descent from Abraham could guarantee salvation to anyone, the Baptizer provocatively claimed that "God is able from these stones to raise up children for Abraham" (Mt 3.8-9 & par Lk 3.8). Remembering that prophetic words which had seemed incredible in other times had proven true (such as Jeremiah's prophecy that Yahweh would abandon

---

[162] For a reconstruction of the more rigorous observance of the Sabbath and circumcision regulations by the Samaritans than by the Pharisees, see R.J. Coggins, *Samaritans and Jews* (Atlanta: John Knox, 1975), 134-5.

[163] This assertion does not deny the theological significance of Jerusalem and the Temple for the mission, also in Mt. But Sundkler's thesis (*op.cit.*, 481) requires modification to take account of the Galilean center.

[164] The four Gospels and Acts testify to the Baptist's interaction with Jesus and his continuing influence on the Jesus movement after his death and even after Jesus' death. Using form- and redaction-criticism, W. Wink attempts to answer the question, "Why is John the Baptist granted such an important role in the Gospel tradition?" *John the Baptist in the Gospel Tradition* (Cambridge: University Press, 1968), 107. Mandaean literature provides evidence for John's independence from (and competition with) Jesus, but "there is no objective evidence of the establishment of Mandaeism earlier than the second century AD." E.M. Yamauchi, "Mandaeism", *IDB* Suppl, 563.

[165] "The complete absence of any reference to John's Messianic preaching and expectations" in Josephus' account (*Antiq* xviii.115-19) is noted by Charles Scobie who concludes that "here certainly his bias is to be detected." *John the Baptist* (Philadelphia: Fortress, 1964), 19. Josephus registers Herod's alarm at the impact of John's eloquence on the crowds (xviii.118), however, which Scobie might have counted as an implicit reference.

Jerusalem to destruction in that prophet's day), some in John's audience might well have accepted the Baptizer's words as truly meaning that the fundamental distinction between 'Israel' and 'the nations' was now finished.[166] "Descent from Abraham will not guarantee membership in the new Israel, nor will lack of it be a disqualification."[167]

In conjunction with this preaching, John's baptism seems to have been a ritual renunciation by Israelites of their old claims to a special relationship with God and an acceptance of equality with the nations— who were able to be received into 'the Kingdom of heaven' as the Messianic Age dawned. If proselyte baptism already was established in John's time, such an interpretation of his baptism would have been inescapable. "Proselyte baptism is certainly attested by the end of the first century AD" and Markus Barth notes that

> if it existed as early as John the Baptist's public activity (*ca.* AD 28) and was known to him, then John's baptism of Jews (John 1.32; Acts 13:24) was an affront to Jewish self-consciousness.[168]

Many Jewish scholars, following the classic statement of Maimonides, have affirmed that proselyte baptism existed before the appearance of the John the Baptist: "By three things did Israel enter into the Covenant, by circumcision and baptism and sacrifice."[169] At the end of the nineteenth century Emil Schürer surveyed the evidence and arguments and concluded that only dogmatic prejudice had led Christian scholars in previous years to deny the obvious.[170] Thomas Torrance, in his 1954 essay "Proselyte Baptism" again marshalled the Rabbinic and Patristic evidence in a strong statement of the case for Jewish antecedents to John's baptism.[171] Nevertheless, the evidence still allows contrary arguments.[172] What must be acknowledged on all sides is what David Hill terms the "profound originality" of John's baptism.[173]

---

[166] Jeremiah's prediction that Jerusalem would actually fall (Jer 26.4-8 *cf.* 38.2-3) contradicted the strongly held article of faith in his time that eternal inviolability of the Temple and the Holy City was the last remaining proof that Yahweh had not and would not abandon his covenant with Israel.

[167] G.B. Caird, *Jesus and the Jewish Nation* (London: Athlone Press, 1965), 7.

[168] M. Barth, "Baptism", *IDB* Suppl, 86.

[169] This 12th century AD statement dates baptism to the wilderness (Ex 29.10) and is based on tractates in the Babylonian and Jerusalem Talmuds. Quoted at length by T.F. Torrance, "Proselyte Baptism", *NTS* 1 (1954-55), 150.

[170] E. Schürer, *The History of the Jewish People in the Time of Jesus Christ* vol 2 (New York: Scribner's, 1891), 311.

[171] T.F. Torrance, *op. cit.* 150-154. *Cf.* O. Cullmann, *Baptism in the Early Church* (London: SCM, 1950), 9; and C.H. Dodd, *Founder*, 122.

[172] See G.R. Beasley-Murray's reservations and bibliography in *Baptism in the New Testament* (Grand Rapids: Eerdmans, 1973 [1962]), 18-25.

[173] D. Hill, *Matthew*, 92. *Cf.* M. Barth's earlier and fuller discussion of this point in *Die Taufe—Ein Sacrament?* (Zürich: Evangelische Verlag, 1951), 16.

The Gospels represent John's ministry as the turning point in God's dealing with mankind (Mt 11.11, par Lk 7.28) and John's baptism can be described as "the proleptic symbol of admission to the Israel of the new age". This interpretation by G.B. Caird in his essay *Jesus and the Jewish Nation* is based on the premise that "John ... summoned the Jews to a national movement of repentance" and that Jesus submitted to John's baptism precisely because Jesus "accepted his own involvement in the national life of his people".[174] In other words, John's ministry, like Jesus' own, was 'Israel-centric'. Caird's meaning of the term 'national' here reflects the statement in Acts 13.23-24 that John prepared the way for Jesus by "preaching a baptism of repentance to all the people of Israel".

If, indeed, John accepted repentant individuals from the nations for baptism[175] as well as Jews and Samaritans, this would not have contradicted the 'Israel-centric' and 'centripetal' nature of his ministry. But such a program could account for the cross-examination by "priests and Levites" sent to John by "the Jews from Jerusalem" (Jn 1.19), and especially their question, "Why are you baptizing?" (Jn 1.25).

The Fourth Gospel's account of the Baptizer's subsequent mission in Samaria "at Aenon near Salim" (Jn 3.23) is consistent with the general description of his territory as "the whole region around the Jordan" (Mt 3.5, par Lk 3.3-6). It is also consistent with the recollection that John's ministry was to "all the people of Israel" (Acts 13.23-24). This move, which has recently received careful attention from a number of New Testament scholars,[176] doubtless was prompted by the Baptizer's understanding of his role in the Messianic mission. His Samaritan experience, no doubt, further developed this understanding.

John's second thoughts about his identification of Jesus as 'the Coming One' (ὁ ἐρχόμενος) are recorded in the First Gospel immediately after the first mission of the Twelve (Mt 11.2-3). It seems most likely that John's question had to do with the pace and sequence of eschatological events related to Jesus. John had seen "the axe laid to the root of the tree" (Mt 3.10, par Lk 3.9) already before he saw Jesus anointed by the Holy Spirit (Jn 1.32, par Lk 3.21-2, Mt 3.16, Mk 1.10).

If the First Gospel's narrative follows historical sequence here, the Baptizer would have heard of the mission of the Twelve in Galilee. This small beginning must have looked disappointing to the powerful reformer who had confidently assured his own followers that Jesus was "the Coming One" who was "more powerful" (Mt 3.11-12; par Mk 1.7, Lk 3.15-17/ Jn 1.30). To John, the prohibition in Jesus' instructions to the Twelve for their first mission might have seemed to represent regressive policy.

---

[174] G. Caird, *Jesus and the Jewish Nation*, 7.

[175] This is implied by the questions from soldiers recorded in Lk 3.14.

[176] J.A.T. Robinson, "The 'Others' of John 4.38", *Twelve New Testament Studies* (London: SCM, 1962), 62-64 responding to O. Cullmann's "Samaria and the Origins of the Christian Mission" [1953-54], *The Early Church* (Philadelphia: Westminster, 1958), 183-92. *Cf.* Scobie, "The Samaritan Ministry", *John the Baptist*, 173-6.

7

PROSELYTIZING

Οὐαὶ ὑμῖν, γραμματεῖς καὶ Φαρισαῖοι ὑποκριταί,
ὅτι περιάγετε τὴν θάλασσαν καὶ τὴν ξηρὰν ποιῆσαι ἕνα προσήλυτον,
καὶ ὅταν γένηται ποιεῖτε αὐτὸν υἱὸν γεέννης διπλότερον ὑμῶν.

Woe to you, scribes and Pharisees, you play-actors!
You travel over sea and land to make a single proselyte
and when he is converted, you make him a child of hell
 even more divided than yourselves.   Matthew 23.15

The Matthean text which records Jesus' "stern judgment upon the Jewish mission"[1] has not been neglected by New Testament scholars. But even those who accept the text as derived from an authentic saying of Jesus often seize on one or another element in the saying to discount the possibility of discovering in the text itself detailed and interrelated historical information about the contemporary Jewish mission and Jesus' response to it.

The three lines in the text have provoked three disputes in older and more recent commentaries. As it stands in the First Gospel, the saying is directed specifically against "scribes and Pharisees", and so Jesus' condemnation might be understood to be not so much against Jewish proselytism as against party recruitment. This, indeed, is the position taken by Alfred Plummer: "Converts to Pharisaism are meant, and not converts to Judaism."[2]

---

[1] This phrase is taken from the first of J. Jeremias' "Three Important Negative Conclusions" in *Jesus' Promise to the Nations*, 11. Jeremias accepts Mt 23.15 as genuinely representative of Jesus' thought and traces the saying to "an old Aramaic tradition"(*ibid.*, 17).

[2] A. Plummer, *An Exegetical Commentary on the Gospel According To S. Matthew* (London: Elliot Stock, 1909), 317. For a statement of this position which relates it with

F.M. Derwacter rejects this interpretation, however, noting that no parallel can be cited "for the use of the term *proselyte* for *party convert*".³ Joachim Jeremias declares absolutely that "προσήλυτον never has this connotation."⁴ Although Jeremias is right in his insistence that Jewish proselytism is the issue here, the question of partisan connotations still calls for close attention in an integrated interpretation of the text.

The second element of the text ("for you travel over sea and land to make a single proselyte") has been interpreted as a scornful reference to "the comparative failure of the effort".⁵ This focus is maintained plausibly when the judgment is taken as being directed only to the Pharisees' part in the proselyte movement or —if the saying is taken to originate with Matthew— as a slighting comparison of Jewish to Christian missionary results. Johannes Munck is inclined to this latter view,⁶ but he uncovers a much deeper line of approach to this text when he cites Justin Martyr's distinction between 'proselytes' and 'nations': "Judaism thought only of proselytes, and did not consider that it had any obligation toward the Gentile nations as a whole."⁷ This way of contrasting individual proselytizing initiative for single proselytes with a corporate effort and goal is an important clue not only for assessing apparently contradictory evidence about the nature and extent of 'the Jewish mission' but also for interpreting Jesus' judgment against the movement.

The third element in the text ("and when he is converted you make him a child of hell even more divided than yourselves") is the most jarring, but it seems to provide the key to interpretation for most modern commentators. If Jesus' judgment had not been eschatological but simply ethical, then the scribes and Pharisees' pattern of life, imitated and exaggerated by their converts, would have been the basis for the judgment. "It should not be overlooked," says David Garland, "that the target of the woe is not proselytism *per se* but the final outcome of the proselytism of the scribes and Pharisees."⁸ Jeremias goes a long way towards accepting this view: "his [Jesus'] saying was aimed at the smug self-righteousness of the Pharisees and the fanaticism of their converts ...

---

some persuasiveness to the "single proselyte" *cf.* Willoughby Allen *A Critical and Exegetical Commentary on the Gospel According to S. Matthew* (Edinburgh: T&T Clark, 1907), 246.

³ F. Derwacter, *Preparing the Way for Paul: The Proselyte Movement in Later Judaism* (New York: Macmillan, 1930), 44. Derwacter considers Mt 23.15 important but not derived from an authentic saying of Jesus.

⁴ J. Jeremias, *Jesus' Promise*, 18.

⁵ Derwacter, *Preparing the Way*, 42, citing Wetstein.

⁶ J. Munck, *Paul and the Salvation of Mankind*, 266.

⁷ *Ibid.*, 268, citing Justin's *Dialogue with Trypho* 121f and 123f. *Cf.* M. Friedländer's suggestion that the Pharisees' individualistic approach opposed mass conversions, cited and rejected by M. Simon, *Verus Israel: A Study of the Relations between Christians and Jews in the Roman Empire (135-425)*(Oxford: University Press, 1986 [1945]), 283.

⁸ D.E. Garland, *The Intention of Matthew 23* (Leiden: E.J. Brill, 1979), 129.

his woe could hardly have been pronounced against the Gentile mission itself."[9] Specific ethical judgment was involved to be sure, and David Hill's suggestion is appropriate for this level of interpretation: the phrase "twice as much a child of hell (*Gehenna*) may indicate that some further privilege or requirement was made for proselytes which was not in accordance with the Law".[10] But Jeremias' generalizations conjure up modern prejudice and weaken the point he himself is driving at. This point (which is still a "riddle" in the stage of Jeremias' argument cited here) is that the saying reflects a fundamental theological confrontation between Jesus and the "scribes and Pharisees". Sharp ethical judgments mark this confrontation, but the real issue, in relation to Jesus' time and teaching, seems certainly to have concerned the revelation of God's will and the End.[11]

A. "Scribes and Pharisees"
ΓΡΑΜΜΑΤΕΙΣ ΚΑΙ ΦΑΡΙΣΑΙΟΙ

According to Sjef van Tilbourg the very conjunction of "scribes and Pharisees" in Matthew 23.15, as elsewhere in the First Gospel, is evidence against the authenticity of this saying. In his book, *The Jewish Leaders in Matthew*, Tilbourg claims that "the historical differences between the various groups [of Jesus' day] could not be understood any longer" when Matthew wrote his Gospel. Consequently, "the groups themselves could be combined."[12] Tilbourg's thesis is carefully argued and challenging. But his confident assumption, that our knowledge of "the various groups" in Jesus' day and specifically our knowledge of "the Pharisees" is sufficient to expose Matthew's ignorance, is a presupposition of his work which must be challenged.

"Information on the Pharisees before 70 comes from three sources, all of which reached their present state after that date," as Jacob Neusner reminds us.[13] Evidence from each of these three sources —Josephus' writings, the Gospels, and the Mishnah-Tosefta— demands special critical caution when used

---

[9] *Jesus' Promise*, 19. Jeremias' next word is "nevertheless" with reference to "the riddle". Exactly what Jeremias means by "the Gentile mission itself" (and how this is exempted from Jesus' negative judgment) is not altogether clear. (*Cf.* below n36.)

[10] D. Hill, *The Gospel of Matthew*, 312 citing E. Lernle and P. Bonnard.

[11] Whether or not it is possible to go 'beyond ethics' in speaking of God's will and the End is a question which goes some way towards clarifying the issue. A modest answer can be given in terms of U. of Michigan William Frankena's 'meta-ethics'; an outrageous answer was given by the 17th-century messiah Sabbatai Svi's program of "Redemption Through Sin". Gershom Scholem, *The Messianic Idea in Judaism* (New York: Schocken 1971), 78 ff.

[12] S. van Tilbourg, *The Jewish Leaders in Matthew* (Leiden: E.J. Brill, 1972), 3. Tilbourg's strongest argument on this point relates to Matthew's use of the phrase οἱ Φαρισαῖοι καὶ Σαδδουκαῖοι, "a formulation proper to him that gathers under one definite article two widely divergent groups" (*Ibid.*, 2).

[13] J. Neusner, *The Glory of God Is Intelligence* (Salt Lake City: Publisher's Press, 1978), 14

in support of historical arguments. This is so not only because of the dates of the documents but also because each of the three sources has a sharp bias for or against the Pharisees, as Neusner has demonstrated persistently and convincingly.[14] The late date which Tilbourg assigns to Matthew's Gospel is a crucial part of his argument against its usefulness as an historical record of Jesus' controversy with the Pharisees and others. But Tilbourg's readers should note that Josephus' *Antiquities* was written *ca.* AD 93-94[15] and the Mishnah and Tosefta were not written before *ca.* AD 200. Even those who argue for a late appearance of the written Gospels usually date them before AD 90.

In building his case against the First Gospel as a source of historical information about the Judaism of Jesus' day, Tilbourg cannot be said to have neglected the earliest documentary evidence altogether. Some of his most persuasive arguments are based on a close comparative analysis of material in the four Gospels. But the standard by which his judgments are made appears to be a 'normative Judaism' deduced from documentary evidence much later and no less biased than Matthew's Gospel itself —even by Tilbourg's own reckoning.

For our present purposes it is not necessary to attempt an exact identification of the "scribes and Pharisees".[16] It is enough to note that however related or opposed to each other the two groups thought themselves to be, Jesus could have linked them together in his judgment on the proselyte movement. Whether they usually agreed or disagreed amongst themselves and with each other about the standards to be set for accepting proselytes, and whether the initiative taken was united or competitive, these representative leaders of Israel

---

[14] For a basic statement see *From Politics to Piety: The Emergence of Pharisaic Judaism* (Englewood Cliffs: Prentice-Hall, 1973). *Cf.* "Bibliographic Reflections", *The Rabbinic Traditions About the Pharisees Before 70*, Part III (Leiden:E.J. Brill, 1971), 320ff and "'Judaism' after Moore: A Programmatic Statement", *JJS* 31/2 (1980).

[15] J. Goldin, "Josephus, Flavius", *IDB* 2. 987. As Neusner points out, "Josephus's picture of the predominance of the Pharisees is drawn not in War but in Antiquities, written twenty years after the War." *Rabbinic Traditions About Pharisees Before 70*, III, 329.

[16] These scribes may be 'scribes of the Pharisees'. For the relationship between *Pharisaioi*, *grammateis*, and *nomikoi cf.* Phillip Sigal, *The Halakah of Jesus of Nazareth According to the Gospel of Matthew* (Lanham: University Press of America, 1986), 163, n15. Michael Cook, leaning heavily on his assumption of Marcan priority, reaches a judgment which coincides with Tilbourg's on the value of Matthew as a source for historical information: "Precisely because Matthew and Luke lack personal familiarity with most of these groups, they often obscure rather than clarify the Markan information." *Mark's Treatment of the Jewish Leaders* (Leiden: E.J. Brill, 1978), 3. A more balanced survey of the three sources notes that "the references to Pharisees in Mark ... appear to reflect, with very great precision indeed, the transition from the *parisaioi* of Josephus to *perushim*, attacked as extremists, of the rabbinic sources." John Bowker, *Jesus and the Pharisees* (Cambridge: University Press, 1973), 38. *Cf.* Phillip Sigal's similar analysis of Matthew's usage, *op. cit.* "When Jesus differed with Pharisees he frequently was differing on the same grounds as proto-rabbis differed with Pharisees." "Matthew in Judaic Context", *Reformed Journal*, 1984.

were engaged in the movement, according to this text. The saying itself, taken together with widespread evidence of the proselyte movement, provides an important but often overlooked clue to Jesus' strong disapproval of the direction they provided to that movement.

B. "A Single Proselyte"
ΠΟΙΗΣΑΙ ἜΝΑ ΠΡΟΣΗΛΥΤΟΝ

As we have seen, when sent out on a mission to Israel even Jesus' own disciples were prohibited from preaching to the nations (Mt 10.5b-6). That prohibition itself implies that Jesus anticipated that *the mission to Israel* would result in the revelation of the Kingdom of heaven to the nations also. Accordingly, his disapproval of the scribes and Pharisees' proselytizing activity was, in part, a strategic judgment.

The scribes and Pharisees were undertaking a mission which, according to Jesus' expressed convictions, must be delayed until a further revelation of God's will. But Jesus' condemnation also indicates his disapproval of the scribes and Pharisees' basic intent and purpose for proselytizing. They had failed to perform the mission they had been given, and now they were exporting their failure.[17] They had not given direction to "the scattered sheep of the house of Israel" in following the will of God. Now, instead of preparing Israel for the Kingdom of heaven, they were traversing sea and land to add to the number of lost sheep.

Before pursuing this line of analysis further, we should answer the question raised in the introduction to the present study: Was there a Jewish mission in Jesus' day? More specifically, did the "scribes and Pharisees" have an active part it in? If 'mission' is simply equated with 'intense proselytizing' the text of Matthew 23.15 provides an affirmative answer, and this answer is credible in relation to the established facts of the expansion of Judaism. Moreover, this text can be interpreted in such a way as to clarify the practical question, how this activity was carried out.

Samuel Sandmel, after noting the important distinction "between welcoming into a community an outsider who volunteers to enter" and "pursuing an active aggressive movement to persuade outsiders to enter" observes that "virtually all the evidence available concerning outsiders joining themselves to Judaism deals with passive reception." Sandmel goes on, however, to say that "the testimony of Matthew 23.15 need not be put aside; it should rather persuade us that at least the Pharisees maintained or countenanced something of

---

[17] As leaders of Israel, the scribes and Pharisees have a 'mission' in the sense of divine assignment. This assumption by Jesus helps explain helps explain the force of his censure. For an attempt to reconstruct Jesus' teaching regarding Israel's mission see Lane McGaughy, "The Fear of Yahweh and the Mission of Judaism", *JBL* 94 (1975), 235-245.

a missionary movement."[18] Sandmel's judgment here is sound, and his qualification ("or countenanced") does not undercut his position.

Another historian, Salo Baron, integrates the same judgment into a broader description which restates the qualification programmatically:

> Although there were no professional missionaries, uninterrupted religious propaganda seems to have gone on throughout the dispersion. There must have been Jews among the numerous itinerant preachers and rhetoricians who voyaged from city to city, propagandizing for one or another idea. To this extent the well-known denunciation of the Pharisees by Jesus —...(Matt 23:15)— reflects reality. To be sure, there is not the slightest evidence that the official leaders ever made an organized attempt to spread Judaism among the nations, but *at least in that period they did not discourage individual efforts.* [Emphasis added.] Many converts must have become propagandists even more zealous than their teachers. The extensive travels of Jewish merchants, a steadily increasing factor in international commerce, helped familiarize even distant peoples with the main tenets of Judaism. Ananias, the Jewish merchant-missionary who converted the royal house of Adiabene, may indeed have been prompted no more by religious zeal than by a wish to enlist royal support for his commercial transactions.[19]

The account by Josephus of the conversions in Adiabene was written somewhat later than the First Gospel, but the conversions Josephus reports occurred within ten years of Jesus' teaching ministry, close enough to be considered exactly contemporary for our purposes.[20]

Josephus had a special interest in the proselyte movement —a fact which is relevant here, since he claimed to be a Pharisee— but his account seems trustworthy, not tendentious. The facts as he relates them help focus questions of method and individual initiative in the proselyte movement of the day.

Ananias' pattern of instructing influential women seems to have been a strategy, supporting Baron's appraisal of Ananias as "the Jewish merchant-missionary".[21] It is noteworthy also that "about the same time" queen Helena "was instructed by a certain other Jew" (*Antiq* xx.35). But most important, with reference to Mt 23.15, is the account which follows of the struggle (between the young king Izates on the one side and his mother and Ananias on the other) concerning the question of circumcision, and the appearance of yet "another Jew named Eliazar, who came from Galilee and who had a reputation for being

---

[18] S. Sandmel, *The First Christian Century in Judaism and Christianity: Certainties and Uncertainties* (New York: Oxford University Press, 1969), 22.

[19] S. Baron, *A Social and Religious History of the Jews*, vol I (New York: Columbia University Press, 1952 [1937]), 173.

[20] Josephus' *Antiquities* appeared *ca.* AD 93-94; Mt's Gospel is dated AD 80-90 by a majority of NT scholars today (according to G.M. Stanton, "Matthean Scholarship 1945-1980" *ANRW* 25.3, 1991), but as early as *AD* 55 by some, see J.A.T. Robinson, *Redating the New Testament* (London: SCM, 1976), 117.

[21] Baron, *loc. cit.*; *Antiq* xx.34.

extremely strict when it came to the ancestral laws" (*Antiq* xx.43). This "learned Jew" persuaded the young king that he had been right in his own decision to be circumcised and that he should no longer defer to the compromising judgment of his mother and Ananias (*Antiq* xx.43).

This story, as Josephus tells it, provides clear evidence not only of individual initiative in seeking proselytes[22] but also of partisan intervention by a single 'scribe', which might imply a continuing interest among the Palestinian Jewish leaders in the far-flung proselyte movement. If this learned Jew from Galilee was a Pharisee of the school of Shammai, the question of partisan initiative in seeking proselytes becomes especially intriguing in relation to negative and positive information in the Rabbinic sources about regulations for reception of proselytes.[23]

Mention of the Rabbinic sources raises questions about how to evaluate documentary evidence which was written later than Matthew 23.15 and this story in Josephus' *Antiquities*. The lack of information in the Rabbinic sources about initiative —individual or organizational— in the proselyte movement is remarkable, especially if the early Tannaitic period was a time of unprecedented and subsequently unparalleled proselytizing activity.[24] This silence of the Rabbis can be interpreted to mean that there was no significant intentional dimension to the proselyte movement. More appropriately, this silence can be understood to imply the individualistic and largely unorganized character of this side of the movement. But the silence also appears to have a deeper, theological significance analogous (and related) to another remarkable silence in the Rabbinic sources.

---

[22] Jn 7.35 is also evidence of individual Jewish initiative in proselytizing. The Apostle Paul's characterization of Jews as those who "feel certain that they can guide the blind" (Rm 2.17-21) is cited by Schürer/Vermes along with the last lines of Horace's Fourth Satire (Book I) as evidence of "the Jewish eagerness to make converts". *HJP* vol III/1, 160.
Horace's poem was written within the time-frame at issue (between Pompeii's conquest of Palestine 63 BC and the Fall of Jerusalem AD 70). John Noland has argued that the relevant reference for the line *ac velati te Judaei cogemus in haec concedere turban* is mobs of unemployed Jews ready to express their opinion in concert to sway Roman officials. *Vigiliae Christianae* 33 (1979), 347-355. But the very existence of a large Jewish population in Rome at this time suggests increases in synagogue membership beyond natural birth rates.

[23] "There were Pharisees in Galilee, but ... Finkelstein's evidence suggests that they belonged to the school of Shammai." Sherman Johnson, *Jesus in His Own Times* (London: A&C Black, 1957), 19. It is often assumed that if there was active encouragement of proselytism from the Pharisees it was from the school of Hillel. But "the aggadic narratives (which are as much legend as history) do not show Hillel as more eager for converts than Shammai, but as possessing a more even and lovable disposition." Bernard Bamberger, *Proselytism in the Talmudic Period* (New York: Ktav, 1968 [1939]), 278.

[24] Whether or not later movements equalled or surpassed the movement 68 BC — AD 70 in intensity of involvement and success is an interesting question which lies outside the scope of the present study. For a convenient account of the 8th century AD conversion of the Khazars see Arthur Koestler's *The Thirteenth Tribe: The Khazar Empire and Its Heritage* (London: Pan, 1977), 52-73.

152 Earliest Christian Mission to All Nations

Two Rabbinic Silences

The reticence about the Messiah in the Mishnah, which amounts to almost complete silence, has already been noted. Joseph Klausner's subtle explanation of this silence has also been noted, along with his conviction that "it was not because these earliest Tannaim rejected the Messianic idea."[25] In a similar way, but more forcefully and positively, Bernard Bamberger and William Braude have interpreted the many sayings about the *reception* of proselytes to prove that the Rabbis did not oppose proselytism. Bamberger presses beyond the Rabbinic evidence when he concludes that *"the Pharisees and the Rabbis were eager for converts, highly successful in winning them, and friendly in their treatment of them."*[26] But the second-to-last chapter in Bamberger's book is a commentary on Matthew 23.15, which does give some solid support to his conclusion.

The relationship between these two Rabbinic silences —about intentional proselytizing and Messianic expectations in the first generation of Tannaim (before *AD* 70)— may be so close as to require a single complex explanation. This explanation can be represented by the commentary of a later Rabbi on *Song of Songs* 2.7 "Do not stir up love until it is ready." Three of the four stern warnings in this commentary seem directed against Jewish initiative in Messianic movements and in the proselyte movement.

> Four vows are contained here. The Israelites are adjured not to revolt against the kingdoms of the world [the secular powers], not to press for the End, not to reveal their mystery to the nations of the world, and not to come up from exile like a wall [in great masses]. But, if so, why does King Messiah come? To gather in the exiled of Israel.[27]

This third-century view, chastened by reflection on the events which followed Jesus' ministry, is strikingly congruent with Jesus' own as represented by his "woe". Accordingly, the reticence of the Rabbis about intentions and methods

---

[25] J. Klausner, *The Messianic Idea in Israel From Its Beginning to the Completion of the Mishnah* (New York: Macmillan, 1955), 392.

[26] B. Bamberger, *Proselytism in the Talmudic Period*, 274, *cf.* 7: Bamberger emphatically rejects the view that the proselyte movement fell into sharp decline after AD 132. Bamberger says that such an assessment as Derwacter's is possible only through "the power of preconceived notions to disregard the facts."
Both Bamberger and William Braude (*Jewish Proselytizing in the First Five Centuries of the Common Era, the Age of the Tannaim and Amoraim*. Providence: Brown University Press, 1940) deal mainly with documentary evidence later than our period and most proselytes they consider are from after AD 70. *Cf.* M. Simon, *Verus Israel: A Study of the Relations between Christian and Jews in the Roman Empire (135-425)* (Oxford: University Press, 1986 [1948]). Simon is uncritically dependent on Braude's conclusions, according to D. Rokeah, *Jews, Pagans and Christians in Conflict* (Jerusalem/Leiden: Magnes/Brill, 1982), 42.

[27] Amora Rabbi Helbo, quoted (with glosses) by G. Scholem, *The Messianic Idea in Judaism* (New York: Shocken, 1971), 14. In the Talmud, Rabbi Helbo complains that "Proselytes are as hard for Israel to endure as a sore." Quoted by J. Klausner, *Messianic Idea in Israel*, 478. This saying indicates a disapproval of proselytizing as strong as that of Jesus.

might be construed as a rebuke of the earlier involvement in the proselyte movement of the "scribes and Pharisees". But the rebuke, if such it is, does not have the same point and thrust as Jesus' "woe".

Before turning finally to Jesus' condemnation itself, we should attempt to discover from Mt 23.15 something more about the *method* and *results* of first-century Jewish proselytism. Sandmel, Baron, and other historians not only accept Matthew's testimony about intentional proselytizing but also suggest an interpretation of ἕνα προσήλυτον which has been overlooked by most New Testament commentators. This support for the idea that there were efforts to persuade *individual* proselytes emerges from historians' synthesis of the established facts about proselytism in the period.

Josephus' account of the conversions in Adiabene certainly reveals an individualistic approach, both in terms of the proselytizer's personal initiative and in terms of the immediate achievement. To Helena the implications of her son's decision were clear, circumcision would isolate him from his people:

> If his subjects should discover that he was devoted to rites that were strange and foreign to themselves, it would produce much disaffection and they would not tolerate the rule of a Jew over them (*Antiq* xx.39).

It must be admitted that the individualistic direction supplied to the proselyte movement by the Pharisees is somewhat paradoxical, not least because *ethnic solidarity* was and remained strong in Judaism. But what Ellis Rivkin describes as a "hidden revolution" together with the witness of Matthew 23.15 provides a radical and coherent explanation for the lack of Rabbinic references to intentional mission to the nations. "For the individual who internalized the system of the two-fold law and guided his life by it, there was the promise of an eternal individuation," according to Rivkin.[28]

Individual proselytes became Jews, according to the formulas applied and discussed by the "scribes and Pharisees" already in Jesus' time. In the later Rabbinic records, references to proselytes are almost exclusively concerned with establishing and defining their Jewishness. This scheme eliminated the need for a mission to the nations.[29] Popular messianic expectations no doubt inspired many of the common people to see eschatological meaning in the proselyte movement. But, if Rivkin's hidden revolution was already underway, this was not the meaning of the direction given to the movement by the "scribes and Pharisees". As the subsequent silence in the Mishnah indicates, and as Rivkin

---

[28] E. Rivkin, "The Meaning of Messiah in Jewish Thought", *USQR* 26 (1971), 390. *Cf.* *A Hidden Revolution* (Nashville: Abingdon, 1978), *passim*.

[29] Justin Martyr makes this point with his distinction between τῶν ἐθνῶν τῶν περφωτισμένως and τοὺς προσηλύτους in his polemic commentary on Mt 23.15 in "Dialogue with Trypho the Jew", chapter 122 (written *ca.* AD 155 in a setting *ca.* AD 140). Migne, *Patrologiae Series Graeca*, vol 6, 760 B.

explains "this system needed no messianic concept,"[30] and no mission to the nations.

C. "A Child of Hell Even More Divided Than Yourselves" [31]
ΥΙΟΝ ΓΕΕΝΝΗΣ ΔΙΠΛΟΤΕΡΟΝ ΥΜΩΝ

The impossibility of gaining precise knowledge about "the scribes and Pharisees" in Jesus' time and about the development of Jesus' own messianic consciousness make caution necessary in interpreting Jesus' judgment on the Jewish mission. But if we press a few simple points already considered, we may be in a position to grasp the basic theological issues involved in the confrontation.

The assertion that each proselyte becomes "a child of hell even more divided" than the scribes and Pharisees is clearly not a judgment directed at the proselytes themselves but at the Jewish leaders. Their mission is premature and misguided. Jesus' own response to non-Israelite inquirers, which will be considered in relation to the design of the First Gospel, shows that he does not blame representatives of the nations for coming to Israel's light. It is the scribes and Pharisees who are to blame for deceiving the proselytes about God's will for Israel and the nations.

This negative judgment involves more than censure of individual leaders or sharp disapproval of the views and behavior of certain groups. The scribes and Pharisees are teachers of Israel, "blind leaders of the blind" (Mt 15.14). The "woe" stands in the biblical tradition of "prophetic anti-Judaism"[32] and despite Jeremias' hesitancy on this point —it *does* appear to be directed "against the Gentile mission itself".[33] But this perspective is easily distorted, and perhaps inevitably so when separated from its original context. Jesus was a Jew calling the scribes and Pharisees back to their own deepest theological commitments.[34]

Jesus, like many other Jews in Palestine and the Diaspora, probably saw the nations' initiative in coming to Israel's light as a positive sign of the End.[35]

---

[30] E. Rivkin, "Meaning of Messiah", 393. *Cf.* J. Neusner, *Messiah in Context*, 74.

[31] Eduard Schweizer's translation of διπλότερον as 'more divided' resonates both with the ancient image of mask/face (ὑποκριτής) and with the modern image of 'a split personality' or 'a character lacking integrity'. *The Good News According to Matthew* (Atlanta: John Knox, 1975), 440.

[32] This very important concept is developed briefly but with admirable clarity by D. Hare in his essay "The Rejection of the Jews in the Synoptic Gospels and Acts", *Antisemitism and the Foundations of Christianity*, ed. A. Davies (New York: Paulist, 1979), 29.

[33] J. Jeremias, *Jesus' Promise*, 19.

[34] Like the later Rabbis, who sharply criticized the *perushim*, "Jesus appears as an essentially Pharisaic Jew." Salo Baron, *History of the Jews*, vol II, 67.

[35] Many references in the Hebrew Bible to "the eschatological pilgrimage of the Gentiles" to Zion are cited by J. Jeremias, *Jesus' Promise*, 60 *et passim*; *cf.* E.P. Sanders' summary appraisal: "The majority of Jews" supposed (at least) that "at the end, some Gentiles would be admitted to the people of God." *Jesus and Judaism*, 221.

In this sense he would not have been against *the proselyte movement* itself. But if, indeed, Jesus thought that the Pharisees were forcing the End, his strong disapproval of their involvement in the movement would be understandable. If we follow the analysis already begun above, however, we arrive at a basis for condemnation which is at once deeper and more subtle than disapproval of 'the impiety of forcing the End'. The Pharisees' system was moving away from an eschatological focus, disregarding Israel's need for atonement and circumventing personal repentance.[36]

The thought and lifestyle of the Pharisees is almost always misrepresented by the modern term 'legalism'. Modern Jewish writers are also correct in their objection to the translation of "Torah" as "law", even though this basis for outsiders' misunderstanding of Judaism has existed since the time the Septuagint represented תורה as νόμος.[37] Besides the distance which separates us from Jesus and the Pharisees of his day, long histories of development in both Christian and Rabbinic doctrine make it hazardous to reconstruct Jesus' judgment in precise theological terms. And yet it seems certain that his judgment was theological and precise.

Christian interpretations in the past which tended towards slander and libel usually (if not always) failed to press beyond Jesus' ethical judgment to its theological (or trans-moral) basis. In objective terms, it seems fair to say that two revolutionary developments in theology, represented by Jesus on the one side and the Pharisees on the other, are in confrontation here. Each side presumes to reach beyond ordinary ethics to an understanding of God's Torah and ultimate salvation.

The Pharisees' notion of individual salvation through the Law was as much a revolutionary departure from the ancient faith of Israel as was Jesus' teaching.[38] This Pharisaic assurance of salvation through precise observance of the Torah was increasingly inaccessible to "the scattered sheep of the house of Israel" even though it included provisions for changing individuals from the nations into Jews. But Israel itself was under the judgment of God and doomed

---

[36] *"Die jüdische Mission erklärt sich nicht aus der eschatologischen Erwartung des Judentums."* Heinrich Kasting, *Die Anfänge der urchristlichen Mission* (München: Kaiser, 1969), 30. But for Jesus' disciples, as Schuyler Brown emphasizes, "precisely because Jesus' coming was already the beginning of the end, a non-eschatological missionizing was impossible." "The Matthean Community and the Gentile Mission", *NovT* 22 (1980), 197.
With specific reference to Mt 23.15a, F. Hahn concludes that "even this proselytizing cannot be described as mission in the real sense: for ... what is finally decisive is not that the Gentiles worship the true God and make the right faith their own, but that they become Jews; the aim is their 'naturalization'." *Mission in NT*, 1961 [1959]), 24.

[37] "The tendency to ethicize Judaism, to understand it as a moral law, disconnected and isolated from the controlling reality of the covenant" is a distortion which can be traced to the LXX, according to H.J. Schoeps, *Paul: The Theology of the Apostle in the Light of Jewish Religious History* (Philadelphia: Westminster, 1961 [1959]), 27.

[38] H. Loewe asks, regarding Jesus' conception of faith, "Is it not perhaps something very old and even superseded?" "On Faith", Appendix I to C.G. Montefiore's *Rabbinic Literature and Gospel Teachings* (New York: Ktav, 1970 [1930]), 377.

to hell along with the heathen. Refinement of legal requirements for individuals which divert attention from the coming Kingdom of heaven are a deadly illusion.[39] The term 'hypocrites' or 'play-actors' in conjunction with 'scribes and Pharisees' does not imply that all of them were engaged in fraudulent practices which would create public scandals if discovered. Rather, everyone who sees himself or herself truly in relation to God's will must be scandalized into the realization of the need for salvation as a gift from God, quite independent of systems-refinement.

---

[39] E.P. Sanders' protest against the (Christian) caricature of "a degeneration of the biblical view in post-biblical Judaism" is justified. *Paul and Palestinian Judaism* (Philadelphia: Fortress, 1977), 419. Sanders' own descriptive term "covenantal nomism" is apt, encompassing the Pharisaic revolutionary development described briefly here. Certainly the idea of covenant was fundamental in 'the zeal for the law' noted above in relation to the Apostle Paul's opponents and Paul's own earlier commitments.

8

THE NATIONS IN THE DESIGN OF THE GOSPEL:
SIGNALS OF THINGS TO COME

Within the structure of the First Gospel, the fundamental theme of *promise and fulfillment* is expressed in many ways. We have designated the early chapters "signals of things to come" (1.1—16.20), and the later chapters "the establishment of the Kingdom" (16.21—28.20). Alternatively, the Gospel as a unit could be described as *signals of things to come*, the middle term between the earlier prophetic writings and the consummation of the Kingdom.

The *prima facie* claim of the First Gospel to be considered part of the literature of Israel is one basis for structural analysis of the book.[1] Acceptance of this claim determines the Gospel's literary context for the critical reader.[2] That the life and literature of Israel is the basic context within which Matthew's Gospel should be interpreted is a precritical idea, both in the sense that this

---

[1] "When ... we claim to speak of one kind of Judaism at a given period, we must not be accused of neglecting other kinds of Judaism ... of the same time and place. These too claimed to be not merely a part of 'Israel' but 'the true Israel'. The testimonies to these other kinds of Judaism are contained not only in the parts of the New Testament, *for example, Matthew*, produced in the later first century in the Holy Land. They also persist ... in those massive and important compilations under the names of Baruch, Ezra and Pseudo-Philo....". J. Neusner, "'Judaism' after Moore: A Programmatic Statement", *JJS* 31 (1980), 155 [emph added]. *Cf.* J. Jeremias, "*Die Muttersprache des Evangelisten Matthäus*", *ZNW* 50 (1959), 270-4.

[2] Just as a sentence defines a phrase, a collection of writings defines a single document within the collection, in "a hierarchy of tagmemes" (Kenneth Pike). Besides the literary and historical reasons for locating the First Gospel within the literature of Israel, see Brevard Childs, "The Canon as the Context for Biblical Theology", *Biblical Theology in Crisis* (Philadelphia: Westminster, 1970), 97-122.

assumption antedates the modern, critical period of biblical scholarship and in the sense that the notion has been abandoned if not explicitly repudiated in many modern critical studies.³

All of the New Testament writings claim continuity with the literature of Israel, of course, and this claim is advanced by the Christian collection of Old and New Testament books in one Bible. But Matthew's Gospel appears first on all extant lists of Gospels, and first in the New Testament canon.⁴ This order seems to have been based at least partly on the early Church's appreciation of the strong links with the older writings which are obvious in the First Gospel and which serve to tie the two Testaments together. The book begins with the declaration that Jesus is the Messiah, "son of David, son of Abraham" (Mt 1.1). This declaration, supported throughout the Gospel by references to biblical prophecies fulfilled by Jesus' words and deeds, leaves no doubt about the basic context within which the writer himself intended the book to be interpreted.

A. Arguments from Design

Besides reasserting our presupposition of the Gospel's 'Jewishness', we should further define our understanding of the evangelist's 'originality' as we consider the structure and design of Matthew's Gospel. The evangelist announces revolutionary good news. What God has done and continues to do in the Messiah Jesus is surprisingly new, although anticipated by the prophets long ago. As a motif this claim is clear throughout the First Gospel from the opening words (Βίβλος γενέσεως Ἰησοῦ Χριστοῦ Mt 1.1) to the conclusion (καὶ ἰδοὺ ἐγὼ μεθ' ὑμῶν εἰμι 28.19-20). But whatever originality Matthew displays in presenting this claim to newness, the claim itself is shared by all New Testament writers. Moreover, the originality of the Jesus Movement is not the only new thing which can be seen emerging from the traditions of Israel in Matthew's day. Radical changes were also taking place in what Jacob Neusner describes as "formative Judaism". We should emphasize once again that the

---

³ See K.W. Clark, "The Gentile Bias in Matthew", *JBL* 66 (1947), 165-72, especially Clark's assertion that "there is real difficulty in ascribing it to a Jew" (166). *Cf.* Poul Nepper-Christensen, *Das Mattäusevangelium: Ein Judenchristliches Evangelium?* (Aarhus: University Press, 1958), 297; Georg Strecker, *Der Weg der Gerechtigkeit* (Göttingen: Vandenhoek & Ruprecht, 1962), 15-35; and Wolfgang Trilling, *Das Wahre Israel: Studien zur Theologie des Matthäusevangeliums* (München: Kösel, 1964 [1958]), 197, responding to the 1928 argument of E. von Dobschütz.

Dobschütz' argument is interesting because he construes Matthew's 'Jewishness' as a *late*, 'catholicizing' feature of the Gospel, "Matthew as Rabbi and Catechist", *The Interpretation of Matthew*, ed. G. Stanton (Philadelphia: Fortress, 1983 [1928]), 28.

⁴ See Daniel Theron, *Evidence of Tradition* (London: Bowes & Bowes, 1957), 107. For a brief partisan review of attempts to claim also *chronological priority* for Mt among the Gospels see G. W. Buchanan, "Current Synoptic Studies: Orchard, the Griesbach Hypothesis, and Other Alternatives", *Religion in Life* 46 (1977), 415-425.

newness or originality of primitive Christianity must not be measured anachronistically against the Judaism defined later by the *Mishnah* and subsequent writings.[5]

As for Matthew's creativity as an editor, a number of Matthean scholars continue to speak of "contradictions"[6] and to imply in other words that Matthew was unable to maintain control of his material throughout the Gospel. But a strong current tendency of redaction critics is to emphasize Matthew's "theological and literary art"[7] to the point of insisting that Matthew (and the other evangelists of the canonical Gospels) should be acknowledged as "creative writers".[8] Going so far as to insist that any other view fails to give the Gospel writers the credit they deserve, some critics imply that the evangelists' historical (or 'historicizing') mode is very like the modern genre of historical novel.[9]

Since Jesus himself made up stories for use in proclaiming the Gospel (καὶ χωρὶς παραβολῆς οὐδὲν ἐλάλει αὐτοῖς Mt 13.34), we cannot rule out the possibility that some of the material in the First Gospel is likewise made up in patterns familiar to us from later Jewish and Christian writings. But in the following pages, our appeal to structure and design in the First Gospel credits Matthew with the creativity of a historian and theologian rather than that of a novelist.[10]

Albert Outler's maxim is relevant to current debates about Gospel genre:

> Historical truth *is* stranger than fiction and more difficult to make sense of. The plot of a novel gets its 'intelligibility' from the coherence of the author's imagination. Historical accidents have no such *logos*.[11]

---

[5] See earlier caveats (chapter 2, n2) on Kittel's *TDNT*, Moore's *Judaism*, and Strack-Billerbeck's *Kommentar*. Diachronic evidence can be used in valid linguistic and theological arguments, but the different dates must be factored into the analysis.

[6] Kenzo Tagawa considers "contradictory ideas expressed side by side with no attempt to harmony" as paradoxes of Mt's own community and ecclesiology. "People and Community in Matthew", *NTS* 16 (1969-70), 150. Georg Strecker emphatically states the widely-held notion that Mt, as a redactor, unwittingly carried forward expressions of earlier thought which categorically contradicted his own. *Weg der Gerechtigheit*, 16 *et passim*.

[7] E.g. Robert H. Gundry, *Matthew: A Commentary on His Literary and Theological Art* (Grand Rapids: Eerdmans, 1982).

[8] M.S. Enslin concludes "Luke and Matthew, Compilers or Authors?" with a rhetorical flourish, remonstrating against those who would "deprive the original gospel writers of the freedom and responsibility of being creative writers to whom the term 'author', not 'compiler', is certainly warranted". *ANRW: Principat* II.25.3 (1985), 2388.

[9] Gerd Theissen has adapted the historical novel to Gospel criticism, *The Shadow of the Galilean: The Quest of the Historical Jesus in Narrative Form* (London: SCM, 1987).

[10] Without attempting to define the relationship between *history* and *historiography*, we can observe that in some situations it is easier and less honest to 'make up stuff' to complete a report than to write a coherent account of what is known to have happened.

[11] A.C. Outler, "Theodosius' Horse: Reflections on the Predicament of the Church Historian", *Church History* 57 Suppl. (1988 [1965]), 11.

But the term "historical accidents" is not congenial to reflection on Matthew's composition, for it is *logos* that the evangelist has discovered in his materials. A theologian's creative discovery of intelligibility (in what was believed to have happened) is not the same thing as imaginative creation of materials.

The First Gospel is a historical document in the obvious sense that it is datable to the first century AD. But it is also historical in the sense that it relates historical information which can be compared, at least in part, to information from other sources. With reference to the Gospel's background, we have suggested a date of composition *ca.* AD 60, and a process of redaction involving some independence as well as strong relationships to the other canonical Gospels. Because an enormous amount of scholarly work has been devoted both to dating the Gospels and to determining Synoptic relationships, and because the arguments used for dating bear significantly on an understanding of the earliest Christian mission, we again briefly consider these questions before claiming information from the Gospel's structure and design.

The Date of Composition

According to Graham Stanton in his 1985 survey of recent Matthean scholarship,[12] "almost all scholars have accepted that the gospel was written after the fall of Jerusalem in 70 AD and before Ignatius uses Matthew about 115 AD.." Stanton's tally of published positions in the field is no doubt right, but in meaningful discussions arguments must be weighed, not counted. For determination of the outside boundary, Stanton might have mentioned the fact that second-century fragments of Matthew's Gospel have been discovered as far away as Egypt.[13] More significantly, by balancing AD 70, on the one hand, with the last possible date for composition of the Gospel on the other hand (AD 115), Stanton implies that 70 is the earliest conceivable date for the appearance of the written Gospel in its present form. But in objective, historical terms the earliest possible date for composition (*terminus a quo*) must follow Jesus' crucifixion (AD 30 or 33) and the last possible date (*terminus ad quem*) must precede Ignatius' quotations (AD 107 or 115). Within this uncontroversial time frame, four dates are noteworthy in relation to arguments based on the nature of the document itself: AD 62, AD 65, AD 70, and AD 90. Assumptions about the relative dating of Matthew-Luke, on the one hand, and about the relative dating of Mark-Matthew, on the other hand, have established boundaries for the absolute dating of Matthew's Gospel in the field of New Testament studies. Accordingly, we review these two sets of assumptions in anticipation of our reference to the Synoptic Problem.

Bo Reicke's assertion that Matthew's Gospel was written before the appearance of Luke-Acts is itself unremarkable. But his further claim that

---

[12] G. Stanton, "The Origin and Purpose of Matthew's Gospel: Matthean Scholarship from 1945 to 1980", *ANRW: Principat* II.25.3 (Berlin: W. de Gruyter, 1985), 142.

[13] Birger A. Pearson, *The Roots of Egyptian Christianity*, B.A. Pearson & J.E. Goehring, eds. (Philadelphia: fortress, 1986), 133.

"Luke composed Acts exactly in the year 62,"[14] if accepted, ends discussion of any later date for the composition of Matthew's Gospel. Reicke's position is based on the judgment that Luke-Acts is a single, two-volume (or two-scroll) book written by a single author. Arguing that the author would not have written the concluding sentence (Acts 28.30-31) if he had known of the martyrdoms of James and Peter (and Paul), Reicke concludes that Acts, and in turn Luke and Matthew (and Mark), must have been completed before AD 62.[15]

J.A.T. Robinson also accepts the date of AD 62 as marking the completion of Luke-Acts, emphasizing and elaborating Harnack's mature position (1911),: "Acts was written at the stage at which the narrative terminates."[16] Johannes Munck, likewise dates Luke-Acts in the early 60s and notes that the requirements of various theories about Synoptic relations provide no firm basis for a later dating of Acts.[17]

If Bo Reicke's AD 62 *terminus ad quem* is rejected or disregarded, normal procedures in current New Testament studies indicate AD 65 as the earliest date to be considered for the synoptic Gospels. Floyd Filson provides a convenient example of the majority opinion endorsed by Graham Stanton's 1985 survey article. Assuming Marcan priority, Filson arrives at a date of AD 80-90 for Matthew's Gospel after proposing AD 65 as the earliest plausible date for the appearance of *Mark's Gospel*.[18] This anchor point in AD 65, however, is itself arbitrary and the ten or twenty years allowed for development along the lines of the Two Document Hypothesis are approximate. Those who start with AD 65 quickly come to two historical phenomena represented by the dates AD 70 and AD 90 which demand consideration in their further reckoning.

The events of AD 66-70 had a formative influence on the church and its mission, as well as on Judaism. This is acknowledged on all sides. The Gospels could be expected to reflect the Fall of Jerusalem if they were written after these events. Accordingly, the several predictions in the Gospels of Jerusalem's destruction often have been considered to be prophecies *ex eventu* by critical scholars of the New Testament. For Graham Stanton such an understanding of Matthew 22.7 is the solid foundation upon which any reasonable discussion of the date of Matthew's Gospel must be built.[19] But

---

[14] Bo Reicke, "The New Testament Era and the Date of the Gospels", *Die Nuwe Testamentiese Wetenskap Vandag* (Pretoria: University Press, 1982), 67.

[15] Bo Reicke, *The Roots of the Synoptic Gospels* (Philadelphia: Fortress, 1986), 177-80.

[16] A. von Harnack, *Date of Acts and the Synoptic Gospels* (1911); summary statement by J.A.T. Robinson, *Redating the New Testament* (London: SCM, 1976), 91.

[17] J. Munck, *The Acts of the Apostles* (Garden City: Doubleday, 1967), liv; *cf.* J.M. Rist *On the Independence of Matthew and Mark* (Cambridge: University Press, 1978), 5.

[18] "If ... this Gospel depends on Mk. as its basic source ... we must date Matt. later than AD 66. The earliest possible date would be in the seventies, and a date in the eighties or even in the nineties would be preferable." F.V. Filson, *The Gospel According to St. Matthew* (London: A&C Black, 1977 [1960]), 15.

[19] G. Stanton, "Origin and Purpose", *op.cit.*, 1943; *contra* K.H. Rengstorf, *Judentum-Urchristentum-Kirche*, Fs. J. Jeremias, ed. W. Eltester (Berlin: Töpelmann, 1960), 106-129.

Stanton's dismissal of K.H. Rengstorf's 1960 article *"Die Stadt der Mörder (Mt 22.7)"* as an eccentric statement, easily dismissed, suggests that epistemological convictions which are stronger and deeper than exegetical arguments inform the judgment of critical orthodoxy on this text.

Already in 1947, C.H. Dodd demonstrated that nothing in Luke 19.42-44 or 21.20-24 indicates formulation after AD 66-70.[20] Stanton does not mention this article or Bo Reicke's 1972 essay on "Synoptic Prophecies on the Destruction of Jerusalem",[21] although he chides J.A.T. Robinson for citing Rengstorf's article without mentioning the responses of Wolfgang Trilling and Rolf Walker. But if C.H.Dodd, K.H.Rengstorf, Bo Reicke and J.A.T. Robinson are right in their exegesis of these texts (against W. Trilling, R. Walker and Stanton's majority), these very texts are strong evidence for dating Matthew and Luke before AD 70. Moreover, since Matthew's style allowed for references to the narrator's time (μέχρι τῆς σήμερον Mt 28.15), Robinson's starting point is also relevant: it is odd that the Fall of Jerusalem "is never once mentioned as a past fact".[22]

For scholars attempting to identify the time of the composition of Matthew's Gospel *after* the Fall of Jerusalem, the date AD 90 is a challenge because of the sharp division between church and synagogue represented by the anathemas associated with Jamnia. Any reconstruction of the evangelist's situation must account for some special 'Jewish' features of the First Gospel, so there is wide agreement that the Gospel's appearance could not have been much later than AD 90.[23]

The Diachronic Written Gospel

The diachronic nature of Matthew's Gospel is more significant for our study than its exact date of composition. Except for the words of the risen Jesus in the conclusion, all of the teachings and narrative in the Gospel represent the time before the Messianic mission to all nations. But the Gospel was written after this mission had been thoroughly established. Accordingly, *problems involved in claiming this Gospel as a source of information about the earliest Christian mission to all nations are not fundamentally changed whatever possible date is assigned to the document.* This point demands emphasis because most of the New Testament studies to which we refer assign a date later than *ca.* AD 60 to the Gospel in its present form. Some specific implications

---

[20] C.H. Dodd, "The Fall of Jerusalem and the 'Abomination of Desolation'", *Journal of Roman Studies* 37 (1947), 47-54.

[21] Bo Reicke, *Studies in New Testament and Early Christian Literature*, Fs. A.P. Wikgren, ed. D.W. Aune (Leiden: E.J. Brill, 1972), 121-134.

[22] J.A.T. Robinson, *Redating the NT*, 13.

[23] G. Stanton, "Origin and Purpose", *loc. cit.*; *cf.* W.D. Davies, *The Setting of the Sermon on the Mount* (Cambridge: University Press, 1964), 292 & 315; "The Council of Jamnia and its alleged date of about A.D. 90 is ... a convenient symbol for the culmination of long processes in early Judaism." Jack P. Lewis "Jamnia" *ABD* 3 (1992), 634.

of a date of composition in the 50s or 60s, rather than in the 80s or 90s, should be noted briefly.

The *earliest* Christian mission to all nations was nearer AD 33 than AD 66.[24] If the First Gospel was composed before AD 62 the book itself is a document of the three-decade period, not much later than the composition of the major Pauline epistles.

Many of the arguments for a late dating of Matthew's Gospel are based on assumptions which systematically preclude the possibility of gaining information about the earliest mission from the document. All such assumptions relate to what has been termed 'the criterion of dissimilarity'.[25] But where a saying or model of action can be shown to be particularly relevant to a situation later than AD 62 the possibility must be considered that the teaching or act was *remembered* because of new or continued relevance to the community.[26]

Synoptic Relations

Three fundamentally different understandings of the literary relationship between the synoptic Gospels are represented by the Griesbach Hypothesis, as advocated by W.F. Farmer and Bernard Orchard; the Two Document Hypothesis, which continues to dominate New Testament studies; and Multiple Traditions Hypotheses, such as the one outlined by Bo Reicke.[27] Among the scholars grouped together in these sharply divided parties there are significant differences which demand acknowledgement even in a summary listing.

Griesbach and his modern disciples propose the sequence *Matthew, Luke and Mark* as the solution to the Synoptic Problem, as indicated by the title of Bernard Orchard's 1976 book. In this scheme, as in the Augustinian solution which accepts the canonical order as chronological, the idea of *The Originality*

---

[24] If the earliest Christian mission galvanized Saul/Paul into violent opposition to the Jesus Movement before his turnabout (as we argued briefly in Chapter 4), this mission to the nations would have been in its third decade in the early 60s. See M. Hengel, "Beginning of the Gentile Mission in Antioch, *c* AD 34/38", *Acts and the History of Earliest Christianity* (London: SCM, 1979), 137.

[25] No doubt Mt was "written in order to adapt the traditional material to the current needs of the church in the author's day". But G.D. Caird correctly insists that "it is a *non sequitur* to argue that, because the form of a *pericope* has its *Sitz im Leben* in the needs or interests of the church, the content of the *pericope* so formulated must also have had its origin in those needs." "The Study of the Gospels", *ExpT* 87 (1976), 102 & 139.

[26] Gerd Theissen treats the synoptic Gospels as "the most important sources of the Jesus movement ..., the renewal movement within Judaism brought into being through Jesus and existing in the area of Syria and Palestine between about AD 30 and AD 70". *Sociology of Early Palestinian Christianity*, 3; *cf.* 1 & 4.

[27] W.R. Farmer, *The Synoptic Problem* (Dillsboro: Western North Carolina University Press, 1976 [1964]); Bernard Orchard, *Matthew, Luke and Mark* (Manchester: Koinonia, 1976); Bo Reicke, *The Roots of the Synoptic Gospels* (Philadelphia: Fortress, 1986).

of St. Matthew[28] is not restricted by the limits of the Two Document Hypothesis.

The dating of the Gospels and of component units are basic considerations in any calculation of Synoptic relationship. It is surprising, therefore, and noteworthy that two leading advocates of the modern Griesbach Hypothesis hold polar positions on the date of Matthew's Gospel. W.R. Farmer argues for a "post-war setting in Antioch of Syria" with Luke and Mark correspondingly later.[29] Orchard posits a date in the 40s for Matthew, with Luke and Mark in the early 60s.[30]

Critical Orthodoxy

The Two Document Hypothesis is a point of reference for very many current New Testament studies. It has become a kind of first principle for much of the recent redaction criticism of Matthew and Luke.[31] E.P. Sanders has protested that "the dominant hypothesis is frequently held too rigidly."[32] Even so, there are very significant differences in the way the Two- or Multi-Document Hypothesis is used by leading scholars. In part this is because one of the documents, '*Q*', is not now extant, if it ever existed. Already in his pioneering work in form criticism, Rudolf Bultmann allowed for the possibility that Matthew or Luke, as well as Mark, could represent the more primitive form of a synoptic unit.[33] Dating the penultimate stage of Matthew's Gospel, T.W. Manson concludes that "the compilation of what we now call *M* [Matthean material not in Mark or in '*Q*'] ... took place not later than about AD 65."[34]

---

[28] B.C. Butler is the most notable modern advocate of 'the Augustinian solution', but he neither claims Augustine's authority nor cites his arguments in this book. *The Originality of St Matthew: A Critique of the Two-Document Hypothesis* (Cambridge: UP, 1951), 8 & 66. Augustine himself came to see that the actual order of composition of the Gospels was likely to have been Mt, Lk, Mk, according to W.R. Farmer, *The Gospel of Jesus: Pastoral Implications of the Synoptic Problem* (Philadelphia: Westminster/ John Knox, 1994), 17.

[29] W.R. Farmer, "The Post-Sectarian Character of Mattthew and Its Post-War Setting in Antioch of Syria", *Perspectives on Religious Studies* 3 (Dansville, Virginia: 1976), 235-47. *Cf.* "Some Thoughts on the Provenance of Matthew", *The Teacher's Yoke*, eds. E. Vardaman & J. Garrett (Waco: Baylor University Press, 1964) 109-16.

[30] B. Orchard, "Thessalonians and the Synoptic Gospels", *Biblica* 19 (1938), 39 cited by J.A.T. Robinson, *Redating*, 106.

[31] "The whole edifice of redaction criticism is largely built upon the acceptance of the priority of Mark...." C.S. Rood, "The Synoptic Problem", *Expository Times* 78/9 (1977), 257. Nevertheless, as Norman Perrin points out, "redaction criticism really began with work on the Gospel of Mark." *What Is Redaction Criticism?* (London: SPCK, 1970), 2.

[32] E.P. Sanders, *The Tendencies of the Synoptic Tradition* (Cambridge: UP, 1969), 279.

[33] R. Bultmann, *The History of the Synoptic Tradition* (Oxford: Blackwell, 1968 [1931]), 3; see E.P. Sanders, *Tendencies*, 290-3 for a compilation of Bultmann's judgments.

[34] T.W. Manson, *The Sayings of Jesus* (London: SCM, 1954 [1937]), 24.

The assumption of Marcan priority is the lynch-pin of the Two-Document Hypothesis, and James M. Robinson is not alone in thinking that

> perhaps the most important new argument for Markan priority is the success of *Redaktionsgeschichte* in clarifying the theologies of Matthew and Luke on the assumption of the dependence on Mark.[35]

But much of the best work in these redaction- or composition- critical studies can be understood equally well in terms of structural linguistics, quite apart from any conviction about precedence in Synoptic relationships. Moreover, the persuasiveness of W.R. Farmer's reconstruction of Mark's *Redaktionsgeshichte* is ironic within the context of James Robinson's appraisal.[36] Perhaps "our entire study of the Synoptic Gospels would profit from a period of withholding judgments on the Synoptic problem while the evidence is resifted."[37] This proposal, stated by E.P. Sanders as part in his study of *The Tendencies of the Synoptic Tradition*, anticipates "a new view of the Synoptic problem ... more flexible and complicated than the tidy two-document hypothesis".[38]

Since 1969, when Sanders published this proposal, variations of the idea have been expressed by many others. As the small number of serious scholars committed to the revived Griesbach Hypothesis continues to grow within a field still dominated by the Two Document Hypothesis, some observers have sought ways "to preserve the solid acquisitions of both theories".[39] M.E. Boismard has suggested that recognition of "two different levels of redaction in Matthew" could be the key to such a compromise.[40] But a more fundamental realignment of both literary hypotheses would result from recognition of what Gordon Fee reconstructs as "the continuing tenacity of the oral tradition *alongside* the written documents as they came into existence".[41] Earle Ellis works to similar effect from another direction, insisting on the "probability for some written transmission of Gospel traditions from the time of Jesus' earthly ministry".[42]

Views of Dissenters

The third view of Synoptic relations, which we have labelled "Multiple Traditions Hypotheses", is not directly comparable to the Two Document Hypothesis or the Griesbach Hypothesis. If all significantly non-conforming

---

[35] J.M. Robinson, quoted by Orchard, *Mt, Lk & Mk*, 15.

[36] W.R. Farmer, *Synoptic Problem*, 233-83.

[37] E.P. Sanders, *Tendencies*, 279; echoed by Lamar Cope, *Matthew: A Scribe Trained for the Kingdom of Heaven* (Washington: Catholic Biblical Association, 1976), 5.

[38] Sanders, *ibid*.

[39] M.E. Boismard, "The Two-Source Theory at an Impasse", *NTS* 26 (1979), 1.

[40] *Ibid.*, 11.

[41] G.D. Fee, "A Text-Critical Look at the Synoptic Problem", *NovT* 22 (1980), 24.

[42] E. E. Ellis, "New Directions in Form Criticism", *Jesus Christus in Historie, Fs. H. Conzelmann*, ed. G. Strecker (Tübingen: Mohr, 1975), 304, with reference to Qumran.

ideas about Synoptic relationships were grouped together, their differences from the dominant hypothesis would hardly constitute a unity which could be considered 'a new view'. But three examples of views which have a certain generic relationship to each other can be cited which are 'more flexible and complicated than the tidy two-document hypothesis' (E.P. Sanders).

The published work of Birger Gerhardsson can be described as a sustained effort towards a solution of the Synoptic Problem, even though the questions he asks and answers in his studies are altogether different from those suggested by either the Two Document Hypothesis or the Griesbach Hypothesis. His own suggestion that Mark's Gospel was the first of the Synoptics to appear in its present form, for example, has almost none of the significance of 'Marcan Priority' in the Two Document Hypothesis.[43] He himself has not formulated his method and reconstructions as a 'Multiple Traditions Hypothesis', but he has emphatically warned against analyses of the synoptic Gospels which assume that "all elements in the gospel tradition originated in one and the same way".[44]

John M. Rist's study *On the independence of Matthew and Mark* challenges one of the few major points agreed upon by advocates of both the Two Document Hypothesis and the Griesbach Hypothesis. In this study the author's agnosticism over against the faith of critical orthodoxy is balanced by a remarkable readiness to believe the testimony of ancient witnesses.[45] All of Rist's arguments are worth considering, but his specific conclusions are not so important as his general procedure of treating the Gospels as historical documents. Some of the points made by Rist have long been disregarded by New Testament scholarship but are no less important for being obviously true. For example, he reminds us that we can be confident that Jesus said many things "twice or even three times, in more or less the same words .... What preacher doesn't?"[46] And, as Gerhardsson also notes in somewhat different terms, "The 'eyewitnesses' were not all eyewitnesses of every event."[47]

For Bo Reicke (as for John Rist), the judgment that the Gospels were composed before AD 62, during the period of living traditions (*vox viva*), is important for an understanding of Synoptic relations. This social context explains why their material "does not appear in the form of coherent firsthand accounts but mainly in the form of traditional pericopes".[48] Reicke's assessment of separate "local aspects" includes not only recognition of formative influences in Jerusalem and Galilee, but even "the contacts of Mark and Luke in Caesarea".[49] These specific contacts, attested by Paul's letter to Philemon (assuming a Caesarean imprisonment here), "are a convenient explanation for

---

[43] B. Gerhardsson, *The Gospel Tradition* (Malmö: Gleerup, 1986), 49, cited above.

[44] B. Gerhardsson, *The Testing of God's Son (Matt 4:1 & Par): An Analysis of an Early Christian Midrash* (Lund: Gleerup, 1966), 12.

[45] J. Rist, *Independence of Matthew and Mark*, 10-108.

[46] *Ibid.*, 92.

[47] *Ibid.*, 101.

[48] Bo Reicke, *Roots*, 47.

[49] *Ibid.*, 52.

the similarities between the Gospels which they were going to write ... preferable to any theory of literary utilization".[50]

To conclude this survey, we should admit that strict adherence to *either* the Two Document Hypothesis *or* the Griesbach Hypothesis imposes a methodological discipline on the interpreter of Matthew's Gospel which readers of the present study may feel the right to expect. For example, if the Two Document Hypothesis were followed, the striking omission of 'all nations' in Matthew's account of the incident in the Temple (Mt 21.10-14/ Mk 11.12-14, Lk 19.41-44 & Jn 12.12-19) would seem to be a statement in itself. For an alternative example, if the Griesbach Hypothesis were followed we would not lightly dismiss the longer or shorter endings of Mark's Gospel (which have a *prima facie* importance to the present study) since Matthew and Luke's similar endings would be considered already written before Mark concluded his Gospel.

One final note: the material found only in Matthew's Gospel is easily supposed to be secondary when the Two Document Hypothesis is followed —but not when either a Multiple Traditions Hypothesis or the Griesbach Hypothesis is accepted. In any case, Rudolf Bultmann's warning in his introduction to *The History of the Synoptic Tradition* is still relevant: The Two Document Hypothesis —even if basically correct— does not justify all of the methodological assumptions that have been derived from it.[51]

Structure and Intent

"Matthew exhibits a most precise and organized mind. His Gospel is most systematic."[52] A growing number of scholars concur with this judgment of Samuel Sandmel even if they cannot agree with each other in identifying the system. The very fact that so many different descriptions of Matthew's design can be defended, however, suggests that the redactor used different levels and types of structural elements to form a complex of traditional material into a coherent and compelling narrative. If this complexity is granted, descriptions of the structure of the Gospel are not so much right or wrong as simply more or less helpful to the interpreter.

Benjamin Bacon's 'Five Books' analysis has been attractive to very many of Matthew's commentators. But what makes the scheme so easy to remember, the idea that the First Gospel is a new Pentateuch, is tied to Bacon's quite mistaken view of the redactor's "neo-legalistic conception of 'the gospel'".[53] Accordingly, the usefulness of this rough division of the material in the Gospel is offset by the distortion insinuated by the mnemonic.

The most helpful outline for our purposes emphasizes the two "new beginnings in 4:17 and 16:21".[54] Whether or not the evangelist himself

---

[50] *Ibid.*, 52; *cf.* 166

[51] R. Bultmann, *The History of the Synoptic Tradition*, 1-3.

[52] S. Sandmel, *Judaism and Christian Beginnings* (New York: Oxford, 1978), 354.

[53] B.W. Bacon, *Studies in Matthew* (London: Constable, 1930), 131.

[54] Ned B. Stonehouse, *The Witness of Matthew and Mark to Christ* (Grand Rapids: Eerdmans, 1958 [1944]), 129.

intended the phrase *"from that time Jesus began..."* (ἀπὸ τότε ἤρξατο ὁ Ἰησοῦς) to be a section heading, Jack Kingsbury has shown that it can serve very well to divide the Gospel into three main sections which we have entitled *"Presentation"* (1.1 - 4.16), *"Proclamation"* (4.17 - 16.20), and *"The Establishment of the Kingdom"* (16.21 - 28.20).[55] The eschatological inauguration of the ingathering of the nations is certainly also a new beginning. Accordingly, a fourth division, "Exaltation of Jesus Messiah and Proclamation to the Nations" (28.16-20), would be consistent with our analysis. But this proleptic scene marks the beginning of the stage which extends beyond the Gospel narrative, so it is not part of our outline.

Every one of the three large units identified by Kingsbury has been indicated by some scholar as the section containing the 'key' or 'main thrust' of this Gospel. Herman Waetjen has proposed "The Genealogy as the Key to the Gospel according to Matthew"[56] and many scholars have considered Jesus' *teaching* as the evangelist's main interest. Certainly a strong case could also be made for the centrality of *the cross* in the structure of this Gospel. As a *resurrection* appearance, Matthew 28.16-20 is rightly included in Kingsbury's third unit, but in this final scene the exalted Messiah reveals God's *mission to the nations* through his disciples. It is the tradition of this revelation, according to Oscar Brooks, which motivated Matthew the evangelist to produce "a Gospel with a unified design".[57]

When considered among the pre-Christian writings of Israel, the First Gospel is certainly a new form. But the Hebrew Bible itself encompasses many different kinds of writings so that the genre 'gospel' (to use Mark's designation) should not be disqualified from a place in Israel's literature simply because it does not follow a form attested earlier.[58] The remarkable number of quotations and allusions to earlier biblical texts suggests that Matthew's 'gospel'

---

[55] J.D. Kingsbury, *Matthew: Structure, Christology, Kingdom* (Philadelphia: Fortress, 1975), 7-9 citing Stonehouse. *Cf.* Joachim Gnilka, *Das Matthäusevangelium*, vol I (Freiburg: Herder, 1986), 99. Kingsbury's titles for the three sections are 1/ "The Person of Jesus Messiah", 2/ "The Proclamation of Jesus Messiah", and 3/ "The Suffering, Death, and Resurrection of Jesus Messiah".

[56] H.C. Waetjen, "The Genealogy as the Key to the Gospel According to Matthew", *JBL* 95 (1976) 204-30.

[57] O.S. Brooks, "Matthew xxviii 16-20 and the Design of the First Gospel", *Journal for the Study of the New Testament* 10 (1981), 16. Otto Michel, in his 1950 essay, focuses his discussion on the last chapter of the Gospel but underscores the claim that *"the very composition of the whole chapter points to the climax in Matt 28:16-20"*. "The Conclusion of Matthew's Gospel", *Interpretation of Mt*, ed. G. Stanton, 31.

[58] With reference to the *term* 'gospel', Mark's use is best understood not as designating his literary genre but as noting the advent of 'the good news about Jesus Messiah'. Bo Reicke, *Roots*, 152. *Cf.* I Cor 15.1 and Ign *Smyr* 7.2. Later 'gospel' became the designation of a written form, specifically of the four canonical Gospels. See O. Cullmann, "The Plurality of the Gospels as a Theological Problem in Antiquity", *The Early Church* (London: SCM, 1956 [1945]), 37-54. With reference to new forms, the later *Mishnah* is also an innovation within the literature of Israel.

is a genre akin to targum or midrash.⁵⁹ But this Gospel is certainly very different from the Aramaic Targums and Tannaitic-Amoraic *Midrashim*, which are derivative in a much more obvious way from the earlier Scripture. Only if the terms 'targum' and 'midrash' are used very loosely (indicating not genre but a certain family relationship to earlier texts), can these terms be useful in locating Matthew's 'gospel' within the literature of Israel.

Like Deuteronomy and Chronicles (which have been compared to targums) and like Jonah (which has been described as a midrash), Matthew's Gospel declares the continuity and amazing development of God's covenant promises and mighty acts. But unlike earlier Scriptures, the Gospel according to Matthew proclaims the climax of God's continuing relationship with his people in the words and action of Jesus the Messiah. What is recorded in this book not only reflects but also *fulfills* earlier Scriptures.

B. Presentation

"The book of the origin of Jesus Messiah, the son of David, son of Abraham" (βίβλος γενέσεως Ἰησοῦ Χριστου ...) echoes Genesis 2.4 and 5.1 of the Hebrew Bible (*LXX*). These opening words can be interpreted to refer to the genealogy that follows immediately (*'the genealogy of Jesus Messiah'* Mt 1.1-17); to the first section of the Gospel (*'the introduction of Jesus Messiah'* 1.1 - 4.16); or to the entire Gospel (*'the book of the history of Jesus Messiah*, from physical conception to exaltation through death and resurrection' 1.1 - 28.20).⁶⁰

Matthew's account of Jesus' genealogy and birth, the visit of the Magi to Bethlehem, flight to Egypt and return to Nazareth, and the baptism of Jesus by John followed by temptation are clearly presented as *signals of things to come*. The focus on Jesus' promise to the nations is unmistakable. Only the explicit commission by the Jesus in the last words of the Gospel focus this promise more sharply. But if the evangelist's bias for the nations is revealed in the structure of his presentation, what might be called his universalism is so tightly bound to Israel as to appear to be a paradoxical expression of Jewish particularism.⁶¹

---

⁵⁹ "It is fairly generally agreed that Matthew makes extensive use of Jewish midrashim on Old Testament texts, yet uses them in an inside-out way: the facts of the Christ story are a commentary upon the Old Testament." J.D.M. Derrett, "Further Light on the narratives of the Nativity", *NovT* 17 (1975), 96. Derrett's term 'midrash' still relates to OT texts, but M.D. Goulder bases his study on the altogether different idea "that Matthew was writing a midrashic expansion of Mark", *Midrash and Lection in Matthew* (London: SPCK, 1974), 4.

⁶⁰ See discussions of Gen 2.4 and Gen 5.1 by H.C. Waetjen, "Genealogy as Key', *JBL* 95, 213-214; and by D. Hill, *The Gospel of Matthew* (London: Oliphants, 1972), 74-75.
Cf. Hubert Frankemölle, *Jahwebund und Kirche Christi* (Münster: Aschendorff, 1973), 362-3 and J.D. Kingsbury, *Matthew: Structure*, 11 contra Raymond Brown, *The Birth of the Messiah* (Garden City: Doubleday, 1977), 58-9.

⁶¹ See K.W. Clark's 1947 *JBL* article cited above, "The Gentile Bias in Matthew" (now also the title of a book of his collected essays). Our argument, sharply modifying Clark's, is that Matthew's bias for the nations is to be explained *in terms of his Jewishness* (Jn 4.22).

As historical (or historicizing) material, *the unit 1.1 — 4.16* is remarkable not only because much of the narrative has no parallel in any of the other canonical Gospels, but also because even the closest of Jesus' disciples could not have witnessed any of the scenes except part of the baptism. Even for the material in this first unit, however, Krister Stendahl's observation is relevant: biblical quotations were more likely to be affected by the facts, in Matthew's construction, "rather than that these are invented as suitable fulfillment of the prophecy. So we must start with the facts, as Matthew knew them."[62] This point is reinforced by Eduard Schweizer when he insists that "only those things that actually occurred in the life of Jesus or his disciples could have any import for the community" for which the Gospel was written. "That community was not interested in fabrication, but in the realities that would affect its members."[63] Matthew's Gospel, unlike later fictional embellishments of what was known of Jesus' life, was written under the constraints of living memory about Jesus of Nazareth and of vital traditions still being shaped by the Jesus Movement.

1. Genealogy

For most modern readers 'the begats' or genealogies are among the most exotic and least interesting sections of the Bible. Recognition of our distance in sympathy and understanding from this genre should warn us against moving quickly to dismiss the opening chapter as an inauspicious beginning to the First Gospel. An instructive preliminary move towards interpretation is a consideration of the meaning and function of genealogies in cultures where this genre of literature continues as a vital form.

In Part One of the present study Tiv (African) genealogies were cited with reference to John Orkar's analysis of "Patterns of Assimilation" in that nation, indicating how very different traditional Tiv genealogies are from the biological charts to which they bear a formal resemblance.[64] Robert R. Wilson's studies of biblical genealogies, which take anthropological studies into account, further expose the error of assuming biblical genealogies to be chronological tables.[65]

Within the Hebrew Bible itself different genealogies serve quite different purposes, and the warning in the Pastoral Epistles against "endless genealogies" (I Tim 1.3-7) indicates Christian disapproval of some of the first-century genealogical speculations which might have claimed continuity with biblical models. The genealogy in the First Gospel is positively significant, as its placement indicates, but we should consider the possibility that it also has significance as negative critique. As an example of Messianic apologetic, the

---

[62] K. Stendahl, *The School of St. Matthew* (Philadelphia: Fortress, 1968 [1954]), 197.

[63] E. Schweizer, *The Good News According to Matthew* (Atlanta: J. Knox, 1975), 11.

[64] J.N. Orkar, *A Pre-Colonial History of the Tiv of Central Nigeria C. 1500-1850* (Halifax, Canada: Dalhousie Ph.D. diss., 1979), 197.

[65] R. Wilson, "The Old Testament Genealogies in Recent Research", *JBL* 94 (1975) 169-89, *cf. Genealogy and History in the Biblical World* (New Haven: Yale, 1977), 2, 6-7, 193.

genealogy clearly intends to be a *final* example.[66] If there is any truth in Joachim Jeremias' assessment of concern for 'racial purity' marking the first-century interest in genealogies following the models in Ezra-Nehemiah,[67] Matthew's pointed inclusion of Tamar, Rahab, Ruth, and Bathsheba is a new direction and, indeed, a reversal. But polemic or negative critique against earlier and contemporary use of genealogies is expressed positively and creatively in this opening statement of the good news of the advent of God's son as the Messiah of Israel and Savior of the nations.

Most of the names in Matthew's genealogy of the Messiah can be found in the Hebrew Bible, but the structure is quite different from that of any other extant list. If IChronicles 1-3 is proposed as a source of Matthew's composition, we must acknowledge the large number of names not useful to Matthew. Moreover, there is a difference even in the first three names that can be compared, with "Jacob" called "Israel" in IChronicles 1.34. If some or all of the structure of the First Gospel's genealogy was already established in an intermediate source or sources[68] between the Hebrew Bible (including Chronicles) and the First Gospel, Matthew has included it into his design in a remarkable way. Three obvious features of the genealogy which relate significantly to the Messianic mission to all nations are the focus on *Abraham and David*; the inclusion of *Tamar, Rahab, Ruth and Bathsheba*; and the division into *three series of fourteen generations*.

Abraham and David

The significance of Abraham for an understanding of Israel and the nations was discussed in the Part One of the present study. No other figure in Israel's tradition so sharply focuses the paradox of particularity and universality in Yahweh's covenant promises. The fundamental role of Abraham in 'Paul's gospel' to all nations has also been noted.[69] Later persistent identification of Abraham with *proselytism* in Rabbinic writings can be seen as part of the continuing stream of interpretation reaching back to biblical texts such as Genesis 12.3 ("...in you all the communities of the earth shall find blessing"). David, like Abraham, focuses particular and universal covenantal themes in surprising ways in the Hebrew Bible. Not only was David an Israelite of the tribe of Judah but he also represents 'all Israel' and —somewhat mysteriously— 'Hebrews' (I Sam 22.2/ 29.3). As Yahweh's anointed, David is the prototype of

---

[66] This does not mean that Mt would have disapproved of Lk's (subsequent) exercise (Lk 3.23-38), but Mt would have disapproved of genealogical arguments for another messiah.

[67] J. Jeremias, *Jerusalem in the Time of Jesus* (Philadelphia: Fortress, 1969 [1937]), 294: "The families of pure race, and they alone, made up the true Israel." *N.b.* n75 below.

[68] H. Waetjen, "Genealogy as Key", *op. cit.* 207 ref Jos *Life* 1.1.6. Also assuming an intermediary source, G. Strecker characteristically attributes the count in the last list to Mt's carelessness in working with the material at hand. *Weg der Gerechtigkeit*, 38 n3.

[69] Rm 4.9-12 "...thus he was to be father of all the uncircumcised who believe." Cf. Gal 3.7 (& 2.11); note also the prominence of Abraham in Stephen's defence.

the Messiah (II Sam 7). But his traditional identification with the Psalms projects him also as a pilgrim and fugitive among the nations, like Abraham.

The conjunction of Abraham and David in the genealogy has significance not only in Matthew's *presentation* of Jesus as the Messiah (Mt 1.1 - 4.16), but also throughout the First Gospel. If Helen Milton is right, there is a specific chiasmic relationship between the conclusion of the Gospel (Mt 28.18-20) and the "special emphasis ... laid upon Jesus' relation to David and Abraham".[70] As the son of David, Jesus fulfills the covenant of II Samuel 7.16 ("your kingdom shall endure forever") and so Jesus can claim finally, "All authority on heaven and earth has been given to me" (Mt 28.18). As the son of Abraham, he fulfills the covenant promises of Genesis 18.18-19 (*cf.* 17.16 & 12.2-3):

> Abraham ... is to become a great and populous nation and all the nations of the earth shall be blessed in him. For I have known him in order that he may command his children and his household after him that they may keep the way of Yahweh to do righteousness and justice.[71]

Accordingly, the risen Jesus can direct his disciples to instruct his household of all nations "to observe everything I have commanded you" (Mt 28.20).

Tamar, Rahab, Ruth, and Bathsheba

Lineage is traced through the males in biblical genealogies, but women's names also appear now and again.[72] Even so, Matthew's reference to four women, besides Mary, in the Messiah's genealogy is extraordinary. Hartmut Stegemann correctly claims that

> *Tatsächlich gehört die Nennung dieser Frauen zu dem Beginn der darstellerischen Entfaltung eines Gedankens, der das ganze Evangelium von Anfang bis Ende wie ein roter Faden durchzieht.*[73] [Mention of these women is actually part of the beginning of a representative unfolding of an idea which runs through the whole Gospel, from start to finish, like a scarlet thread.]

---

[70] H. Milton, "The Structure of the Prologue to St. Matthew's Gospel", *JBL* 81 (1962) 176.

[71] *Ibid.*

[72] M.D. Johnson exaggerates when he says that "names of women are rare in Jewish genealogies." *The Purpose of the Biblical Genealogies with Special Reference to the Setting of the Genealogies of Jesus* (Cambridge: University Press, 1988 [1969]), 153.
Johnson's words here are the same as those in the ET of Gerhard Kittel's θαμάρ article in the *TDNT*, which also cites St-B I, 15. Johnson himself notes a number of women's names listed in the Chronicles genealogies. Perhaps he and Kittel distinguish between biblical and subsequent Jewish genealogical lists.

[73] H. Stegemann, "<*Die des Uria*> Zur Bedeutung der Frauennamen in der Genealogie von Matthäus 1,1-17", *Tradition und Glaube*, Fs. K.G. Kuhn, ed. G. Jeremias *et al.* (Göttingen: Vandenhoeck & Ruprecht, 1971), 246.

Even if Matthew's first readers had not paid special attention to the names of Tamar, Rahab and Ruth, they could hardly have failed to notice the astonishing reference to Bathsheba as "the wife of Uriah".[74] Against a strong current of opinion in Jesus' and Matthew's day, this list insists that representatives of the nations had honored positions as members of the people of God.[75] The inclusion of these four women also reminds readers of the First Gospel that God's grace defies pious calculations.

Whether or not Tamar was a Canaanite,[76] mention of her irregular sexual union with Judah incidentally reminds the reader that Judah's legitimate wife *was* "a Canaanite woman, Bathshua" (I Chr 2.3 /Gen 38.2). In a way reminiscent of Paul's argument about the faith of Abraham preceding the rite of circumcision (Rm 4.11), Matthew compels his reader to face the fact that the divine ordinances given by Moses and Joshua preparatory to the Conquest, and by Ezra and Nehemiah at the time of the Restoration, were not yet in force at the time of the Patriarchs. This point is unavoidable with reference to Rahab's acceptance into Israel in the tribe of Judah (Mt 1.5/ Josh 2.14-15; 6.17).

Ruth and Bathsheba ("the wife of Uriah") are also included in the first epoch of the genealogy. In narrative chronology, however, their acceptance into Israel comes after the time represented by the prohibitions of Deuteronomy 23.3 ("no Moabite may ever be admitted") and Exodus 34.16 ("neither shall you take their daughters as wives for your sons" *cf.* Deut 7.3). Ruth was certainly a Moabite, and Bathsheba —whose name is the same as that of the Patriarch Judah's wife— was probably a Canaanite or Hittite.[77]

---

[74] *Ibid.*, 253.

[75] "The whole community of Judaism at the time of Jesus was dominated by the fundamental idea of the maintenance of racial purity." J. Jeremias, *Jerusalem*, 270. This unrevised 1937 opinion must be viewed with suspicion. (See above, page 35 n64.) Nevertheless, something like 'concern for racial purity' can be traced back to Jesus' time. *Cf.* M.D. Johnson *Purpose*, 85. Earlier Johnson distinguished between the purpose of Ezra-Nehemiah and the purpose of the Chronicler in composing genealogies, a distinction emphasized by H.G.M. Williamson, *Israel in the Books of Chronicles* (Cambridge: University Press, 1977), 61, 71-82.

[76] That Tamar was a Canaanite seems obvious from the story in Gen 38.6-30 and could be implied in I Chr 2.3-4, which includes the name of her Canaanite mother-in-law Bathshua. *Cf.* Ruth 4.11-12. So, on the one hand, S.J. DeVries identifies her as "the Canaanite wife of Judah's eldest son, Er". "Tamar", *IDB* 4, 515. On the other hand, the stories in *Jubilees* 4 and *The Testaments of the Twelve Patriarchs: Judah* 10-15 make a point of identifying Tamar as an Aramaean. But these later stories seem less likely to have accurate information than to have been inspired in part by the challenge of extricating the matriarch of the Tribe of Judah from the ban on the Canaanites.

[77] Many commentators suggest that Bathsheba was originally an Israelite who lost 'caste' by marrying a Hittite. Dubbing this into the story makes her volitional move seem more blameworthy in an ethics of 'maintenance of racial purity' than the happenstance of birth. In any case, Bathsheba —like Judah's second wife— seems to have been a Canaanite; stories identifying her as an Israelite probably were composed for that purpose.

The biblical book of *Ruth* implies a fundamental resolution to the problem posed by a literal application of the earlier ban in the time of the Judges and later. Without disregarding or relaxing the absolute force of the prohibition against accommodating the ethos and religion of the Moabites, the biblical solution allows for —and celebrates— Ruth's conversion and 'coming over' into covenant with the God of Israel (Ruth 1.16-17/ 2.11-12). If, alternatively, the absolute prohibition were defined in terms of national origin and 'blood lines' David himself would be posthumously 'excluded from Israel'. A casuistic solution to the problem defined in these terms in the second century AD is recorded in the *Mishnah*.[78]

The threat to Solomon's 'legitimacy of ancestry' is immediate if, indeed, Bathsheba was a Canaanite or Hittite. 'The concern for genealogical purity' can be traced back at least as far as the time of Ezra and Nehemiah and certainly became a major issue in second-century Rabbinic Judaism.[79] This 'narrowing of genealogical interest' together with messianic speculation would have made David's miscegenation more troublesome to some pious minds than his admitted adultery and murder. Confident of his readers' commitment to the idea of a Davidic Messiah, Matthew confronts them with the absurdity of 'blood-line' definitions of covenant so stringent as to disqualify even David and Solomon from membership.

If the four women listed in the genealogy are representatives of the nations who are to be united with Israel through the Messiah, each in a different way also represents the transcendent power of God to transform human relationships and possibilities. The very term ἔθνη can serve as a synonym for sinners.[80] But Ruth, the faithful daughter-in-law, elicits the acknowledgement that there are also some righteous among the nations, even if Rahab the prostitute in her former state fits the stereotype of the heathen. David is clearly guilty for establishing his relationship with "the wife of Uriah", even though God is able to transform this evil beginning to a good end. (Bathsheba herself seems not to be blamed in the biblical text or in traditional interpretations.) If we accept Judah's relative judgment that Tamar is "more righteous" than he (Gen 38.26), her deliberate action is so shocking, nevertheless, that the guilt of both seems obvious. Nevertheless, the tradition of excusing Tamar completely and praising her as a model of faith might already have influenced Matthew and his readers.[81] The tradition of praising Rahab is easier to affirm since her

---

[78] *Yebomoth* 8.3, Danby trans. 229. This is a bizarre early example of arguments which deny that male grammatical forms in the Bible are sometimes inclusive.

[79] M.D. Johnson, *Purpose*, 85-6. J. Jeremias notes that "the greater part of the references concern membership of *the tribe of Judah*, and especially among them those concerning membership of *the line of David*". Jeremias does not mention —and perhaps did not notice— the irony of such a focus in the quest for 'racial purity'. *Jerusalem*, 276.

[80] Consider also modern connotations of *'Heiden'*, 'heathen', and 'pagans'.

[81] Renée Bloch emphasizes this strongly, but does not deal with the question of dating the tradition, "'Juda Engengre Pharés et Zara, de Thamar' Matth. 1,3", *Melanges Bibliques Fs. Andre Robert* (Paris: Bloud & Gay, 1957), 381-9. *Contra* St-B and G. Kittel,

decision of faith itself makes a story which can be explained to children without embarrassment (Josh 2), and she can be assumed to have led a changed life thereafter. That she continues as a symbol of God's transforming power as well as an example of faith is emphasized by her citation elsewhere in the New Testament as "Rahab the prostitute" (Heb 11.31 & Jas 2.25).

The Messiah's identification with sinful humanity, in his origin as in his baptism and temptation, is stunningly complete, yet transcendental. Some interpreters have pressed the stories of these four women into a single paradigm proving that the Messiah's "grace is to fulfil its work through the fall of man".[82] Such a neat *felix culpa* formulation is seriously amiss. It is also a mistake to identify these women as 'types of Mary', and it would be even less appropriate to designate the four as 'types of the Holy Spirit' (Mt 1.18). Nevertheless, the reference to the four women does prepare the reader for the 'holy irregularity' of Jesus' conception by the Holy Spirit.[83] The shifts in grammar and logic (such as the tally of the third fourteen) are not lapses on the part of the writer but rather signals of Jesus' 'paternity on two levels'.[84]

Counting the Messiah

The long series which repeats the phrase 'he became the father of' (δὲ ἐγέμμησεν τόν ... 39 times) "is unexpectedly broken at the very end" with the appearance of Joseph, 'the husband of Mary from who was born Jesus who is called the Messiah' (Mt 1.16), as Herman Waetjen notes.[85] As a matter of fact, what is so carefully detailed up to this point "is not the divine paternity of Jesus but the genealogy of Joseph that legitimates Jesus as king of the Jews".[86] When 'the origin of Jesus Messiah' is restated in verses 18-25, Mary is declared

---

H. Stegemann declares, "*Keine einzige dieser Frauen betrachtete man damals unter dem Aspekt der 'Sünderin'.*" <*Die des Uriah*> 260.

[82] G. Kittel, Θαμάρ, Ῥαχάβ, Ῥούθ, ἡ τοῦ Οὐρίου, *TDNT* 3 (Grand Rapids: Eerdmans, 1965 [1938]), 1.

[83] K. Stendahl, "Matthew', *Peake's Commentary on the Bible*, ed. Matthew Black & H.H. Rowley (London: Nelson, 1962), x. *Cf.* Raymond Brown, *Birth*, 73-74. The suggestion that the four are introduced in an apologetic effort to combat Jewish slurs on Mary is anachronistic even if the First Gospel is dated as late as AD 95. Moreover, the list makes no sense as apologetic, perhaps "it was the birth narratives themselves that actually stimulated such calumnies." W.D. Davies, *The Setting of Sermon on the Mount* (Cambridge: UP, 1964), 66. *The Samaritan Chronicle II*, a medieval text which claims neutrality in Jewish-Christian disputes, laments the unnecessary reference "to non-Israelite elements in Jesus' ancestry and the (alleged) improper relationships between certain male and female ancestors" in the first Gospel's genealogy. J. MacDonald & A.J.B. Higgins, "The Beginnings of Christianity According to the Samaritans", *NTS* 18 (1971-72) 54.

[84] See Cyrus H. Gordon, "Paternity at Two Levels", *JBL* 96 (1977) 101.

[85] H.C. Waetjen, "Genealogy as Key", 205.

[86] C.H. Gordon, "Paternity", 101.

the human parent who begat Jesus ἐκ πνεύματος ἁγίου.[87] Jesus is the adopted son of Joseph, the natural son of God.[88]

Whether or not the schematized form of this genealogical table can be traced back to Matthew the tax collector, we can be sure that the evangelist knew how to count.[89] The Messiah is the fourteenth name in the third list. He marks the end of an era and the beginning of a new age. The identity of Jesus with the Messiah is fundamental to the Gospel, of course, and so it is possible and even apparently necessary for us to count "Jesus ... the Messiah" as a single, thirteenth, entry in this list. But Waetjen is surely right in insisting that "no solution that hopes to be adequate can ignore the fact that the genealogy is incomplete" in this reading.[90] The fundamental solution, which is not explained in the genealogy itself and only becomes obvious in the Gospel's concluding statement, is that "Jesus is the one who begets a new beginning."[91] In his own person, through death and resurrection, he represents two generations.[92]

The three epochs, the number fourteen, and individual names besides those of the four women have significance that could be explored.[93] Certainly much more than we have briefly noted could be said about Abraham and David as types of the Messiah. But we conclude this discussion of the genealogy by suggesting one more argument from design.

Everything in the genealogy points to the Messiah and can be referred to him. But since everything that follows explains his significance, the genealogy itself simply ends with his name. In the first epoch, the phrase "Judah and his brothers" (Mt 1.2) represents 'all Israel'. In the second epoch, "Jechoniah and

---

[87] J. LaGrand, "How Was the Virgin Mary 'Like a Man'? (ܐܝܟ ܓܒܪܐ) A Note on Mt.i 18b and Related Syriac Christian Texts", *NovT* 22 (1980), 106-7.

[88] See Adolf Schlatter's apt section heading for Mt 1.18-25: *"Die Einpflanzung Jesus in das Geschlecht Davids", Der Evangelist Matthäus* (Stuttgart: Calwer, 1929), 7.
The term υἱοθεσία does not appear in the First Gospel, but the application of the concept to Israel and the nations is fundamentally important in the quotation from Hos 11.1 (Mt 2.15), in the teaching on prayer (Mt 6.8), and throughout. *Cf.* Paul, Rm 8.15-17.

[89] Various explanations are given by commentators for the total of the three fourteens, including G. Strecker's (already cited above) that the redactor overlooked an error in his source. *Weg der Gerechtigkeit*, 38 note 3. E.J. Goodspeed claims "the strange quasi-mathematical feature of the genealogy" as evidence that Mt the tax-collector is the author of the First Gospel. "There is an arithmetical subtlety about this which can only be regarded as the literary device of a practiced mathematician." *Matthew, Apostle and Evangelist* (Philadelphia: Winston, 1959), 60.

[90] H.C. Waetjen, "Genealogy as Key", 214.

[91] *Ibid.*, 215. Waetjen cites Hofmann (1841) and T. Zahn (1905).

[92] "Mt counts the Messiah the 14th, while Jesus is the 13th. 'Christ' should then refer to Jesus in his risen state and/or at his coming (parousia) at the end of time." K. Stendahl, *Peake's Commentary*, 770.

[93] The rhetorical significance of three epochs beginning, in turn, with Abraham, David, and the Exile is obvious. Since the number fourteen equals the three consonants of David's name (4+6+4), J. Jeremias has suggested a Davidic stamp on the whole list, along with more complicated systems related to I Enoch 93.1-10 and 91.12-27. *Jerusalem*, 292.

his brothers" (Mt 1.11) represents the solidarity of God's people in Exile. In the third epoch, beginning the new age, the reader can project this pattern in anticipation of the reunion of the Messiah 'and his brothers' from all nations (Mt 28.19-20 cf. 28.10).

2. Bethlehem — Egypt — Nazareth

"It is obvious that the birth narratives are woven from materials that had been frequently used in regular worship," according to Paul Minear.[94] This appraisal seems particularly apt with reference to Matthew's second chapter. The story of the adoration of the Magi, the escape to Egypt from Herod's jealousy, and the return of Joseph, Mary and the infant to Nazareth has long been celebrated in pictures, pagents, and songs. Besides manger scenes and Sunday School plays in our own time, art representing the motifs of this story from other centuries and different cultures is familiar to most modern readers of the First Gospel. But however the elements of the story were formed and came to the evangelist, the narrative he presents is coherent and challenging. If we are willing to suspend judgments about the star and the divine warnings in dreams (Mt 2.12, 13 & 22), it is also historically plausible.

The mysterious Magi have often dominated reflections on this story, especially with reference to the evangelist's understanding of the Messianic mission to all nations. These 'wise men from the East' demand close scrutiny. Krister Stendahl's challenging article *"Quis et Unde?"* incidentally points out the importance of geography in the chapter for our theme also.[95]

If the narrative in chapter two begins some weeks or even months after Jesus' birth, Τοῦ δὲ Ἰησοῦ γεννηθέντος ἐν Βηθλέεμ is best translated, "After the birth of Jesus in Bethlehem ...." Assuming this interpretation to be correct, we should note that the First Gospel gives no account of the birth day. Certainly nothing in chapter one qualifies as a story of Jesus' birth. Matthew 1.18-21 is "an extension or explanation of the genealogy," as L. Cantwell rightly insists. By way of warning, Cantwell notes that Bible translations and commentaries most often give that section the heading "The Birth of Jesus".[96]

The only *Kindheitsgeschichte* or 'infancy narrative' in Matthew's Gospel is this second chapter, which is closely linked to the first and moves quickly on to an account of Jesus' baptism and temptation. Adolf Schlatter's summary title, *"Der Kampf der Königs gegen den Christus"*, represents the plot line of the story well and also provides a useful focus of the main theme at this point in the evangelist's presentation of the Messiah.[97] But this title is negative and the story, despite the terrible example of Herod's depravity, is positive good news.

---

[94] P. Minear, "The Interpreter and the Birth Narratives", *Symbolae Biblicae Upsalinenses* 13 (1950), 17.

[95] "Matt. 2 is dominated by geographical names." K. Stendahl, "Quis et Unde?" *Interpretation of Mt*, ed. Stanton.

[96] L. Cantwell, "The Parentage of Jesus Mt 1:18-21", *NovT* 24 (1982), 306.

[97] A. Schlatter, *Matthäus*, 25.

The episodic title "Bethlehem, Egypt, Nazareth" has the advantage of celebrating not only the survival but also the adventure of the refugee family.

The Magi represent the nations attracted to Israel's light. In a story remarkable for its congruence and interrelatedness to biblical traditions, the name 'Magi' itself is in every sense alien. The evangelist's identification of the *"Erstlinge der Heiden"*,[98] therefore, requires further explanation to which we shall return. But first something should be said about what appears to be the most basic Jewish motif in the chapter.

A Star from Jacob

If the evangelist considered the fulfillment of Baalam's ancient prophecy so obvious as not to require citation ("A star shall advance from Jacob ..." Nu 24.17) his narrative judgment is better here, perhaps, than in some similar points in his composition.[99] But the intense study of this passage by Essene monks[100] and the fact that a Messianic pretender (more than fifty years after the appearance of the First Gospel) was called *"Bar Kokhba"*, 'Son of the Star', perhaps allow us to assume the text to be considered read.[101]

Postponing, for the moment, identification of the Magi except as foreigners in the land of Israel, it can be said that in Matthew's telling of the story they are certainly models of faithful submission to divine revelation, in stark contrast to the response of official Judaism in Herod's court. In Jerusalem even the very oracles of God (Rm 3.2) have become instruments of political intelligence. Judea's evil compromise with Roman power seems to have reached its nadir. Protected by God's providence, however, the Magi learn what they need to know from the Jewish scholars and continue following the star in simple faith.

Herod's earlier cross-examination of the travellers about the exact time of the star's appearing (Mt 2.6) and his subsequent slaughter of all boys in the town up to two years old (Mt 2.16) suggest that the Magi appeared about a year after Jesus' birth. If Matthew also knew stories of the birth day, such as those recorded in Luke's Gospel, he nevertheless gives first place in his account to these foreigners for the recognition and worship of Israel's Messiah. The readers' impression that these representatives of the nations have been directed by God to make a beginning in discipleship is confirmed by their faithful response to the divine warning in a dream (Mt 2.10). Accepting the personal risk implied, they return home without reporting to Herod.

---

[98] W.A. Visser't Hooft, "Die Magier und die Mission", *Basileia*, *Fs.* W. Freytag (Stuttgart: Ev. Missionsverlag, 1959), 208.

[99] "Although there is no explicit reference to this astrological oracle, certain features of Matthew's narrative suggest a connection with it." This base hardly supports the weight H. Waetjen gives to Num 24.17-18 in his treatment of Mt 2. *The Origin and Destiny of Humanness* (San Rafel, California: Crystal Press, 1976), 66.

[100] Bo Reicke, *Roots*, 73 citing *IQM* XI. 6ff., *CD* VII. 18-21, and *Q Testim* 9-13.

[101] S.V. McCasland, "Magi", *IDB* 3, 223.

If this summary demonstrates that Matthew's telling of the story is *a signal of things to come* in terms of the Messianic mission to all nations, important questions remain about *"Die Magier und die Mission"*, nevertheless.[102] How, specifically, do these Magi represent the nations?

The portrayal of the Magi as eastern monarchs in later Christian art can be dismissed from consideration of Matthew's account. The Magi are dressed outlandishly in the earliest extant pictures, but never as kings.[103] Moreover, the substitution of kings in later legends can be explained as a solution to the problems which *Magi* posed for the Church in the first centuries.[104] But if not kings, are the Magi 'wise men' (*Weise*) as Martin Luther and most modern translators indicate?[105]

The idea of 'wise men' who are prepared for a divine sign by the integrity of their study of 'natural theology' may have its own value, like the later legend of 'the three kings', but Matthew tells a different story. Already in the book of Daniel (*LXX*), *"Die Weisheit der Magier und ihrer Kollegen ist Torheit."*[106] To be sure, in Matthew's day "some Magi in the Mediterranean area had established a sound reputation for both character and learning",[107] but this learning is not accommodated by Paul's gospel, as Luke's accounts of Paul's confrontation with Bar-Jesus (Acts 13.6-11) and Peter's confrontation with Simon Magus (Acts 8.9-10, 20-23) show. Nor is this learning accepted unchanged in Matthew's Gospel.

Lowther Clarke's interpretation of the gifts of gold, frankincense, and myrrh (Mt 2.11) as symbols of the Magi's craft and of their submission makes sense of the narrative.[108] This interpretation also matches Ignatius' very early comment: by the light of the star which led the Magi all magic was dissolved (ἐλύετο πᾶσα μαγεία Ign Eph 19.3). Visser't Hooft argues that Isaiah 47 is more immediately relevant to an understanding of the scene in Matthew's Gospel than Isaiah 60, and concludes his argument with the graphic suggestion that we

---

[102] W. Visser't Hooft, "Die Magier", 208-11.

[103] *Ibid.*, 208. See cover for Magi *ca.* AD 180.

[104] *Didache* 5.1 lists μαγεῖαι as marking "the Way of Death" (*cf.* 2.2). This 'Two Ways' section was probably formulated before the Gospel of Mt was written. The warning reappears in *Barnabas* 20.1. *Cf.* continuing warnings against magic by Justin Martyr, Tertullian, and Augustine cited by Visser't Hooft, *"Die Magier"*, 210.
The difficulty which the Magi caused the church argues for a solid tradition behind the story, to which Mt was a reluctant witness. *Re* details in Mt 2 see R. France, "Herod and the Children in Bethlehem", *NovT* 21 (1979) 98-120.

[105] W. Visser't Hooft, "Die Magier", 209.

[106] *Ibid.*

[107] S.V. McCasland, "Magi", *IDB* 3, 222.

[108] W.K.L. Clarke, "The Rout of the Magi", *Divine Humanity* (New York: Macmillan, 1936), 47.

illustrate this scene by replacing the pretty kings in our Christmas creches with medicine men or 'witch doctors'.[109]

These foreigners are certainly sympathetic human beings, as Matthew tells the story. But their pilgrimage is more than proof of individual humanity among the nations. Magi, representing heathen thought and life, are drawn by the light to Israel's Messiah.

Haven in Egypt

The escape to Egypt is a motif familiar to readers of the literature of Israel.[110] As a recapitulation of the message of the genealogy, this chapter focuses on Jesus' divine paternity, and God's power to protect his son.[111] But what is most remarkable for the mission to the nations is the transformation of Egypt from a symbol of oppression and bondage (Deut 5.5 & 15) to a haven and protector of Israel's Messiah. The light of this chapter brings out of the shadows the ancient image of Egypt as a place of refuge and salvation also for Abraham (Gen 12.10) and Israel (Gen 42.1-2; 43.1-2; & esp. 46.3). It is not necessary to accept S.G.F. Brandon's suggestion that the First Gospel was composed in Alexandria[112] to see that this chapter would have played a positive part in early missions to Egypt. Matthew's inclusion of these stories, which may even have been shaped in the earliest Christian mission to Egypt, also helps explain evidence of very early circulation of the First Gospel in Egypt.[113]

Galilee of the *Goyim,* where Jesus begins his ministry and where Matthew concludes his Gospel with the command of the risen Lord to his disciples to begin the mission to all nations, is the destination of the journey that began in the city of David. If Krister Stendahl is correct[114] in his identification of 'the shoot' (נצר) of Isaiah 11.1 as the referent of Matthew 2.23, this text is one of many proofs that the adopted son of David, like David himself, is called by God to begin his leadership of Israel as a fugitive and refugee among the nations.

---

[109] W. Visser't Hooft, "Die Magier", 211. *Cf.* C.S. Mann, "The Historicity of the Birth Narratives", *Historicity and Chronology in the New Testament* (London: SPCK, 1965), 50-1.

[110] *N.b.* Gen 46.3 "...go down to Egypt, for there I will make you a great nation." D. Daube cites reference to this text in Ex Rabbah 3.12 as "foreshadowing not only the redemption from Egypt but also the final redemption". *The New Testament and Rabbinic Judaism* (London: Athlone, 1956), 191.

[111] "Jesus is the Son of Abraham ... the entire history of Israel, which bears promise also for the gentiles, reaches its culmination in him (1:17; 8:11). Still ... Jesus is preeminently the 'Son of God'." J.D. Kingsbury, *Matthew* (Philadelphia: Fortress, 1986), 39.

[112] S.G.F. Brandon, "The Gospel of Matthew and the Origins of Alexandrian Christianity", *The Fall of Jerusalem* (London: SPCK, 1951), 217-48.

[113] B. Pearson, "Earliest Christianity in Egypt", *Roots of Egyptian Christianity*, 133.

[114] K. Stendahl, *The School of St. Matthew* (Philadelphia: Fortress, 1968 [1954]), 103 & 199.

3. Baptism by John and the Testing of God's Son

John the Baptist is an imposing figure in each of the canonical Gospels.[115] His significance in the First Gospel is indicated in a striking way by Matthew's characterization of the beginning of Jesus' public ministry with the same words which identified John's preaching: "Reform your lives! The Kingdom of heaven is at hand!" (Mt 3.2/ 4.17). We have already surveyed some of the historical evidence which indicates John's importance in defining the context of Jesus' ministry and the earliest Christian mission to all nations. The Matthean focus on Jesus' baptism by John and the voice from heaven now call for specific attention in the immediate context of Matthew's presentation of the Messiah, and in the design of the whole Gospel.

The opening genealogy has prepared the reader for John's challenge to Jewish claims of descent from Abraham (Mt 3.8-9). The four foreign women in the Davidic line are proof that God (who created mankind from clay) can graft any human being into Abraham's family. The Baptizer declares that physical blood lines are as irrelevant as the stones on the path.[116]

Solidarity with Israel

Jesus' submission to John's baptism is an act of solidarity with the people of Israel who are being called to repentance. Following the genealogy as it does, Jesus' baptism also confirms his adoption into David's line. But Jesus himself declared the deeper specific meaning of this act of submission. It is in order (πρέπον) "to fulfill all righteousness" (Mt 3.15). The meaning of these words could not have been clear to John before the explanatory confirmation by the voice from heaven (Mt 3.16-17). It is the authority of Jesus' person that over-rules John's objection ("John tried to refuse him..." Mt 3.14). The dynamics of the scene demands John's submission to the will of God, paradoxically, by accepting Jesus' submission.[117]

The grammar of Matthew's account of the divine response to Jesus' baptism focuses on Jesus' consciousness of God's confirmation. "He saw the Spirit of God descend like a dove and hover over him" (εἶδον πνεῦμα θεοῦ Mt 3.16). But the voice from heaven which declares Jesus' divine sonship is heard also by the Baptizer and others: "This is my beloved son on whom my

---

[115] The Fourth Gospel includes evidence of special sources of information and particular interest in the Baptizer. The Baptizer appears at the very beginning of Mark's Gospel and special materials in Mt and Lk include record of his teaching.

[116] *Contra* C.H. Kraeling who insists that "there is a difference between the thought of God *being able* to raise new sons to Abraham from the stones, and the thought that he had begun to do so by creating a new community into which Jews and Gentiles come on equal footing." *John the Baptist* (London: Scribners' Sons, 1951), 103. Kraeling (citing *Die urchristlich Taufe im Lichte der Religionsgeschichte* [1928], 27) opposes J. Leipoldt's formulation of proselyte baptism for 'Israel gone astray', but Kraeling does not explain just what John's declaration means, that God *is able* to create new 'sons of Abraham'.

[117] M. Barth, *Die Taufe - Ein Sacrament?* (Zollikon-Zürich: Evangelischer, 1951), 63.

favor rests" (Οὗτος ἐστιν ὁ υἱός μου Mt 3.17). Identification of Jesus as the Son of God is the fundamental motif in the genealogy, in the adoration of the Magi and escape to Egypt, and in the temptation which follows the baptism immediately.

If Matthew understood the words from heaven to be exactly those of the Hebrew text of Isaiah 42.1, his choice of ὁ υἱός μου to translate עבד would not be surprising even if unusual. But since Mark, Luke, and John also record υἱός (instead of παῖς, the more obviously correct translation of עבד), it is reasonable to suppose that the Hebrew word was בני. This word in the divine declaration invites recall of biblical texts such as Genesis 22.2 and Psalm 2.7 as well as Isaiah 42.1. Freedom from exact quotation of Scripture might be considered a mark of authenticity of the voice from heaven. But the Isaiah citation is fundamental for understanding the scene, as Oscar Cullmann has argued emphatically.[118]

In terms of Isaiah 42.1 (following Cullmann' argument), we can see that

> Jesus is baptized in view of his death, which effects forgiveness of sins for all men. For this reason Jesus must unite himself in solidarity with his whole people, and go down himself to Jordan, that 'all righteousness might be fulfilled'.[119]

Jesus submission to baptism is only the beginning of the fulfillment. Georg Strecker correctly emphasizes this, but when he writes *"noch ist nur ein Teil der* δικαιωσύνη" Strecker misleadingly suggests an approximation of 'all righteousness' to the sense of 'every requirement' or δικαίωμα.[120] Baptism is not so much 'a part' of Jesus' task as *the first step* on 'the way of righteousness' (Mt 21.32). Jesus' baptism is the inaugural symbol of everything that Jesus must say, do, and suffer.

This meaning is unfolded in the First Gospel by the story of Jesus' subsequent teaching and action, which marked the way for all who follow him. In the end, through his sacrificial death and resurrection, Jesus decisively opens this way to all nations and authorizes his disciples to baptize "in the name of the Father, and of the Son, and of the Holy Spirit" (Mt 28.19-20), bringing the Baptist's prophecy (Mt 3.1) to fulfillment.[121]

The Law and the Prophets

The terms of Jesus' 'fulfillment of all righteousness' in the First Gospel are best understood in relation to Matthew's characteristic phrase 'the law and

---

[118] O. Cullmann, *Baptism in the New Testament* (London: SCM, 1950), 17. *Cf.* J. Jeremias, *The Proclamation of Jesus* (New York: Scribners, 1971), 55: "From the time of the baptism he was conscious of being God's servant promised by Isaiah."

[119] O. Cullmann, *Baptism in the NT*, 18.

[120] G. Strecker, *Weg der Gerechtigkeit*, 181. *N.b.* M. Barth *Die Taufe*, 64-67, including reference to LXX use of δικαιοσύνη to translate חסד (*e.g.* in Gen 19.19 & 32.10 [.11]).

[121] Cullmann, *Baptism in NT*, 22.

the prophets', not with reference to a narrow view of law.¹²² In this opening scene, John the Baptist not only is recognized as a prophet (or 'The Prophet' Mt 11.9), he even participates in the saving work of the Messiah: Jesus says to him ἐστιν ἡμῖν πληρῶσαι ("it is fitting *for us to fulfill* all righteousness" Mt 3.15). Jesus' lead role is explained, in turn, by the voice from heaven unmistakably reminding all who hear of the prophet Isaiah's message:

> Here is the servant whom I uphold;
> my chosen one with whom I am pleased;
> (I have put my spirit upon him.
> He shall make the right go forth to the nations.) Is 42.1

There is very little historical or literary evidence to control speculation about the development of John's understanding of Jesus' calling. But even if we limit ourselves to the text of the First Gospel, the apparent contradiction between John's description of the powerful Coming One and Jesus' self-identification with Isaiah's suffering servant of Yahwah is remarkable. J.P. Meier expresses the obvious when he says that "Jesus is a different type of Messiah from the one the Baptist and indeed all Israel had expected."¹²³ It would be easy to assume, therefore, that John's later questions from prison indicate continuing dissatisfaction with the specter of a suffering Messiah. But the design of the First Gospel indicates another explanation.

As we have seen, Matthew gives no reason to suppose that John understood Jesus' puzzling statement (Mt 3.15/ 13.34) *before* submitting to Jesus' personal authority. But we can be sure that the prophet John understood the voice from heaven as confirmation of Jesus' declaration, and also as the words from which to interpret and understand Jesus' ministry.

The Questions from Prison

John's faithfulness to Jesus is never in doubt, in the opening scene or when John sends a deputation to Jesus from prison (Mt 11.2-19). Even in Matthew's account of the Baptist's martyrdom, this loyalty is represented by the concluding note that John's disciples travelled to inform Jesus of his death (Mt 14.12). The question from prison in response to the reports of Jesus' messianic deeds (τὰ ἔργα τοῦ χριστοῦ Mt 11.2) certainly expresses radical doubt. But Jesus' eloquent testimony to the Baptist's character which follows the question and answer immediately (Mt 11.7-14) does not encourage the easy assumption that John's own incarceration prompted brooding despair about the future of the movement.

---

¹²² "Law is ... to be understood in relation to, in analogy with, prophecy. *Mt 5:18* explains this relationship or analogy." J.P. Meier, *Law and History in Matthew's Gospel* (Rome: Biblical Institute, 1975), 123 & *passim*. *Cf.* W. Zimmerli, *The Law and the Prophets* (Oxford: Blackwell, 1965); and Chapter 6 above.

¹²³ J.P. Meier, "John the Baptist in Matthew's Gospel", *JBL* 99 (1980), 393.

After the revelation from heaven identifying Jesus as the Son of God, we can assume that John began to apply himself to reflection on Isaiah's prophecy and especially on Isaiah 42.1. The First Gospel, if not its modern commentators, encourages the reader to suppose that John would have been able to submit to the apparent contradiction of a suffering Messiah. If the voice from heaven seemed to demand such submission in faith, however, the very words of that revelation could explain John's question in chapter eleven. This question about 'messianic deeds'[124] appears just after the record of the mission of the Twelve which had been restricted to the 'lost sheep of the house of Israel'. Anyone in prison, thinking again and again about the words of Isaiah 42.1, might respond to reports of such a mission with the question, "What about 'bringing justice (משפט / κρίσιν) to the nations'? When does that start?" Put more bluntly, "Are you the Coming One? Or should we expect another?" (Mt 11.3).

The Testing

Jesus' baptism and temptation are virtually two sides of the same event in Matthew's presentation, as in the other Synoptic accounts. The First Gospel declares Jesus to be the Messiah in the opening sentence which introduces the genealogy, and the baptism is the public presentation of the Messiah to Israel. Although public, this presentation is sharply focused on Jesus's own consciousness and personal commitment. As soon as he has been publicly anointed (τότε Mt 4.1) he is "led by the Spirit into the wilderness".[125]

Even if we understand the account of the temptations as representative of Jesus' personal experience just before beginning his public ministry, it is obvious that "the description which the gospels give of that time of withdrawal is ... highly symbolic."[126] Birger Gerhardsson aptly describes the account as "The Testing of God's Son" and identifies the form as *haggadic midrash* on Deuteronomy 6-8.[127] Certainly Jesus' forty days in the wilderness recapitulates Israel's forty years in the wilderness. Jesus' responses to the three temptations can be understood also to anticipate keynotes of his earthly ministry: 'implicit obedience to the will of God', 'trust in God which asks no proof', and

---

[124] This is the most obvious translation of the phrase. ("The genitive with the function of adjective is the commonest way in which the case is used." Blass-Debrunner/ Funk #162.) Textual critical questions should be dealt with separately (and prior to) questions of interpretation. Readings are either original or not. The textual evidence for this reading in Mt 11.2 is strong, with mss witnesses including P19, ℵ, and B. The discussion of modern commentators suggests that this is *lectio difficilior*. Our interpretation implies an authentic carryover from pre-Christian 'messianic' usage, *contra* the argument that "the language here seems to be that of later Christianity" (D. Hill, *Mt*, 197).

[125] B. Gerhardsson, *The Testing of God's Son* (Lund: Gleerup, 1966), 19.

[126] C.H. Dodd, *The Founder of Christianity* (London: Macmillan, 1970), 123.

[127] B. Gerhardsson, *Testing of God's Son*, 11.

'a dedicated allegiance to God which excludes all lesser claims'.[128] But the third test relates particularly to the nations (Mt 4.8-9).

The devil's offer of 'all the kingdoms of the world' in exchange for token homage can be translated as bowing to Rome. In Jesus' day this was a strong temptation; in Matthew's day it was re-focused by demands for literal Emperor worship. But for Jesus himself the temptation may have been at the other end of the political spectrum: "exploiting the latent forces of violence to wrest from Rome the liberation of his people," as C.H. Dodd proposes for the meaning "in realistic terms" of 'doing homage to the devil'.[129]

If Dodd is correct that 'the zealot option' is in view here, the devil's temptation relates in a particularly subtle way to the divine commands regarding the nations in Deuteronomy 6-8 (*e.g.* 7.2 &.16-17). The devil's promise was not only freedom from the nations but dominion over them. Jesus' simple answer expresses submission to the ancient commands against entanglement in idolatry (Mt 4.10). Implied in this response also is the explanation for the restriction of his own mission to 'the scattered sheep of the House of Israel' until he himself is handed over to the nations for judgment and execution (Mt 20.17-19).

Jesus is physically exhausted at the end of the trial, but he is prepared by his faithfulness and his Father's special provisions (Mt 4.11) to enter the Promised Land, Galilee of the *Goyim* (Mt 4.15-16). The prophetic significance of this region was suggested already in the account of how Joseph "withdrew into the region of Galilee" with Mary and the child, in response to divine direction through a dream (Mt 2.22-23). Now (although the same verb is used, Mt 4.12) Jesus *returns* to his own country[130] despite Herod Antipas, the worldly ruler who had unjustly imprisoned John the Baptist.[131]

The full significance of Galilee is now announced and will be explained in the words and deeds of Jesus Messiah:[132]

---

[128] C.H. Dodd, *Founder*, 124.

[129] *Ibid.*, 123.

[130] This Greek verb illustrates 'systemic ambiguity'. In different contexts it can mean 'go away', 'return', or 'withdraw, retire, take refuge' (Bauer-AG 62-63). Mt has already used this word to mark the strategic move of the Magi to elude Herod (2.12) and the relocation of the refugee family (2.22-23). Jesus' *return* to Galilee is most important.
That the place name 'Galilee' was still heard in Aramaic as an abbreviation for 'District of the Nations' (גליל הגוים) is demonstrated by Mt's quotation of Is 9.1-2.

[131] "'Matthew' clearly implies that John's arrest led Jesus to go to *Galilee*. This move was not a flight from danger ... [rather it was] an answer to Herod; he took up in Herod's territory the work which Herod had tried to stop by arresting John; he began his ministry with a challenge rather than with a retreat." F. Filson, *A Commentary on the Gospel According to St. Matthew* (London: A&C Black, 1960), 72. *Cf.* E. Schweizer, *Good News Mt*, 67.

[132] The projection of this significance in the world mission through his disciples is indicated already in Jesus' inaugural 'teaching from the hillside' ("You are the light of the world" Mt 5.14) and is finally revealed programmatically in 'the Great Commission'.

The people living in darkness have seen a great light;
On those living in a land overshadowed by death a light has dawned.
(Mt 5.16/ Is 9.1)

9

THE NATIONS IN THE DESIGN OF THE GOSPEL:
PROCLAMATION IN WORD AND DEED

The Messiah's identity is paradoxical in the First Gospel. This is apparent already in the genealogy, which emphasizes both continuity and discontinuity. Jesus' divine sonship is the dominant theme in Matthew's opening presentation, and when the narrative of Jesus' own words and deeds begins, the message of the Kingdom of heaven is powerful and clear ('ἀπὸ τότε ἤρξατο ὁ Ἰησοῦς κηρύσσειν ... Mt 4.17). But in this second main section of the book (*4.17 - 16.20*) Jesus' human limitations are sharply drawn also, and his involvement with the nations is strictly curtailed. Even so, the first chapters have given the readers the clues they need to understand the transcendent meaning of Jesus' teaching and action. Following these clues, the readers can understand Jesus' rare responses to faith outside Israel not simply as exceptions, but as *signals of things to come* in the fulfillment of God's promise to the nations through Israel.

The correlation and identity of word and deed in the First Gospel is reminiscent of the semantic range of the term דבר יהוה in the Hebrew Bible.[1] Matthew's special interest in the teachings of Jesus is obvious. But what Jesus *does* is most important, as the climax of the Gospel makes unmistakably clear.[2] The relationship between Jesus' teaching and action is significant, and the evangelist has included explicit references to the necessary bond between 'hearing' and 'doing' the will of God (*e.g.* Mt 7.24; 12.50; 28.19-20). *Sequence* of words and events in the narrative also can be basic to understanding.[3] In

---

[1] In Mt, Jesus is never actually called 'the word of God' as in Jn 1.1 and Ign *Magn* 8.2.

[2] Jesus' sacrificial death and resurrection is the climax of the First Gospel, as in all the canonical Gospels: "the gospels are passion-narrative with extended introductions." Martin Kähler's dictum cited by J.P. Meier, *Law and History*, 31.

[3] The conjunction in the narrative of John's disciples' query to the restricted mission of the Twelve has already been emphasized above. *Re* the order of the narrative *cf.* J.P. Meier, "John the Baptist in Matthew's Gospel", *JBL* 99 (1980) 383-405, *contra* W. Trilling.

other words, the narrative structure is itself constitutive. Description of the Gospel's design with the simile of beads and string is inadequate, no matter how much emphasis is placed on the 'string'.[4]

A. The Call to Discipleship

"Reform your lives! The Kingdom of heaven is at hand!" (Mt 4.17). These words, which described John the Baptist's ministry, are used to characterize Jesus' earliest preaching which defines the context of the discipleship accepted by Peter and Andrew, James and John (Mt 4.18/21).

After a brief description of Jesus' teaching and healing in Galilee, which spread his fame throughout Syria,[5] the stern demands of discipleship are elaborated in 'the Sermon on the Mount'. The unconditional demands of discipleship are re-emphasized in the following chapter with Jesus' words, "Follow me, and let the dead bury their dead" (Mt 8.22). Also in this section of the Gospel *(4.17-16.20)* Jesus associates the call to discipleship in starkest terms with the call to humiliating death (Mt 10.38, anticipating 16.24). If these sayings are lined up next to each other, or recalled out of context, it is easy to overlook the happy excitement and positive force of the beginning of the Jesus movement. Jesus acknowledges and justifies the party atmosphere which his ministry generated. In answer to question from John the Baptist's disciples about fasting he asks, "How can wedding guests go in mourning while the groom is with them?" (Mt 9.12-17, *cf.* 12.19).

Birger Gerhardsson, in his study of *The Mighty Acts of Jesus According to Matthew*, observes that

> Matthew sees the activity of Jesus in Israel as a ministry of two phases: first in 'strength' and then in 'weakness'. All his mighty acts belong to the first of these two phases.[6]

On the one hand, this early phase, which is the context for much of Jesus' teaching recorded in the First Gospel, represents the early popular success which Jesus certainly experienced. On the other hand, the evangelist is fully aware of the paradox that the Kingdom was established –as foretold by the Prophet Isaiah– through the weakness, suffering, and death of the Messiah.

Matthew's understanding of discipleship relates not only to Jesus' earthly ministry but also to the readers of the Gospel. Recent interpreters of the

---

[4] *Contra* O.L. Cope, *Matthew: A Scribe Trained for the Kingdom of Heaven* (Washington: Catholic Biblical Association of America, 1976), 3.

[5] "The whole of Syria" in Mt 4.24 seems to be the Roman province, with Galilee defined here as its center from which Jesus' fame radiated out, drawing crowds not only from Galilee but also from the Decapolis, Judea, and Transjordan (4.25). If so, the subsequent reference to "Judea" can be assumed to include Samaria ('Judea-Samaria').

[6] B. Gerhardsson, *The Mighty Acts of Jesus According to Matthew* (Lund: CWK Gleerup, 1979), 9.

First Gospel have debated whether the concept is 'transparent' in the sense of relating immediately to Matthew's own community or 'historicizing' in the sense of representing a conscious attempt to recount specific situations and developments in Jesus' activity and teaching. Ulrich Luz reviews this debate and concludes that

> for Matthew historicizing is itself the presupposition for genuine transparency. For him true discipleship is at all times only possible as recourse to the historical Jesus.[7]

If we follow Luz here, using the term 'historicizing' without prejudice about Matthew's ability to remember or reconstruct historical information, we can note also the fundamental significance of 'disciples' both in the design of the First Gospel and in the earliest mission to all nations. (The terms 'apostles' and 'the Twelve' are also significant for an understanding of the mission. We shall consider these two terms when they appear before the second discourse.)

Matthew's account of Jesus' recruitment of Peter and Andrew, James and John (Mt 4.18/21) does not identify these men as 'disciples' or 'apostles', and in this first reference they are four, not twelve.[8] When the word 'disciples' first occurs a few verses further on in the text (οἱ μαθηταὶ αὐτοῦ Mt 5.1) it seems to designate the whole crowd following Jesus, or at least those in the crowd willing to take instruction when Jesus seated himself on 'the hillside' (τὸ ὄρος Mt 5.1). The four already appointed to be 'fishers of people' (Mt 4.19) were certainly among these disciples, along with some or all of the others who were to be appointed to the inner circle of twelve disciples.

In the design of the First Gospel, Jesus' introductory challenge to those first called to 'follow' him (Δεῦτε ὀπίσω μου) and become 'fishers of people' (ἁλιεῖς ἀνθρώπων Mt 4.19) anticipates the final commission to 'the eleven disciples' (Mt 28.16-20). If the figure of speech 'fishers of people' was Jesus' own, which seems likely, it fits the pattern of his earliest preaching and the boldness of metaphor in his subsequent parables. As an expression of eschatological hope, echoing Jeremiah 16.16, it carries also dark overtones of judgments. But in any case, this first call to discipleship clearly promised instruction for *engagement* in the dynamics of the coming Kingdom.[9]

---

[7] U. Luz, "The Disciples according to Matthew" [1971], *Interpretation of Mt*, ed. G. Stanton, 112. Luz's use of the term 'historical Jesus' here seems straightforward, not a reference to a construct from 'the quest for the historical Jesus'.

[8] The Evangelist seems to be reporting the facts as he understood them matching the requirements of his narrative. There is no hint of tendentious construction in support of any later doctrine or ideology about a 'college of Apostles' or 'guardians of the Tradition'.

[9] "The metaphor employed suggested that, having been caught themselves, they are to catch others. ... Whatever else the group that Christ gathered around himself was meant to be, it was not meant to be merely a society for the study of theology. It was a group that would make a direct impact on the life of the society round about it." T.W. Manson, *Only to the House of Israel?* (Philadelphia: Fortress, 1964 [1955], 6; *cf.* 16-19.

The recruitment of Matthew from his tax booth (ἐπὶ τὸ τελώνιον Mt 9.9) is singled out as another exemplar of the call to discipleship (also in the other synoptic Gospels where the tax collector is named Levi, son of Alphaeus). In the First Gospel the tax collector appears after the teaching on the hillside (or 'Sermon on the Mount', to which we turn next) and after the rejection of a more respectable applicant (Mt 8.22). This order is significant, as is the tax collector's place in the series of Jesus' mighty acts which involves a leper, a foreigner, and a sharp controversy about the forgiveness of sins (Mt 8.1-4, 5-13; 9.1-7). The tax-collector's appointment draws attention to Jesus' continuing involvement with apparently hopeless humanity, and specifically his table fellowship with 'tax collectors' and 'those known as sinners' (Mt 9.10-11). Since the fundamental meaning of 'discipleship' in the First Gospel is 'following Jesus', the Messiah's example must provide the basic interpretive context for the teaching from the hillside and other instructions to his disciples.[10]

In this second section of the Gospel the basic pattern of Jesus' earthly ministry is strictly maintained, so that his own teaching is represented without any explicit references to his death and resurrection. Clear prophecies and finally a description of the Messiah's crucifixion and vindication are held off until the third, final section (*16.21-28.20*). In the conclusion of the Gospel, when the Eleven are commissioned to baptize (incorporating disciples into his death) and teach all that Jesus taught them, the chiasmic order is completed: teaching-death/ death-teaching. On the one hand, the conclusion of the Gospel (and the order of Jesus' words there) indicates that Jesus' teachings are best understood and explained to new disciples in the light of his death and resurrection. On the other hand, the revelation of Jesus as the Messiah and Son of God includes the teaching ministry, which made sense immediately to his disciples in early first-century Palestine.

The Sermon on the Mount
With reference to the text of the 'Sermon on the Mount' it is impossible to say with certainty which words (or their Aramaic counterparts) Jesus himself spoke. But it is equally impossible to declare with assurance which words he did not speak or could not have spoken. What we have are Matthew's words which he recorded as representing Jesus' first instructions to his disciples.

J.P. Meier's study of Matthew 5.17-20 ("Teaching about the Law") demonstrates the comprehensive significance of this saying for the Messianic

---

[10] L. Schottroff and W. Stegemann, *Jesus and the Hope of the Poor* (Maryknoll: Orbis, 1986 [1978], 36. The designation ἐπὶ τὸ τελώνιον here suggests further characterization of the evangelist's community, even though mention of the call of a tax collector (or 'tax farmer') to discipleship also appears in the Second and Third Gospels.
If τελῶναι and ἐθνικοί are considered together (as in Mt 18.17) and if Matthew the disciple was associated with this Gospel in the minds of its first readers, the point about 'pagans' (*infra*) is strengthened: Having been a 'tax-gatherer' or a 'pagan' would not prejudice a person's standing in the Christian community.

mission to all nations.[11] Specifically, the phrase "until it all comes true" (ἕως ἂν πάντα γένηται Mt 5.18b, cf. Mt 24.34) should be read as a gloss on the immediately preceding end-time reference (Mt 5.18a). Meier argues that "Matthew has reinterpreted this eschatological event as the entire career of Jesus, culminating in his death-resurrection."[12] Besides the function of this discourse in defining and justifying the mission to all nations, some of these instructions for disciples have immediate relevance also to those being trained as missionaries.[13] Notable examples are 'the beatitudes' (Mt 5.3-12), the identification of disciples as "the light of the world" τὸ φῶς τοῦ κόσμου Mt 5.14), the challenge, based on the fatherhood of God, to extend the borders of covenant love beyond the circles of one's countrymen (τὸν πλησίον σου Mt 5.43-45), and the model prayer (Mt 6.9-13).

Linked to the challenge to expand the borders of disciplined love is the command Ἔσεσθε οὖν ὑμεῖς τέλειοι ("Be perfect, therefore, even as your Father in heaven is perfect" Mt 5.48), which Jack Kingsbury appropriately translates "be whole-hearted" in your service of God and humanity.[14] The transcendent reference of the way of better righteousness (Mt 5.10 cf. 6.21) is marked by Jesus' proclamation which preceded this teaching (Mt 4.17) and the impact of his authority (ἐξουσίαν) which amazed those taking instruction even at the very beginning of his ministry (Mt 7.28-29). The placement of 'the Sermon on the Mount' indicates the importance of the teachings, but also warns against any attempt to claim these words as the whole Gospel. However perfect and complete these first instructions might be, Matthew gives no reason to suppose that the first disciples thought that they had already received the final revelation of "the mysteries of the Kingdom" (Mt 13.11).

The development of Jesus' ministry demonstrates the paradox of his identity. The explanation for the restriction of Jesus' mission and that of his disciples to Israel is implicit in Matthew's narrative and is made explicit in the words of the glorified Son of Man (*Mt 28.16-20*). After Jesus has paid the price of mankind's redemption, the crucified Messiah has the power as resurrected Lord to authorize the proclamation of the Gospel to all nations. But the ambiguities of Jesus' own teaching and suffering remain, also in the eschatological mission which he entrusts to his disciples.

---

[11] J.P. Meier, *Law and History*, 42 & *passim*.

[12] *Ibid.*, 64.

[13] *Contra* H.D. Betz who claims "that the SM contains a theology that is independent of Matthew and different at characteristic points" and assumes that Mt's readiness to accept the nations into the Covenant community is one such notable difference. *Essays on the Sermon on the Mount* (Philadelphia: Fortress, 1985), 18. Many of Betz's speculations and arguments support our analysis, *e.g.*, his idea of a "pre-Matthean source originating in the Jewish Church around 50 A.D.", 15.

[14] J.D. Kingsbury, "The Place, Structure, and Meaning of the Sermon on the Mount Within Matthew", *Interpretation* 41 (1987), 137.

ἘΘΝΗ and ἘΘΝΙΚΟΙ in Matthean Usage

No term used by Matthew transmitted these ambiguities more emphatically than 'the nations' (τὰ ἔθνη). The very fact that different forms of this word occur more frequently in the First Gospel (*17x*) than in any of the other three (Mk 5x, Lk 10x, Jn 5x) may help explain why this Gospel has been singled out so often for discussion about the redactor's "Gentile bias"[15] or "anti-Gentile bias".[16] But in a comparison of usage, the relative frequency of the word's occurrence in the First Gospel is less striking than Matthew's inclusion of one particular form of the word, ἐθνικοί. This unusual form appears twice in the 'Sermon on the Mount' (Mt 5.47 & 6.7) and one other time in the First Gospel (Mt 18.17). The word does not appear in the Septuagint translation of the Hebrew Bible and only occurs once elsewhere in the New Testament (III John 7). The term is always used in a derogatory sense and so the NEB translations "heathen" (Mt 5.47; 6.7) and "pagan(s)" (Mt 18.17; III Jn 7) are justified. The RSV translation "Gentiles" in the three Matthean occurrences adds unnecessary conceptual problems to the text, but preserves the ambiguity of the Greek word.

The form ἐθνικοί stands on the far end of the semantic range of ἔθνη and conveniently illustrates the Gospel writer's ability to use the term in its most pejorative sense. Matthew Black correctly identifies the use of τὰ ἔθνη in Matthew 6.32 ("for the heathen seek all these things") as having the same negative meaning as οἱ ἐθνικοί in 5.47 ("Do not even the heathen do the same?") and 6.7 ("And in praying do not heap up empty phrases as the heathen do").[17] In Matthew 10. 18 τοῖς ἔθνεσιν would seem to include every bit of this pejorative force ("and you will be dragged before governors and kings for my sake, to bear testimony before them and the heathen"). But what is remarkable about this last example is that it is *sharply ambiguous* in the larger context of the First Gospel. This extremely negative reference itself allows anticipation of the most positive meaning of 'the nations' being discipled to perfect obedience in the Kingdom of heaven.

Only one of Matthew's ἐθνικοί texts has a parallel in Luke's Gospel (Mt 5.47/ Lk 6.33) where that redactor's choice of the word "sinners" (οἱ ἁμαρτωλοί) leaves little doubt about the intensity of negative connotations in the common source; ("for even sinners do the same" Lk 6.33). If the common

---

[15] See K.W. Clark's article "Gentile Bias" already cited in Chapter 8 (notes 3 and 61), but *cf.* Douglas Hare's response in *The Theme of Jewish Persecution of Christians in the Gospel According to St Matthew* (Cambridge: University Press, 1967), 165: "Matthew speaks as one for whom it [the synagogue] has only recently become an alien institution."

[16] H.D. Betz cites Mt 5.47; 6.7 & 6.32 as examples of "many passages" which "warn against assimilation with them [non-Jews]". *Essays SM*, 19. C.G. Montefiore refers to Mt 10.5b-6 as "one of his anti-Gentile remarks". Montefiore goes on to say that Mt "includes, in the strangest way, some very philo-Gentile and anti-Jewish statements, and some which point precisely in the reverse directions". *The Synoptic Gospels*, vol 2 (New York: Ktav, 1968 [1927]), 146.

[17] M. Black, *An Aramaic Approach to the Gospels and Acts* (Oxford: Clarendon Press, 1967), 177.

source of this saying in the First and Third Gospels were Greek (which seems unlikely and certainly not proven), the question could be asked in a straight-forward way whether Luke, for his own reasons, screened out ἐθνικοί and substituted οἱ ἁμαρτωλοί or, from the other side, whether Matthew dropped a word in order to add ἐθνικοί. Black assumes the (ultimate) common source to have been Aramaic and so depends on hypothetical reconstruction of the Aramaic text for his judgment, but he declares that "Matthew's ἐθνικοί is clearly Jewish interpretation."[18] The question at issue for the present discussion, however, is whether the Greek word here (and in different form but with the same sharply negative connotations elsewhere in Matthew) *faithfully represents* the way Jesus' Jewish disciples (and Jesus himself) spoke.

The answer to this question seems not susceptible of direct proof, but the evidence from the Apocrypha, Pseudepigrapha, and later Rabbinic records of the period, as well as the Hebrew Bible itself, the other three canonical Gospels, and the warp and woof of the First Gospel strongly suggests that the 'strangeness' of verbal appearances of xenophobic bias accurately reflects one side of the ambiguous Jewish attitude to 'the nations' which was brought forward and built upon, not introduced by, the evangelist. If this is so, and if Luke and the other evangelists also knew the word ἐθνικοί but rejected it as unsuitable for their purposes and audiences, a second question—about Matthew's sensitivity to his own situation—calls for an answer and raises further questions.

Ethnic Christians

At the time Matthew wrote, was the term ἐθνικοί so obnoxious as to be abusive and obviously offensive to non-Jewish readers? If so, does Matthew's usage prove that his community was entirely 'Jewish Christian' and only theoretically interested in mission to 'the nations'? Both questions, it seems, can be answered in the negative. Although Christians remain Italians, Ethiopians, and Arabs who are sensitive to racial slurs, they cease to be "heathen" (גוים / ἔθνη / ἐθνικοί) immediately upon becoming Christians. Even when their non-Jewishness and the excesses of their kinsmen according to the flesh are represented by the same term (as in the Pauline epistles, *e.g.* Gal 2.14-15) they seem able to sort out the ambiguity without taking offense.

If there were non-Jewish members in Matthew's community, and if Matthew 18.17 is basically a redactional construct (as many modern critics

---

[18] *Ibid.* Matthew Black's magisterial work incorporates three notable weaknesses in his argument relating to ἐθνικοί in Mt 5.47 and 6.7: a/ His arguments imply that there is only one correct Greek translation for any Aramaic saying. b/ He does not consider 5.47 independently, but generalizes from his analysis of Mt 6.7—apparently on the assumption that a word in one language always is (or should be) translated by the same word in the target language. c/ Black's judgment that "Luke's rendering [11.2] is then literal and correct" over against Mt's inferior and tendentious "Jewish interpretation" at 6.7 is based on his textual-critical judgment that the variant D is the authentic Lucan text.

judge it to be),[19] this passage sharpens the issue to the point of proof: not only did the redactor carry forward this usage in 'the Sermon on the Mount', he could also confidently insert it himself in this saying. Like modern Christians, non-Jewish members of Matthew's congregation knew that they themselves were not 'pagans'; ("and if he will not listen even to the congregation, you must then treat him as you would a pagan or a tax-gatherer" Mt 18.17, NEB.)

As we shall note when we return to this passage in its context (between the parable of 'the single stray sheep' and the parable of 'the unmerciful debtor'), the positive connotations of the term are no less striking in Matthew's usage than the negative connotations. It is precisely as ὁ ἐθνικός that the unrepentant sinner maintains positive claims on the resurrection community.

B. Instructions for the First Mission

The disciples' first mission to Israel was an important event in Jesus' ministry and a significant episode in the design of the First Gospel,[20] as we have already indicated. Our first reference related to the Messianic expectations which surrounded and shaped Jesus' ministry, the second reference was to the narrative context of John the Baptist's question from prison. We turn now to two major themes of the First Gospel which come into focus for the first time in chapter ten: *the disciples as missionaries* and *Jesus as 'the Son of Man'*.

The Apostles

Jesus had chosen twelve men for his inner circle of disciples. Matthew accepts this as fact when he reports their names and their first assignment. The term 'apostles' (ἀποστόλων Mt 10.2) is virtually a participle pointing to their assignment, which the evangelist describes after listing their names. They are never again termed 'apostles' in the First Gospel. Their role as disciples is immediately relevant to Matthew's account of Jesus' words and deeds. The evangelist may also suppose that their role as disciples is more immediately transferable to his readers. Even in the conclusion, when the Eleven take instruction from the glorified Son of Man for the eschatological mission to all nations, they are 'disciples'. Nevertheless, the fact that there is no clear indication in the next chapter that their first assignment was completed suggests

---

[19] When standard form-critical methods are used for analysis this judgment is almost unavoidable, but the judgment itself is not so certain as is commonly supposed. "Everything we know about Jesus goes to show that the creation of the corporate body, called the church ... was not an idea that first occurred to the disciples after the resurrection, but rather an essential part of ... 'the intention of Jesus' from the first days of the Galilean ministry." T.W. Manson, *Only Israel?*, 6 citing J.W Bowan's *The Intention of Jesus* (1943).

[20] "Matthew is probably thinking of the Twelve as prototypes of all the wandering apostles of his own period." E. Schweizer, *Good News Mt*, 237. Schweizer agrees with Schuyler Brown that the evangelist is reporting "an event which he undoubtedly took to be historical". S. Brown, "The Mission to Israel in Matthew's Central Section (Mt 9.35-11.1)", *ZNW* 69 (1978), 75.

that they continue also as apostles on this and subsequent missions, "until the Son of Man comes" (Mt 10.23).

Telescoping related actions into one report is not unusual in the First Gospel, and subsequent missions in Judea (including Samaria) as well as in Galilee might be implied by the reference to completing the tour of "the towns of Israel" (Mt 10.23). David Hill suggests that such a reconstruction is not inconsistent with reports in the other Gospels of a return *"in the course of* their missionary activity", for even "Mk 6.30 probably does not refer to a final return."[21]

The list of the names of all twelve apostles indicates that *the number* is significant to the evangelist.[22] The subsequent eschatological picture of 'twelve thrones' relating to 'the Twelve Tribes of Israel' (Mt 19.28), and in the precise reference to "the eleven disciples" after Judas' defection (Mt 28.16). But the occasional reference in the First Gospel to 'the twelve disciples' seems no more related to modern arguments about a 'College of Twelve in Jerusalem' than does the single reference to 'apostles'.[23] Indeed, already in chapter eleven but especially in the conclusion, the First Gospel anticipates the situation suggested by Acts 21.18 where it appears that the Twelve Apostles had "all gone to the mission field" leaving James and the presbyters in charge of the church in Jerusalem.[24]

The pointed reference to Simon's place at the head of the list (πρῶτος Σίμων ὁ λεγόμενος Πέτρος Mt 10.2) probably represents the evangelist's information about the order of appointment already noted (Mt 4.18), and certainly anticipates Simon's Messianic confession which concludes this section of the Gospel (Mt 16.16-20). The primacy of Simon and his designation as 'Rock' (Cephas/ Peter) should not be interpreted in a hierarchical way but rather in terms of leadership of the *apostles*. As Oscar Cullmann has emphasized, with reference to Acts 8.14, Simon Peter's early leadership in the Jerusalem Church included supervision of "the mission field in Samaria".[25]

---

[21] D. Hill, *Gospel of Matthew*, 190.

[22] The agreement in the synoptic Gospels and Acts on the number of the apostles, and the minor disagreement about their names, is a problem sharply focused by J.R. Harris, *The Twelve Apostles* (Cambridge: Heffer & Sons, 1927). Taking the opposite tack, E.J. Goodspeed notes Matthew's emphasis on the number twelve in 10.1,2,5 & 11.1 and assumes that the evangelist's complete familiarity with the individuals listed allowed him freedom to choose from alternate names. *Matthew: Apostle and Evangelist* (Philadelphia: J.C. Winston, 1959), 134 & 144.

[23] The concept and designation 'apostles' is certainly relevant to the earliest mission to 'all nations', but even a survey of the critical literature on the subject would press us far beyond the bounds of the present study. Walter Schmithals' monograph *The Office of Apostle in the Early Church* (Nashville: Abingdon, 1969 [1961]) surveys modern critical positions.

[24] Kirsopp Lake, "The Twelve and the Apostles", *The Beginnings of Christianity* Part I/V (Grand Rapids: Baker, 1966 [132]), 58, *cf.* 56.

[25] O. Cullmann, *Peter: Disciple - Apostle - Martyr* (Cleveland: World, 1953), 36.

Moreover, "according to the narrative [of Acts 9 and 10], Peter takes the first position also as a missionary to Gentiles and explicitly justifies this mission."[26]

The Son of Man

"The coming of the Son of Man" anticipated in Matthew 10.23 is fundamental to the design of the First Gospel. This verse has been the focus of disagreements among Matthew's interpreters, and the term 'Son of Man' itself has generated debate which has become a sub-field in New Testament studies. The significance of Matthew's use of the term in this section (*4.17 - 16.20*) and in the final section of the Gospel (*16.21 - 28.20*) must be related to earlier usage in the tradition, and in Jesus' own teaching. As we observed of the Scriptures quoted in the First Gospel, we can confidently say also that the 'Son of Man' idea did not originate with Matthew. For although the term is strange 'translation Greek', Matthew's use of the phrase apparently required no explanation for his first readers. Moreover, as in the other canonical Gospels, the phrase is only used by Jesus himself. These agreed facts of usage, to which we shall return, have very great significance for understanding the earliest Christian mission to all nations. But we turn now to the narrative significance of the phrase in Matthew 10.23.

Albert Schweitzer's well-known view that this verse in the First Gospel represents an authentic, failed prediction and the turning point in Jesus' own mission[27] has the advantage of focusing on the time-reference of the saying, but in Matthew's narrative the prediction comes true. Schulyer Brown, who also focuses on the time reference of this verse, is partly right in observing that "the missionary disciples do not return to Jesus because the mission is still going on."[28] But it continues only during the time of Jesus' own earthly ministry. This on-going mission is interrupted by the coming of the Son of Man before all the towns of Israel have been reached. The conclusion of the Gospel (Mt 28.16-20) is a specific fulfillment of this prophecy and a radical expansion of the mission which, henceforth, is to all the nations.[29]

---

[26] Cullmann, *ibid. Cf. supra* Chapter 1.

[27] A. Schweitzer, *The Quest for the Historical Jesus* (New York: Macmillan, 1964 [1906]), 358-60. *Cf.* Barnabas Lindars, *Jesus, Son of Man* (Grand Rapids: Eerdmans, 1983), 122: "It was manifestly not fulfilled in the time to which it refers."

[28] S. Brown, "The Mission to Israel", *op. cit.*, 79.

[29] "The same Jesus who, during his earthly ministry, forbids the Twelve a mission among the Gentiles and Samaritans is also the Jesus who, as the exalted Son of Man, commands the Eleven to make disciples of *panta ta ethne*." J.P. Meier, *Law and History*, 27. *Cf.* Karl Barth, "An Exegetical Study of Matthew 28:16-20", *The Theology of Christian Mission*, ed. G.H. Anderson (New York: McGraw-Hill, 1965 [1945]), 56; Morna Hooker, "Uncomfortable Words: The Prohibition of Foreign Mission (Mt 10.5-6)", *ExpT* 82 (1971), 362; and Harnack, *Mission and Expansion*, 40-41 n2. *Contra*, the many NT scholars who fail to see the consistency in Mt's full account. (B. Lindars does allow for "a proleptic fulfillment in the resurrection" *op. cit.*, 123.)

The reference to 'the coming Son of Man' is an explicit *signal*, in this section of the Gospel, *of things to come*. But the two references to 'the Son of Man' which precede it and those which follow are also significant in the design of the Gospel. The evangelist's first use of the phrase, which can be translated plausibly as 'Everyman' (or *'Jedermann'*), represents a self-reference by Jesus.[30] This quotation of Jesus' circumlocution for the first person singular pronoun 'I'[31] also carries with it unavoidable connotations of corporate personality.[32] T.W. Manson argues persuasively that

> 'Son of Man' in the Gospels is the final term in a series of conceptions, all of which are found in the Old Testament. These are: Remnant (Isaiah), the Servant of Jehovah (II Isaiah), the 'I' of the Psalms, and the Son of Man (Daniel). ... The restriction of the denotation of the term [to Jesus himself] is the outcome of the prophetic ministry of Jesus.[33]

'The representative human being' who has 'no fixed abode' (Mt 8.20) anticipates references to 'the Son of Man' who explicitly identifies with 'the least of his siblings' (Mt 25.31/ 40 & 45). But the first reference to 'the Son of Man', emphasizing his earthly circumstances, is also parallelled within the section itself *(4.17 - 16.20)* by the reference to 'the Son of Man eating and drinking' (Mt 11.19) which refuted the falsely spiritual arguments of Jesus' (and Matthew's) opponents.

The second occurrence of the term 'Son of Man', in the order of the narrative, also emphasizes Jesus' solidarity with mankind through the still-to-be-explained declaration that the authority to forgive sins has been given (by God) to human beings (Mt 9.6). This saying parallels the somewhat later declaration that "the Son of Man is lord of the Sabbath" (Mt 12.8). Jesus' incorporation in mankind is then re-emphasized by the saying that "[mistaken] speaking against

---

[30] "It is inconceivable that the evangelists thought that Jesus was referring to anyone but himself when they incorporated these sayings into their gospels." B. Lindars, *ibid.*, 3.

[31] G. Vermes has won wide agreement for this position with his 1965 essay "The Use of בר נש / בר נשא in Jewish Aramaic", reprinted as appendix to the 1967 edition of M. Black's *Aramaic Approach to the Gospels and Acts*. Vermes subsequently sharpened his position to insist that "in its Synoptic presentation ... [it is] an unambiguous and unprovocative phrase always used by Jesus alone." *Jesus the Jew* (Glasgow: Collins, 1976 [1973]), 162.

[32] H. Wheeler Robinson relates the concept of 'corporate personality' in Israel to the individual prophet who "temporarily becomes the nation, and makes its needs articulate" and to "the 'I' of the Psalms and of the Servant of Yahweh". *Corporate Personality in Ancient Israel* (Philadelphia: Fortress, 1980 [1935-'37]), 36 & 37.

[33] T.W. Manson, *The Teaching of Jesus* (Cambridge: University Press, 1963 [1931]). 227. *Cf.* C.F.D. Moule's term 'Corporate Christ' and his designation of Jesus as "an inclusive personality". *The Phenomenon of the New Testament* (London: SCM, 1967), 24.

the Son of Man will be forgiven" (Mt 12.32), even though fundamental contradiction of the Holy Spirit is unpardonable.[34] Still another 'Son of Man' saying in this chapter (Mt 12.40-41) relates the Son of Man to the important time-designation 'this generation' (τῆς γενεᾶς) and to 'the Sign of Jonah', which we shall consider further in relation to Jesus' mighty acts.

In chapter thirteen and in the introduction to Simon Peter's confession in chapter sixteen the term is closely related to its use in Matthew 10.28 and to its use in the final section of the Gospel. In this final section the term typically refers to Jesus' death, resurrection and exultation. In Simon Peter's confession the Son of Man is explicitly equated with "the Son of God" (Mt 16.6). The previous occurrence of the phrase in the narrative was Jesus' prophecy of "the Son of Man dispatching his angels" (Mt 13.41) which concludes with an unmistakable echo of Daniel 12.4: "Then the righteous will shine like the sun in their Father's Kingdom" (Mt 13.41).

A Structural Homologue

The layered connotations of the term and its systematic ambiguity are important in all its occurrences in Matthew's Gospel. This can be illustrated by the first of the two occurrences in chapter thirteen where the sower in the parable is identified as "the Son of Man" (Mt 13.37). This means that Jesus sows the seeds of the Kingdom of heaven with his words and deeds. By way of qualifying Joachim Jeremias' correct emphasis on divine initiative in the eschatological ingathering of the nations,[35] we should note that Matthew's text here undeniably indicates human agency. Moreover, a correspondence between Jesus and his followers is encompassed in the systematic ambiguity of the term 'Son of Man'. Gerd Theissen calls this correspondence "a structural homologue"[36] and claims that "the figure of the Son of man was central for the Jesus movement."[37]

The four canonical Gospels themselves provide ample documentation for Theissen's claim, but surprisingly "'Son of Man' was not at all a common title for Jesus in the early Church," as Oscar Cullmann notes with reference to later literature.[38] Indeed, the term does not even appear in the Pauline epistles which were written before the Gospels. Attempts to analyze the evidence (in the four Gospels) that Jesus himself used the term have resulted in many

---

[34] H.B. Green explains this saying (par Mk 3.28 & Lk 12.10) as "deriving from the Beelzebul controversy". *The Gospel according to Matthew* (Oxford: University Press, 1975), 127. G. Theissen cites Mt 12.32 as proof that some of "the earliest Christian preachers set themselves above the Son of man." *Sociology of Early Palestinian Christianity*, 28. No doubt such use of the text was made in the first century (as in every subsequent century), but Theissen's inference that the saying *originated* with arrogant preachers is unwarranted.

[35] J. Jeremias, *Jesus' Promise*, 71 & *passim*.

[36] G. Theissen, *op.cit.*, 26 citing L. Goldman, *Die Soziologie der Literature*.

[37] *Ibid.*, 30.

[38] O. Cullmann, *The Christology of the New Testament* (Philadelphia: Westminster, 1963 [1957]), 155.

significant studies, but no clear agreement about *how* he used the term and with what meaning.[39] Paul's letters prove that Christological titles were ascribed to Jesus already before the Gospels were written, but 'the Son of Man' is certainly not a title formulated by the evangelists or their immediate sources. Geza Vermes has argued that the phrase, used by Jesus himself, was first connected with Daniel 7.13 by the Gospel writers.[40] But the evidence in the New Testament and near-contemporary writings supports the contrary argument that various uses and levels of ambiguity, including clear allusions to Daniel 7.13-14, can all be understood in terms of Jesus' own self-expression.[41]

"No term was more fitted both to conceal, yet at the same time to reveal to those who had ears to hear, the Son of Man's real identity."[42] This summary solution to the Son of Man problem by Matthew Black was anticipated by Oscar Cullmann in his 1955 Zenos Lectures when he insisted that "we must reckon with the possibility that Jesus always used 'Son of Man' in a deliberately ambiguous sense."[43] Following this same tack, Seyoon Kim concludes that

> God's resurrection of Jesus confirmed his claim to be 'the Son of Man' of Dan 7, i.e. the Son of God who is the inclusive representative of God's eschatological people (= the sons of God), and it confirmed his death as the vicarious, atoning and covenant-establishing death which has brought about a new eschatological people of God.[44]

Kim's theological interpretation corresponds to the historical evidence. The complexity of his formulation reflects the systematic ambiguity of the phrase 'the Son of Man' which is not simply two-sided but multi-layered as Cullmann and Black also indicate.[45]

In Daniel 7.13-14. "all peoples, tribes, and languages" will serve the Son of Man. In the design of Matthew's Gospel this goal is never out of sight. But even without reference to Daniel's prophecy, the term 'Son or Man' or 'Everyman' is "universalistic ... by its very nature," as L. LeGrand points out.[46]

---

[39] Carsten Colpe surveys the critical literature to 1969 in his complicated analysis of the sources of the concept and its NT development. *TDNT* 8 (1972) 400-477. "The only sound conclusion is that Jesus Himself was a prophet in the apoc. tradition and that He proclaimed himself to be the Son of Man" (438).

[40] "The formal association of 'the *son of man*' in the Synoptics with Daniel 7:13 appears to be derivative and can scarcely be ascribed to Jesus himself." Vermes, *Jesus the Jew*, 184.

[41] "It can at least be shown that the application of the title Son of man to Christ is *early Palestinian tradition*." J. Jeremias, *New Testament Theology* vol 1: *The Proclamation of Jesus* (New York: Scribners, 1971), 264.

[42] M. Black, *Aramaic Approach to the Gospels and Acts* (1967), 329.

[43] O. Cullmann, *Christology*, 154.

[44] S. Kim, *The 'Son of Man' as the Son of God* (Tübingen: J.C.B. Mohr, 1983), 100.

[45] The term 'ambiguity' itself implies a two-sidedness and perhaps a proportionality between the two sides. Here the ambiguity is systemic, but not devisable by two.

[46] L. LeGrand, "Was Jesus Mission-Minded?" *Indian Ecclesiastical Studies* 3 (1964), 90. If the analysis above is sound, R. Pesch errs in omitting the term 'Son of Man' from

Jesus' persistent use of this term as a self-designation (according to all four canonical Gospels) points to *"Jesus als Begründer der Heidenmission"*, which Matthew explicitly indicates in the conclusion to the First Gospel.[47]

C. Parables — To Know the Mysteries

"The parables are the most characteristic part of the record of the teaching of Jesus."[48] This critical opinion of C.H. Dodd coincides with the intuitive judgment widely held through the centuries by those who claim to follow Jesus. This rare confirmation of popular judgment by critical New Testament scholarship has been repeated and emphasized in recent years. Our comments which relate the earliest Christian mission to Jesus' parables follow Amos Wilder's short, appreciative essay on "The Parable" as rhetorical form.[49] The prominence of parables in the First Gospel testifies not only to their continuing relevance to the evangelist's community, but also to Matthew's faithful representation of the Jesus tradition.

"Jesus' speech had the character not of instruction and ideas but of compelling imagination ... and transformation."[50] In the design of the Gospel, this form of proclamation is not only appropriate but necessary. Since the establishment of the kingdom depended on the sacrificial death of Jesus himself and his resurrection, his teaching during his earthly ministry necessarily pointed forward to the coming Kingdom. Within the context of the First Gospel, at least, John J. Vincent is correct in identifying the basic purpose of the parables as "not instruction or apologetics or controversy but self-revelation" by Jesus.[51] Like Jesus' characteristic term of self-designation 'the Son of Man', his parables are at once specifically Jewish and unmistakably universal in reference and application.

Following the lead of C.H. Dodd and Joachim Jeremias, recent studies of the parables have emphasized the Jewishness of their form and content. The basic assumption "that action is significant"[52] together with an approximation of the *mashal* form (riddle *et c.*), and the perception that "man's destiny is at

---

the apparently comprehensive list of *"neutestamentliche Terminologie zur Bescreibung der <urchristlichen Mission>"* in *"Voraussetzungen und Anfänge der urchristlichen Mission"*, *Mission im Neuen Testament*, ed. K. Kertelge (Freiburg: Herder, 1982), 14-15 (11-70).

[47] L. LeGrand, *ibid.*, citing M. Meinertz, *Zeitschrift für Missionwissenschaft* 1 (1911), 21-41.

[48] C.H. Dodd, *The Founder of Christianity* (London: Macmillan, 1970), 54; *cf. The Parables of the Kingdom* (London: Nisbet, 1936), 11.

[49] "It is the revelatory character of Jesus' parables which is to be stressed." A.N. Wilder, *Early Christian Rhetoric: The Language of the Gospel* (London: SCM, 1964), 80, citing Maxime Hermanink and Ernst Fuchs.

[50] *Ibid.*, 92.

[51] J.J. Vincent, "The Parables of Jesus as Self-Revelation", *Studia Evangelium* vol 1, ed. K. Aland et al. (Berlin: Academie-Verlag, 1959), 82.

[52] A.N. Wilder, *Christian Rhetoric*, 79.

stake in his ordinary creaturely existence, domestic, economic and social"[53] are all firmly grounded in first-century Palestine, usually Galilee. Jesus was a prophet of Israel, "the spokesman of the potent and dynamic word that acts".[54] As Justin Martyr confessed, "his word was the power of God."[55] The immediate relevance of the parables to mission to the nations is undeniable. But this universal applicability demands explanation, paradoxically, in terms of the parables' Jewishness.

Transformation and Growth
Two parables of the Kingdom, included in the thirteenth chapter of Matthew's Gospel, can serve to illustrate the originality of Jesus' use of Jewish forms and the relevance of these forms to the mission to the nations. The parable of the leaven (Mt 13.33) is notable for its reversal of the traditional imagery of leaven as an agent of insidious corruption (from Ex 12.15, *e.g.* Gal 5.9, I Cor 5.1-8, and Jesus' own words in Mt 16.6, 11-12). In this parable leaven become a symbol of positive transformation and astonishing growth. As in the parable of the mustard seed which immediately precedes it (13.31-2), the nature of this growth of the Kingdom contradicts, or at least radically realigns, some strong current Jewish expectations about the formation of the Messianic Kingdom.

C.H. Dodd has argued, with reference to Daniel 4.12 and Ezekiel 31.6 and 17.23, that the growth of the mustard seen "up to a point at which the tree can shelter the birds" specifically refers to the Kingdom accommodating the nations.[56] Joachim Jeremias concurs, claiming that κατασκηνοῦν ('building nests') is "actually an eschatological technical term for the incorporation of the Gentiles into the people of God".[57] If this interpretation is correct, this detail would have been significant to Matthew and other Jews (and to some in Jesus' audience if the form is original). But the basic imagery, which proclaims and affirms unexpected, miraculous growth in the Kingdom, would have been most important to inquirers from the nations.

Jack Kingsbury, in describing the redaction-critical method of his study on the parables of Jesus in Matthew 13, asserts that

> Just as Jesus employed parables to meet the demands of his own situation, so Matthew employed parables that had come down to him to meet the demands of the situation of the Church to which he belonged .... This Church was universally oriented, and its members were of both Jewish and Gentile origin.[58]

---

[53] *Ibid.*, 82.
[54] *Ibid.*, 86.
[55] *Ibid.*, 79 citing Justin Martyr's *Apology* I.14.5.
[56] C.H. Dodd, *The Parables of the Kingdom* (London: Nisbet, 1936), 190-1.
[57] J. Jeremias, *The Parables of Jesus* (New York: Scribners, 1963), 147; *cf.* T.W. Manson, *The Teaching of Jesus* (Cambridge: University Press, 1963 [1931]), 133 note 1.
[58] J.D. Kingsbury, *The Parables of Jesus in Matthew 13* (London: SPCK, 1969), 10-11.

If we accept this reconstruction of the redactor's situation and method, the prominence of parables in Matthew's Gospel is itself proof that they were used in the mission to the nations.[59]

The relevance to all nations of Jesus' specifically Jewish parables can be considered in yet another way, related to Matthew's use of the term τὸ μυστήρια (Mt 13.11). This text itself is mysterious —in one sense of the English word— partly because of its place in the narrative, near the beginning of Jesus' ministry. The term in this text, however, points to a basic link between parables and the revelation of the Kingdom. Moreover, Matthew's use of the term is in line with the use of רז (LXX μυστήρια) in Daniel 2.28. ("But there is a God in heaven revealing mysteries, and he has made know to King Nebuchanezzar what things must pass in the last days.") Matthew's use (and Lk 8.10/ Mk 4.11) fits the New Testament development of the Semitic usage.[60]

The Council of the LORD

The basic link between 'parables' and 'the mysteries of the Kingdom' is our present interest, but the difficulties of the specific formulation of Matthew 13.1-23 demand some attention before we try to claim the broader implications of this link. It is hard to imagine the disciples making sense out of Jesus' explanation at the time, even with the special knowledge he attributes to them in this text.

For modern readers, the statement of purpose (Mt 13.11-17) seems to say that parables are intended to obscure rather than to clarify the message of the Kingdom. The application of the prophecy of Isaiah seems only to compound confusion.[61] Any detailed, prosaic translation and interpretation of this text is bound to miss the point. But we can understand that the crowds are able to hear Jesus' message, if at all, only obliquely. His message finally must grasp the hearer rather than simply be grasped intellectually.

Jesus certainly instructed his disciples by means of parables. The apparent contradiction of this fact by the pointed reference to 'the others' in Matthew's text states a paradox. Even today, as in the time of Jesus' earthly

---

[59] I know of no direct evidence for the use of parables in the earliest mission to the nations. Paul, in his letters, neither cites Jesus' parables nor composes his own. (Some of his quotations of Scripture might be counted as parables: *e.g.* "You shall not muzzle an ox while it treads out grain" Dt 25.4/ I Cor 9.8-10.) Of Paul's preaching we have only the scanty evidence in Acts, but it seems unlikely that he was gifted in formulating parables (II Cor 10.10). But even if the earliest mission, like Paul's, centered in towns and cities, the survival of parables in the written Gospels is proof that Jesus' Parables retained a central place in the mission and also in the life of churches established by Paul.

[60] J. LaGrand, TO MYΣTHPION: *The New Testament Development of the Semitic Usage* (Grand Rapids: Calvin Th.M. diss., 1976), 21-25.

[61] E. Schweizer's solution to the problem is attractive: "The hardness of men's hearts is ... not in accordance with God's purpose; on the contrary, Jesus speaks in parables because their hearts are already hardened. *Good News Mt*, 299.

ministry, outsiders are sometimes seized by a parable and so are brought into a position to begin to understand the mysteries of the Kingdom. But whereas most hearers simply dismiss the parables as anecdotes (Mt 13.13-15) those already committed to the Way find these very 'stories for beginners' to be an amazing source of enrichment (Mt 13.12). Despite the apparent meaning of verses ten and eleven, it is reasonable to assert that Matthew himself identified Jesus' parables of the Kingdom as a means of communicating τὰ μυστήρια τῆς βασιλείας τῶν οὐρανῶν (Mt 13.11).

Joachim Jeremias concludes his study of the parables saying that "all the parables of Jesus compel his hearers to come to a decision about his person and mission"[62] In other words, "the parables imply a Christological self-attestation".[63] This surely is Matthew's understanding of the parables, already in this section of the Gospel where they are still signals of things to come. The disciples, even if puzzled by the attribution of special knowledge to themselves at this point, 'stand in the council of the Lord' like the ancient prophets.

This biblical image becomes unmistakable in Matthew 28.16-20, when the Eleven stand in the presence of the risen Lord and receive the mysteries of the Kingdom brilliantly revealed. But from the very beginning of the Gospel, Jesus is presented by Matthew as the Son of God. So the disciples are being introduced to the mysteries of the Kingdom from the start of his teaching ministry. In retrospect, all of the parables can be understood to be good news for all the nations.[64]

D. Mighty Acts and the Sign of Jonah

All of Jesus' acts recorded in the Gospels are significant, but many of his prophetic deed or 'acted parables' were not miraculous, or even unusual except within a specific dramatic setting. Eating and drinking with social outcasts, which was one of Jesus' most characteristic acts signalling the coming Kingdom, was a simpler pattern of behavior than the scrupulous system of discrimination practiced by the Pharisees. Jesus' trial and crucifixion, so far from demonstrating his divine authority and power, might serve as warnings about what can happen when well-meaning persons fall into circumstances beyond their control after conflicting with leaders of the religious and political establishment. But the main point and thrust of the Gospel is that Jesus' death was not only his most important act but the greatest achievement in human history and, together with his vindicating resurrection, the greatest act of God since the creation of the world.

---

[62] J. Jeremias, *Parables of Jesus*, 159.

[63] *Ibid.*

[64] "The Gospel has been designed to support the conclusion that Jesus is endowed with authority and that his teachings are worthy to be transmitted by the disciples." O. Brooks, "Matthew xxviii 16-20 and the Design of the First Gospel" *JSNT* 10 (1981), 2.
The Pauline definition of τὸ μυστήριον in Eph 3.8-12 makes sense as commentary on the Parables of Jesus taken together.

Within such a paradoxical framework, Matthew's restraint in narrating the acknowledged miracles which accompanied Jesus' ministry is understandable. These mighty acts were astonishing evidence of the coming Kingdom breaking into the present.

Now and Then

In our own time it is problematical to speak of 'miracles' at all. What C.F.D. Moule labels 'the thoroughgoing materialist position' assumes that any miracle story must be explained, finally, by 'natural laws' or as a false report.[65] That the evangelists themselves believed the reported mighty acts of Jesus is often accepted by those who take this position. Indeed, such critics sometimes exaggerate the superstitious gullibility of those living in the first centuries in terms of "a rampant jungle of ancient credulity with regard to miracles".[66]

Gerd Theissen has demonstrated the importance of distinguishing different patterns or fashions of thought about miracles in different periods of antiquity. The popularity of miracle stories in the third century AD must be recognized as representing a very different social and intellectual context from the one in which Matthew wrote. In the third century, typically, conversions to Christianity were related to miracle stories. Moreover, according to Ramsey MacMullen, the same can be said of conversions to non-Christian religions: "pagan sources tell of the same kind of stories as the Christians."[67] Whereas the first-century evangelists themselves regarded the stories of Jesus' mighty acts as evidence in some sense for the truth of the Gospel (*e.g.* Jn 20.31), the phenomenal persuasiveness of miracle stories in the third century and subsequent periods of history tends to discredit rather than recommend the biblical accounts to inquirers today. In an essay on "The Evidential Value of Biblical Miracles", C.F. Woods has shown that there have been wide fluctuations in patterns of arguments about the miracles even in comparatively recent time. Elements of the Gospels previously used to demonstrate the truth of Christianity have become the elements most demanding defense.[68]

The existence of charlatans and frauds in every age and mankind's enormous capacity for self-deception must be taken into account, but theists can scarcely deny the possibility of miracles if they believe that God created the

---

[65] C.F.D. Moule, *Miracles: Cambridge Studies in their Philosophy and History* (London: A.R. Mowbray, 1965), 14.

[66] G. Klein, "*Wunderglaube und Neues Testament*" (1970) quoted by G. Theissen, *The Miracles Stories of the Early Christian Tradition* (Philadelphia: Fortress, 1983 [1974]), 265.

[67] R. MacMullen, *Paganism in the Roman Empire* (New Haven: Yale, 1981), 96.

[68] C.F. Woods, *Miracles*, ed. C.F.D. Moule, 19-32. *Cf.* G. Theissen's observation: "The ancient Church's pride in the miracles has turned into its opposite." *Op. cit.*, 299.

world and continues to govern it.[69] C.F.D. Moule proposes 'a consistent theist position' over against the 'thoroughgoing materialist position'. "This position refuses to treat the material and the trans-material as separate systems, even though they may be distinguishable."[70] In any case, the analysis of Gerd Theissen, Birger Gerhardsson and others has demonstrated the significance of the miracle stories in the canonical Gospels and at the same time has proven that they cannot be subtracted or even minimized without collapsing the Gospels.[71] Moreover, "the resurrection and empty tomb" which climax each of the canonical Gospels "are miracles which dwarf anything that has gone before"[72]

Some of the special significance for the nations has already been noted of the miracles which marked Jesus' conception and baptism as well as his own refusal to perform miracles in response to the devil's seduction (1.1 - 4.16). Accounts of the miracles which Jesus himself performed are concentrated mainly in chapters 4.17 - 16.20. But for Matthew, certainly, "there is no doubt that Jesus worked miracles, healed the sick and cast out demons."[73] The record of the miracle stories in the First Gospel itself, like the record of Jesus' teaching in parables, can be claimed as documentary evidence for the relevance to the nations of these stories. But more to the point, "the existential meaning of the primitive Christian miracle stories" as "a revelation of the holy [and] its power to break into the normal course of the world"[74] can be interpreted as an analogue to the coming breakthrough of the Kingdom into the world of nations.

The universal implication of some non-therapeutic miracles such as the calming of the storm (Mt 8.23-27) are obvious. But Gerhardsson correctly identifies the particular reference of the healing miracles as "Jesus' therapeutic activity in Israel".[75] Even so, this particular reference has relevance to the nations, since Jesus' ministry to Israel related to Israel's indispensable role in the mission to the nations. So it is that the most 'particularistic' words and

---

[69] Ludwig Wittgenstein, after declaring that "God does not reveal himself *in* the world," concludes that "Not *how* the world is is the mystical, but *that* it is." (<*Nicht w i e die Welt ist, ist das Mystische, sondern, d a s s sie ist.*>) *Tractatus Logico-Philosophicus* ed. & trans. D.F. Pears and B.F. McGuiness (New York: Humanities Press, 1961), 6.432 & 6.44. Without revelation, nothing more can be said.

[70] C.F.D. Moule, *Miracles*, 16.

[71] In response to Kertelge's assertion that "the Marcan miracles have a tendency 'to make themselves superfluous'", Theissen asks, "Can Mark really have told sixteen miracle stories solely in order to war against belief in miracles? It seems rather a clumsy way of doing it." *Miracle Stories*, 294. *Cf.* J. LaGrand, "The First of the Miracle Stories According to Mark (1:21-28)", *Currents in Theology and Mission* 20/6 (1993) 479-84.
Theissen distinguishes sharply between magicians and "charismatic miracle-workers" (242) and B. Gerhardsson notes that "part of the character of the mighty acts ...[is that] they are ambiguous." *The Mighty Acts of Jesus According to Matthew* (Lund: Gleerup, 1979), 18.

[72] G. Theissen, *Miracle Stories*, 295.

[73] *Ibid.*, 277.

[74] *Ibid.*, 291.

[75] B. Gerhardsson, *Mighty Acts*, 20.

deeds of Jesus are the most promising to the nations. Matthew's use of Isaiah 53 (Mt 12.15-21) to explain the significance of Jesus' healings anticipates the apocalyptic vision of "the healing of the nations" in the Kingdom (Rev 22.2).

The Sign of Jonah

Matthew's testimony to the incomparability of Jesus' mighty acts (e.g. Mt 9.33) must be taken into account in any attempt to interpret the Gospel miracles. Related to this testimony is Jesus' sharply negative judgment against the demand for a 'sign', recorded in Matthew 12.38-42 and again in 16.4. Without attempting to consider all the implications of these important texts, we can point to broad and deep significance in these saying for the mission to the nations.

Jesus' repeated reference to the biblical book of Jonah, according to Matthew, is itself noteworthy for our theme. But the meaning of 'the sign of Jonah', which has sometimes been judged by New Testament scholars to be a riddle without a solution, can be interpreted —correctly, I believe— as an implicit prediction of the apostolic mission to all nations.

'The vocabulary of miracle' in the New Testament is instructive. But as C.F.D. Moule points out, it would be a mistake to suppose that because σημεῖον is usually used negatively in the Synoptics (with δύναμις being the characteristic word for miracles) Matthew, Mark, and Luke have a view of miracles fundamentally different from that of Josephus and the author of the Fourth Gospel.[76] Without digressing into a word-study here, we can profit by noting Matthew's use of the term σημεῖον in Jesus' negative judgment. K.H. Rengstorf observes that "the miracles give rise to the demand" for a 'sign' that Jesus' power was divinely ordained.[77] The demanded proof itself would not necessarily or even probably involve a miraculous act. More likely, it would have involved the accurate prediction of an event or portent. As the challenge is put here, it is reminiscent of Jesus' temptation by the devil. To give in to the demand, like bowing down to the devil, would contradict Jesus' ministry and the significance of the mighty acts which prompted the challenge.

Appeals to Jonah by Jesus, and specifically to 'the preaching of Jonah' (Mt 12.41), are a challenge to Matthew's readers to re-read the book for the proof of Jesus' divine vocation. Like the basic references to the Isaiah scroll in Matthew 8.17 and 12.18-21, the two references to Jonah provide a glimpse into Jesus' own understanding of the Scriptures as directive for his ministry. Jesus' response to the scribes and Pharisees (and again to the Pharisees and Sadducees), like the story of Jonah, is directed to recalcitrant Israel. George Landes characterizes "the central thrust" of the book of Jonah as "related to the way in which the author understood the implications of 4:2b": ("You are a gracious and merciful God, slow to anger and rich in clemency, loath to punish.")[78] The book of Jonah, like Jesus' teaching and healing ministry,

---

[76] C.F.D. Moule, "The Vocabulary of Miracle", *op. cit.*, 235. *Cf.* George MacRae, "Miracle in the *Antiquities* of Josephus", *ibid.*, 127-47.

[77] K.H. Rengstorf, *TDNT* 7, 236.

[78] G. Landes, *IDB* Suppl, 489b.

projects a strong and undeniable promise to the nations which awaits explication and application. The miracle of Jonah's deliverance from watery death by the fish is an astonishing act of God, symbolizing Yahweh's mercy to undeserving Israel.

Turning now specifically to the representation in the First Gospel of 'the sign of Jonah', τὸ σημεῖον Ἰωνᾶ, we can be confident that this 'sign' will not conform to the demand and expectations of those requesting the proof of Jesus' divine authority.[79] The grammar of the sentence and of the whole *pericope* (and the summary parallel in Mark's Gospel) make Rengstorf's concern about doing "justice to the meaning of σημεῖον" misdirected.[80] Jesus defines the meaning here in a riddle. The possibility that the 'sign' is specifically and exclusively defined by his current preaching is precluded by Matthew's inclusion of the pointed reference to Jonah's deliverance from *sheol* and the future tense of the verb ἔσται in verse 40 (cf. δοθήσεται in Mt 12.39 & par).[81] But what *the present generation* will witness is precisely related to Jonah's preaching to the heathen after being raised from the dead. Just as Jonah himself was shocked and dismayed by the transforming power of God on those who heard his message, so will this perverse generation be astonished when the nations turn to the God of Israel in response to the apostolic preaching, after the resurrection of the Son of Man.

E. Two Exceptional Responses to Non-Israelites

Miracles are exceptional by any definition, and Matthew repeatedly emphasizes the astonishment which attended Jesus' mighty acts. In Theissen's terms, Jesus was a "charismatic miracle worker ... looking for new patterns of life applicable to society", in contrast to contemporary magicians.[82] If we express this in theological terms, interpreting Matthew's account of Jesus' mighty acts as the coming Kingdom breaking into the present, there is no contradiction in Jesus' extension of his healing power also to the nations. Even so, there is a special

---

[79] J. Jeremias characterizes Jesus' response as "a riddle"; our solution differs from his, but we agree that "there is no discrepancy between the absolute refusal to give a sign (Mt. 8:11) and the intimation of the sign of Jonah. Both statements make it clear that God will not give any sign that is abstracted from the person of Jesus and that does not give offence." *TDNT* 3, 410. R.A. Edwards gets tangled up in his brief comparison of the studies by J. Jeremias and K.H. Rengstorf of this 'sign'. *The Sign of Jonah in the Theology of the Evangelists and Q* (London: SCM, 1971), 15, note 40.

[80] K.H. Rengstorf, *loc. cit.*, 233.

[81] With reference to the narrative sequence in the story of Jonah, note that Jonah does not call to Yahweh until he is plunging to *sheol*. But Jonah does compose a psalm of thanksgiving after God has saved his life by means of the great fish (Jonah 2.1-2). At least since early medieval times many Jewish and Christian interpreters (*e.g.* J. Jeremias, *loc. cit.*, 410 n28) have misread the story as a tale of "deliverance from the monster" instead of a story of divine deliverance from watery death. See G. Landes, *IDB* Suppl, 488-91.

[82] G. Theissen, *Miracle Stories*, 242.

element of surprise in the telling of the healing of the centurion's servant (Mt 8.5-13) and of the Canaanite woman's daughter (Mt 15.21-28).

As Gerhardsson rightly observes, Jesus' healing is limited to Israel by design.[83] The special emphasis on the faith of the centurion and the Canaanite woman indicates that these representatives of the nations are proleptically joined to Israel in anticipation of the time when God's people will be formed from all the nations. But except for their faith, neither could pass for a Jew. Each in different ways was emphatically foreign.

A Leader of the Opposition?

Jesus insistently demonstrated his willingness to associate with tax collectors, who were Jewish collaborators with the foreign occupation forces. But reaching out to such 'wandering sheep' was quite different from personal involvement with a leader of the Roman army. A centurion epitomized the heathen forces from which many hoped Jesus would liberate Israel. Luke's account of this story has its own plausibility, but Jesus' rhetorical question recorded by Matthew is the obvious rejoinder to the statement of the centurion in context: "Am I to come and cure him?" (Ἐγὼ ἐλθὼν θεραπεύσω αὐτόν; Mt 8.7b.)[84] If, indeed, this is an expression of Jesus' first surprise at the centurion's presumption, Jesus' amazement at the centurion's statement of faith is the more emphatic and unambiguous: "In the case of no one in Israel have I found such faith." Clearly,

> the pagan centurion has made the kind of response to the ministry of Jesus that Jesus himself was looking for, a response which had not been forthcoming to the same degree in the place where one would have expected it — in Israel.[85]

'Jesus' promise to the nations' is brilliantly clear and tightly bound to his mission to Israel in the *logion* which Matthew includes in this story: "I tell you, many will come from east and west to sit at table with Abraham, Isaac, and Jacob in the Kingdom of heaven" (Mt 8.11). The echo of Psalm 107.2-3 might suggest a first reference to dispersed Jews, but the placement of the saying here

---

[83] Specifically Northern Israel. B. Gerhardsson, *Mighty Acts*, 35. *Cf.* Theissen, *Miracle Stories*, 247: "Most of the miracle stories are set in Galilee."

[84] For punctuation of Mt 8.7b as a question, see Chapter 2, note 27. "In the context of the whole, the better understanding undoubtedly results from regarding it as the astonished or indignant question of Jesus." H.J. Held, "Matthew as Interpreter of the Miracle Stories", *Tradition and Interpretation in Matthew* ed. Bornkamm *et al.* (Philadelphia: Westminster, 1963), 194. See 1982 *Gute Nachricht im heutigem Deutsch* & *NEB* footnote, *contra* UBS Greek *NT* editors, *Zürcher Bibel, NRSV et al.*
There are no objective controls for this textual-critical decision except the meaning of the words in context. The earliest extant MSS marks of interrogation are AD 9th cent. F. Blass and A. Debrunner, *A Greek Grammar of the New Testament and Other Early Christian Literature*, trans. R.W. Funk (Chicago: University Press, 1961), 10 #16.

[85] T.W. Manson, *Only Israel?*, 21.

relates directly to the pilgrimage of the nations pictured in Isaiah 25.6. If the *logion* represents an authentic saying of Jesus, the saying may have been repeated by him many times. Its placement in this story may be redactional, but there is no reason to contradict Eduard Schweizer's suggestion that it might well have been "uttered under circumstances like those described here".[86]

How the promise will be fulfilled and precisely *when* is not yet clear. But in the End, God will enable people from all the nations to share the joys of the Kingdom of heaven with Israel. The promise recorded here is not only to the centurion as an individual but as a representative of his nation, which can hope to join in table fellowship with Israel's patriarchs. Ferdinand Hahn is right in his insistence that "the promises for all nations and the narratives of the acceptance of individual Gentiles must not be torn apart."[87]

Crumbs for Dogs

The incident involving the centurion is an isolated incident in the First Gospel, a signal of things to come. When a Canaanite woman pleads for mercy and healing for her daughter, Jesus again appears to be surprised by the presumption of the request (Mt 15.21-28). The clear priority of his ministry has remained the same as in the instructions to his disciples sent out 'to the wandering sheep of the House of Israel'. Jesus' positive commitment is explicitly restated here: Οὐκ ἀπεσάλην εἰ μὴ εἰς τὰ πρόβατα τὰ ἀπολωλότα οἴκου Ἰσραήλ (Mt 15.24).

Jesus' censure of the scribes and Pharisees' involvement in the far-flung campaign to bring individuals from distant lands into Israel through proselytizing, which we have already considered, comes later in Matthew's narrative. As we indicated, this censure must be understood in relation to the discipline which Jesus accepted for himself and his disciples regarding Israel and the nations. The censure is immediately preceded in Matthew 23 by condemnations of the scribes and Pharisees' failure to carry out their corporate responsibilities as leaders of Israel (Mt 23.1-13). So when Matthew tells of Jesus' travels to Tyre and Sidon in search of Israel's wandering sheep, it is important to show that Jesus resists the temptation to win over to his movement the relatively rich and powerful non-Israelite individuals there.[88] If, as seems

---

[86] E. Schweizer, *Good News Mt*, 213.

[87] F. Hahn, *Mission in the New Testament* (London: SCM, 1965 [1963]), 39 [31]. With reference to Mt 8.11, Hahn rejects Jeremias' rigid stereotype of 'the pilgrimage of the nations'. The *combination* of the meal in the Kingdom with the nations' pilgrimage cannot be documented earlier, according to Hahn. But this conjunction makes new expectations possible "in a way characteristic of Jesus" (35 n1). Jeremias himself, in a later work, makes this point with reference to Mt 11.5 / Lk 7.22f where "the fulfillment goes far beyond all promises, hopes and expectations". *NT Theol* vol 1: *Proclamation*, 103 & 105.

[88] The woman was "probably a member of the Hellenized upper class". G. Theissen, *Miracle Stories*, 253. Theissen's reference is to Mk but applies equally to Mt. B.C. Butler argues persuasively for the priority of the Matthean form of this *pericope* (Mt 15.21-8 / Mk 7.24-30). *The Originality of St Matthew* (Cambridge: University Press, 1951), 130-1.

likely, the Canaanite woman is wealthy, her petition represents a temptation and challenge to the integrity of the teacher who declared in another context that "it is harder for a wealthy person to enter heaven than for a camel to pass through the eye of a needle" (Mt 19.24). But this woman's remarkable faith, like the centurion's, shows that she is indeed "poor in spirit" (Mt 5.3) and ready to receive the Kingdom of heaven.

Jesus' commitment to Israel is positive and has positive implications for the nations. These implications could only be worked out through the work which he was sent to do. Representation of the self-understanding of others must always be attempted cautiously, but T.W. Manson's formulation correlates with what is known from the Gospels about Jesus' early ministry:

> I think that Jesus saw the immediate task as that of creating ... a [disciplined] community within Israel, in that faith that it would transform the life of his own people, and that a transformed Israel would transform the world.[89]

If we allow also for Jesus' anticipation, already at this time, of his own sacrificial death, the importance of working within Israel to this conclusion is no less clear. But that is a theme which dominates the narrative only in the final section of the Gospel (*16.21 - 28.20*), where the focus is on Judea and specifically Jerusalem.

Joachim Jeremias is quite right in judging that Jesus' response to the Canaanite woman and to the Roman centurion are exceptions that prove the rule. Jesus' own unqualified statement of the rule in his confrontation with the woman is an indication of his commitment to the will of God, as he understood it (Mt 15.29). The fact that he relented in response to the woman's expression of faith, which included acceptance of the divine election of Israel ("yet even the dogs eat the crumbs" Mt 15.27), indicates not sentimentality on Jesus' part, but acceptance of this revelation of "what is now God's will for him".[90] For the evangelist certainly, and apparently also for Jesus himself, this encounter pointed to the time when even Canaanites, who stood under an ancient curse (Gen 9.25), would be received into the Kingdom of heaven as children of God through faith.

Our view is *contra* that of R.H. Gundry who thinks that Mt emphasizes "Jesus' departure into a territory of Gentiles" and intends "to make the story a dominical example of ministry to Gentiles". *Matthew: A Commentary on His Literary and Theological Art* (Grand Rapids: Eerdmans, 1982), 310.

[89] T.W. Manson, *Only Israel?*, 23-24.//
[90] J. Jeremias, *Jesus' Promise*, 32.

10

THE NATIONS IN THE DESIGN OF THE GOSPEL:

ESTABLISHMENT OF THE KINGDOM

Jesus' proclamation of the Kingdom to Israel is complete, in principle, when Simon Peter makes his confession that Jesus is the Messiah, the Son of the living God (16.16). The narrative of Jesus' words and deeds continues, broken only by Jesus' death itself and the three days (Mt 27.50 - 28.1). But 'απο τότε ἤρξατο ὁ Ἰησοῦς ... /[1]

> From then on Jesus began to show his disciples that it was necessary for him to go to Jerusalem and there suffer many indignities from the elders, ruling priests, and scribes, to be put to death and the third day be resurrected. (Mt 16.21.)

Peter's protest focuses the apparent contradiction between Jesus' vocation as the *suffering* Messiah and his identity as the Son of God. The clarity of Jesus' response to Peter's outburst reveals the strength of maturity the Messiah has gained since his initial temptation by the devil (Mt 4.10/ 16.23).

The story goes on without any immediate change of scene, and Peter's abrupt turn-about is explicable in terms of previous characterization (*e.g.* Mt 14.28/30). But "from this point" Matthew narrates *the establishment of the Kingdom*. The event being described in the third and last main section of the Gospel (*16.21 - 28.20*), is the Messiah's death-resurrection. This is explicitly announced at the beginning of the section and again in 17.22-23 and 20.17-19.

---

[1] "Jesus Messiah" (Ἰησους Χριστος) is the reading of both ℵ and B. This Christological reading, if original, implies Mt's *intentional* use of this sentence to announce the establishment of the Kingdom.

John Meier has demonstrated that this two-sided event is "an eschatological turning point" in the design of the First Gospel.[2]

"Jerusalem ... now supersedes Galilee as the focus of attention" even though much of the action is still set in Galilee.[3] The evangelist's faithfulness to the demands of narrative form —and Jesus' faithfulness to his calling— requires some reports of continuing mighty acts, parables, and *halakah*. But these forms themselves now stand under the shadow of the Messiah's death, even as they provide proof of the Kingdom being established.

A. The Messiah's Death

The Messiah is relinquishing power, ever more clearly, "from this point on". With the solution to the problem of sin having been announced, even the significance of healing acts in Israel is eclipsed.[4] Coming down from the mount of transfiguration, Jesus is confronted with his disciples' failed attempt to heal a demon-possessed boy. Jesus' response to the father's plea for mercy is linked to his own focused attention on the radical response required for the malaise of this "faithless and perverse generation" (Mt 17.17). Jesus "spoke sternly to the boy, and the demon left him" (Mt 17.18). But Jesus' answer to the obvious question from his disciples ("Why couldn't we do it?") demonstrates his concern for their faith rather than for specific instruction about future healings.

As Jesus finally approaches Jerusalem, the two noisy blind men outside Jericho appear in the narrative almost as stragglers who had missed out on Jesus' earlier healing ministry. His query, "What do you want me to do for you?" (Mt 20.32), is not a calloused response but a riddle (*mashal*). Compassion demands healing, which Jesus provides. But his own preoccupation is now with the cure for spiritual blindness which, ironically, seems to afflict the two rather less than the others.

1. Three Predictions
(Matthew 16.21; 17.22-23; 20.17-19; cf. 26.1-2)

The three predictions reveal death-resurrection as two sides of the same event. Nevertheless, the directness of Matthew's account of the first prediction, followed by Peter's vociferous objection, dramatically emphasizes the side of suffering and death (Mt 16.21-22). The twelve disciples, like Martha in the Fourth Gospel (Jn 11.24), were probably prepared to profess belief in resurrection from the dead. But their attitude was informed by ordinary experience with human mortality, and the threatening signs gathering around

---

[2] J.P. Meier, *Law and History in Matthew's Gospel* (Rome: Biblical Institute, 1976), 23.

[3] J.D. Kingsbury, *Matthew: Structure, Christology, Kingdom* (Philadelphia: Fortress, 1975), 23.

[4] The eclipse is not total. A burst of miraculous energy accompanies the Messiah's appearance in the Temple (Mt 21.14-15 *cf.* Jn 2.23).

Jesus' ministry now focus their attention on 'death' more sharply than on 'resurrection'.

In his report of the second and third predictions, likewise, the evangelist projects the twelve disciples' sense of immediate threat of humiliation and death to Jesus (and themselves). The first prediction was convincing in its directness and the specification of opposition to Jesus by Israel's leaders. The second broadens and deepens the description in terms of 'betrayal to human agency' (παραδίδοσθαι εἰς χεῖρας ἀνθρώπων), poignantly balancing Jesus' reference to himself as ὁ υἱὸς τοῦ ἀνθρώπου. The emotional point strikes home and the disciples are "filled with grief" (Mt 17.22-23). The third prediction recapitulates both earlier formulations but adds narratively convincing details which are eschatologically significant: Jesus takes the twelve disciples aside to prepare them for what is about to happen in the Holy City.

> Look, we are coming into Jerusalem. There the Son of Man will be betrayed to the ruling priests and scribes, who will condemn him to death and hand him over to the nations; the heathen will ridicule him, whip him, and crucify him; and the third day he will be raised from the dead (Mt 20.18-20).

Events are moving quickly. The narrator says nothing about grief or despair in response to this most explicit prediction of imminent disaster. Nevertheless, the reader understands that the disciples are experiencing emotional over-load. Perhaps in desperation they seize on the hope of the resurrection. Whether desperate or not, James and John have vivid projections of the future in their minds.

Comic Relief

In a scene that begins like comic opera, the mother of these two disciples from Jesus' closest circle of three confidants comes bowing respectfully to petition top spots for her sons in Jesus' Kingdom. Apparently assuming that James and John had put their mother up to the request, Jesus reprimands them and sharply focuses their attention again on his anticipated crucifixion. The two seem quite unable to understand Jesus' words, most likely because paralyzed by embarrassment at being discovered in their political maneuver. But for the reader with ears to hear, Jesus' question and his response to James and John's answer in this *pericope* clearly explain the meaning of the Messiah's death, both for the gathered community and for the whole world.

The contrast between Jesus' disciples and "world rulers" (οἱ ἄρχοντες τῶν ἐθνῶν Mt 20.25) has been sketched in some detail by Matthew in the immediately preceding discourse on the new community (Mt 17.22-18.35). Earlier, in the second main section of the Gospel (*4.17 — 16-20*) the pattern of the Son of Man's service was established. In this final section Matthew concludes the story of how Jesus came "to give his life as a ransom for many" (διακονῆσαι καὶ δοῦναι τὴν ψυχὴν αὐτοῦ λύτρον ἀντὶ πολλῶν Mt 20.28).

2. From Death to Life in the New Community

To the reader who knows the outcome of the drama, it is clear that the discourse on life in the new community is addressed to those redeemed by the Messiah's death. What was already anticipated in Jesus' baptism "to fulfill all righteousness" (Mt 3.15) and represented proleptically in the authority of his teaching (Mt 7.29) and mighty acts (Mt 8.27) is a transcendent righteousness which the community receives as a gift from God through Jesus' redeeming death. The radical freedom to forgive, which characterizes the new community, is compellingly represented by the cautionary tale of the unmerciful debtor which concludes the discourse (Mt 18.21-35). In the context of ordinary experience, it is all too believable that a clever scoundrel who manages to be forgiven a debt of millions should press the letter of the law in demanding repayment of a couple of hundred dollars from his own debtor. But members of the new community forgive as they have been forgiven.

Forgiving our debtors is not itself a work of righteousness which earns divine forgiveness, but to refuse to forgive small debts in response to God's forgiveness of our massive debt of sin is to break faith. Forgiveness is a gift from God, which must be received in faith.

The encounter with the rich young man (Mt 19.16-30) and the parable of the day laborers in the vineyard (Mt 20.1-16) declare that life is a gift from God which defies human calculations. The parable includes a demand for work according to ability as an expression of faith, but stunningly insists that God gives the full wages of eternal life to all the faithful alike. This parable and many others in this last section of Matthew's Gospel invite interpretation also in terms of 'Israel' and 'the nations'.[5] The faithful in Israel receive the full reward; but the heathen who are accepted as laborers in the vineyard only at the end of the day likewise receive the full reward of life everlasting.

Before pressing on to the fundamental issue of the 'ransom for many' in Jerusalem, we should consider one more vineyard parable which comes somewhat later in the narrative. The parable of the two sons includes the phrase "in the way of righteousness" (ἐν ὁδῷ δικαιοσύνης Mt 21.32), which we cited earlier with reference to Georg Strecker's emphasis on the concept of 'righteousness' in Matthean theology. In the narrative context, the challenge to Jesus' authority to teach in the Temple which introduces this parable has symbolic significance. Specifically, the ruling priests and elders of the people ask, "Who gives you this authority?" (Mt 21.23). After parrying with a question

---

[5] J.D. Kingsbury and others see Israel's rejection of Jesus and his rejection of Israel, in turn, as a major Matthean theme. But Kingsbury does not sufficiently account for the disciples as a faithful remnant of Israel when he writes of "the rejection of Jesus by all segments of Israel (11:2 - 12:50) [and] the negative responses of Jesus to Israel which the people themselves prompted". *Mt: Structure*, 19. *Cf.* D. Verseput's thesis on *The Rejection of the Humble Messianic King* (Frankfort: Peter Lang, 1986), which gives scant attention to 'this generation' of Mt 11.16-19 (106).
When even the disciples abandon Jesus before the Trial, Mt's point seems to be that 'all mankind' rejected Jesus. See below on "*Gethsemane, Trial and Crucifixion*".

about John the Baptist which they do not dare to answer for fear of the mob's reaction, Jesus declares that he will not answer either. But the parable which follows immediately is aimed at his interrogators and relates directly to their question.[6] If we accept the text which has the first son answer his father's command with a disrespectful refusal, followed by repentance and unannounced obedience, we can accept Jesus' "amen" as confirmation that the priest and elders correctly identified the first son as the one who did the will of his father. The second son said the right words, but did not act accordingly. The willingness of the priests and elders to give an honest answer to the *mashal* may have been governed in part by their inability to imagine themselves as the second son, with the *'am ha'aretz* as the first son. Several observations relevant to 'the way of righteousness' can be made here.

On the one hand, it is consistent with Matthew's narrative, and with the multiple tradition, for Jesus to give priority in this parable to the *'am ha'aretz* as 'the wandering sheep of the House of Israel' (Mt 10.6/15.24). But the reader should not be so eager to assign roles as to miss the point that the verbal answer of the first son is shockingly wrong. Those represented by him are indeed 'sheep that have gone astray', sinners who depend on the forgiveness and mercy of God in response to their repentance. On the other hand, the leaders of Israel —including "those who sit in the chair of Moses" (Mt 23.12)— are capable of saying the right words. But they have made an artifice of the law and separated their lives from the will of God. Consequently, they were unable to recognize the authority of the word of God spoken by the Baptizer in the wilderness or now by Jesus in the Temple.

Just as John's proclamation of the Kingdom 'in the way of righteousness' had been a call to repentance, so Jesus' teaches that "actual performance is to be approved, not lip service."[7] Deeds of faith connect the repentant sinner to God's covenant faithfulness. But neither John's preaching (Mt 3.8) nor this parable allows interpretation of the sinners deeds of faith as 'fulfilling all righteousness' (Mt 3.15). God brings in the Kingdom from beyond ordinary human achievement, just as the father in the parable provided the vineyard.

The link between salvation and righteousness is important and indissoluble.[8] As Birger Gerhardsson observes, "Matthew stresses, in quite

---

[6] This analysis accepts the difficult reading of ℵ (*Siniaticus*) as the original Matthean text (21.28-32), following the UBS editors. Alternatively, J.D.M. Derrett's very challenging proposal is based on the B (*Vaticanus*) text. He identifies "the chief priests and elders" with the elder son, citing J. Jeremias and A. Jülicher. In Derrett's view, verse 32 is "an old soteriological amplification, which ought to be eliminated before study of the parable". "The Parable of the Two Sons", *Studia Theologica* 25 (1971), 110 note 3.

[7] J.D.M. Derrett, "Parable of the Two Sons", 115.

[8] In Chapter **8** (182) we criticized Georg Strecker's formulation of 'righteousness', but his summary of Mt as "The Way of Righteousness" is exactly right.
B. Przybylski, in his monograph *Righteousness in Matthew and His World of Thought* (Cambridge: University Press, 1980), surprisingly concludes that "the concept of righteousness does not play a crucial role in Matthew's self-understanding as a follower of

explicit terms, that Jesus' ministry was for the purpose of taking away sin and creating righteousness."[9] This ministry certainly involves ambiguity and paradox, which Brian Nolan has expressed in terms of Matthew's "participatory Christology".[10] God himself enables "the Son of Man ... to give his life as a ransom for many" (Mt 20.28). But divine initiative does not eliminate or trivialize human response. "Matthew's stress on mercy is not impaired by his respect for justice."[11]

3. Jerusalem, the Temple, and the Passover Sacrifice

The focus on Jerusalem, the place of sacrifice, in this final section of Matthew's Gospel indicates the meaning of the Messiah's death (*16.21-28.15*, excepting the concluding commission in Galilee). This focus defines the reference of 'a ransom for many'.[12] The Temple itself figures prominently in this section, with references to it in the trial and in Matthew's description of the crucifixion. But it is *the Passover* which is the central motif in the Last Supper (with what are now called the eucharistic words of Jesus), and in the crucifixion narrative. The Passover-Exodus motif also informs the concluding scene where the Promised Land is 'the whole world' (πάντα τὰ ἔθνη Mt 28.19 cf. ἐν ὅλῳ τῷ κόσμῳ 26.13) viewed from the mountain in Galilee of the *Goyim*.[13]

There are many different kinds of sacrifice described in the Hebrew Bible, and a bewildering variety of references to sacrifice in the New Testament itself, as Markus Barth reminds us in his essay, "Was Christ's Death a Sacrifice?"[14] The picture is further complicated if we consider, on the one hand, the varied

---

Jesus"(116). Correctly observing that "the Gospel of Matthew clearly indicates that salvation is the gift of God", Przybylski separates Mt's view of this gift from Mt's concept of righteousness: "righteousness is seen [by Mt] only as the demand of God made upon man" (*ibid*). Przybylski's conclusions and his stated method of analysis are opposite from ours in several ways. Most notable is his determination of "what in fact constitutes the appropriate background literature for the Gospel of Matthew"(3). At the higher levels of what we term 'the hierarchy of tagmemes' Przybylski insists that the Dead Sea Scrolls and the Tannaitic literature should be used as the basic context for interpreting Mt's Gospel, *not* the NT (and the canon of the Hebrew Bible and the NT taken together).

[9] B. Gerhardsson, "Sacrificial Service and Atonement in the Gospel of Matthew", *Reconciliation and Hope*, ed. R. Banks (Grand Rapids: Eerdmans, 1974), 25.

[10] B. Nolan, *The Royal Son of God: The Christology of Matthew 1-2 in the Setting of the Gospel* (Göttingen: Vanderhoeck & Ruprecht, 1979), 115.

[11] *Ibid.*, 124.

[12] M. Barth, *Was Christ's Death a Sacrifice?* (Edinburgh: Oliver & Boyd, 1961), 4. E. Lohse's comment on the Marcan text applies equally to Mt 16.21: "This 'must' ... is not an expression of the inexorableness of fate but points rather to the fact that in the passion of Christ is it the will of God that is to be fulfilled." *History of the Suffering and Death of Jesus Christ* (Philadelphia: Fortress, 1967 [1964]), 20. *Cf.* J. Jeremias, *The Eucharistic Words of Jesus* (Philadelphia: Fortress, 1977 [1960]), 225, and M. Hengel, *The Atonement: The Origins of the Doctrine in the New Testament* (Philadelphia: Fortress, 1981), 73.

[13] N.A. Dahl, "The Passion Narrative in Matthew", *Interp Mt*, ed. G. Stanton, 52.

[14] M. Barth, *Was Christ's Death a Sacrifice?*, 10-27.

prophetic evaluation of Israel's cultic practice in the Bible itself[15] and, on the other hand, the sharply divergent practices of sacrifice in Israel by different sects such as the Samaritans, the Elephantine colony, the group at Leontopolis, and the Essenes.[16] Despite its suspension during the Babylonian Captivity, Jerusalem Temple sacrifice was of fundamental importance for the faith and life of Israel in the time of Jesus. The annual *Hanukkah* celebration of the recapture and purification of the Temple by Judas Maccabeus in the second century BC reflects this importance. The elaborate regulations recorded in the *Mishnah* for sacrifice in Jerusalem, even though physical sacrifices were no longer possible after AD 135, indicates the persistent importance of *the idea of sacrifice* also in Rabbinic Judaism.[17]

In the midst of all this variety, the earliest Christian community appears to have been united in its understanding of the central importance for their faith of the suffering and death of the Messiah. The Gospel narratives do not allow the kind of systematic development of this theme that can be found in the Pauline and Petrine epistles and in the Epistle to the Hebrews. But Matthew's exploitation of the idea of 'fulfillment' shows that he understands the Messiah's sacrificial death to be the recapitulation and goal of all the forms of sacrifice in Israel. The Apostle Paul's characterization of this understanding of the crucified Messiah as "a stumbling block to Jews and an absurdity to Greeks" (I Cor 1.23) is a forceful reminder that even, and especially, for Jews the idea is offensive. Simon Peter's protest at the beginning of this final section of Matthew's Gospel (16.22) is understandable in these terms.[18] But Jesus' immediate response is even more emphatic than Peter's strong protest. "From this point on" Jesus insistently directs his path towards Jerusalem. As the narrative of the First Gospel unfolds, it becomes clear that the meaning of *Jesus' death must be understood in terms of sacrifice in Israel.* Only in these terms can his death have significance and promise for the nations.

According to Exodus 19.6, Israel is "a kingdom of priests". This text is not cited in the First Gospel, but the logic of Jesus' journey to Jerusalem with

---

[15] M.A. Schmidt, *Prophet und Tempel: eine Studie zum Problem der Gottesnähe im Alten Testament* (Zollikon-Zürich: Evangelischer, 1948). *Cf.* various critical appraisals of Jesus' quotation of Hosea 6.6 in Mt 9.13 & 12.7.

[16] Reference to post-Exilic temple in Leontopolis (Egypt) in Josephus *Antiq* xiii.62-73. *Cf.* "Hebrew sanctuaries and temples (those besides Jerusalem)" in G.A. Barrois, "Temples", *IDB* 4, 566-68. *Re* 'Cleansing of the Temple', L. Gaston, *No Stone on Another, Studies in the Significance of the Fall of Jerusalem in the Synoptic Gospels* (Leiden:Brill, 1970), 112-19. The Essene boycott of the Jerusalem Temple resulted in a spiritualized abstinence which can be compared, at least superficially, to later Christian and Rabbinic practice. But the Essenes seem to have understood their system as a temporary measure —until the pollution could be removed from Jerusalem to allow for properly administered sacrifice.

[17] *N.b.* the eleven tractates in the Fifth Division, *Kodashim*, Danby ed. 467-602.

[18] M. Hengel, *Atonement*, 40.

his disciples conforms to this pattern.[19] Immediately following the first of the predictions of death in Jerusalem is the saying, "If anyone will come with me, he must take up his cross and follow me" (Mt 16.24). Jesus alone is finally delivered up as the 'ransom for many', but "the Matthean Jesus stresses forcefully that every true believer must be prepared to make even the utmost sacrifice," as Birger Gerhardsson correctly notes.[20] In the Fourth Gospel the threat of the journey to Jerusalem to the disciples, as well as to Jesus, is explicitly expressed by Thomas' declaration of faith: "Let us go along to die with him" (Jn 11.16). A faithful remnant of Israel travels to the Holy City in submission to the will of God for mankind's atonement.[21]

Entry into Jerusalem and Cleansing of the Temple

The narrative prominence of Jesus' entry into the Holy City and his cleansing of the Temple are not unique to the First Gospel. These Matthean features must be explained in terms of the earliest Christian tradition which related Jesus' action and Messianic consciousness to the 'suffering servant' scriptures.[22] Such common elements of the story must not be supposed to be less characteristic of Matthew's theology than are the elements peculiar to his account. Neither should we suppose that the Scriptures quoted here (with one text attributed to the crowds and two to Jesus) are the only texts which the evangelist considered relevant to the occasion. In a full and adequate reflection on the meaning which Matthew —and Jesus— might have understood in these events, very many other texts should also be considered. For our theme, however, there is particular significance in the scriptures quoted from Zechariah (Mt 21.5) and Isaiah 56 (Mt 21.13).

Since Mark quotes the complete sentence from Isaiah 56.7, "My house shall be called a house of prayer for all the nations" (Mk 11.17), Matthew's omission of the phrase "for all the nations" seems odd, especially to critical scholars who assume Marcan priority. C.H. Dodd solves the puzzle by saying what many have felt: "Matthew and Luke, in copying Mark, have left out 'for all the nations', missing the point."[23] But another explanation is possible. The words which follow in Scripture immediately after those just quoted by the narrator from Zechariah 9.9 (Mt 21.5) also are strikingly relevant to the theme:

---

[19] As pilgrims to Jerusalem for the Passover celebration, the disciples were reenacting the Exodus pattern in a general way. More specifically, the evangelist enables us to see that Jesus' band is moving to the place where the salvation of mankind will be enacted. "*Intervenair dans le centre, c'est transformer l'organisme entier.*" B. Sundkler, "Jésus et les païns", *Revue d'histoire et de philosophie Religieuses* 16 (1936) 466-99.

[20] B. Gerhardsson, "Sacrificial Service and Atonement", *op. cit.*, 32.

[21] This view contradicts all arguments about 'the rejection of Israel'.

[22] With reference to identification of Jesus as the *ebed Yahweh*, it can be said confidently that this is a distinctive NT theme "which does full justice to the total witness of the New Testament". O. Cullmann, *Christology*, 80.

[23] C.H. Dodd, *The Founder of Christianity* (London: Macmillan, 1970), 180 note 12.

> He shall banish the chariot from Ephraim
> and the war horse from Jerusalem.
> The warrior's bow shall be banished
> and he shall proclaim peace to the nations.

Both of these sequels are so explicit that it seems probable that Matthew is pointing his readers to them.[24] If so, his restraint in not spelling out the lines may be explained in terms of the requirements of the narrative which is still focused here on Israel itself.

Following Jesus' last discourse this restraint is lifted with his declaration that "the Son of Man will be handed over to be crucified, at the Passover, in two days" (Mt 26.2). After a short note about the priests' and elders' plot to kill Jesus, Matthew records the action of the woman pouring costly perfume on Jesus at the house of Simon the Leper in Bethany. This demonstration is accepted and affirmed by Jesus as "preparation for my burial", with an explicit reference to the future mission to all nations: "I assure you, wherever the good news is proclaimed throughout the world, what she did will be spoken of as her memorial" (Mt 26.12).

The Last Supper

No single incident in the Gospels is more 'transparent' than the Last Supper, which clearly represents the eucharistic celebration of the resurrection community. Earlier in the present study we emphasized the tradition of 'the eucharistic words of Jesus' in the community liturgy as the starting point for the writing of the canonical Gospels. Acknowledgement that the community was formed around these words is no judgment about the claim that the words can be traced back to Jesus. What we can say confidently is that Matthew did not make up all these words or the incident.

In all four Gospels the scene is presented as historical. As just noted in another connection, the words peculiar to the First Gospel —or in any of the Gospels— should not be assumed by that very fact to be either the most important elements in Matthew's account or his own composition. What can be assumed is that every word included in this section had special significance for Matthew and his first readers. What Jesus said and did "on the night in which he was betrayed" (I Cor 11.23; Mt 26. 21-25 & par) is presented here as prophetic or parabolic, relating back to the Exodus of Israel from Egypt and forward to Jesus' own sacrificial death on the cross.

The coincidence of this acted parable with the subsequent drama of Jesus' trial and crucifixion is uncanny. But although this correspondence or coincidence is almost unbelievable, it remains within the realm of historical possibility. Indeed, correspondence of Jesus' words to the events which began

---

[24] "It is the habit of ancient Jewish authors to cite merely the first words when quoting texts of this kind and to leave it to the informed reader to insert the whole text, even where it is the later words, not even included in the passage cited, which contain the really pertinent matter." E. Stauffer, *Jesus and His Story* (London: SCM, 1960), 112.

to unfold immediately could explain, in part, both the power of the eucharistic symbol in the earliest church and the pattern of Jesus' submission to his accusers and executioners. Without pressing ahead of the narrative, we should note that the account of the Last Supper by Matthew and the other evangelists has sustained close scrutiny in terms of historical analysis.[25] This is especially striking in modern research which has discovered details not known, or long forgotten, in the liturgical tradition of the churches.[26] For our present purposes the main point to note is that the Last Supper was a Passover meal.[27] Two other points of specific significance for the earliest Christian mission to all nations can be discovered in the single sentence which refers to 'the many' and 'forgiveness of sins' (Mt 26.28).

With reference to "the pre-Pauline passover *haggadah* preserved in I Cor. 5.7f." which calls Jesus 'our passover lamb', Joachim Jeremias argues the probability "that Jesus had prepared the way for this comparison of himself [with bread and wine representing his flesh and blood sacrifice] ... in the passover meditation" interpreting *"the passover lamb in terms of himself".*[28] Noting that "the crucifixion itself was a bloodless form of execution,"[29] Jeremias further argues for the historicity of these words which follow Scriptural usage (*e.g.* Lev 17.11) but seem unlikely to have been formulated after the event.

The 'many' certainly refers to persons in Israel, but just as certainly to the nations. The pre-Christian interpretations of Isaiah 53 (and 52) must be our guides to interpreting these words of Jesus, as Jeremias rightly insists.[30] Later Rabbinic interpretations of Isaiah 53, which typically confine the 'many' to Israel, reflect a new pattern of thought which was shaped in part by reaction to the persistent Christian references to this text.

The explicit reference to 'forgiveness of sins' in connection with 'covenant' echoes Jeremiah 31.34 (and Is 42.6 & 49.7-8), indicating that "Matthew thus looks upon the death of Jesus as the basis for the forgiveness of sins, albeit in such a way that the forgiveness is exercised by the community."[31] Eduard Schweizer suggests that in addition to the perception of atoning sacrifice, Matthew "sees Jesus going to his death ... as a pioneer, who opens the way of a new life to those who follow him".[32]

---

[25] Besides J. Jeremias, *Eucharistic Words, cf.* I. H. Marshall, *Last Supper and Lord's Supper* (Exeter: Paternoster, 1980) and M. Barth, *Das Mahl des Herrn: Gemeinschaft mit Israel, mit Christus and unter den Gästen* (Neukirchen-Vluyn: Neukirchener, 1987).

[26] J. Jeremias, *Eucharistic Words*, 7. Such claims of new discoveries will not be accepted immediately and universally, *e.g.* Jeremias' claim that "Jesus neither ate of the passover lamb nor drank of the wine; probably he fasted completely" (212).

[27] "All three of the Synoptic Gospels affirm that Jesus' last meal was a Passover meal." M. Barth, *Rediscovering the Lord's Supper* (Atlanta: John Knox, 1988), 15, *cf.* 9-10.

[28] J. Jeremias, *op. cit.*, 222.

[29] *Ibid.*, 223.

[30] *Ibid.*, 179-82; *cf.* M. Barth, *Rediscovering the Lord's Supper*, 24.

[31] E. Schweizer, *Good News Mt*, 491.

[32] *Ibid.*

Jeremias concludes that at this time "Jesus did expect a violent death,"[33] and what he claimed at the Last Supper was that

> his death is the vicarious death of the suffering servant, which atones for the sins of the 'many', the peoples of the world, which ushers in the beginning of the final salvation and which effects the new covenant with God.[34]

4. Gethsemane, Trial, and Crucifixion

The scene in Gethsemane emphasizes Jesus' deliberate thought and action in approaching his sacrificial death. The substantial agreement of the multiple tradition, represented also in the Epistle to the Hebrews 5.7-10, indicates the importance attached to this scene by the earliest church. The narrative description of Jesus facing death self-consciously, including the remarkable record of his words of anguish and grief (Mt 26.37-38), obviously supports the church's claim that Jesus in his human frailty already anticipated a violent death, and vindication through resurrection.[35] If this scene in Gethsemane is historical, it adds plausibility to Jesus' earlier predictions of his death and resurrection. Seen from this vantage point, even his sayings which projected a world-wide mission to the nations become conceivable within the context of Jesus' earthly ministry.

Strategic time is clearly at issue in the Gethsemane scene, both in Jesus' repeated remonstrance to the three disciples and in his ironic question to the posse about their failure to apprehend him previously during his daily teaching in the Temple (Mt 26.55). This 'hour' is even more sharply focused in Jesus' struggle with God in prayer;[36] and his insistence that the disciples should 'watch' might reflect the tradition —attested in later Rabbinic writings— that the Messiah would be revealed at the time of Passover.[37] And, perhaps with the lynch mob in sight, Jesus declares that *this is the hour*: "Look, the time has now arrived for the Son of Man to be betrayed into the hands of sinners" (Mt 26.46).

---

[33] J. Jeremias, *Eucharistic Words*, 225.

[34] *Ibid.*, 231.

[35] Not even the three disciples (who stayed some distance away) would have witnessed the *words* of Jesus' prayer, unless he cried aloud in his distress. It is hard to imagine the three falling asleep from nervous exhaustion while actually within hearing of such cries. This adds a difficulty (not unlike that encountered with the temptation accounts at the beginning of Jesus' ministry) to the assessment of this as an historical account.
That the three were in some sense witnesses suggests that this was a continuation of the Passover liturgy. "If during the Passover celebration members of the company fell into a deep sleep, and could not answer at all, then the celebration was regarded as terminated." W.F. Albright and C.S. Mann, *Matthew* (Garden City: Doubleday, 1971), 327 citing D. Daube, *NT and Rabbinic Judaism*, 333-5.

[36] Mt 26.38 and the repeated prayer itself make it clear that Jesus considered this to be the final hour of trial for him. He states this explicitly when 'the time is up' in 26.45.

[37] M. Barth, *Mahl des Herrn*, 23.

Matthew focuses his narrative sharply on Judas' betrayal, but in terms of what follows —with "all the disciples" fleeing (26.56) and Peter emphatically denying any association with Jesus (26.70/.72/.74)— even the show of loyalty by "one of those with Jesus" (26.51) is a sign of misunderstanding. This defensive act is a prelude to the betrayal of Jesus by all mankind. Only the few women at the foot of the cross remain with Jesus as a faithful remnant of Israel in the hour of divine judgment.[38]

Jesus' prediction that "the Son of Man is to be handed over to be crucified" (Mt 26.2) picks up the theme specified in the third (Synoptic) death-resurrection prophecy, that he would be delivered up to the heathen for final degradation and execution (Mt 20.17-19 & par). In fact, Jesus was sentenced by Roman authority and put to death with Roman penal procedure, as Oscar Cullmann emphasizes in his study of *The State in the New Testament*, and as Matthew's narrative itself indicates.[39] But the role played by the Sanhedrin is also significant and has been brought up for reconsideration in a number of recent studies.[40]

The Pharisees are not mentioned in Matthew's account of the trial and crucifixion, which is noteworthy,[41] although their involvement is implied in the reference to "the whole Sanhedrin" (Mt 26.59). Together with the earlier reference to "all the disciples" deserting Jesus (Mt 26.56) and the subsequent reference to "all the people" calling for Roman force (Mt 27.25), this inclusive designation indicates the theological answer to the question "Who crucified Jesus?" We all did. Certainly Matthew's account implicates both Israel and the nations.

That Generation

When the question "Who crucified Jesus?" is submitted to historical analysis, the only certain answer is "That generation." This certain answer could bear more emphasis than it has been given by European and American

---

[38] That the faithful remnant with Jesus appears to have been reduced finally to a few *women* has not been sufficiently recognized in modern times, until recently. Women are also the first witnesses of the Resurrection, according to the multiple tradition.

[39] O. Cullmann, *The State in the New Testament* (New York: Scribners, 1956), 42.

[40] *E.g.* D.R. Catchpole, "The Problem of the Historicity of the Sanhedrin Trial", *The Trial of Jesus* ed. Ernst Bammel (London: SCM, 1970), 47-65 responding to Paul Winter, *On the Trial of Jesus* (Berlin: W. de Gruyter, 1961). See Catchpole's *The Trial of Jesus: A Study in the Gospels and Jewish Historiography from 1770 to the Present Day* (Leiden: E.J. Brill, 1971) for a survey of earlier discussions.

[41] Paul Winter's analysis focuses on the significance of this omission, *op. cit.*, 125, but *cf.* Winter's evaluation of Mt's perspective (126).
This omission does not weaken C.F.D. Moule's argument that "Jesus' way of life and teaching were already recognized during his ministry as dangerous to Pharisaic Judaism." The *Birth of the New Testament* (San Francisco: Harper & Row, 1982 [1962]), 96. With reference to the Third Gospel, David Moessner notes that "for one reason or another, Luke intentionally absolves the Pharisees from direct involvement in the arrest and execution of Jesus." "The 'Leaven of the Pharisees' and 'This Generation'", *JSNT* 34 (1988), 23.

scholars, since Matthew's Jesus repeatedly and pointedly refers to that "wicked generation" (Mt 12.39, 16.4; 17.17; *cf.* 23.36; 24.34; & 12.41-2 /Mk & Lk; Acts 2.40 & Php 2.15).⁴² Historical arguments which are used to prove that Jews of subsequent generations bear specific responsibility for Jesus' execution not only outrun available evidence but twist it cruelly. Indeed, the tradition of representing the vicious shout of the mob as an expression of the will of God ("Let his blood be upon us and our children" Mt 27.25) has gained demonic force through the centuries of such interpretation.

The reformulation of the question "Who crucified Jesus?" to "What crucified Jesus?", proposed by Ellis Rivkin, has the advantage of maintaining the historical focus on that 'wicked generation' in terms of Jewish collaboration with Roman imperial policy. Rivkin uses the writings of Josephus to reconstruct "an objective framework of time, place, structure, and circumstance" for Jesus' trial and crucifixion.⁴³

It was not uncommon for Roman officials to use violence to suppress expressions of Jewish 'zeal for the Law' which transgressed imperial authority. Recalling that such violence in Jesus' time included the execution by Herod the Great of the individuals who tore down the golden eagle from the Temple entrance, and the crucifixion by Quintilius Varus of about 2,000 insurrectionists,⁴⁴ Rivkin gives a convincing explanation for Josephus' designation of the ideology of resistance formulated by Judas of Galilee and Zadok the Pharisee as a "fourth philosophy" comparable to the teachings of the Sadducees, the Pharisees, and the Essenes.⁴⁵ What was new, according to Josephus' disapproving appraisal, was the unreasonable refusal of those following 'the fourth philosophy' to accommodate Roman authority.⁴⁶

Even though Sadducees, Pharisees, and Essenes differed sharply and bitterly from each other, each of these groups assumed what Rivkin calls a political doctrine of 'two realms' and a religious policy of 'live and let live'.⁴⁷ The Sadducees and Pharisees were even able to work together "in many areas of mutual concern, especially those that might endanger the very existence of

---

⁴² The term 'generation' is ambiguous in Greek, Aramaic and Hebrew as in English, so that 'a wicked generation' or 'a righteous generation' might be interpreted in terms of 'seed' (or modern 'genetics' / 'heredity'). But as a time-set referring to 'age-mates' or, more broadly, 'everyone living at that time' it seems to have functioned powerfully as a referent for corporate responsibility, disgrace, and pride both in the Hebrew Bible (Deut 32.5 & 20) and in the NT.
In our time this concept of age-cohort is still strong in China, Japan, Korea and among the Tiv in Nigeria. Even in the individualistic West, analogous sets of family, nationality, and economic class function in a similar way.

⁴³ E. Rivkin, *What Crucified Jesus? The Political Execution of a Charismatic* (Nashville: Abingdon, 1984), 6.

⁴⁴ *Ibid.*, 20 citing Josephus, *War* ii. 66-75.

⁴⁵ *Ibid.*, 21.

⁴⁶ *Ibid.*, 22.

⁴⁷ *Ibid.*, 39.

the people and the sanctuary".⁴⁸ Thus, when crowds were rallying around the charismatic Jesus, the Sanhedrin ("a privy council and not a religious body") was convened to address what was perceived as a real and present threat to their political compact.⁴⁹ Caiaphas the high priest, Pilate's appointee and agent, made the conservative decision that this charismatic (but not his disciples) should be handed over for crucifixion. No one would have been surprised if the language Caiaphas used in formulating his decision was the religious language of his office, as represented in the Gospels.⁵⁰

The only near-contemporary historical records of the trial and crucifixion still extant are those in the four Gospels. But Paul Winter correctly raises fundamental questions about these 'primary documents':

> No testimony was available of eye-witnesses present either at a preliminary examination of Jesus or at the court session in which sentence of death was passed.⁵¹

Nevertheless, the picture that Rivkin has drawn of the interrelatedness of mutually antagonistic Jewish sects in Jesus' day suggests the likelihood that second-hand eye-witness accounts were available to Matthew. Even though Rivkin dismisses the Fourth Gospel as an historical source,⁵² his own reconstruction encourages us to follow C.H. Dodd in supposing that John 18.15-16 is a clue to the sources of information behind the Gospels.⁵³

It seems likely that the council (βουλευτής Mk 15.43) of which Joseph of Arimathea was a respected member was not the political Sanhedrin but a *bet din* of the Pharisees.⁵⁴ But surely the over-lapping membership of these councils would facilitate the circulation of reports on these momentous events. So even the detail of Pilate's wife's testimony regarding "that righteous man" (Mt 27.19), which admittedly fits established patterns in Matthew's narrative, might be based on reports from eye-witnesses:

> Pontius Pilate, as we know from Josephus, had his own political agendas. As one who was given to provoking Jews with wily stratagems, Pilate was not beyond using a politically naive charismatic, one who claimed to be their King, to entrap the Jews. By giving the crowds a choice between the release of a revolutionary such as

---

⁴⁸ *Ibid.*, 53.

⁴⁹ *Ibid.*, 34; *cf.* 64 & 83.

⁵⁰ Mt 26.62-63; 65-66 & par. E. Rivkin, *op.cit.*, 31. Part of Caiaphas' staying power, no doubt, was his facility in using pious phrases and manipulating pious emotions.

⁵¹ P. Winter, *On the Trial of Jesus*, 6

⁵² The Fourth Gospel "presupposes a different time, a different space, and a different mind set". E. Rivkin, *op.cit.*, 91.

⁵³ John notes "that a disciple of Jesus who was acquainted with the High Priest had found his way into the house ...which we may possibly take as a hint that he had good information at this point". C.H. Dodd, *The Founder of Christianity*, 157.

⁵⁴ E. Rivkin, *op. cit.*, 54.

Barabbas, who made no claim to being King of the Jews, and a charismatic who did make such a claim, Pilate was, in effect, compelling the crowd to choose the revolutionary. They would fear to choose the other, lest Pilate loose his soldiery on them for acknowledging a king other than Caesar.[55]

The utter disgrace resulting from the intentional degradation which crucifixion involved was identified by Jews in Jesus' day specifically with divine judgment (Deut 21.23 *LXX*). None of this is mitigated by the narrative account of Jesus' crucifixion in the First Gospel. Matthew records Jesus' dying words in Hebrew, "My God, my God, why have you forsaken me?" (27.46), and Rivkin's socio-political assessment of these words is apt: "The historian has no choice other than to read these words of Jesus on the cross as among the most pathetic ever uttered in the annals of history."[56] But when Matthew recorded this first line of Psalm 22 in the light of the Resurrection, he was fully aware that the entire scene as he has recorded it can be understood as an enactment of what was prophesied by the Psalmist. The recorded signs in nature clearly point to vindication and the centurion's testimony, "Clearly this was [the] son of God!" (Mt 27.54), is the beginning of the fulfillment of the Psalm's conclusion: "All the families of the nations shall bow down before him!" (Ps 22.28).

Finally, the mention of "the women from Galilee" (Mt 27.55) and the report of the courageous decency of Joseph of Arimathea, "another of Jesus' disciples" (Mt 27.57) are signs of the beginnings of the new community in Israel. The reappearance of the Pharisees in the narrative, joining the chief priests in voicing concern about Jesus' earlier claim that he would rise from the dead (Mt 27.62-64), not only shows the influence of the Pharisees' doctrine of resurrection on their actions but also indicates to the reader that Jesus' prediction is about to come true.

B. *Resurrection of the Lord*

'Resurrection' was a theme in the Messianic expectations which formed the historical context of Jesus' ministry, as we have seen.[57] Jesus' own predictions of his death and resurrection are clearly stated in the First Gospel, and 'resurrection' becomes a prominent theme in the final section which immediately follows Simon Peter's confession (Mt 16.21 - 28.20). The narrative witness to the resurrection of the crucified Messiah does not include any description of the event itself, but the resurrection is precisely dated as 'the third day' after Jesus' death on the cross (Mt 27.64 & 28.1). Further details in the narrative, including a final appearance of the risen Lord to the eleven disciples, confront the reader with the faith-challenge to accept the resurrection of Jesus as a meaningful event in the history of the world.

---

[55] E. Rivkin, *What Crucified Jesus?* 104.
[56] *Ibid.,* 108.
[57] Chapter **6** (125-6), and "Three Predictions" above (212-213).

1. Prediction and Anticipation

In response to Simon Peter's confession of faith, Jesus declares that "the gates of Sheol (or 'the powers of death') will not be able to withstand (or 'prevail against') the community built upon this rock" (Mt 16.18). Jesus' three predictions (Mt 16.21; 17.22-23; 20.17-19) which punctuate the beginning of this final section (*16.21-28.20*) insistently link resurrection to his sacrificial death. This link defines the meaning of his resurrection as vindication over against the judgment of God, excluding the kind of pagan hope for resurrection (or 'life after death') which is a perennial human temptation, even for God's people (Hos 6.1-4).[58] In the Hebrew Bible the clearest projection of resurrection hope (Dan 12.23) also emphatically relates resurrection to divine judgement. Moveover, Daniel's prophecy, which obviously influenced much of the material included in this final section of Matthew's Gospel, provides the way to view Jesus' resurrection as the coming of the Son of Man to receive dominion over the nations (Dan 7.14). We shall return to this picture in our reflections on the commission to the eleven disciples which concludes the First Gospel.

Earlier indications in Matthew's Gospel that the twelve disciples were given authority to "raise the dead" on their first mission (Mt 10.8), and Jesus' reference to "dead being raised" in his review of τὰ ἔργα τοῦ χριστοῦ for the Baptist's disciples (Mt 11.5), if taken literally, mean that there were instances of persons being brought back from death to life at Jesus' command.[59] Although Matthew nowhere abandons narrative form to explain the theological implications of these resuscitations, the narrative itself makes it clear that they point forward to (and draw power from) Jesus' death and resurrection. The difference in kind between the raising of the dead in Jesus' ministry and his own resurrection is most simply explained by noting that the reader must assume that all except Jesus himself subsequently died again and were buried. In Matthew's account of the crucifixion, his report of "many bodies of sleeping saints raised" in direct response to Jesus' death (Mt 27.51-53) seems to most commentators to represent the evangelist's enthusiasm for the subject of resurrection rather than a sober report of reliable tradition. But apart from the difficulty of translating the sentence in such a way as to explain just *what* happened *when*, even this report introduces no narrative or theological inconsistency to the account.

---

[58] Careless proof-texters have often suggested Hosea 6.2 as the obvious reference in Paul's letter to the Corinthians ("in accordance with the Scriptures he rose on the third day" I Cor 15.4). Only as an ironic riddle can Jesus' resurrection be seen as fulfilling the (false) hope expressed in Hos 6.2. More likely references are Ps 16.10 and Jonah 1.17.

[59] "In the OT and the Orient generally, the expression 'dead' can often mean 'dying'," according to Albright-Mann, *Matthew*, 136. *Cf.* comment on Mt 9.18-34, "We are in no position to determine whether Jesus was saying ... the girl was not dead but in a coma. The evangelist and the witnesses are certainly represented as believing that a miracle of raising the dead had occurred." (*Op. cit.*, 111-112.)

Note also the raising of the widow's son in Lk 7. 11-16, which is *not* recorded by Mt.

Instructions about Discipleship in the Perspective of Eternity

Jesus' death-resurrection can be considered as the one event which establishes the Kingdom, and we have already considered material from the discourse on the new community (Mt 18) in terms of one side of this event, the Messiah's death. But the other side, resurrection, brings the perspective of eternity to the instructions about discipline —and exclusion from the community— of unrepentant brothers and sisters. So we return now to consider the context of the instructions which we briefly reviewed in our analysis of Matthew's use of the term ἐθνικοί.

Few passages in the New Testament have been distorted so much from interpretation-out-of-context as these instructions. Gerhard Barth in his essay on "Matthew's Understanding of the Law" rightly insists that Matthew 18.15-18 be interpreted in relation to the parable of 'the single stray sheep' which immediately precedes it (Mt 18. 12-14) and the injunction to united prayer (Mt 18.19-20) and the parable of 'the unmerciful debtor' (Mt 18.21-35) which follow it. G. Barth's conclusion is that

> the one who has gone astray should be sought as the shepherd seeks the lost sheep, trusting in the promise of the hearing of prayer and the presence of the Risen One in the Church, thinking of forgiveness received and the judgment to come.[60]

Following the same line of interpretation, Herman Waetjen notes that even the final step in the patient process outlined by the instructions is not so much exclusion or ostracism as acknowledgment that the individual has withdrawn himself or herself from the community. Waetjen concludes that "he or she is to be the object of the same mission ... that is directed towards pagans and tax collectors".[61] As noted earlier, it is precisely as ὁ ἐθνικός that an unrepentant sinner maintains positive claims on the resurrection community.

In the light of the Resurrection, the importance of Jesus' quotations of Leviticus 19.18 becomes clear for the mission to the nations: "You shall love your neighbor as yourself." Already in his first instructions on discipleship Jesus made the apparently impossible demand of perfection. Specifically he applied the love command not only to those foreigners who had been assimilated through their acceptance of Israel's law (as in the *LXX* translation of גר as προσήλυτος Lev 19.33), but also to 'resident aliens' in the most threatening sense of 'the enemy next door' (τοὺς ἐχθροὺς ὑμῶν Mt 5.44). Now, as the Kingdom is being established, Jesus responds to a wealthy inquirer in a way which makes the possibility of attaining perfection in the new order as obvious as child-play. But the rich, sophisticated inquirer cannot attain the simplicity represented by the children (Mt 19.13-15) and goes away sorrowful.

---

[60] G. Barth, "Matthew's Understanding of the Law", *Trad & Interp*, Bornkamm ed., 84, citing A Schlatter, and G. Bornkamm's understanding of "the love-command to be the canon for the interpretation of the whole Torah" in Mt (78).

[61] H. Waetjen, *The Origin and Destiny of Humanness: An Interpretation of the Gospel According to Matthew* (California: Omega, 1976), 188.

When Jesus again quotes this text from Leviticus immediately after answering questions about resurrection, he relates love of neighbor directly to the glory of God and 'the greatest commandment' (Mt 22.34-39 cf. 5.48). In anticipation of the Resurrection, and with reference to the earlier demand for the extension of the borders of covenant love, the projected witness to the nations must be understood as an expression of gratitude and praise to Yahweh. Just as love for brothers and sisters is an expression of love for parents, so δευτέρα δὲ ὁμοία αὐτῇ flows from perfect obedience to the first and great commandment (Mt 22.38-39).

Immediately following Jesus' entry into Jerusalem 'the Great Eschatological Discourse' begins (Mt 21.1-17) and includes, somewhat awkwardly, the long warning against the practice of 'the scribes and Pharisees' (Mt 23). The Jerusalem setting is significant, and in the context of Matthew's narrative all of this teaching anticipates Jesus' crucifixion and vindicating Resurrection. This material is remarkable both for its immediate applicability to the earliest Christian mission and for its links with existing apocalyptic literature, which strongly support claims for its origin in Jesus' own teaching ministry. Perhaps most striking of the sayings is the poetic description of the final judgment which concludes the discourse (Mt 25.31-46/ 26.1).

"This word-picture of the Last Judgment has no parallel in the other Gospels," but, as T.W. Manson observes, "it certainly contains features of such startling originality that it is difficult to credit them to anyone but the Master himself."[62] What is most impressive about this *pericope* is Jesus' dramatic identification with 'the least of his siblings' (25.40/45). This is a confrontational statement of what C.F.D. Moule sees as "a generally accepted Christian estimation of Jesus, as an inclusive, incorporate personality" after the Resurrection.[63] What Moule discovers throughout the New Testament is particularly noteworthy here because of its expression in the category of τῶν ἐλαχίστων. It can be argued that the 'little ones' are Jesus' disciples, representing Israel and sent out to 'the nations'. Echoes of earlier apocalyptic representations of the final judgment suggest such a division between 'Israel' and 'the nations'. But specific echoes of Daniel 7.13-14 and Enoch suggest rather that Jesus himself, and Matthew, understood πάντα τὰ ἔθνη inclusively. (*Cf.* Enoch 48.4b "And he shall be the light of the nations.")

Cognitive Dissonance

Before reviewing Matthew's account of Jesus' resurrection, and the question whether Christian faith in the resurrection of the crucified Messiah allows and perhaps demands belief in the event as a fact in history, we should consider briefly what John Gager and others have called 'cognitive dissonance'. Certainly the ignominious death of Jesus was a shocking event in the life of the

---

[62] T.W. Manson, "The Sayings of Jesus", *The Mission and Message of Jesus*, Major, Manson, and Wright (London: Nicholson & Watson, 1967), 541.

[63] C.F.D. Moule, *The Phenomenon of the New Testament* (London: SCM, 1967), 24.

Establishment of the Kingdom

disciples, which must have brought crashing to the ground any vivid hopes James, John, and the others had of the coming Kingdom.

In modern times, the suggestion has often been made with varying degrees of sophistication, sympathy, and piety (by persons attempting to salvage Christian faith —and with a different point by those wishing to swamp this faith) that the disciples' experience of the Resurrection was induced by the intensity of their commitment, rebounding from profound defeat. Quite recently this line of explanation has been projected to account specifically for the earliest Christian mission to all nations.[64] Without attempting a thorough critique of this explanation, we should note obvious implications for assessing the claims in the First Gospel that Jesus anticipated and predicted his own resurrection.

With reference to the earliest Christian community and mission, 'cognitive dissonance' is the jarring contradiction between the disciples' commitment of faith and their everyday experience. Not only the crucifixion, but especially the delay of Jesus' return in glory is proposed by Gager as an explanation for the initiation of Christian mission to the nations. The theory states that

> under certain conditions a religious community whose fundamental beliefs are disconfirmed by events in the world will not necessarily collapse and disband. Instead it may undertake zealous missionary activity as a response to its sense of cognitive dissonance, *i.e.*, a condition of distress and doubt stemming from the disconfirmation of an important belief.[65]

The usefulness of this theory in explaining the response to failed predictions of certain modern religious groups is undeniable. Its application, in stages, to Jesus' disciples' responses to the crucifixion, the delay of the parousia, and the failure of 'all Israel' to accept the Gospel is intriguing if not altogether compelling.

If Jesus had predicted his own resurrection, as the multiple tradition claims, it can be argued that these predictions themselves would have been one of the props on which the disciples would have constructed their delusion and 'resurrection faith'.[66] But Jesus' projection beyond his death and resurrection, to the reception of the nations into the Kingdom, complicates the application of the 'cognitive dissonance' theory.

If Jesus' promise to the nations was a fundamental element of his words and deeds before his death, and if he looked forward to, and predicted, the apostolic mission to the nations, the Christian mission was a coherent expression of the earliest Christian faith. In this case, delay in evangelizing the nations

---

[64] J. Gager, "Christian Missions and the Theory of Cognitive Dissonance", *Kingdom and Community: The Social World of Early Christianity* (Englewood Cliffs: Prentice-Hall, 1978), 37-57.

[65] J. Gager, *ibid.*, 39 citing L. Festinger, *When Prophecy Fails* (1956).

[66] Texts such as Mt 24.4 /Mk 13.10 which represent Jesus referring explicitly to a world mission before the End might be accepted as authentic sayings which were a *cause* of deluded 'resurrection faith'. *Cf. supra* Chapter 6 and S.G. Wilson's assessment of these texts (n25).

would naturally produce the 'cognitive dissonance' of failure to act in faith. But if we take this view we could expect to discover from historical records that when successful mission activity was carried out it produced social and psychological reassurance to the faithful. Such reassurance would have at least some validity, representing the real achievement of bringing the community's practice in line with their faith. If the anticipation and prediction of the mission to the nations antedated the crucifixion, the historical beginnings of this mission cannot simply be said to be an alternate focus or cover-up for failed expectations.

2. The Resurrection as a Narrative Event

The scene for the resurrection in Matthew's narrative (Mt 27.62-66) is set by the petty calculations of the religious establishment, and their scheming with the representatives of the mightiest military power of the day. For readers who already know the outcome, the Roman seal is laughable (Ps 2.2-4). The sealed stone can be understood by faith to represent the powers of death (πύλαι ᾅδου Mt 16.18) which Jesus breaks through as the leader of the new community. In another sense, the seal is a disproportionate but not insignificant detail marking Jesus' resurrection itself as an act of civil disobedience.[67]

The faithful community is represented by the women who come to watch the tomb (θεωρῆσαι τὸν τάφον Mt 28.1). Following Thomas Longstaff's reading, we interpret their action as conforming to "a well-known practice required by Jewish burial custom".[68] According to this interpretation,

> the very persons charged with insuring that the laws of Judaism are kept (the chief priests and the Pharisees) make it difficult, if not impossible, for those who want to keep the law (the followers of Jesus) to do what the law requires

because of the connivance with the Romans to have the tomb sealed.[69]

The Women's Report

The earthquake, the appearance of the angel of the Lord with the announcement that "he has been raised exactly as he predicted" and the invitation to examine the empty tomb (Mt 28.6), followed by the command to tell

---

[67] The literal, categorical claim of the Gospels that Jesus' resurrection violated a government ordinance is eloquently restated in the NT Epistles (Eph 1.20-23; Phlp 2.9-11). "The resurrection is thus proclaimed as a political event of universal import." V.H. Fletcher, "Resurrection and Politics", *Acquittal by Resurrection*, Markus Barth & V.H. Fletcher (New York: Holt, Rinehart & Winston, 1964), 99.

[68] T. Longstaff, "The Women at the Tomb: Matthew 28:1 Re-Examined", *NTS* 27 (1981), 278 citing Talmudic *Semahot* 8:1 which he dates to the third century AD, Longstaff argues that "some of the customs described in this tractate can be assigned a date in the first century, C.E., if not earlier" (280).

[69] *Ibid.*, 282.

the disciples that Jesus is already on his way to Galilee where they will see him, clearly indicate the narrator's understanding of the event that has occurred.

The women, who had undertaken the sad duty of confirming Jesus' death, are thus confronted with an unexpected —and until then unimaginable— experience. The angel had begun by telling them not to be frightened and ended urging them to hurry to the disciples, and the narrative says they rushed off to tell the good news. But the next scene suggests that their flight from the tomb may not have taken the most direct route to the disciples (cf. Mk 16.8). In any case, before they tell anyone anything, the risen Jesus himself meets them. After they have embraced him, he urges them not to be afraid to carry the news to 'his brothers' (τοῖς ἀδελφοῖς μου Mt 28.10), referring here to the disciples — with special emphasis, perhaps, on Jesus' identification with the 'new generation', as suggested above with reference to the First Gospel's genealogy. The risen Jesus also repeats the angel's directive to the disciples that they are to meet him in Galilee.

The narrative returns briefly to the guards and the chief priests with reference to the cover-up story "which circulates among the Jews to this very day"[70]. Then the promise of a meeting in Galilee is fulfilled. This Galilean resurrection appearance demands thorough analysis because of its importance for our subject and —as we have already noted in anticipation— for the whole design of the First Gospel. But some further narrative elements should be noted briefly because of the focus they give to the problem of interpreting resurrection appearances as history.

The Resurrection Appearance in Galilee

The phrase "the eleven disciples" (Mt 28.16), used also in Luke-Acts, is a shockingly accurate designation of the Twelve at this time. This historical (or 'historicizing') description is a ragged match with "the new world" (ἐν τῇ παλιγγενεσίᾳ Mt 19.28) previously predicted by Jesus, where his faithful disciples were to "sit on twelve thrones, judging the twelve tribes of Israel". Less plausible, in terms of factual reporting, is the "worship" (προσεκύνησαν) of verse 17. Although consistent with what follows, it is historically problematic in a way typical of resurrection scenes. The "doubt" (οἱ δὲ

---

[70] This tradition (Mt 28.11-15) appears only in the First Gospel. The phrase παρὰ Ἰουδαίοις is striking, since the designation 'Jews' is used only by foreigners elsewhere in the Gospel (2.2 Magi; 27.11, 29, 37 Romans). E. Schweizer argues that the evangelist's own use of the term here "reveals the origin of the whole story about the guards: [anti]-Jewish propaganda". *Good News Mt*, 526. If we suspend judgment on the story, a different explanation for the use of the term 'Jew' here is equally convincing. Relating to the term's earlier use in the Hebrew Bible and near-contemporary use in the Fourth Gospel, the *prima facie* regional sense of 'Judean' is obvious: "This is a rumor which continues to circulate in the capital region among those Israelites tied in with the Jerusalem establishment." In any case, the term here is polemical and may anticipate later usage. *Cf.* T.L. Schram, "Emphasis on Polemic", *The Use of* ΙΟΥΔΑΙΟΙ *in the Fourth Gospel* (Utrecht diss, 1974), 192-205.

ἐδίστασαν) in this same verse is realistic, reminding the reader how sensible men would react to a resurrection appearance.[71]

In verse 18 the reference to Jesus' προσελθών can be plausibly translated in such a way as to form an awkward transition from the preceding verse. But Eduard Schweizer is correct in identifying this as a peculiar idiom which Matthew frequently uses to introduce traditional material: 'Jesus drew near and said to them ...'. Here it indicates "that Jesus is not speaking from heaven but is walking the earth".[72] *How* and *if* it is reasonable, or in any way possible, to accept reports that a man who had died was 'walking the earth' is a question we must face before attempting an analysis of 'the Great Commission'.

One last narrative element to note is the abrupt ending of the First Gospel with these words of the risen Jesus.

3. Interpreting Jesus' Resurrection as an Event in History

Belief in Jesus' resurrection from the dead is central to Christian faith and to the history of the church. Nevertheless, the words which Gustav Warneck wrote in 1892 seem strangely inappropriate today:

> *Da uns die Auferstehung des gekreuzigten Jesu eine objektive geschichtliche Thatsache und die Erscheinungen des aus dem Grabe Auferstandenen vor seinen Jüngern nicht subjektive Visionen sind, so gelten uns auch die Reden des Auferstandenen wirklich als Reden Jesu, speziell der Sendungsauftrag.*[73]
>
> [For us, the resurrection of the crucified Jesus is an objective, historical fact and the appearances of the resurrected one from the grave to his disciples are not subjective visions. Accordingly, the sayings of the resurrected one —especially the instructions for mission— are valid as authentic sayings of Jesus.]

Warneck correctly identifies Jesus' resurrection as the decisive starting point for the mission to the nations, and it is only fair to emphasize his words *"da uns"* in defining *"objective geschichte Thatsache"*. Nevertheless, Günther Bornkamm's statement in the conclusion of his book *Jesus of Nazareth* seems a much more accurate formulation of the problem:

> the event of Christ's resurrection from the dead, his life and eternal reign, are things removed from historical scholarship. History cannot ascertain and establish conclusively the facts about them as it can with other events in the past. The last historical fact available ... is the Easter faith of the first disciples.[74]

Karl Barth makes the same point more simply when referring to the New Testament accounts of the Resurrection: "these texts speak of an 'historically'

---

[71] "This is in accordance with what is said of christophanies in the NT generally; they were not of such a kind as to make doubt utterly impossible." D. Hill, *Gospel of Mt*, 361.

[72] E. Schweizer, *Good News Mt*, 528.

[73] G. Warneck, *Evangelische Missionslehre* vol. 1 (Gotha: Perthes, 1892), 183-4.

[74] G. Bornkamm, *Jesus of Nazareth* (New York: Harper & Row, 1960), 180.

inconceivable event."⁷⁵ And even at the second remove, this "inconceivable event" is more problematical than Bornkamm admits when he defines "the last historical fact available" to historical scholarship in this matter as "the Easter faith of the first disciples".

In a footnote to his discussion of Matthew 28.19f., Harnack protests that

> it is impossible and quite useless to argue with those who see nothing but an inadmissable bias in the refusal to accept traditions about Jesus eating and drinking and instructing his disciples after death.⁷⁶

But such traditions certainly express "the Easter faith of the first disciples", and the theological judgment of Hans Frei impinges on historical judgments relating to this faith when he concludes that

> the New Testament authors ... were right in insisting that it is more nearly correct to think of Jesus as factually raised, bodily if you will, than not to think of him in this manner.⁷⁷

When we turn to 'the Great Commission', we should consider whether belief in the resurrection of Jesus allows —and perhaps demands— acceptance of the possibility that the risen Lord engaged in "instructing his disciples after death". Within the boundaries of the area Bornkamm defines as susceptible to historical analysis, we can be confident at least of *the evangelist's belief* that Jesus was resurrected bodily and that the risen Lord gave instructions to his disciples.

---

[75] K. Barth, "An Exegetical Study of Matthew 28:16-20", *The Theology of the Christian Mission* ed. G.H. Anderson (New York: McGraw-Hill, 1961 [1945]), 57.

[76] A. von Harnack, *Mission and Expansion*, 41 note 1.

[77] H. Frei, "Theological Reflections on the Gospel Accounts of Jesus' Death and Resurrection", *The Christian Scholar* 49 (1966), 302.

11

THE GREAT COMMISSION

(Matthew 28. 16-20)

Ἐδόθη μοι πᾶσα ἐξουσία ἐν οὐρανῷ καὶ ἐπὶ γῆς.
πορευθέντες οὖν μαθητεύσατε πάντα τὰ ἔθνη,
βαπτίζοντες αὐτοὺς εἰς τὸ ὄνομα τοῦ πατρὸς καὶ τοῦ υἱοῦ καὶ τοῦ ἁγίου πνεύματος,
διδάσκοντες αὐτοὺς τηρεῖν πάντα ὅσα ἐνετειλάμην ὑμῖν·
καὶ ἰδοὺ ἐγὼ μεθ᾽ ὑμῶν εἰμι πάσας τὰς ἡμέρας ἕως τῆς συντελείας τοῦ αἰῶνος.

Designation of the concluding sentences of Matthew's Gospel as "The Great Commission" reminds today's reader of the influence which this text has had on the modern missionary movement and on the ancient legendary accounts of missionary activity by the Twelve disciples.[1] But three major questions demand answers if information about the earliest Christian mission is to derived from the text of this 'Great Commission'.

Textual criticism poses the first, obvious question: Does the conclusion to the First Gospel, as it now stands, belong to Matthew's original formulation?

---

[1] William Carey's 1792 publication of *An Enquiry into the Obligation of Christians to use Means for the Conversion of the Heathen* broke with the sixteenth-century Reformers' idea that the apostolic commission was restricted to the eleven disciples (and Paul). This break marks the beginning of the modern missionary movement. "The Great Commission" is the first chapter title in the three-volume *History of the Church Mission Society* (London, 1844) cited by H. R. Boer, *Pentecost and Missions* (London: Lutterworth, 1961), 16 & 25. Legendary accounts of missions by the Twelve such as *The Acts of Thomas* seem to have been written in the second and third centuries. The earliest and most significant extant documentary evidence outside the NT for missionary activity of the Twelve is the *Didache*.

Or was this resurrection appearance, which includes 'the Great Commission', added by one of the evangelist's successors?

A second question: Does this text control the other parts of Matthew's Gospel? This second question, when answered affirmatively, supports our textual critical conclusion that the abrupt ending is an integral part of the First Gospel. But a third question becomes more difficult to answer as proof of the Matthean character of the text grows stronger: What were the author's sources? Some critics insist that the composition of 'the Great Commission' is to be explained entirely in terms of Matthew's literary creativity. Questions of his sources remain, nevertheless, even if only to ask where Matthew got his ideas.

A. Textual and Literary Criticism

The strongest argument for the acceptance of Matthew 28.16-20 as an integral part of the original text of the First Gospel is based on the internal evidence of structure. If we allow for reservations about verse 19b, assent to this argument appears to be unanimous today. But it was not always so.

The *external evidence* of the manuscripts for this part of the Gospel is solid. But it was with obvious reluctance that Harnack acknowledged that "no positive proofs can be adduced for regarding xxviii 19f. as an interpolation."[2] Indeed, the evidence is consistent even for the Trinitarian baptismal formula: "there is not a single manuscript which does not have it."[3] But having acknowledged this, Hans Kosmala goes on to argue for textual emendation at verse 19b. His argument is based on the omission of the line referring to baptism from every quotation of the text in Eusebius' ante-Nicene writings.[4] The fact that the baptismal formula in the Gospel's text appears also in Didache 7.1, however, is much stronger evidence for Matthean authenticity than Kosmala admits.[5] Accordingly, the entire text of Matthew 28.16-20 (as it stands in the 26th edition of the Nestle-Aland text) should be accepted as a secure basis for an examination of Matthew's understanding of the commission from the resurrected Lord.

With reference to "the importance of this closing composition of Matthew for the Gospel as a whole", Otto Michel declares that

> the whole Gospel was written under this theological premise of Matt. 28:18-20 (*cf.* 28:19 with 10:5ff. 15:24 v. 20 with 1:23; also the return to baptism, *cf.* 3:1).

---

[2] A. von Harnack, *Mission and Expansion*, 40 note 2.

[3] H. Kosmala, "The Conclusion of Matthew", *Studies, Essays and Reviews II: New Testament* (Leiden: E.J. Brill, 1978), 132.

[4] *Ibid.*, 133 citing F.C. Conybeare's earlier argument for "The Eusebian Form of the Text Matthew 28,19", *ZNW* 2 (1901) 275-288.

[5] For the date of the *Didache*, Audet sees "the last decades of the first century" as "the extreme end of probabilities". The parallel reference to baptism "in the Lord's name" (εἰς ὄνομα κυρίου) in *Did* 9.5 enables Audet to press his case for a date pre-AD 70. Jean-Paul Audet, *La Didachè instruction des Apôtres* (Paris: J. Gabalda, 1958), 190-192.

... *Matt. 28.18-20 is the key to the understanding of the whole book.*[6]

Noting the emphasis in this scene on "the recognition by all nations" of Jesus' authority and rule, Michel cites Daniel 7.12-14 as the relevant allusion to Scripture. Jesus' authority "proceeds from the exaltation" in the Easter event.[7]

Following different lines of analysis, Oscar Brooks similarly declares that "the concluding *pericope* (xxviii 16-20) has controlled the entire design of the Gospel of Matthew."[8] Paying particular attention to the narrative development of the themes 'authority' and 'teaching', Brooks correctly focuses on the one finite verb in the commission: "make disciples" (μαθητεύσατε).[9] The two present participles which follow this imperative verb in the commission, "baptizing" (βαπτίζοντες) and "teaching" (διδάσκοντες), summarize in chiasmic order the narrative development of the whole Gospel: Jesus taught and finally suffered humiliating death // through baptism his disciples identify with his death in order to continue his teaching.[10]

The chiasmic order should not be interpreted as implying that no instructions precede baptism.[11] But baptism declares the necessity of transcendental transformation, so that disciples can be taught and teach as Jesus taught. In other words, baptism implies the preaching of repentance and forgiveness of sins (as in Lk 24.46-48). Jesus did not bring a new law or a new refinement of the law through which individuals can achieve personal salvation. Through his sacrificial death he achieved *atonement* between God and mankind; his *vindication through resurrection* validates all that he taught regarding the Kingdom. Baptism unites his disciples with the Father and with the vindicating Spirit. Through identification with the crucified and exalted Messiah, the disciples themselves now teach 'with authority' (Mt 7.29).

In the context of the immediately preceding verses, this meeting of Jesus with the Eleven marks an abrupt change of scene from Jerusalem (Mt 28.15) to "Galilee at the hillside which Jesus had designated" (28.16). This footing in

---

[6] O. Michel, "The Conclusion of Matthew's Gospel: A Contribution to the History of the Easter Message", *Interp Mt* ed. G. Stanton, 35.

[7] *Ibid.*, 36.

[8] O. Brooks, "Matthew xxviii 16-20 and the Design of the First Gospel", *JSNT* 10 (1981), 2.

[9] *Ibid.*, 3. This imperative verb has a two-fold connotation made explicit by the following participles. *Cf.* n 20 below.

[10] Chiasm in the design of the Gospel is not recognized by Brooks, who speaks only of "the bipolar emphasis of authority and teaching". Although he warns that "the importance of baptism must not be minimized" Brooks neglects its relation to Jesus' death-resurrection.

[11] *Kerygma* and *didache* are never completely separated in practice, but 'proclamation' is represented here by baptism which is followed by 'instruction' within the fellowship of Christ's death and resurrection. "Disciples are to be initiated into the ἐκκλησία by baptism and then taught to observe the commands of Jesus which are the substance of the community's life." Benjamin Hubbard, *The Matthean Redaction of a Primitive Apostolic Commissioning: An Exegesis of Matthew 28:16-20* (Missoula: Scholars Press, 1974), 89.

Galilee is the necessary context for detailed interpretation of the Commission. But it also completes the Matthean theme introduced in 2.2-23 and developed from 4.12-16 onward. After Jesus' sacrificial death in Jerusalem, the Galilean setting of the Commission was prepared by his instructions in a resurrection appearance to the women (28.10) and in the announcement to them by the angel (28.7 cf. Mt 26.31-32 /Mk 14.27-28). The end of the scene is as abrupt as its beginning. This abrupt ending calls for further consideration, not only in interpreting the words of the Commission itself but also in placing the First Gospel in canonical and historical context.

As already noted, Jesus has his feet on the ground when he meets the disciples.[12] Nevertheless, his words clearly reveal him to be the exalted Son of Man envisioned by the prophet Daniel (Dn 7.14): "To me has been given all authority in heaven and on earth" (Mt 28.18b). Gerhard Barth interprets this statement as a revelation to the disciples of what has already taken place: "This exaltation happened at Easter and the Risen one here makes it known to the disciples."[13] We shall return to questions about how the Christian tradition identifies and relates resurrection, exaltation, ascension, and enthronement. The important point to note in the design of Matthew's Gospel is that "the exaltation of Jesus to be the eschatological ruler of the worlds provides the basis for the missionary command to go to all nations, which now follows (28. 19f)."[14]

The relationship of the Commission to Daniel 7.14, emphasized in Otto Michel's 1950 essay, is now generally acknowledged. But the direct bearing of this interpretation of the Son of Man prediction in Matthew 10.23 seldom has been made so explicit as in Karl Barth's "Exegetical Study of Matthew 28:16-20":

> The disciples truly were not to go through all the towns of Israel before the Son of Man came (Mt. 10:23). Now he came, and now 'all these things' happened. [Reference to Mk 13.30]. ... It became manifest, in other words, that the *eschaton* had really begun.[15]

If Matthew 28.18b is the decisive fulfillment of 10.23 ("You will not have completed your mission to all the towns of Israel before the Son of Man comes") the mandate to the disciples for the first mission (10.5b-6) has come to

---

[12] E. Schweizer, *Good News Mt*, 528; cf. supra Chapter 10 (232).

[13] G. Barth, "Matthew's Understanding of the Law", *Trad & Interp*, 133. Cf. F. Hahn, *Mission in NT*, 66: "The words about authority in 18b are not a direct saying about the act of enthronement, but one of revelation which makes known the exaltation that has been accomplished."

[14] G. Barth, ibid., 134.

[15] K. Barth, *Theology of Christian Mission* ed. G.H. Anderson, 56.

a definite end.¹⁶ John Meier expresses this explicitly in terms of the design of the First Gospel:

> Mt has very consciously and carefully drawn up a scheme of salvation-history. ... The great turning point in the schema is the death-resurrection seen as apocalyptic event, the definitive breaking-in of the new aeon. Such a schema allows Mt to preserve stringent Jewish-Christian statements (*e.g.*, 10:5-6; 15:24) by referring them to the time before the turning point, the time of restricted ministry to the land and people of Israel. As 28:16-20 shows, after the turning point such restrictions fall in favor of a universal mission free of circumcision.¹⁷

Meier's reference to Matthew 10.5-6 and 15.24 as "stringent Jewish-Christian statements" implies the form-critical judgment that these statements were formed (or repeated, as having continuing validity) by some Christians long after the Resurrection. But Meier's main point, which we emphasize here, is that for Matthew these particular 'sayings of Jesus' are neither contradictions nor isolated surds. They are important elements in his own theological argument. Morna Hooker, somewhat earlier than Meier, arrived at the same conclusion: "Matthew ... sees the limitation of 10.5b-6 as a temporary one, no longer applicable to the post-resurrection situation."¹⁸

A Decisive New Command

As the Commission stands in Matthew's Gospel, with its setting in Galilee, the aorist imperative marks a decisive new command to "make disciples of all nations" (28.19); the concluding assurance of the Lord's presence "to the consummation of the age" indicates the term of the new mandate's validity (28.20). The familiar translation of the first two words as "Go therefore" (*"Darum gehet hin ... "*) expresses this well, but the aorist participle can be interpreted equally well as a simple fact:¹⁹ "Going therefore ..." or even, "As you go ...". In its original narrative setting, the application is to Galilee of the *Goyim*.

The Eleven were to *begin the mission* to all nations, but the command does not send them scurrying to the ends of the earth. The previous announcement, "he is going before you to Galilee" (Mt 28.7 par Mk 16.7),

---

¹⁶ *Contra* Schuyler Brown, "The Mission to Israel in Matthew's Central Section (Mt 9.35 - 11.1)", *ZNW* 69 (1978), 80. Brown correctly notes that "there is no temporal limit to the mission except the coming of the Son of man (10.23)," but he fails to recognize 28.16-20 as this fulfillment, and so supposes that "the [first] mission is still going on" for Mt (79).

¹⁷ J.P. Meier, *Law and History*, 40.

¹⁸ M. Hooker, "Uncomfortable Words: The Prohibition of Foreign Mission (Mt 10.5-6)", *Expository Times* 82 (1971), 362.

¹⁹ "The distinction of the Aorist Participle is not that it expresses a different time-relation from that expressed by the present or Perfect, but that it conceives of the action denoted by it ... as a simple fact." E.D.W. Burton, *Syntax of the Moods and Tenses in New Testament Greek* (Edinburgh: T & T Clark, 1898), 60 #132.

projected campaign strategy. The mission to all nations is to be inaugurated in Galilee. This new stage of the messianic mission not only begins symbolically in the same place as the first mission, but it also implies the same concentric gathering —"make disciples". This command is a reaffirmation of the incarnational pattern of mission already exemplified by Jesus.

The two present participles "baptizing" and "teaching" summarize Jesus' earthly ministry, but the chiasm emphasizes the new order which now allows extension of the model to reach all nations. The participles themselves should probably be construed as 'participles of identical action' which describe the action of the main verb ("make disciples") from different points of view.[20]

The closing words of assurance project beyond the inauguration of the world-mission by the resurrected Lord to "the consummation of the age" (Mt 28.20b). No more information is given of the 'time between the times' of Jesus' exaltation and his return in glory except the assurance of his presence πάσας τὰς ἡμέρας. In the context of the Commission itself, this phrase can be interpreted "the whole of the day".[21] Today and tomorrow —as well as "to the end of the age"— the Eleven will need this assurance as they attempt to carry out the immediate assignment in their home district, Galilee of the *Goyim*.

It goes beyond the bounds of literary criticism to ask whether Matthew himself understood this Galilean mission as a training model for the world-mission which would begin at Pentecost, or as the beginning of an uninterrupted final mission to the nations.[22] But the evangelist clearly indicates that 'the end of the age' lies beyond this abrupt ending of his narrative.

Our confidence that Matthew knew some subsequent history, and that his first readers also had some awareness of what happened next, challenges us to go beyond his text itself in search of answers to further questions. Before moving from the text to its historical context and its wider literary context in the New Testament canon, however, we should consider once again the question whether these words —reported as spoken by a man after his death— can in any way guide us to an understanding of the earliest Christian mission to all nations.

B. Sayings of the Risen Jesus

It seems reasonable enough to try to imagine what the earliest version of 'a redactional formulation' might be. In many cases it would even be reasonable to hope that the original statement could be recovered or reconstructed. But the current agreement about 'Matthean redaction' is superficial, covering two quite

---

[20] *Ibid.*, 55, #120 & #121.

[21] C.F.D. Moule, *An Idiom-Book of New Testament Greek* (Cambridge: UP, 1963), 34.

[22] E.J. Goodspeed presses a popular assumption to a consistent conclusion, without any attempt to include a regrouping in Jerusalem: "The silence of the Book of Acts about their specific labors is no doubt mainly due to the fact that they had gone forth from Galilee in different directions in obedience to Jesus' recorded order to go into all the world and preach the gospel, perhaps twenty years before Luke himself came on the scene in A.D. 49-50." *Matthew: Apostle and Evangelist* (Philadelphia: J.C. Winston, 1959), 2.

different meanings of the term even with reference to pre-Easter material. Simply put, the view of some critics is that 'redactional material' is Matthean in the sense that an *editorial* is the work of an editor; others use the same phrase to refer to received material which the editor shaped or *edited*.

G.D. Kilpatrick formulates the first view clearly, if not quite absolutely, with reference to the conclusion of the First Gospel:

> From xxviii.9 onward Matthew is without the guidance of Mark's narrative ... and the two sections xxviii.9f, 16-20 are the evangelist's attempt to fill the gap. ... The materials available for the evangelist in his attempt ... were poor in the extreme.[23]

Having said all this, Kilpatrick adds that "it may be admitted that there is probably an element of tradition behind the assertion of an appearance in Galilee and a formal commission of the disciples."[24] Schuyler Brown does not discuss the composition of this text in detail, but when he writes that "Mt xxviii 19 is clearly redactional" his readers understand from the force of the assertion and the shape of his argument that he implies 'editorializing', not 'editing'.[25] Referring to 'early tradition' in a sense that calls for further examination, F.W. Beare goes so far as to insist that "even the command to 'make disciples of all the nations' is not conceivable as an *early* tradition of a word of the risen Lord."[26]

Each of the scholars quoted above is cautious enough not to rule out the possibility of "an element of tradition behind the assertion",[27] but the tenor of each argument is clear: this 'saying of the risen Jesus' was not re-cast but originally composed in response to a situation in the evangelist's own time and place, many decades after the crucifixion. Other scholars, however, reckon seriously with Matthew as a redactor of traditional material.

Günther Bornkamm cites Kilpatrick in support of his judgment that the commission bears a "Matthean stamp in both language and content",[28] but Bornkamm's view that "a very complex tradition is embedded in ... the words of

---

[23] G. Kilpatrick, *The Origins of the Gospel According to St. Matthew* (Oxford: Clarendon, 1946), 48-9.

[24] *Ibid.*, 49.

[25] S. Brown, "The Matthean Community and the Gentile Mission", *NovT* 22(1980), 199. *Cf.* G. Stanton's confident assertion that "the evangelist himself has expanded the traditions of the words of Jesus to which he has access." "Matthew as a Creative Interpreter of the Sayings of Jesus", *Das Evangelium und die Evangelien* ed. P. Stuhlmacher (Tübingen: JCB Mohr, 1983), 273.

[26] F. Beare, "Sayings of the Risen Jesus in the Synoptic Tradition: An Inquiry Into Their Origin and Significance", *Christian History and Interpretation: Studies Presented to John Knox* ed. W.R. Farmer *et al.* (Cambridge: University Press, 1967), 165.

[27] G.D. Kilpatrick, *op. cit.*, 49, cited above.

[28] G. Bornkamm, "The Risen Lord and the Earthly Jesus: Matthew 28.16-20", *The Future of Our Religious Past: Essays in Honour of Rudolf Bultmann* ed. James Robinson (London: SCM, 1971 [1964]), 206.

the Risen Lord"[29] is notably different from Kilpatrick's. The three elements of the Commission "were certainly not a free formulation of the evangelist", according to Bornkamm. "Rather they came to him from the tradition."[30] When he notes that "the universal extension of his [Jesus'] ἐξουσία over heaven and earth" is "the only new thing in Matt. 28" Bornkamm refers to the internal development of the Gospel narrative, not to a Matthean innovation.[31] Ferdinand Hahn, whom Bornkamm cites with approval, is confident that in the tradition of "Hellenist Jewish Christianity", which Hahn sees Matthew faithfully and creatively representing "the command to missionize ... is traced to the exalted Jesus", because "Jesus is indeed already installed as ruler over the whole world ... the bringing in of the Gentiles can now begin".[32]

Working along different lines from those pursued by Bornkamm and Hahn, Benjamin Hubbard also concludes that the basic material in Matthew 28.16-20 —including the juxtaposition of the Resurrection with the command to preach the gospel to all nations— did not *originate* with Matthew. Hubbard argues that this tradition was current in Christian communities already before AD 48.[33] He locates the *Sitz im Leben* of the text "one step removed from the actual narration of a Christophany and commissioning on the lips of one of the 'eleven'".[34]

Edition or Editorial?

Those who argue that 'the Great Commission' is an edition of traditional material (rather than simply 'editorializing' by Matthew) surely have the stronger case, and Hubbard's speculative reconstruction of the "proto-commissioning" which he sees behind Matthew's edited version warrants careful consideration. Before turning to Hubbard's evidence and arguments, however, we should note once again the fundamental challenge to faith raised by any text attesting the Resurrection.

Statements of faith in the Resurrection do not fit into normal categories of historical research. The phrase 'sayings of the risen Jesus', as a technical term of New Testament scholarship, focuses this challenge in a peculiar way which seems designed to avoid the question whether Jesus actually spoke to his disciples in the days immediately following the first Easter. Rudolf Bultmann and Martin Dibelius differed sharply in their respective use of 'post-Easter

---

[29] *Ibid.*

[30] *Ibid.*

[31] *Ibid.*, 208.

[32] F. Hahn, *Mission in NT*, 68.

[33] B. Hubbard, *Matthean Redaction of Apostolic Commissioning*, 117. Hubbard's reconstructed "proto-commission" (131) is speculative, but much of his argument is persuasive.

[34] *Ibid.*, 134. Hubbard's hypothesis requires a "Gentile missionary" to add "the stress on the Gentile mission ('all nations')" to "the narrative of one of the eleven disciples".
But if this stress was an element of the Christophany itself (or an addition by one of the eleven) an extra figure is not necessary.

sayings' in relation to the recorded sayings attributed to Jesus' public ministry, but both used the category 'sayings of the risen Jesus' to identify *additions* to the Christian tradition, inspired by the Spirit or 'the Risen Lord'.[35] We should note, in appreciation of Bultmann and Dibelius, that both focus on the Resurrection as the great turning point not only for faith but also for analytical method. Their common assumption is also correct, historically and theologically: the church, from earliest times, identified Jesus of Nazareth with the living Resurrected Lord who still speaks through the Spirit to his disciples.

Recent attempts to achieve a clearer understanding of the role of contemporary prophets in the formation of the New Testament follow the lines already marked out. But Bultmann and Dibelius and their successors have not differentiated clearly between sayings from the risen Jesus in heaven and saying attributed to the risen Jesus with his feet on the ground. This modern consensus contrasts sharply with the ancient Christian tradition, where the sayings of the risen Jesus during the forty days between Easter and Pentecost are clearly distinguishable from sayings of the risen Jesus from heaven (*e.g.* Rev 1.17f, Acts 9.4f).[36]

Returning now to Hubbard's arguments, we can agree that the supporting evidence in Luke 24.36-53 and John 20.19-23 implies the existence of 'a primitive commissioning'.[37] Hubbard's analysis of the literary form of commissionings in the Hebrew Bible convincingly projects the form which such a commissioning would have received.[38] Agreeing with Bultmann and others that "the universal missionary command is hardly *ipsissima verbal Jesu*", Hubbard reconstructs

> a Gentile missionary who had come in contact with the narrative of one of the eleven disciples and added the stress on the Gentile mission ('all nations').[39]

This contrived reconstruction is no more plausible than the narrative setting of the commission in Matthew's Gospel —except for the inherent impossibility that the words could have been spoken by someone who had already died. The

---

[35] For a survey of these earlier discussions see M.E. Boring, *Sayings of the Risen Jesus: Christian Prophecy in the Synoptic Tradition* (Cambridge: University Press, 1982), 1-14.

[36] With reference to passages from the last book in the NT canon which are important in Bultmann's argument, D. Hill insists that "these passages from Revelation suggest nothing about the attribution to the historical Jesus of the words of the exalted Christ spoken through the Spirit." "On the Evidence for the Creative Role of Christian Prophets", *NTS* 20 (1974), 267.
Odes of Solomon 42.6 suggests a possible line of justification for identifying later sayings with memories of Jesus' earlier words ("Then I arose and am with them,/ And will speak by their mouths"). But these lines themselves could fit with the conservative Christian theology and poetic license of a 19th or 20th century hymn writer.

[37] B. Hubbard, *Matthean Redaction of Apostolic Commissioning*, 113-122.

[38] *Ibid.*, 25-67.

[39] *Ibid.*, 134.

conclusion of Hubbard and others that the commission indicates 'a very old tradition' is perhaps as far as we can press historical evidence for a Resurrection appearance.

Controls on Sayings of Jesus

In an examination of the evidence for "The Creative Role of Christian Prophets", David Hill argues convincingly against Bultmann's suggestion that words of Christian prophets, addressed to interests and concerns of the church, could have found their way to acceptance as 'words of Jesus' identified with specific incidents in his public teaching ministry.[40] Hill's argument, which follows some of the lines established by Dibelius in earlier debate, carefully limits the discussion to pre-Easter 'sayings of Jesus'. Nevertheless, an extension of Hill's argument to some post-Easter sayings seems warranted. Specifically "the part played by tradition in the early Christian community, and the importance of the Twelve as witnesses of the tradition of Jesus' words"[41] would seem likely to have safeguarded also the sayings attested in resurrection appearances. Indeed, some of the controls described by Hill seem to rule out Hubbard's mid-century 'Gentile missionary' as the creator of the commissioning 'words of Jesus'. The sharply limited number of New Testament 'sayings of the risen Jesus' in the New Testament indicates that stringent controls were in place for stories about the period between Easter and Pentecost.

C. Preparation for Pentecost

Any attempt to gain information from the First Gospel about the earliest mission to all nations must also reckon with the canonical *Acts of the Apostles*, the earliest extant narrative account of this mission. The title "Acts", which tradition assigns to Luke's second book, is best understood as "the Acts of Jesus through his Spirit", as the opening sentence in that document indicates. Ernst Haenchen suggests that the "*acta omnium apostolorum*" listing in the *Canon Muratori* "shows what people hoped to find in the book".[42] The document's silence about individual activity by any of the Twelve besides Peter and John is notable, and this silence is susceptible to different interpretations. But what is

---

[40] D. Hill, "Creative Role", *op. cit.*, 262-274. *Contra* R.Bultmann: "The Church drew no distinction between such utterances by Christian prophets and the sayings of Jesus in the tradition, for the reason that even the dominical sayings in the tradition were not the pronouncements of a past authority, but sayings of the risen Lord who is always a contemporary for the Church." *The History of the Synoptic Tradition* (Oxford, 1968), 127f.

[41] D. Hill, *ibid.*, 264. Hill concedes that "prophets and other teachers in the Christian community may have played a part in the process where *logia* of Jesus were adapted to the post-Easter situation of the Church ... : but that is not the same thing as ascribing to them the creation *de nova*, indeed *ex nihilo*, of sayings of Jesus."

[42] E.Haenchen, *The Acts of the Apostles: A Commentary* (Philadelphia: Westminster, 1971 [1965]), 136.

most immediately relevant to an interpretation of Matthew 28.16-20 is Luke's emphasis on the Ascension and Pentecost in Acts 1-2.

The Ascension of Jesus forty days after his Resurrection and the miraculous happenings at Pentecost are now well established in Christian tradition. Can we assume that Matthew, Mark, and John also knew these events and would have agreed with Luke's account of their significance?[43] Or does the evidence of the First Gospel itself compel us to suppose that Matthew knew nothing of an ascension and an outpouring of the Spirit at Pentecost? (Or, perhaps, that he knew the stories but disbelieved, and disapproved of the telling?) "Nothing is said about the departure and ascension of the Risen Lord" in the abrupt ending of Matthew's Gospel.[44] And, in terms of literary criticism, the opinion can be argued that "there is no room in Matthew for a special act of ascension."[45] But is it reasonable to claim from Matthew's formulation "the fact that there is not, and cannot be, any later 'ascension' of the Jesus who here speaks —'I am with you always, to the close of the age'"?[46]

The Ascension and the miracles of Pentecost, like the Resurrection itself, are articles of faith which are hardly susceptible to historical analysis. And yet, if faith claims them as divine events breaking into human history, some attempt to relate them to history is not only appropriate but necessary. Since only Luke tells of these events, we must look to *Acts* for the basis of any judgment about whether the abrupt ending of the First Gospel can or cannot be understood as preparation for Pentecost.

In his essay "The Ascension - Acts i.9", C.F.D. Moule acknowledges the intimate theological relationship between the Resurrection, Ascension, and Pentecost, "but that does not necessarily mean that, in narrative form, the 'moments' were not from the first distinguishable."[47] Turning next to a consideration of the 'forty days', Moule argues that the Galilean disciples would have left Jerusalem very soon after Passover and would not have returned until Pentecost. "Nothing but an express command ... would have kept them in Jerusalem."[48] Such a command does occur in Luke 24.49, but for a correct understanding of the sequence of events, Moule argues, we should note that "Acts i.4 puts it shortly before Pentecost."[49] In the meantime —as indicated in

---

[43] Jn 20.19-23 anticipates both the commissioning (Mt) and Pentecost (Lk-Acts).

[44] G. Bornkamm, "Risen Lord & Earthly Jesus", *op.cit.*, 20.

[45] *Ibid.*, 206 note 16. H.B. Green presses this point to an historical judgment: "the earliest Christian thinking did not distinguish sharply between the resurrection and the exaltation; the idea of the ascension as a separate stage is peculiar to Lk-Acts." *The Gospel According to Matthew* (Oxford: University Press, 1975), 229. But see *infra* n 47.

[46] M.E. Boring, *Sayings of the Risen Jesus*, 47.

[47] C.F.D. Moule, "The Ascension - Acts i.9", *Essays in New Testament Interpretation* Cambridge: University Press, 1982), 57.

[48] *Ibid.*, 58.

[49] "In the interval between Passover-Unleavened Bread and Weeks (Pentecost), the disciples had naturally gone home to Galilee and had seen Jesus there, just as they had seen him in Jerusalem during the pascal octave." *Ibid.*

Mark 16.7, John 21, and in the First Gospel— Jesus appeared to his disciples in Galilee.

In canonical context (and in lectionary readings), the First Gospel no less than the Third is read as complementary to *Acts*. It goes beyond our present purposes to argue, as Moule does, for the acceptance of "the resurrection and ascension of Christ as two moments in the anticipation of the ultimate home-gathering of the whole people of God".[50] Neither can we inquire here how "the event of Ascension is related to time and space".[51] But we can note that the conclusion of Matthew's Gospel stands appropriately within the 'forty days' which Luke-Acts and later Christian tradition considered necessary for

> the training of the disciples through a manifestation of Christ, in whom the thoughts of suffering and glory, of humiliation and exaltation, were bound together in his own Person in indissoluble union.[52]

Turning finally to a consideration of 'the Great Commission' as an abrupt ending of the First Gospel, we focus once again on the diachronic nature of the document. In canonical context it is obvious that Matthew, like Luke, wrote about "what Jesus began to do and teach" (Acts 1.1). Although it has been said that "Matthew is the only gospel which has anything that can properly be called an ending,"[53] it is only satisfactory to readers who understand that this ending represents the beginning of the consummation of the Kingdom of heaven. Whatever date is assigned to the document, it must be agreed that this conclusion was written more than forty days after Easter. So Matthew's cut-off point is by design.

God with Us

The final assurance of Matthew 28.20b καὶ ἰδοὺ ἐγὼ μεθ' ὑμῶν εἰμι is a satisfactory fulfillment of τὸ ὄνομα αὐτοῦ Ἐμμανουήλ of 1.23 in literary terms. But no interpretation of these words is satisfactory which insists that Matthew considered the Risen Jesus to be physically present still at the time of writing. The evangelist's own emphasis on the physical details of the empty tomb (Mt 27.57 - 28,15) and the hillside meeting in Galilee make it far more reasonable to suppose that Matthew knew and accepted the stories of the Ascension and Pentecost, as recorded in Luke-Acts. But why, then, does he break off his narrative where he does?

Like Mark's abrupt ending (Mk 16.8), Matthew's ending in Galilee describes an emotional crisis, not the misty tapering into the endless future

---

[50] *Ibid.*, 62.

[51] T.F. Torrance, *Space, Time and Resurrection* (Grand Rapids: Eerdmans, 1976), 122.

[52] *Ibid.*, citing William Milligan, *The Ascension of Our Lord*, and Karl Barth, *Church Dogmatics* IV/2, 150: "The resurrection and ascension of Jesus Christ are two distinct but inseparable moments in one and the same event. The resurrection is to be understood as the *terminus a quo*, its beginning, and the ascension as its *terminus ad quem*, its end."

[53] Albright-Mann, *Matthew*, 361.

which some literary critics suppose.⁵⁴ This last recorded confrontation of the disciples with the crucified, vindicated Messiah is designed to confront the faithful reader also in his home district with the resurrected Lord.

Even more clearly than elsewhere in the First Gospel, it is the details of the disciples' situation which makes 'the Great Commission' readily transferable to Matthew's readers in the 60s, and through the ages to the 1990s and beyond. "It is precisely the past event which is transparent for the present."⁵⁵ The Eleven are apostles to the nations only because of their commission from the Risen Lord, and this commission is passed on to persons whom they disciple. There can be no doubt of the extent of the mandate "to all the nations", but the beginning (πορευθέντες) is with kinsmen and resident aliens, with Jews and foreigners who make their home in Galilee of the *Goyim*.

If we can suspend objections to belief that Jesus actually returned from the dead to instruct his disciples for forty days, it is reasonable to project Jesus' known pattern of instruction by acted parable to a practice-mission to the nations in Galilee. As preparation for Pentecost, the command to the Eleven has obvious subsequent relevance to all disciples of Jesus.

The Gospel's abrupt ending allows all of the faithful to stand in the Council of Yahweh for the final revelation of the mystery of the Kingdom of heaven. All who have heard the Gospel are then dismissed with their marching orders: "As you go, make disciples of all nations ...."

---

⁵⁴ *Contra* H. Waetjen, *Origin and Destiny of Humanness*, 256.

⁵⁵ U. Luz, "The Disciples in the Gospel According to Matthew", *Interp Mt*, ed. G. Stanton, 106.

12

CONCLUSION

Comparing historical discoveries to aesthetic awakenings, David Steinmetz recently observed that

> only a relatively small percentage are prompted by the discovery of wholly new and previously unknown evidence. The great majority are stimulated by fresh insight into evidence so familiar that its significance has been underestimated or disregarded.[1]

In a well-cultivated field of inquiry, even such 'discoveries' are often only re-discoveries of what has been long forgotten or denied.

Concepts are human achievements, but the first step towards progress in new understanding sometimes involves the dismantling of one or more well-established concepts which stand in the way of an adequate perception of reality. So we have argued that the established concepts of 'Petrinism' and 'Paulinism' must be dismantled. More threatening than these concepts themselves is the assumption (expressed in the base points of the 'Hegelian triads') that 'there are two sides to every issue.' This idea of 'two sides' is useful in its simple proverbial form, and can be a defense against dogmatism. But when developed into academic systems and maintained by persistent habits of seeing 'two sides, and only two', both unity and multiplicity are often misconstrued.

---

[1] D. Steinmetz, "Calvin and Abraham: The Interpretation of Romans 4 in the Sixteenth Century", *Church History* 57 (1988), 443.

The fundamental conclusion of this study is theological: Israel's mission to the nations is constitutive of the Christian Gospel, which was understood by the earliest Christian community as expressing God's will for the world through his Son. The linguistic, historical, and theological evidence and arguments leading to this conclusion can be summarized in terms of 'the single people of God' and 'Israel's Messiah, Lord of the nations'. We review here, briefly, the method which we followed in adducing evidence and pressing arguments.

We have attempted to allow our sample of documents to define 'the earliest Christian mission to all nations' in the way that words together define the meaning of a sentence. Trajectories outside this sample have been briefly noted, but we insist (*contra* Helmut Koester) that the linguistic and historical assignment is necessarily "limited to a fresh reading of the known sources".[2] As surely as different words change the meaning of a sentence, different documents would change our understanding of 'the earliest Christian mission to all nations'.

Two important criteria governed our choice of documents: 1/ *the dates of the documents*, and 2/ *the relationship of the documents to the Christian mission*. Precise dating is almost always open to question, but in most cases the question whether a document was written before or after AD 135 can be answered confidently. So too, it is beyond dispute that such documents as the Pauline epistles and the *Didache* are intimately related to the Christian mission to all nations. We have chosen such documents, along with Matthew's Gospel, as our core linguistic sample. Not surprisingly, 'Matthew and his world of thought' are reconstructed quite differently by Benno Przybylski after he substitutes the Qumran literature and the much later Rabbinic material for the Pauline epistles in his core linguistic sample.[3]

One of the controversial decisions taken in this study is the dating of the First Gospel before AD 70. This decision itself is not critical to our arguments or conclusion, since it is agreed on all sides that the Gospel was written before AD 135. It might have been easier to claim a hearing by accepting current majority opinion in the field. But very many of the arguments for dating Matthew's Gospel *after* AD 70 are based on assumptions about evolutionary developments in the mission to all nations which this study challenges.

---

[2] With the emphasis on Koester's phrase 'the conventional picture' we can agree with his statement that "The task is not limited to a fresh reading of the known sources and close scrutiny of the new texts in order to redefine their appropriate place within the conventional picture of early Christian history." "GNOMI DIAPHOROI: The Origin and nature of Diversification in the History of Early Christianity", *Trajectories through Early Christianity* (Philadelphia: Fortress, 1971), 114.

[3] B. Przybylski, *Righteousness in Matthew and His World of Thought*, 3: "In Comparison to the Pauline literature, the concept of righteousness has an entirely different function in the Gospel of Matthew." *Cf. supra*, Chapter 10, n8.

A. The Single People of God

The racial definition of 'the Jews' which emerged in early modern times and was sharpened by vicious racism in quite recent times can be dismissed from our consideration of the earliest Christian mission to the nations. Similarly, the Rabbinic definitions which accompanied 'the closing of the ranks' after AD 135 (first documented in the *Mishnah*) are anachronistic. But the accounts in the Hebrew Bible of God's election of Israel as his people are certainly relevant, since these Scriptures were the constitutional documents of the Christian mission.

That the one true God created all peoples and nations is emphasized again and again in the Bible. That he elected Israel from among the nations to be his peculiar possession is a basic theme: God reveals himself as Israel's creator and redeemer. His Covenant with Abraham was reconfirmed in the Exodus and in the Conquest of Canaan. When the Hebrews were delivered from bondage in Egypt, 'no people' became 'the people of God'.

The establishment of monarchy focused the question whether Israel could finally take its place as an equal among the nations, but the development of the divided kingdoms demonstrated more clearly than anything else in Israel's history the impossibility of 'numbering Israel among the nations'. David's kingship came to symbolize the Messianic hope of the Kingdom of God, which transcended even the bitter experience of the Exile. This persistent hope is itself proof of God's providential faithfulness and abiding love for his people.

God did not abandon Israel through any of the subsequent attempts at 'ethnic' definition. But, as John the Baptist rightly declared, only God's electing love guaranteed Israel's existence as his people, the children of Abraham. Finally, God sent his Son, Jesus the Messiah, to recapitulate Israel's history in his own person and to gather to himself the redeemed from all the nations of the world.

B. Israel's Messiah, Lord of the Nations

Jesus' whole life, from his miraculous conception to his vindicating Resurrection from death, must be understood as fulfillment of the Scriptures. Moreover, Jesus' own teaching ministry and all his actions clearly indicate that he himself accepted the Scriptures as directives for his ministry.

Much of what Matthew wrote can be discovered also in the testimony of the other Gospels to Jesus, including his choice of twelve disciples for training in leadership. This group, together with the larger congregation of disciples gathered from the scattered sheep of the House of Israel, at once represented the faithful 'remnant' of Israel and symbolized the hope that all faithful people will finally be gathered into the Kingdom of God. The Twelve themselves, as well as the crowds, carried the marks of many different divisions in Israel. As disciples they were prepared as God's agents —in ways they themselves could not yet fully understand— for *Israel's mission to the nations*.

The preparation of Israel for its mission to the nations was focused by Matthew's emphasis on Jesus' teaching ministry. But the breaking into the present age of the coming Kingdom was already signalled by signs of the Messiah's miraculous power, especially in Jesus' acts of healing.

The betrayal of Jesus into the hands of the Roman government brought a shocking end to the Messiah's ministry in Israel. But his astonishing Resurrection, witnessed first by the faithful women, then by the Eleven, demonstrated the true meaning not only of his death but of the whole sacrificial order which had been revealed to Israel in ancient times. Now, indeed, 'all that the prophets had announced' (Lk 24.25) became brilliantly clear with the Messiah of Israel revealed as the Lord of the nations.

In Galilee, the Eleven stood in the presence of the risen Lord, like the ancient prophets in the Council of Yahweh, to receive the final revelation of the mystery of the Kingdom. All power and authority has been given to the Messiah and the whole world has become the Promised Land. The disciples themselves were commissioned as God's agents to make disciples of all nations, incorporating them into the fellowship of the Messiah's death and resurrection and instructing the gathered people of God all that Jesus had taught them, in preparation for the consummation of the age.

SELECT BIBLIOGRAPHY:
Texts, Resources for Analysis, Monographs

(For complete listing of works cited, see "Authors" index and bibliographic data in notes.)

A. TEXTS & TRANSLATIONS

1. Hebrew Bible & New Testament

Biblia Hebraica Stuttgartensia, ed. Rudolf Kittel/ A.Alt, O. Eissfeldt, P. Kahle; K. Ellinger, W. Rudolph *et al.* Stuttgart: Deutsche Bibelstiftung, 1967/77 [1919].

Septuaginta Id est Vetus Testamentum graece iuxta LXX interpretes, ed. Alfred Rahlfs. Stuttgart: Deutsche Bibelanstalt, 1962 [1935].

The Greek New Testament, eds. Kurt Aland, Matthew Black, Carlo M. Martini, Bruce M. Metzger, Allen Wikgren. New York/ London/ Edinburgh/ Amsterdam/ Stuttgart: United Bible Societies, 1975 [1966].

Nouum Testamentum Latine, Secundum Editionem Sancti Hieronymi/ Iohannes Wordsworth et Henricus Iulianus White. Oxford: Clarendon Press, 1920 [1911].

The Holy Scriptures according to the Masoretic Text. Hebrew-English eds. & trans. Max L. Margolis, Solomon Shechter, Cyrus Adler, Joseph Jacobs, Kaufman Kohler, David Philipson, Samuel Schulman. Philadelphia: Jewish Publication Society of America, 1955. (London: Socino Press,1916 [Hebrew]).

The New American Bible, trans. Catholic Biblical Association. Nashville: Thomas Nelson, 1983 [1970].

The New English Bible. Oxford & Cambridge: University Presses, 1961.

New Revised Standard Version, Bible with the Apocryphal/Deuterocanonical Books, trans. 1611 revised 1881-1885 & 1901; 1952 & 1971;1989. New York: Oxford University Press, 1991.

Version Synodale, Le Nouveau Testament 7e Edition. Paris: Alliance Biblique Française, 1957.

Zürcher Bibel, Die Heilige Schrift des Alten und des Neuen Testaments. Zürich: Verlag der Zürcher Bibel, 1978.

2. Intertestamentary & Biblical-Parallel Literature

The Amarna Letters, ed. and trans. W.L. Moran. Baltimore: The Johns Hopkins University Press, 1992 [1987].

Apocrypha and Pseudepigrapha of the Old Testament in English, ed. R.H. Charles. Vol I: **Apocrypha**. Vol II: **Pseudepigrapha**. Oxford: Clarendon Press, 1931.

The Old Testament Pseudepigrapha: Apocalyptic Literature and Testaments, ed. James H. Charlesworth. Garden City: Doubleday & Company, 1983.

The Dead Sea Scrolls in English, ed. & trans. Geza Vermes. Baltimore: Penguin Books, 1965 [1962].

Joseph and Aseneth, trans. Chr. Burchard, 92-110 *Outside the Old Testament*, ed. M. de Jonge. Cambridge: University Press, 1985.

The Biblical Antiquities of Philo [Pseudo-Philo's *Liber Antiquitatum Biblicarum*], trans. M.R. James, "Prolegomenon" by Louis H. Feldman. New York: Ktav, 1971 [1917].

3. Philo & Josephus

On the Migration of Abraham, trans. F.H. Colson & G.H. Whitaker. (Loeb Classical Library: *Philo IV*.) London: Heinemann, 1932.

On Abraham, On the Special Laws, On the Virtues, Every Good Man Is Free, trans. F.H. Colson. (Loeb: *Philo IV, VII, VIII & IX*.) London: Heinemann, 1935, 1937, 1939.

Questions and Answers on Exodus, trans. from the ancient Armenian version of the original Greek by Ralph Marcus. (Loeb: *Philo Supplement II*.) London: Heinemann, 1953.

The Jewish War, Books i-vii trans. H.St.J. Thackeray. (Loeb: *Josephus II & III*.) London: Heinemann, 1961 [*ca*. AD 73].

Jewish Antiquities, Books i-v trans. H.St.J. Thackeray, vi-xi; Ralph Marcus, xii-xx Louis Feldman. (Loeb: *Josephus IV-IX*.) London: Heinemann, 1930-34 [*ca*. AD 93]

Life of Josephus, Against Apion, trans. H.St.J. Thackeray. (Loeb: *Josephus I*.) London: Heinemann, 1926.

4. Other First- & Second-Century Literature

Didache, 1 Clement, The Epistles of Ignatius, The Epistle of Barnabas, The Epistle to Diognetus, trans. Kirsopp Lake. (Loeb: *The Apostolic Fathers I & II*.) London: Heinemann, 1912-13.

The Odes of Solomon: The Syriac Texts, ed. & trans. J.H. Charlesworth. Missoula: Scholars Press, 1977 [1973].

Justin Martyr, *Dialogue with Trypho the Jew*, ed. J.P. Migne. (*Patrologiae cursus completus, Series Graeca*, vol 6.) Paris: Petit Montrouge, 1857.

The Gospel of Thomas, trans. B.M. Metzger, 511-530 *Synopsis Quattuor Evangeliorum* ed. Kurt Aland. Stuttgart: Wurttembergische Bibelanstalt, 1965.

Celsus, *On the True Doctrine: A Discourse Against the Christians*, trans. R.J. Hoffman. New York: Oxford University Press, 1987.

5. Documents from the Third Century and Later

The Mishnah, trans. Herbert Danby. Oxford: University Press, 1933 [*ca*. AD 200].

Babylonian Talmud, ed. & trans. I. Epstein. Vol II. London: Socino Press, 1935.

"The Beginnings of Christianity According to the Samaritans", *Samaritan Chronicle II*. Introduction, Text, Translation & Notes by John Macdonald with Commentary by A.J.B. Higgins. *New Testament Studies* 18 (1971-72) 54-80.

New Testament Apocrypha, ed. E. Hennecke & W. Schneemelcher/ R.McL. Wilson. Vol I, *Gospels and Related Writings*. Vol II, *Writings Related to the Apostles, Apocalypses and Related Subjects*. London: SCM, 1963 & 1965 [1959 & 1964].

Origen, *Commentary on Matthew*, trans. John Patrick. 411-512 vol 10 *The Ante-Nicene Fathers*, ed. Allan Menzies. Grand Rapids: Eerdmans, 1951 [AD 246-48].

Eusebius Pamphilius, *Ecclesiastical History*, trans. C.F. Cruse. Grand Rapids: Baker Book House, 1962 [1850] [*ca*. AD 325].

Augustine of Hippo, *Confessions*, trans. V.J. Bourke, vol 21 *The Church Fathers*. Washington: Catholic University of America Press, 1953 [*ca*. AD 400]

The Meaning of the Glorious Koran: An Explanatory Translation, ed. & trans. Marmaduke Pickthall. London: George Allen & Unwin, 1930.

Bede, *Ecclesiastical History of the English People*, eds. B. Colgrave & R.A.B. Mynors. Oxford: Clarendon, 1969 [*ca*. AD 734].

B. RESOURCES FOR ANALYSIS

1. Grammars and Textual Criticism

Blass, F. & Albert Debrunner/ Robert W. Funk trans. & rev. *A Greek Grammar of the New Testament and Other Christian Literature*. Chicago: University of Chicago Press, 1961 [1913].

Burton, Ernest DeWitt. *Syntax of the Moods and Tenses in New Testament Greek*. Edinburgh: T.& T. Clark, 1898.

Metzger, Bruce M. *et al. A Textual Commentary on the Greek New Testament*. London/ New York: United Bible Societies, 1971.

Moule, C.F.D. *An Idiom-Book of New Testament Greek*. Cambridge:University Press, 1963.

2. Lexicons & Concordances

Aland, Kurt. *Vollständige Kondordanz zum griechischen Neuen Testament* 3 volumes. Berlin: W. de Gruyter, 1978-1983.

Bauer, Walter/ W.F. Arndt & F.W. Gingrich trans. & rev. *A Greek-English Lexicon of the New Testament and Other Christian Literature*. Chicago/ Cambridge: University Presses, 1957 [1952].

Gesenius, William/ Francis Brown, S.R. Driver, C.A. Briggs eds. *A Hebrew and English Lexicon of the Old Testament*. Oxford: Clarendon, 1975 [1907].

Goodspeed, Edgar J. *Index Patristicus sive Clavis Patrum Apostolicorum Operum*. Naperville: Allenson, 1960 [1907].

Hatch, Edwin & Henry A. Redpath. *A Concordance to the Septuagint and the Other Greek Versions of the Old Testament (Including the Apocryphal Books)*, 3 volumes. Grand Rapids: Baker, 1983 [1897].

Jones, Putnam Fennel, ed. *A Concordance to the Historia Ecclesiastica of Bede*. Cambridge, U.S.A.: Medieval Academy of America, 1929.

Koehler, Ludwig & Walter Baumgartner. *Lexicon in Veteris Testamenti Libros*. Leiden: E.J. Brill, 1958.

Kuhn, K.G. *et al. Konkordanz zu den Qumrantexten*. Göttingen: Vandenhoeck & Ruprecht, 1960.

Kuhn, Sherman M., ed. *Middle English Dictionary*. Ann Arbor: University of Michigan Press, 1963.

Lampe, G.W.H. *A Patristic Greek Lexicon*. Oxford: Clarendon, 1961.

Liddell, Henry George & Robert Scott/ H. S. Jones rev. ed. *A Greek-English Lexicon*. Oxford: Clarendon, 1968 [1843-1940].

Moulton, James Hope & George Milligan. *The Vocabulary of the Greek Testament Illustrated from the Papyri and Other Non-Literary Sources*. Grand Rapids: Eerdmans, 1980 [1930].

Moulton, W.F. & A.S. Geden. *A Concordance to the Greek Testament*. Edinburgh: T.&T. Clark, 1963 [1897].

Murray, James A.H. *et al.* eds. *Oxford English Dictionary (A New English Dictionary on Historical Principles)*. Oxford: University Press, 1884-1928.

Powell, J. Enoch. *A Lexicon to Herodotus*. Cambridge: University Press, 1938.

Rengstorf, Karl Heinrich, ed. *A Complete Concordance to Flavius Josephus*, 3 volumes. Leiden: E.J. Brill, 1975.

Webster's Third New International Dictionary of the English Language. Unabridged, ed. Philip Babcock Gove. Springfield: G.&C. Merriam Company, 1963.

3. Charts, Maps et c.

Aland, Kurt. *Synopsis Quattuor Evangeliorum: Locis parallelis evangeliorum apocryphorum et patrum adhibitis*. Stuttgart: Wurttembergische Bibelanstalt, 1964.

Barr, Allan. *A Diagram of Synoptic Relationships*. Edinburgh: T.& T. Clark, 1938.

May, Herbert G. ed. John Day. *Oxford Bible Atlas*. Third edition. New York: Oxford University Press, 1984 [1962].

McEvedy, Colin. *The Penguin Atlas of Ancient History*. Hammondsworth: Penguin, 1967.

Meer, Frits van der. *Die ursprunge christlicher Kunst*, trans. F. Stoks. Greidburg: Herder, 1982.

4. Essays in Linguistics, Philosophy & Sociology

Albright, William Foxwell. "Gerhard Kittel and the Jewish Question in Antiquity", 229-240 *History, Archaeology, and Christian Humanism*. New York: McGraw-Hill, 1964.

Arendt, Hannah. *Antisemitism*. New York: Harcourt, Brace & World, 1968 (1951).

Austin, J.L."The Meaning of a Word", *Philosophical Papers*, J.O. Urmson & G.J. Warnock, eds. Oxford: University Press, 1961.

Banton, Michael & Jonathan Harwood, *The Race Concept*. London: David & Charles, 1975.

Barr, James. *The Semantics of Biblical Language*. Oxford: University Press, 1961.

Berge, Pierre van den, *The Ethnic Phenomenon*. New York Elsevier, 1981.

Bruce, F.F. *The English Bible: A History of Translation from the Earliest English Version to the New English Bible*. London: Lutterworth Press, 1970 [1961].

Bynon, Theodora. *Historical Linguistics*. Cambridge: University Press, 1977.

Caponigri, A. Robert. *Philosophy from the Age of Positivism to the Age of Analysis*. (A History of Western Philosophy, Volume 5.) Notre Dame/ London: University of Notre Dame, 1971.

Cook, Walter A. *Introduction to Tagmemic Analysis*. New York: Holt, Reinhart & Winston, 1969.

Culler, Jonathan. *Saussure*. Glasgow: Fontana, 1976.

Grant, Frederick C. *Translating the Bible*. Edinburgh: Thomas Nelson, 1961.

Handlin, Oscar. *Race and Nationality in American Life*. Garden City: Doubleday, 1957.

Hobsbawm, E.J. *The Age of Revolution: Europe 1789-1848*. London: Weidenfeld & Nicolson, 1962.

Jenkins, Paul. "Exploring the Historic Nationalism of the Ewes", *Transactions of the Historical Society of Ghana* 12 (Accra, 1971).

Koestler, Arthur. *The Thirteenth Tribe: The Khazar Empire and Its Heritage*. London: Pan, 1977.

Levi-Strauss, Claude. *Race and History*. Paris: UNESCO, 1958.

Lyons, John. *Introduction to Theoretical Linguistics*. Cambridge: University Press, 1968.

Marx, Karl & Friedrich Engels, *Communist Manifesto* [1848].

Montagu, Ashley. *Man's Most Dangerous Myth: The Fallacy of Race*. New York: Oxford University Press, 1974.

Nida, Eugene A. *Message and Mission: Communication of the Christian Faith*. New York: Harper & Row, 1960.

Pike, Kenneth L. *Language in Relation to a Unified Theory of the Structure of Human Behavior*. The Hague/ Paris: Mouton, 1971 [1959].

Read, Allan Walker. *Current Trends in Linguistics* Volume 10, Thomas A. Sebeok, ed. The Hague/ Paris: Mouton, 1973.

Sartre, Jean-Paul. *Anti-Semite and Jew*. New York: Schocken, 1965 [1946].

Smith, Anthony D. *The Ethnic Revival*. Cambridge: University Press, 1981.

Steinmetz, David C. "Calvin and Abraham: The Interpretation of Romans 4 in the Sixteenth Century", *Church History* 57 (1988) 443-55.
Ulmann, Stephen. *Semantics: An Introduction to the Science of Meaning*. Oxford: Basil Blackwell, 1962.
Waismann, Friedrich."Language Strata" and "Verifiability" 226-247 & 122-150 *Logic and Language*, ed. Antony Flew. Garden City: Doubleday Anchor, 1965 [1946].
----- *The Principles of Linguistic Philosophy*, ed. R. Harre. London: Macmillan, 1965.
Whorf, Benjamin Lee. *Language, Thought, and Reality*, ed. J.B. Carroll. Cambridge, U.S.A.: MIT Press, 1964 (1956).
Wittgenstein, Ludwig. *Philosophical Investigations*. trans. G.E.M. Anscombe. Oxford: Basil Blackwell, 1958.
----- *Tractatus Logico-Philosophicus*, trans. D.F. Pears & B.F. McGuinness. London: R.& K. Paul, 1961 [1921].

C. MONOGRAPHS: COMMENTARIES AND STUDIES

Albright, William Foxwell. *Archeology and the Religion of Israel*. Johns Hopkins University Press, 1953 [1942].
----- *Yahweh and the Gods of Canaan: A Historical Analysis of Two Contrasting Faiths*. Garden City: Doubleday, 1968 [1965].
----- & C.S. Mann. *Matthew: A New Translation with Introduction and Commentary*. Anchor Bible. Garden City: Doubleday, 1971.
Audet, Jean-Paul. *La Didachè Instruction des Apôtres*. Paris: J.Gabalda, 1958.
-----"A Hebrew-Aramaic List of Books of the Old Testament in Greek Transcription", *Journal of Theological Studies*, New Series I (1950).
Baeck, Leo. *Judaism and Christianity*, trans. Walter Kaufmann. Cleveland: World, 1961 [1958].
Bamberger, Bernard Jacob. *Proselytism in the Talmudic Period*. New York: Ktav, 1968 [1939].
Barnett, P.W. "'Under Tiberius All Was Quiet'", *New Testament Studies* 21 (1975).
Baron, Salo. *A Social and Religious History of the Jews*. Volumes 1 & 2. New York: Columbia University Press, 1952 [1937].
Barth, Gerhard. "Matthew's Understanding of the Law", *Tradition and Interpretation in Matthew*, eds. G. Bornkamm, G. Barth, H.J. Held, trans. P. Scott. Philadelphia: Westminster, 1963.
Barth, Karl. "An Exegetical Study of Matthew 28:16-20", trans. T. Wieser, *The Theology of the Christian Mission*, ed. G.H.Anderson. New York: McGraw-Hill, 1965.
-----"Israel and the Church", *Church Dogmatics* II/2, trans. G.W.Bromily. Edinburgh: T.& T. Clark, 1957.
----- *Jesus und das Volk*. Zürich: A.G. Zollikon, 1944.
Barth, Markus. "Baptism", *IDB Suppl Vol*, 85-89 (1976).
----- *Israel and the Church*. Richmond: John Knox, 1969.
----- *Jesus the Jew*, trans. F. Prussner. Atlanta: John Knox, 1978.
----- *Das Mahl des Herrn: Gemeinschaft mit Israel, mit Christus und unter den Gasten*. Neukirchen-Vluyn: Neukirchener Verlag, 1987.
----- *The People of God*. Sheffield: JSOT Press, 1983.

Brueggemann, Walter. *David's Truth in Israel's Imagination and Memory*. Philadelphia: Fortress, 1985.
----- "Trajectories in Old Testament Literature and the Sociology of Ancient Israel", *JBL* 98 (1979) 161-85.
Buchanan, George Wesley. "The Samaritan Origin of the Gospel of John", *Religions in Antiquity: Essays in memory of Erwin Ramsdell Goodenough*, ed. J. Neusner. Leiden: E.J.Brill, 1968.
Bultmann, Rudolf. *The History of the Synoptic Tradition*, trans. J. Marsch. Oxford: Blackwell, 1968 [1931].
----- *Primitive Christianity in its Contemporary Setting*, trans. R.H. Fuller. London: Thames & Hudson, 1956.
Burchard. Chr. "Introduction", *Joseph and Aseneth* 92-110 *Outside the Old Testament*, ed. M. de Jonge. Cambridge: University Press, 1985.
Butler, B.C. *The Originality of St Matthew: A Critique of the Two-Document Hypothesis*. Cambridge: University Press, 1951.
Cadbury, Henry J. "The Hellenists","The Titles of Jesus in Acts", *The Beginnings of Christianity* Vol 5, eds. F.J. Jackson & K. Lake. Grand Rapids: Baker, 1966 [1932].
Caird, George B. *Jesus and the Jewish Nation*. London: Athlone, 1965.
----- "The Study of the Gospel", *Expository Times* 87 (1976) 102-139.
Cantwell, L. "The Parentage of Jesus Mt 1:18-21", *NovT* 24 (1982).
Catchpole, D.R. "The Problem of the Historicity of the Sanhedrin Trial", *The Trial of Jesus*, Fs. C.F.D. Moule, ed. E. Bammel. London: SCM, 1970.
----- *The Trial of Jesus: A Study in the Gospels and Jewish Historiography from 1770 to the Present Day*. Leiden: E.J.Brill, 1971.
Childs, Brevard. "The Canon as the Context for Biblical Theology", 97-122 *Biblical Theology in Crisis*. Philadelphia: Westminster, 1970.
----- *Myth and Reality in the Old Testament*. London: SCM, 1957.
Clark, Kenneth W."The Gentile Bias in Matthew", *JBL* 66 (1947) 165-72.
Clarke, W.K.Lowther."The Rout of the Magi", 41-51 *Divine Humanity*. New York: Macmillan, 1936.
Coggins, R.J. *Samaritans and Jews: The Origins of Samaritanism Reconsidered*. Oxford: Blackwell, 1975.
Cross, Frank Moore. *The Ancient Library of Qumran*. Garden City: Doubleday, 1961.
----- "Aspects of Samaritan and Jewish History in the Late Persian and Hellenistic Time", *Harvard Theological Review* 59 (1966).
Cullmann, Oscar. *The Christology of the New Testament*. Philadelphia: Westminster, 1963 (1957).
----- "Dissension Within the Early Church", *Union Seminary Quarterly Review* 22 (1967) 83-92.
----- *Peter: Disciple-Apostle-Martyr*, trans. F.V. Filson. Cleveland: World, 1958.
----- "The Plurality of the Gospels as a Theological Problem in Antiquity" 39-54, "Samaria and the Origins of the Christian Mission" 183-192, *The Early Church*, trans. A.J.B.Higgins. London: SCM, 1956 [1945 & 1953].
----- *The State in the New Testament*. New York: Scribners, 1956.

----- "St.Paul -- A Good Jew", trans. L. Gaston, *Horizons in Biblical Theology: An International Dialogue* 1 (1979) 7-45.
----- *Was Christ's Death a Sacrifice?* Edinburgh: Oliver & Boyd, 1961.
----- & Verne H. Fletcher. *Acquittal by Resurrection*. New York: Holt, Reinhart and Winston, 1964.
Bauer, Walter. *Orthodoxy and Heresy in Earliest Christianity*, ed. R.A. Kraft. London: SCM Press, 1972 [1934].
Baur, Ferdinand Christian. *The Church History of the First Three Centuries*, trans. A. Menzies. London: Williams & Northgate, 1878 [1853].
Bennoit, Pierre. "Ascension","The Inspiration of the Septuagint", *Jesus and the Gospel*, vol 1 trans. B. Weatherhead. London: Darton, Longman & Todd, 1973 [1961].
Betz, Hans Dieter. *Essays on the Sermon on the Mount*., trans. L.L. Welborn. Philadelphia: Fortress, 1985.
Bimson, John J. *Redating the Exodus and Conquest*. Sheffield: JSOT, 1978.
Black, Matthew. *An Aramaic Approach to the Gospels and Acts*. Oxford: Clarendon, 1967 [1946].
Boer, Harry R. *Pentecost and Missions*. London: Lutterworth, 1961.
Bornkamm, Günther. "End-Expectation in Matthew" [1954],"The Stilling of the Storm in Matthew"[1948], *Tradition and Interpretation in Matthew*. Philadelphia: Westminster, 1963.
----- "The Risen Lord and the Earthly Jesus: Matthew 28: 16-20", *The Future of Our Religious Past: Essays in Honor of Rudolf Bultmann*, ed. James Robinson. London: SCM, 1971 [1964].
Bosch, David T. "'Jesus and the Gentiles' -- A Review After Thirty Years', *The Church Crossing Frontiers, Fs.* Bengt Sundkler, eds. P. Beyerhaus & C. Hallencreutz. Uppsala: Gleerup, 1969.
Bowker, John W. "Speeches in Acts: A Study in Proem and Yelammedunu Form", *New Testament Studies* 14 (1967-68) 96-111.
Bowman, John. *The Samaritan Problem: Studies in the Relationship of Samaritanism, Judaism, and Early Christianity*, trans. A. Johnson. Pittsburgh: Pickwick Press, 1975 [1959].
Brandon, S.G.F. "Tübingen Vindicated?" *Hibbert Journal* 49 (1950) 41-47.
Braude, William G. *Jewish Proselytizing in the First Five Centuries of the Common Era, the Age of the Tannaim and Amoraim*. Providence: Brown University, 1940.
Bright, John. *Early Israel in Recent History Writing: A Study in Method*. London: SCM, 1956.
----- *The Kingdom of God: The Biblical Concept and Its Meaning for the Church*. Nashville: Abingdon, 1953.
Brooks, Oscar S. Sr. "Matthew xxviii 16-20 and the Design of the First Gospel", *Journal for the Study of the New Testament* 10 (1981) 2-18.
Brown, Raymond E. *The Semitic Background of the Term "Mystery" in the New Testament*. Philadelphia: Fortress, 1968 [1958].
Brown, Schuyler."The Matthean Apocalypse", *JSNT* 4 (1979) 2-27.
-----"The Matthean Community and the Gentile Mission", *NovT* 22 (1980) 193-221.
-----"The Mission to Israel in Matthew's Central Section", *Zeitscrift für Wissenschaftliche Theologie* 69 (1978) 73-90.
-----"The Two-Fold Representation of the Mission in Matthew's Gospel", *Studia Theologica* 31 (1977) 21-32.
Bruce, F.F. *Israel and the Nations: From the Exodus to the Fall of the Second Temple*. Exeter: Paternoster, 1963.
----- "The People of God", *This is That*. Exeter: Paternoster 1976.

Dahl, Nils. "Nations in the New Testament", *New Testament Christianity for Africa and the World: Essays in Honour of Harry Sawyerr*, eds. M. Glasswell, E. Fashole-Luke. London: SPCK, 1974.

----- "The Passion Narrative in Matthew" *The Interpretation of Matthew*, ed. G. Stanton. Philadelphia: Fortress, 1983 [1976].

Danielou, Jean. *The Theology of Jewish Christianity*, trans. J.A.Baker. Vol I, *A History of Early Christian Doctrine Before the Council of Nicea*. London: Darton, Longman & Todd, 1964 [1958].

----- "A New Vision of Christian Origins: Judaeo-Christianity", *Cross Currents* 18 (1968) [1967].

Daube, David. *The New Testament and Rabbinic Judaism*. London: Athlone, 1956 [1952].

Davies, Philip R. *IQM, The War Scroll from Qumran: Its Structure and History*. Rome: Biblical Institute Press, 1977.

----- *The Damascus Covenant: An Interpretation of the "Damascus Document"*. Sheffield: JSOT Press, 1983.

Davies W.D. "From Schweitzer to Scholem: Reflections on Sabbatai Svi", *JBL* 95/4 (1976).

----- *The Setting of the Sermon on the Mount*. Cambridge: University Press, 1964.

Dentan, Robert C. *The Knowledge of God in Ancient Israel*. New York: Seabury, 1968.

Derrett, J.Duncan M. "Further Light on the Narratives in the Nativity", *NovT* 17 (1975) 81-105.

----- "Jesus' Fishermen and the Parable of the net", *NovT* (22) 1980.

-----"The Parable of the Two Sons", *Studia Theologica* 25 (1971) 109-116.

Dexinger, Ferdinand. "Limits of Tolerance in Judaism: The Samaritan Example", *Aspects of Judaism in the Graeco-Roman Period*, vol 2 *Jewish and Christian Self-Definition*, ed. E.P. Sanders *et al*. Philadelphia: Fortress, 1981.

Dix, Gregory. *Jew and Greek: A Study in the Primitive Church*. New York: Harper and Brothers, 1953.

Dobschütz, E. von. "Matthew as Rabbi and Catechist", *The Interpretation of Matthew*, ed. G. Stanton. Philadelphia: Fortress, 1983 [1928].

Dodd. C.H. *According to the Scriptures: The Sub-Structure of New Testament Theology*. London: Collins, 1965 [1952].

----- "The Fall of Jerusalem and the 'Abomination of Desolation'", *Journal of Roman Studies* 37 (1947) 47-54.

----- *The Founder of Christianity*. London: Macmillan, 1970.

----- *Historical Tradition in the Fourth Gospel*. Cambridge: University Press, 1965.

Donner, Herbert. "The Separate States of Israel and Judah", *Israelite and Judaean History*, eds. J. H.Hayes and J.Maxwell Miller. Philadelphia: Westminster, 1977.

Eichrodt, Walter. *Theology of the Old Testament*, trans. J.A. Baker. Two volumes. London: SCM, 1961 & 1967 [1933].

Ellis, E. Earl. "'Those of the Circumcision' and the Early Christian Mission", 380-399 vol 4 *Studia Evangelica*. Berlin: Akademie-Verlag, 1968.

Elon, Amos. *The Israelis: Founders and Sons*. Jerusalem: Adam, 1981.

Emerton, John A. "Some Problems of Text and Language in the Odes of Solomon", *JTS* 18 (1967).

Enslin, Morton Scott."Luke and Matthew: Compilers or Authors?" *Principat*, ed. W. Haase *ANRW* II 25.3.) Berlin/ New York" W. de Gruyter, 1985.

----- *The Prophet From Nazareth*. New York: McGraw-Hill, 1961.

Farmer, William R. "Essenes", *IDB* 2 (1962) 143-9.
----- *Maccabees, Zealots and Josephus: An Inquiry into Jewish Nationalism in the Grecian Roman Period*. New York: Columbia University Press, 1956.
----- *The Synoptic Problem: A Critical Analysis*. Dillsboro: Western North Carolina Press, 1976.
----- "Zealot", *IDB* 4 (1962) 936-9.
Feldman, Louis H. *Jew and Gentile in the Ancient World: Attitudes and Interactions from Alexander to Justinian*. Princeton: University Press, 1993.
Finley, Moses I. "The Ancient Greeks and Their Nation", *The Use and Abuse of History*. New York: Viking, 1975.
France, Richard T. "Herod and the Children in Bethlehem", *NovT* 21 (1979) 98-120.
----- *Jesus and the Old Testament: His Application of Old Testament Passages to Himself and His Mission*. London: Tyndale, 1971.
Frei, Hans. "Theological Reflections on the Gospel Accounts of Jesus' Death and Resurrection", *The Christian Scholar* 49 (1966).
Gager, John G. *Kingdom and Community: The Social World of Early Christianity*. New York: Scribner's Sons, 1965.
Gerhardsson, Birger. *The Gospel Tradition*. Malmo: CWK Gleerup, 1986.
----- *The Mighty Acts of Jesus According to Matthew*. Lund: CWK Gleerup, 1979.
----- "Sacrificial Service and Atonement in the Gospel of Matthew", *Reconciliation and Hope*, ed. R. Banks. Grand Rapids: Eerdmans, 1974.
----- *The Testing of God's Son (Matt 4:1 and Par): An Analysis of an Early Christian Midrash*. Lund: CWK Gleerup, 1966.
Goodenough, Erwin Ramsdell. *Goodenough on the History of Religion and on Judaism*, eds. E.S. Frerichs & J. Neusner. Atlanta: Scholars Press, 1986.
-----"Philo Judeus", *IDB* 3 (1962) 796-9.
Goodspeed, Edgar J. *Matthew, Apostle and Evangelist*. Philadelphia: J.C. Winston, 1959.
Gordon, Cyrus. "Paternity at Two Levels', *JBL* 96 (1977) 101.
Greenberg, M. *The Hab/piru*. New Haven: American Oriental Society, 1955/1961.
Gundry, Robert Horton. *The Use of the Old Testament in St.Matthew's Gospel With Special Reference to the Messianic Hope*. Leiden: E.J.Brill, 1967.
Hahn, Ferdinand. *Mission in the New Testament*, trans. F.Clarke. London: SCM, 1965 [1963].
Halpern, Baruch. *The Emergence of Israel in Canaan*. Chico: Scholars Press, 1983.
Hare, D.R.A. *The Theme of Jewish Persecution of Christian in the Gospel According to Saint Matthew*. Cambridge: University Press, 1967.
-----"The Rejection of the Jews in the Synoptic Gospels and Acts", *Anti Semitism and the Foundations of Christianity*, ed. A.T. Davies. New York: Paulist Press, 1979.
Harnack, Adolf von. *Bible Reading in the Early Church*, trans. J.R. Wilkinson. New York: G.P. Putnam's Sons, 1912.
----- *History of Dogma*, vol 1 trans. N. Buchanan. New York: Dover, 1961 [1900].
----- *The Mission and Expansion of Christianity in the First Three Centuries*, vol 1 trans. James Moffat. New York: Harper, 1962 [1908].
Harris, J. Rendel. *The Twelve Apostles*. Cambridge: Heffer & Sons, 1927.
Hengel, Martin. *Acts and the History of Earliest Christianity*, trans. John Bowker. Philadelphia: Fortress, 1983 [1971].
----- *The Atonement: The Origins of the Doctrine in the New Testament*, trans. J. Bowden. Philadelphias: Fortress, 1981.

----- *Between Jesus and Paul: Studies in the Earliest History of Christianity*, trans. John Bowker. Philadelphia: Fortress, 1983 [1971].
----- *Judaism and Hellenism: Studies in the Encounter in Palestine During the Early Hellenistic Period*, trans. John Bowker. Philadelphia: Fortress, 1974.
----- *The Zealots: Investigation into the Jewish Freedom Movement in the Period from Herod I until 70 A.D.*, trans. David Smith. Edinburgh: T&T Clark, 1997 [1961].
Hill, David. *The Gospel of Matthew*. London: Oliphants, 1972.
----- "On the Evidence for the Creative Role of Christian Prophets", *NTS* 20 (1974).
Hooker, Morna. "Uncomfortable Words: The Prohibition of Foreign Mission (Mt 19.5-5)", *Expository Times* 82 (1971).
Horsley, Richard A. & John S. Hanson. *Bandits, Prophets, and Messiahs: Popular Movements at the Time of Jesus*. Minneapolis: Winston Press, 1985.
Hubbard, Benjamin J. *The Matthean Redaction of a Primitive Apostolic Commission: An Exegesis of Matthew 28:16-20*. Missoula: Scholars Press, 1974.
Jenni, Ernst."Messiah, Jewish","Remnant", *IDB* 3&4 (1962).
Jeremias, Joachim. *The Eucharistic Words of Jesus*, trans. N. Perrin. Philadelphia: Fortress, 1977 [1964].
----- *Jerusalem in the Time of Jesus: An Investigation into Economic and Social Conditions During the New Testament Period*, trans. S.& C. Cave. London: SCM, 1969 [1923-1937].
----- *Jesus' Promise to the Nations*, trans. S.H. Hooke. London: SCM, 1967 [1956].
Johnson, Marshall D. *The Purpose of the Biblical Genealogies with Special Reference to the Setting of the Genealogies of Jesus*. Cambridge: University Press, 1988 [1969].
Jonge, M. de. "The Use of the Word 'Anointed' in the Time of Jesus", *NovT* 8 (1966) 132-48.
Käsemann, Ernst. *New Testament Questions of Today*. Philadelphia: Fortress, 1969 [1965].
Kasting, Heinrich. *Die Anfänge der urchristlichen Mission: Eine historische Untersuchung*. München: Kaiser, 1969.
Kertelge, Karl, ed. *Mission im Neuen Testament*. (*Quaestiones Disputatae* 93.) Freiburg: Herder, 1982.
Kim, Seyoon. *The 'Son of Man' as the Son of God*. Tübingen: J.C.B. Mohr, 1983.
Kingsbury, Jack Dean. *Matthew: Structure, Christology, Kingdom*. Philadelphia: Fortress, 1975.
----- *The Parables of Jesus in Matthew 13: A Study in Redaction Criticism*. London: SPCK, 1969.
Kittel, Rudolf. *Geschichte des Volkes Israel*. Gotha: Perkes, 1922 [*Geschichte des Hebräers* 1892].
Klausner, Joseph. *The Messianic Idea in Israel from Its Beginning to the Completion of the Mishnah*, trans. W.F. Stinespring. New York: Macmillan, 1955.
----- *Jesus of Nazareth His Life, Times, and Teaching*, trans. H. Danby. New York: Macmillan, 1927 [1922].
Klijn, A.F.J. "The Study of Jewish Christianity", *NTS* 20 (1974) 419-31.
Kline, M.G. *Treaty of the Great King: The Covenant Structure of Deuteronomy*. Grand Rapids: Eerdmans, 1963.
Koch, K. "Ezra and the Origins of Judaism", *Journal of Semitic Studies* 19 (1974) 1973-97.
Koester, Helmut. "Apocryphal and Canonical Gospels", *HTR* 73 (1980) 105-130.
----- & James M. Robinson. *Trajectories Through Early Christianity*. Philadelphia: Fortress, 1971.

Koestler, Arthur. *The Thirteenth Tribe: The Khazar Empire and Its Heritage*. London: Hutchinson, 1976.
Kohler, Kaufmann. "Atonement", *Jewish Encyclopedia* vol 1. New York: Funk & Wagnalls, 1902.
Kosmala, Hans."The Conclusion of Matthew", *Studies, Essays and Review*, vol 2: *New Testament*.
Lake, Kirsopp. "Proselytes and God-Fearers", "The Twelve and the Apostles", 74-96 & 37-59 *The Acts of the Apostles*, vol 5 *The Beginnings of Christianity*, eds. F.J. Foakes Jackson & Lake. Grand Rapids: Baker, 1966 [1932].
Landes, George. "Jonah", *IDB* Suppl (1976) 489-90.
LeGrand, L. "Was Jesus Mission Minded?" *Indian Ecclesiastical Studies* 3 (1964) 87-104.
Lemche, Niels Peter. "'Hebrew' as a National Name for Israel", *Studia Theologica* 33 (1979) 1-23.
Lindars, Barnabas. *The New Testament Apologetic: The Doctrinal Significance of the Old Testament Quotations*. London: SCM, 1961.
Loewe, H. "On Faith", Appendix I to C.G. Montefiore's *Rabbinic Literature and Gospel Teachings*. New York: Ktav, 1970 [1930].
Lohmeyer, Ernst. "<*Mir ist gegeben alle Gewalt*>, *Eine Exegese von Mt 28, 16-20*", *In Memorium E. Lohmeyer*, ed. W. Schmauch. Stuttgart: Evangelisches Verlagswerk, 1951 [1945].
Lohse, Eduard. *History of the Suffering and Death of Jesus Christ*, trans. M.O. Dietrich. Philadelphia: Fortress, 1967 [1964].
Longstaff, Thomas. "The Women at the Tomb: Matthew 28:1 Re-Examined", *NTS* 27 (1981).
Luz, Ulrich. "The Disciples according to Matthew", *The Interpretation of Matthew*, ed. G. Stanton. Philadelphia: Fortress, 1983 [1971].
Macdonald, John. *The Theology of the Samaritans*. London: SCM, 1964.
MacMullen, Ramsay. *Paganism in the Roman Empire*. New Haven: Yale University Press, 1981.
Malina, Bruce. "Jewish Christianity or Christian Judaism: Toward a Hypothetical Definition", *Journal of the Study of Judaism in the Persian, Hellenistic and Roman Period* 7 (1976)
Manson, T.W. *The Mission and Message of Jesus*. London: Nicholson & Watson, 1937. [301-639 reprinted as *The Sayings of Jesus*. London: SCM Press, 1949.]
----- *Only to the House of Israel? Jesus and the Non-Jews*. Philadelphia: Fortress, 1964 [1955].
Marshall, I.Howard. *Last Supper and Lord's Supper*. Exeter: Paternoster, 1980.
----- "Slippery Words: Eschatology", *Expository Times* 89/9 (1978).
Meier, John P. "John the Baptist in Matthew's Gospel", *JBL* 99 (1980) 383-405.
----- *Law and History in Matthew's Gospel: A Redactional Study of Mt. 5:17-48*. Rome: Biblical Institute Press, 1976.
-----"Nations or Gentiles in Matthew 28:19?" *Catholic Biblical Quarterly* 39 (1977) 94-102.
Mendenhall, George E. "The Hebrew Conquest of Palestine", *The Biblical Archaeologist Reader* 3, eds. E.F. Campbell & D.N. Freedman. Garden City: Doubleday, 1970 [1962].
----- *Law and Covenant in Israel and the Ancient Near East*. Pittsburgh: Biblical Colloquium, 1955.
----- "Social Organization in Early Israel", *Magnalia Dei*, *Fs*. G.E. Wright. 1976.
----- *The Tenth Generation: The Origins of the Biblical Tradition*. Baltimore: Johns Hopkins University Press, 1974.
Moessner, David P. "The 'Leaven of the Pharisees' and 'This Generation': Israel's Rejection of Jesus According to Luke", *Journal for the Study of the New Testament* 34 (1988) 21-46.
Montgomery, James Alan. *The Samaritans: The Earliest Jewish Sect, Their History, Theology, and Literature*. Philadelphia: Winston, 1907.

Montefiore, C.G. *The Synoptic Gospels*, vol 2. New York: Ktav, 1968 [1927].
----- *Rabbinic Literature and Gospel Teachings*. New York: Ktav, 1970 [1930].
Moule, C.F.D."Adoption", *IDB* 1 (1962) 48-9.
-----"The Ascension - Acts 1.9", *Essays in New Testament Interpretation*. Cambridge: University Press, 1982.
----- *The Birth of the New Testament*. San Francisco: Harper & Row, 1982 [1962].
-----"Fulfillment Words in the New Testament: Use and Abuse", *NTS* 14 (1967-68) 293-320.
-----"Once More, Who Were the Hellenists?" *Expository Times* 70 (1958-59).
----- *The Phenomenon of the New Testament*. London: SCM, 1967.
-----"Saint Matthew's Gospel: Some Neglected Features", *Studia Evangelica* vol 2/1, ed. F.L.Cross. Berlin: Akademie-Verlag, 1964.
Mowinckel, Sigmund. *He That Cometh*, trans. G.W.Anderson. Oxford: Blackwell, 1956 [1951].
Munck, Johannes. *Christ and Israel: An Interpretation of Romans 9-11*, trans. I. Nixon. Philadelphia: Fortress, 1967 [1956].
----- *Paul and the Salvation of Mankind*, trans. F. Clarke. Richmond: John Knox, 1959 [1954].
Murphy-O'Connor, Jerome. "An Essene Missionary Document?" *Revue Biblique* 77 (1970) 201-29.
Murray, Robert. "Defining Judaea-Christianity", *The Heythrop Journal* 15 (1974) 303-10.
-----"On Early Christianity and Judaism: Some Recent Studies", *Heythrop Journal* 13 (1972) 441-51.
----- *Symbols of Church and Kingdom: A Study in Early Syriac Christianity*. Cambridge: University Press, 1975.
Neusner, Jacob. *Aphrahat and Judaism: The Jewish-Christian Argument in Fourth-Century Iran*. Leiden: E.J.Brill, 1971.
----- "The Conversion of Adiabene to Judaism", *JBL* 83 (1964).
----- *From Politics to Piety: The Emergence of Pharisaic Judaism*. Englewood Cliffs: Prentice-Hall, 1973.
----- *The Glory of God Is Intelligence*. Salt Lake City: Publisher's Press, 1978.
----- "Judaism after the Destruction of the Temple", 663-77 *Israelite and Judaean History*, eds. J.H.Hayes & J.M.Miller. Philadelphia: Westminster, 1977.
----- *Judaism in the Beginning of Christianity*. Philadelphia: Fortress, 1984.
----- "'Judaism' after Moore: A Programmatic Statement", *Journal of Jewish Studies* 31/2 (1980). (Reprinted in *Method and Meaning in Ancient Judaism* second series 19-33. Chico: Scholars Press, 1981.)
----- "Map without Territory: Mishnah's System of Sacrifice and Sanctuary", *History of Religions* 19 (1979) 103-27.
----- *Messiah in Context: Israel's History and Destiny in Formative Judaism*. Philadelphia: Fortress, 1984.
----- *Rabbinic Traditions About Pharisees Before 70*, Part 3. Leiden: E.J. Brill, 1971.
Nock, Arthur Darby. *Early Gentile Christianity and Its Hellenistic Background*. New York: Harper and Row, 1964 [I&II 1928, III 1952].
Noland, John. "Proselytism or Politics in Horace Satires I,3, 138-143?" *Vigiliae Christianae* 33 (1979) 347-355.
O'Neill, J.C."The Silence of Jesus", *NTS* 15 (1968-69) 153-67.
Orchard, Bernard. *Matthew, Luke & Mark*. Manchester: Koinonia, 1976.
Orkar, John Ngusha. *A Pre-Colonial History of the Tiv of Central Nigeria C. 1500-1850*. Halifax: Dalhousie Ph.D. dissertation, 1979.

Pearson, Birger. "Earliest Christianity in Egypt: Some Observations", *The Roots of Egyptian Christianity*, eds. B. Pearson & J. Goehring. Philadelphia: Fortress, 1986.
Pope, Marvin. "Proselytes", *IDB* 3 (1962).
Purvis, James. *The Samaritan Pentateuch and the Origin of the Samaritan Sect*. Cambridge, U.S.A.: Harvard University Press, 1968.
Rabinowitz, Isaac. "Government", *IDB* 2 (1962).
----- "The Meaning and Date of 'Damascus' Document IX,1", *Revue de Qumran* 6 (1968) 433-5.
----- "A Reconsideration of 'Damascus' and '390 Years' in the 'Damascus' (Zadokite) Fragment", *JBL* 73 (1954) 11-35.
Rad, Gerhard von. "Israel, Judah and Hebrews in the Old Testament", *TDNT*, vol 3, 356-9.
Reicke, Bo. *The New Testament Era: The World of the Bible from 500 B.C. to A.D. 100*, trans. D.E.Green. Philadelphia: Fortress, 1964.
----- *The Roots of the Synoptic Gospels*. Philadelphia: Fortress Press, 1986.
----- "Synoptic Prophecies on the Destruction of Jerusalem", 121-34 *Studies in New Testament and Early Christian Literature*, Fs. A.P. Wikgren, ed. D.W. Aune. Leiden: E.J.Brill, 1972.
Rengstorff, Karl H. "Die Stadt der Mörder (Mt 22.7)", 106-129 *Judentum, Urchristentum, Kirche*, Fs. Joachim Jeremias, ed. W. Etester. Berlin: Topelman, 1960.
Richardson, Peter. *Israel in the Apostolic Church*. Cambridge: University Press, 1969.
Ridderbos, Herman. *The Coming Kingdom*, trans. H. de Jongste. St. Catherines: Paidea Press, 1978 [1962].
Rist, John H. *On the Independence of Matthew and Mark*. Cambridge: University Press, 1978.
Rivkin, Ellis. *A Hidden Revolution*. Nashville: Abingdon, 1978.
----- "The Meaning of Messiah in Jewish Thought", *USQR* 26 (1971) 383-406.
----- *What Crucified Jesus?* Nashville: Abingdon, 1984.
Robinson, H. Wheeler. *Corporate Personality in Ancient Israel*. Philadelphia: Fortress, 1980 [1935 & 1937].
----- "The Council of Yahweh", *Journal of Theological Studies* 45 (1945) 151-7.
Robinson, John A.T. "The 'Others' of John 4:38: a Test of Exegetical Method", *Twelve New Testament Studies*. London: SCM, 1962.
----- *Redating the New Testament*. London: SCM, 1976.
----- "Resurrection in the NT", *IDB* 4 (1962).
Rokeah, David. *Jews, Pagans and Christians in Conflict*. Jerusalem/ Leiden: Magnes/ Brill, 1982.
Rosenthal, Erwin I.J. *Studia Semitica*. Volume 1: *Jewish Themes*. Cambridge: University Press, 1971.
Sanders, E.P. *The Tendencies of the Synoptic Tradition*. Cambridge: University Press, 1969.
Sanders, J.A. *Torah and Canon*. Philadelphia: Fortress, 1972.
Sandmel, Samuel. *The First Christian Century in Judaism and Christianity: Certainties and Uncertainties*. New York: Oxford University Press, 1969.
----- *Judaism and Christian Beginnings*. New York: Oxford University Press, 1978.
----- "Parallelmania", *JBL* 81 (1962) 1-13.
----- *The Several Israels*. New York: Ktav, 1971.
Scharlemann, Martin H. *Stephen: A Singular Saint*. Rome: Pontifical Biblical Institute, 1968.
Schlatter, Adolf. *Der Evangelist Matthäus: Seine Sprache, sein Ziel, seine Selbstandigkeit*. Stuttgart: Calwer, 1929.

Schoeps, H.J. *Jewish Christianity*, trans. D.R.A. Hare. Philadelphia: Fortress, 1969.
----- *Paul: The Theology of the Apostle in the Light of Jewish Religious History*, trans. H. Knight. Philadelphia: Westminster, 1961 [1959].
Scholem, G. *The Messianic Idea in Judaism*. London: Allen & Unwin, 1971.
Schürer, Emil. *The History of the Jewish People in the Age of Jesus*, trans. S. Taylor & P. Christie. Second Division, vol 2. New York: Scribner's Sons, 1891.
----- & Geza Vermes *et al.* revision. Volume III.1 & 2. Edinburgh: T.&T. Clark, 1986 & 1987.
Schwartz, D.R. "'To Join Oneself to the House of Judah' (Damascus Document IV,11)", *Revue de Qumran* 39 (1981).
Schweizer, Eduard. *Church Order in the New Testament*, trans. F. Clarke. London: SCM, 1961.
----- *The Good News According to Matthew*, trans. D.E.Green. Atlanta: John Knox, 1975.
Scobie, C.H.H. "Jesus or Paul? The Origin of the Universal Mission of the Christian Church", *From Jesus to Paul*, eds. P.Richardson & J.C.Hurd. Waterloo, Canada: Wilfred Laurier University Press, 1984.
----- "North and South: Tension and Reconciliation in Biblical History", *Biblical Studies in Honour of Wm. Barclay*, eds. J. McKay & J. Miller. London: Collins, 1976.
----- "The Origins and Development of Samaritan Christianity", *NTS* 19 (1972-73) 390-414.
Sevenster, J.N. *Do You Know Greek? How Much Greek Could the First Jewish Christians Have Known?* Leiden: E.J.Brill, 1968.
----- *The Roots of Pagan Anti-Semitism in the Ancient World*. Leiden: E.J.Brill, 1975.
Segal, Alan. "The Costs of Proselytism and Conversion", *SBL Annual Meeting Seminar Papers*. Atlanta: Scholars Press, 1988.
----- "Matthew's Jewish Voice", *Social History of the Matthean Community: Cross Disciplinary Approaches*, ed. D.L. Balch. Minneapolis: Fortress, 1991.
Sigal, Phillip. *The Emergence of Contemporary Judaism*, Volume 1, Part 1: *From the Origins to the Separation of Christianity*. Pittsburgh: Pickwick, 1980.
----- *The Halakah of Jesus of Nazareth According to the Gospel of Matthew*. Lanham: University Press of America, 1986 [1976].
Simon, Marcel. *Verus Israel: A Study of the Relations between Christians and Jews in the Roman Empire (135-425)*, trans. H. McKeating. Oxford: University Press, 1986 [1948].
Speiser, E.A. "'People' and 'Nation' of Israel", *JBL* 79 (1959) 157-163. [Reprinted in *Oriental and Biblical Studies*, eds. J.J. Finkelstein & M. Greenberg. Philadelphia: University of Pennsylvania Press, 1967.]
Spiro, Abram. "Stephen's Samaritan Background", eds. W.F.Albright & C.S.Mann 285-300 *The Acts of the Apostles, Introduction, Translation and Notes* by Johannes Munck. Anchor Bible. Garden City: Doubleday, 1967 [1965].
Stegemann, Hartmut. "<Die des Uria>. Zur Bedeutung des Frauennamen in der Genealogy von Matthaus 1,1-7", 246-76 *Tradition und Glaube: Das frühe Christentum in seiner Unwelt*, Fs. K.G.Kuhn, ed. G.Jeremias *et al.* Gottingen: Vandenhoek & Ruprecht, 1971.
Stendahl, Krister. "Matthew", 769-98 *Peake's Commentary on the Bible* eds. M. Black & H.H. Rowley. London: Thomas Nelson, 1962.
----- "*Quis et Unde?*" *The Interpretation of Matthew*, ed. G.Stanton. Philadelphia: Fortress, 1983.
Stonehouse, Ned B. *The Witness of Matthew and Mark to Christ*. Grand Rapids: Eerdmans, 1958 [1944].

Strecker, Georg. *Der Weg der Gerechtigkeit*. Göttingen: Vandenhoek & Ruprecht, 1962.
----- "On the Problem of Jewish Christianity", Appendix 1 to Walther Bauer's *Orthodoxy and Heresy in Earliest Christianity*. London: SCM, 1972 [1964].
Sundkler, Bengt. "Jésus et les païens", *Revue d'histoire et de philosophie Religieuses* 16 (1936) 466-499.
Tagawa, Kenzo. "People and Community in the Gospel of Matthew", *NTS* 16 (1969) 149-162.
Theissen, Gerd. *The Miracle Stories of the Early Christian Tradition*, trans. F. McDonagh. Philadelphia: Fortress, 1983 [1974].
----- *Sociology of Early Palestinian Christianity*, trans. J.Bowden. Philadelphia: Fortress, 1978 [1977].
Thomson, J.E.H. *The Samaritans: Their Testimony to the Religion of Israel*. Edinburgh: Oliver & Boyd, 1919.
Torrance, Thomas F. "Proselyte Baptism", *NTS* 1 (1954-55) 150-154.
----- *Space, Time and Resurrection*. Grand Rapids: Eerdmans, 1976.
Vaux, Roland de. "Method in the Study of Early Hebrew History", *The Bible and Modern Scholarship*, ed. J.Philip Hyatt. London: Kingsgate Press, 1966.
Vermes, Geza. *Jesus the Jew: A Historian's Reading of the Gospels*. Glasgow: Collins, 1976 [1973].
----- "The Use of ברנש / בר נשא in Jewish Aramaic", published in Matthew Black's *An Aramaic Approach to the Gospels and Acts* 310-328. Oxford: Clarendon Press, 1967 [1965].
Vincent, John J. "Did Jesus Teach His Disciples to Learn by Heart?" 104-118 *Studia Evangelica* III/ii, ed. F.L.Cross. Berlin: Akademie-Velag, 1964.
----- "The Parables of Jesus as Self-Revelation", 79-99 *Studia Evangelium* I, ed. K. Aland *et al*. Berlin: Akademie-Verlag, 1959.
Visser't Hooft, Willem A. "Die Magier und die Mission", *Basileia, Fs*. Walter Freytag. Stuttgart: Evangelische Missionsverlag, 1959.
Waetjen, Herman C. "The Genealogy as the Key to the Gospel According to Matthew", *JBL* 95 (1976) 205-230.
Walbank, F.W. "The Problem of Greek Nationality", *The Phoenix: The Journal of the Classical Association of Canada* 5 (1951) 41-60.
Wilder, Amos N. *Early Christian Rhetoric: The Language of the Gospel*. London: SCM, 1964.
Williamson, H.G.M. *Israel in the books of Chronicles*. Cambridge: University Press, 1977.
Wilson, Robert R. *Genealogy and History in the Biblical World*. New Haven: Yale University Press, 1977.
Wilson, Stephen G. *Gentiles and the Gentile Mission in Luke-Acts*. Cambridge: University Press, 1973.
Winter, Paul. *On the Trial of Jesus*. Berlin: W. de Gruyter, 1961.
----- "Psalms of Solomon", *IDB* 3 (1962).
Wisse, Frederick. "The Nag Hammadi Library and the Heresiologists", *Vigiliae Christianae* 25 (1971) 205-223.
Woods, C.F. "The Evidential Value of the Biblical Miracles", *Miracles*, ed. C.F.D. Moule. London: Mowbray, 1965.
Zeitlin, Solomon. "The Origin of the Idea of the Messiah", *In the Time of Harvest, Fs*. Abba Hillel Silver, ed. D.J.Silver. New York: Macmillan, 1963.
----- "Zealots and Sicarii", *JBL* 81 (1962) 395-398.
Zimmerli, Walther. *The Law and the Prophets: A Study of the Meaning of the Old Testament*, trans. R.E. Clement. Oxford: Blackwell, 1965.

A. ANCIENT TEXTS CITED

OLD TESTAMENT

Genesis
2 .4	169	46 .3		180
.17	435	46 .20		81
.1	169	50 .20		44
6 .5-8	65			
9 .25	210	Exodus		
12 .1	60	1 .15, 16, 19		52
.2-3	171, 172	2 .6, 7		52
.10	180	.11,13		53
14 .13	55	.24		50
15	50	3 .6,14,15		49
.1-3, 19	59	.9, 18		53
17	50	4 .22-23		49
.16	172	.23		50
18	59	5 .3		53
.18-19	172	7 .16		53
19 .19	182	9 .1, 13		53
21	60	10 .3		53
22 .2	182	12 .4, 19, 27		50
23 .4	55	.10		180
25	60	.15		201
32 .10	182	.38		50, 61, 97
.23	49	16 .2		50
34	73, 82	19 .4		50
35 .9	49	.5		58
38 .2, 6-30	173	.6		217
.26	174	20 .4-5		51
39 .14, 17	52	21 - 23		51
40 .15	52	22 .20		54
41 .12	52	23 .9		54
.45, 50-52	81	.19, 28, 32		51
42 .1-2	180	29 .10		143
43 .1-2	180	31 .3		32
.32	52	32		73

(Exodus cont.)		26 .18	58
34 .10	51, 58	29 .29	43
.16	173	32 .5, 20	223
42 .1-2	180	.21	72
43 .1-2	180		
46 .3	180	Joshua	
		2	175
Leviticus		.14-15	173
17 .11	220	6 .17	173
18 .26	71	10 .24-25	57
19 .18, 33	227	14 .6, 8	59
Numbers		Judges	
11 .4, 12	50	1 .16	59
13 .3, 6	59	2 .4	62
.30	60	3 .9	62
14 .6, 24, 30	60	5	62
23 .9	58, 65	8 .23	62
24 .17-18	178	9 .7-21	62
25 .6-9	74		
		Ruth	
Deuteronomy		1 .1, 16-17	60, 174
2 .12	56	2 .11-12	174
5 .5	180	4 .11-12	173
.15	54, 180	.11	60
6 - 8	184, 185		
6 .1	56	I Samuel	
7 .3	173	4 .6, 9	53
.6	58	8 .5, 7	63
10 .22	61	10 .1	63
13 .1-3	60	11 .12	63
14 .2	58	13 .3, 4 , 6-7	53
.28-29	71	.19	53
15 .12	55	14 .11	53
17 .14-17	64	.21, 22-23	54
21 .23 LXX	225	22 .2	171
23 .3-6	69, 173	25 .10	54
.3	73	29 .3	54, 171
25 .4	202		
26 .5	55		
.12	71		

II Samuel	
5 .1	63
7	172
7 .16	64, 172

I Kings	
3 .12	64
12 .30	116
19 .18	65
22	87

II Kings	
17	141

I Chronicles	
1 - 3	171
1 .34	171
2 .3-4	173

Ezra	
6 .17, 21	69

Nehemiah	
1 .6	69
10	69
13 .1-3, 23-25	72
.1	60
.3	69

Esther	
4 .14	70
8 .17	71
9 .21, 27, 29, 31, 32	71
absence in Mt citations	123

Psalms	
2 .2-4	230
.7	63, 182
16 .10	226
22 .28	225
78	123
89 .27	63
107 .2-3	208
117	130
118 .22-23	119
136 .4	58

Song of Solomon	
2 .7	152

Isaiah	
6	87
7 .3	65
9 .1	186
11 .1	180
25 .6	209
42	64, 115
.1	13, 182, 184
.4	113
.6	220
47	179
49 .6	138
.7-8	220
52	220
53	206, 220
56	131
.7	108, 130, 218
60	130, 179

Jeremiah	
16 .16	189
23 .1-8	138
.18	87
26 .4-8	143
31	64
.34	220
32 .8	56
34 .9, 14, 15	55
35 .18	59
38 .2-3	143
44 .14	65
50 .4-7	138

Ezekiel		6 .1-4	226
5 .10	65	.6	217
17 .23	201	11 .1	176
31 .6	201		
.34	220	Amos	
34	138	9 .7	39
37	64		
.19, 22-23, 28	141	Jonah	
		1 .9	55, 73
Daniel		.17	226
2 .18-19	87	2 .1-2	207
.28	202	4 .2	206
4 .6	87		
.12	201	Zephaniah	
7 .12-14	237	2 .3, 7	65
.13-14	199, 228	3 .12-13	65
.13	199		
.14	226, 238	Zechariah	
11 .31	122	9 .9	218, 219
12 .2	139	12 .15 LXX	81
.4	198		
.23	226	Malachi	
		1 .11	94
Hosea		3 .17	58
1 .10	49, 54		

APOCRYPHA AND PSEUDEPIGRAPHA

Tobit		14 .10	73
1 .1, 3-4, 8	71	16 .17	73
13. 3, 5	71		
14. 6-7	72	Ecclesiasticus (Sirach)	
		Prol. 24	72
Judith		24 .6, 8, 23	72
1 .1	73	36 .1-2, 11	72
5 .6	73	44 .18, 19	72
9 .2, 4	73	45 .23	72
10 .12	73	48 .2	72

(Ecclesiasticus cont.)		17 .9	78
49 .13	72	18 .12	77
50 .25-26	72		
		Wisdom of Solomon	
I Maccabees		3 .8	77
1 .11, 41-43	74	10 .5, 15	77
.56	118	11 - 19	77
2 .10, 12, 15, 23,		17 .2	77
.26, 27, 54, 58	74		
3 .10	74	Additions to Daniel	
4 .30	73	Susanna 56 Θ	77
.58	131		
5 .9	74	Additions to Esther	
.23	131	1 .1 f	70
6 .58	74	3 .13 d	70
8 .23, 25	74	3 .13 e	70
14 .16, 18	131	4 .17 e	70
		10 .3 f	70
II Maccabees		10 .3 g	70
1 .1, 7, 10	77		
2 .21	78	Psalms of Solomon	
4.2	77	2 .24	784
5 .22	77	4 .3	78
6 .12	77	17	126
7 .1-15	77	.26, 28	78
.16, 38	77	.30-34	132
.31	78	18	126
8 .1	78		
11 .13	78	I Enoch	
14 .38	78	48 .4	228
15 .37	78	91 .12-27	176
		93 .1-10	176
III Maccabees			
1 .3	78	Book of Jubilees	
2 .28	77	4	173
4 .26	78	25 .4, 10	79
8 .14	77	30 .7	79
		.17	72
IV Maccabees			
4 .26	78		
8 .1	78		

Testaments of the Twelve Patriarchs		15 .7	81
Levi 6	72	23 .1-13	82
Judah 10-15	173		
Naphtali 3.3	79	II Baruch	
		1 .5	82
Pseudo-Philo (LAB)		41 .4	82
9 .3-4	80	42 .4, 5	82
Joseph and Aseneth		IV Ezra	
1 .5	81	4 .23	82
.9	81	6.56	82
8 .9	81	7.46	82

DEAD SEA SCROLLS

Damascus Document (CD=6QD)		War Scroll (IQM)	
4.11	133	xii. xiv. xix	132
6	133		
11.13-14	79	Testimony Book	
14	133	4QTestim	119
17.3	80		
		Non-Canonical Psalms	
Manual of Discipline (1QS)		4Q380	80
1.4	79		

PHILO

Migration of Abraham		On the Virtues	
20	84	181-2	85
On Abraham		Questions and Answers on Exodus	
273-6	85	ii .2	86
On the Special Laws		On the Preliminary Studies	
i .51-52	85	51	85
ii .253	85		

JOSEPHUS

The Jewish War		xx	85
ii.66-75	223	.35	150
.232	84	.39	153
vi.312	128	.43	151
		.264	117
Jewish Antiquities			
i .46	84	Life of Josephus	
ix .227-91	141	6	171
xi .173, 344	84	24	84
.322	141		
.344-347	84	Against Apion	
xii .36	84	i .8	11
xiii .62-73	217		
xv .372	80		
xviii	85		
.30	84		
.115-119	128, 142		

NEW TESTAMENT

Matthew		2 .12, 13, 22	177
1-16.20	157	.14-15, 17-18	123
1-4.16	169, 170, 172, 205	.22-23	123, 185, 238
		.23	180
1.1-17	169, 172	3 .1	182
.1	158	.2	181
.2	176	.3	123
.3	174	.5, 10, 11-12, 16	144
.5	60, 173	.8-9	142, 181, 215
.11	177, 179	.11	142
.16, 18-25	175	.13-15	124, 142
.18-21	176, 177	.14, 16	181
.22-23	123	.15	181, 183, 214, 215
2 .2	231		
.6, 10, 16	178	.17	182

(Matthew cont.)

Reference	Pages
4 .1	184
.8-9, 10-12, .15-16	185, 211
.13-16	123, 142, 144, 238
.17	167, 181, 187-188, 191
.18	188-189, 195
.19	189
.21	188-189
.24-25	188
5 .1	189
.3-12	1
.3	210
.10	191
.14	185, 191
.16	186
.17-20	190
.17	124
.18	183, 191
.43-45	191, 227
.47	84, 111, 192-193
.48	191, 228
6 .7	84, 111, 192-193
.8	176
.9-13, 21	191
.32	110, 192
7 .2, 16-17	185
.12	123
.24	187
.28-29	191, 214, 237
8 .1-4	190
.5-13	109, 190, 208
.7	25, 208
.11	207-208
.16-17	123, 206
.20	197
.22	188, 190
8 .23-27	205, 214
9 .1-7	190
.6	197
9.9, 10-11	190
.12-17	188
.13	217
.18-34	226
.33	206
10	134
.2	135, 194-195
.3, 4	135
.5-6	133-139, 149, 192, 196, 215, 236, 238-239
.7	138
.8	226
.18	192
.23	2, 139, 195-196, 238
.28	198
.38	188
11 .2-19	183
.2-3	144, 184
.5	209, 226
.9	183
.11	144
.13	124
.16-19	214
.19	197
12 .7	217
.8	197
.15-21	113, 123, 206
.32	198
.38-42	206-207
.40-41	198, 207
.41	206, 223
.50	187
13 .1-23	202
.6	126
.11	191, 202-203
.12-15	203
.31-32, 33	201

(Matthew cont.)		21 .42	119
13 .34-35	123, 159	.43	77, 108
.37, 41	198	22 .7	162
.52	124	.34-39	228
14 .12	183	.40	123
.28, 30	154	23	228
15.		.1-13	209, 215
.21-28	208-210	.15	145-156
.29	210	.35	117
.24	209, 215, 239	.36	223
16 .4	206, 223	24 .2	117
.6	117, 198, 201	.4	111
.11-12	201	.7-8	110
.16-20	195	.15	122
.16	211	.34	191, 223
.21-22	212	25 .31-46	197, 228
.21	167, 210, 211, 216	26 .2	219
.22	217	.13	216
.23	211	.21-25	219
.24	188, 218	.28	220
17 .17	223	.37-38, 45f	221
.22-23	211, 213	.51, 59, 70f	222
18 .17	190, 192-194	.56	117, 124, 222
.21-35	214	27 .9-10	123
19 .16-30	214	.11, 29, 37	231
.24	210	.19	224
.28	126, 195, 231	.25	222, 223
20 .1-16	214	.46	225
.17-19	110, 185, 211, 222	.51-53	226
		.54f, 62-64	225
.18-20	213	28 .1	225
.25	110, 213	.6	126, 230
.28	213, 216	.7	113, 238-239
21 .1-17	228	.10	177, 231
21 .4-5	123	.11-31	231
.5, 13	218	.15	162, 237
.10-14	167	.16-20	113, 168, 189, 191, 196, 203, 231-232, 235-247
.12	126		
.23	214	.16	195
.32	182, 214	.18-20	172

(Matthew cont.)		
28 .19-20		17, 136, 158
		177, 182, 187
		190
.19		216, 233, 236
.20		172

Mark
1 .7, 10	144
3 .6	80
4 .11	202
6 .30	195
7 .24-30	109. 209
10 .32-34, 42	110
11 .15f	117
.17	108, 218
13 .8	110
.10	111
14 .49	117
15 .43	224
16 .6-7	107, 113
.8	107, 113, 231, 246

Luke
1 .1-4	109
2 .23	108
3 .8	142
.9, 14f	144
.23-38	171
4 .16	116
6 .13	135
.33	192
7 .1-10	109
7 .5	108
7 .11-16	226
8 .10	202
9 .53	140
10 .1	140
.9	138
12 .30	110

14 .26	58
15 .21-28	109
17 .18	141
.19	111
18 .31-33	110
19 .10-11	110
19 .41-44	162, 167
21 .20-24	162
22 .25	110
.53	117
23 .2	108
24 .4	124
.6	113
.25	119, 124, 252
.27	118, 124
.36-53	243
.46-49	113, 237
.49	245
.52-53	117

John
1 .1	187
.19, 25, 30	144
.32	142, 143, 144
.35-37	142
2 .23	212
3 .16	111
.23	144
4 .9	32
.22	33, 107, 117, 141, 169
.25	133
.38	144
5 .39	119
7 .14	117
.35	151
10 .16	139
11 .16	218
.24	212
.49-50, 51-52	108
12 .12-19	167

(John cont.)		22 .1-4	86
12 .32	108	24 .25	252
15 .18	111	28 .30-31	161
18 .15-16	224	Romans	
20 .19-23	113, 243, 245	1 .14	41
21 .1f	113, 117, 246	2 .9-10	30
Acts		3 .2	178
1&2	245	.9	33
1 .1	246	4 .9-12	171, 173
.3	117	8 .1	86
.7-8	17, 113	.15-17	176
.9	91, 245	.37-39	86
.11, 12-14	117	9 .1-2	86
2 .1	117	10 .2-4	86
.5	91	.2	89
.7-8	87	11 .1	86
6	87, 89-90	.25-27	88-89
.1	7, 90	15 .11	130
8 .1	86, 91	16 .25	14, 88
.4-25	5	22 .3-4	86
.4	91	I Corinthians	
.5-8, 26-40	92	1 .23	217
.9	5, 179	5 .1-8	201, 220
.14	195	9 .5	5
9 .1-2	86	11 .23	219
.4f	243	15 .1	168
.29	89	.9-10	86
10 .1 - 11 .18	5	II Corinthians	
11 .20	89	11 .2	89
12 .1-4	93	Galatians	
13 .6-8	179	1 .13-14	78
.23-24	144	.17-21	87
.45	86	.18	91
15	5	.19	86
.14	5	2 .9	86
17 .11	119	.11	171
21 .27 - 22 .25	88	.13-14	89
.18	195		
.20-23	13		
.20-21	86		

(Galatians cont.)		I Timothy	
3 .7	171	1 .3-7	170
.28	44		
4 .4	11	Hebrews	
5 .9	201	5 .7-10	221
		7 .14	141
Ephesians		11 .31	175
1 .3-14	25, 26		
.20-23	230	James	
2 .12	88	2 .25	175
3 .1-7	88		
.8-13	86	II Peter	
.8-12	88, 203	1 .1	5
.9	88		
		III John	
Philippians		7	192
2 .15	223		
3 .4-6	86	Revelation	
.5	89	1 .17f	243
		21 .24	130
Colossians		22 .2	206
1 .24-29	88		
2 .1-3	88		
3 .11f	44		
4 .2-4	86, 88		

OTHER EARLY CHRISTIAN WRITINGS

Didache		I Clement	
Title	93	2.2-3	97
9.4	94	4.7,9,11	97
11.3, 4	94	5.4-5	97
13.1f	94	.7	87
14.3	94	6.4	97
		7.3	97
Odes of Solomon		29.3	97
42.6	243		

Ignatian Epistles		Justin Martyr	
Ephesians		*Dialogue with Trypho the Jew*	
19.3	179	29	97
		120	97
Magnesians		121f	146
8.2	187	122	153
10.3	8, 89	123f	146
Smyrnaeans		*Apology*	
7.2	168	I.14.5	201

MISHNAH

Demai		Ketuboth	
5.9	79	7.6	100
Megillah		Nadarim	
4.4	115	11.2	100
Yebamoth		Aboth	
8.31	74	5.21	117
16.7	118		

Kodashim: eleven tractates   217

B. AUTHORS
(including ancient writers from *ca.* AD 200)

Abravanel, I. 126
Aharoni, Y. 116
Aland, K. & B. 120, 122, 126, 236
Albright, W.F. 44, 49-50, 59, 62, 90, 140, 221, 226, 246
Allen, W. 67, 146
Althaus, P. 38, 43
Aphrahat 95-97
Arendt, H. 34
Audet, J.-P. 93, 118, 236
Augustine 21-22, 164, 179
Austin, J.L. 23
Bacon, B. 167
Baeck, L. 126-127
Baker, D.L. 2
Bamberger, B. 9, 11, 151-152
Bammel, E. 12
Banton, M. and J. Harwood 22
Baron, S. 11, 67, 100, 150, 153-154
Barr, J. 18-22, 24, 26
Barrois, G. 217
Barth, G. 227, 238
Barth, K. 19, 123, 233, 238, 246
Barth, M. 4, 112, 143, 181-182, 216, 220-221
Bauer, W. 96
Bauer-Arndt-Gingrich 135, 186
Baur, F. 2, 3, 12
Baxter, C. 123
Beare, F.W. 241
Beasley-Murray, G.R. 143
Beattie, D.R.G. 60
Becker, J. 128
Bede 42
Beer, G. 50
Benoit, P. 76

Berghe, P. van den 39, 52
Bertram, G. 43
Betz, H. 191-192
Billerbeck, P. see Strack-Billerbeck
Bimson, J. 54, 56, 61
Black, M. 120, 140, 192-193, 199
Blass-Debrunner-Funk 184, 208
Bloch, R. 174
Blomberg, C. see Goetz
Boer, H. 235
Boismard, M. 165
Boling, R. 58
Boring, M.E. 112, 243, 245
Bornkamm, G. 87, 103, 107, 227, 232, 241-242, 245
Bosch, D. 17
Bowan, J. 194
Bowker, J. 99, 116, 148
Bowman, J. 90-91, 108
Brandon, S.G.F. 2, 180
Braude, W. 9, 11, 152
Bright, J. 62-63
Brooks, O. 168, 203, 237
Brown-Driver-Briggs 50
Brown, R. 87, 169, 175
Brown, S. 155, 194, 196, 239, 241
Bruce, F.F. 27, 37
Brueggemann, W. 63
Buchanan, G. 122, 158
Bultmann, R. 19, 103, 107, 125, 164, 167, 242-244
Burchard, C. 81
Burton, E.D.W. 239
Butler, B.C. 164, 209
Bynon, T. 29
Cadbury, H. 89-90, 120
Caird, G. 114, 143-144, 163
Cantwell, L. 177

Caponigri, A. 23
Caponigro, M. 72
Carey, W. 235
Carroll, Lewis 6
Catchpole, D. 222
Chamberlain, H.S. 34, 43
Charles, R.H. 71, 82, 99
Charlesworth, J. 75, 96, 126
Childs, B. 49, 51, 64, 157
Clark, K.W. 158, 169, 192,
Clarke, W.K.L. 179
Clines, D. 69-70
Cloete, G.D. 45
Coggins, R. 8, 33, 142
Colpe, C. 199
Colson, F. 21
Conybeare, F. 236
Conzelmann, H. 112
Cook, M. 25
Cook, W. 148
Cope, O.L. 165, 188
Craigie, P. 56-57
Cross, F.M. 67-68, 131-132
Crossan, J.D. 104, 109
Culler, J. 28
Cullmann, O. 3-6, 19, 22, 108, 135, 139, 143-144, 168, 182, 195, 198-199, 218, 222
Dahl, N. 38, 40-42, 100, 216
Danby, H. 36
Danell, G. 49-50
Daniel, C. 80
Danielou, J. 12
Daube, D. 180, 221
Davies, P. 132, 139
Davies, W.D. 109, 126, 162, 176
Delling, G. 22
Dentan, R. 48
Derrett, J. 115, 169, 215
Derwacter, F. 9, 11, 146, 152
DeVries, S. 173
Dexinger, F. 141

Diessmann, G.A. 90
Dix, G. 3-4, 12, 92, 95, 105, 107
Dobschütz, E. von 107, 158
Dodd, C.H. 107, 115, 118-119, 125, 138, 162, 185, 200-202, 218, 224
Donfried, K. 88
Donner, H. 63
Dunlop, D. 35
Edwards, R. 114, 207
Eichrodt, W. 49, 59
Ellis, E. 91, 165
Elon, A. 38
Emerton, J. 96
Enslin, M. 134, 137, 159
Ephrem 96
Ericksen, R. 43
Eusebius 52, 236
Farmer, W.R. 77, 80, 85-86, 131, 163-165
Fee, G. 165
Feldman, L. 32, 80-81
Festinger, L. 229
Filson, F. 161, 185
Finley, M. 42
Fletcher, V. 112, 230
France, R. 179
Frankemölle, H. 169
Frankena, W. 147
Freedman, D. 49
Frei, H. 233
Friedländer, M. 146
Fuerst, W. 70
Gager, J. 229
Gaston, L. 217
Garland, D. 146
Georgi, D. 13
Gerhardsson, B. 106, 109, 166, 185, 188, 205, 208, 215-216, 218
Geus, C. de 49
Gibbon, E. 9

Gill, M. 64
Ginsberg, H.L. 68
Gnilka, J. 168
Gobineau, A. de 34-35, 43
Goetz, S. & C. Blomberg 136
Goldin, J. 83, 148
Goldman, L. 198
Goldstein, J. 73-74, 77
Goodenough, E.R. 83, 86, 130
Goodspeed, E.J. 176, 195, 240
Gordon, C. 175
Gottwald, N. 56, 58
Grant, F.C. 26
Green, H. 198, 245
Greenberg, M. 54
Gundry, R. 120, 122, 159, 210
Gutbrod, W. 84
Haenchen, E. 91, 244
Hahn, F. 10, 13, 37, 108, 136-137, 155, 209, 238, 242
Handlin, O. 34, 35
Hare, D. 67, 154, 192
Harnack, A. von 1, 136, 161, 233, 236
Harrington, D. 80
Harris, H. 3
Harris, J.R. 96, 195
Held, H.J. 208
Hengel, M. 1, 10, 117, 163, 216-217
Higgins, A.J.B. 175
Hill, D. 20, 143, 147, 169, 184, 195, 232, 243-244
Hobsbawn, E. 38
Hooker, M. 196, 239
Horsley, R. and J. Hanson 32, 57
Hort, F.J.A. 12
Hubbard, B. 237, 242-244
Jellicoe. S. 67
Jenkins, P. 40
Jenni, E. 20-21, 65

Jeremias, J. 4, 9, 11, 35, 79, 85, 107, 115, 118, 137, 139-140, 145-147, 154, 157, 171, 173, 176, 182, 198, 199, 201, 203, 207, 209, 216, 220-221
Jesperson, O. 27
Johnson, M. 42, 173-174
Johnson, S.E. 123, 138, 151
Jonge, M. de 129
Jülicher, A. 215
Juster, J. 9
Kähler, M. 187
Käsemann, E. 103, 104, 107
Kasting, H. 17, 155
Kelly, J.N.D. 87
Kilpatrick, G. 241
Kim, S. 199
Kingsbury, J.D. 168-169, 180, 191, 201, 212, 214
Kippenberg, H. 108
Kittel, G. 18, 43-44, 172, 175
Kittel, R. 49
Klausner, J. 20-21, 128, 131, 135, 139, 152
Klein, C. 8, 44
Klein, G. 204
Klijn, A.F.J. 12-13, 82
Knox, W. 121
Koester, H. 13, 99, 109, 250
Koestler, A. 35, 151
Kohler, K. 126
Kohn, H. 38
Kosmala, H. 236
Kraeling, C. 181
Kuhn, K.G. 84
Kuhn, S. 30
L'Heureux, C. 58
Labuschangne, C. 51
LaGrand, J. 31, 49, 88, 100, 176, 202, 205
Lake, K. 9, 92, 97, 195

Landes, G. 206-207
LeGrand, L. 200
Leipoldt, J. 181
Lemche, N. 49, 54
Levi-Strauss, C. 28, 41
Lietzmann, H. 37
Lightfoot, J. 26
Lindars, B. 120, 125, 196-197
Loewe, H. 156
Lohse, E. 88, 216
Longstaff, T. 230
Louw, J. 25
Luz, U. 189, 247
Lyons, J. 28-29, 32
MacDonald, J. 133, 175
MacMullen, R. 204
MacRae, G. 206
Malina, B. 12-13
Mann, C.S. 90, 180, 247
Manson, T.W. 10, 127, 128, 136, 138, 164, 189, 194, 197, 201, 208, 210, 228
Margolis, M. 67
Marr, W. 33
Marshall, I.H. 130, 220
Marty, M. 39
Marx, K. and F. Engels 54
Masson, C. 87
McCasland, S. 113, 117, 179
McGaughy, L. 149
McKelvey, L. 117
McNamara, M. 116
Meier, J.P. 124, 183, 187, 190-191, 196, 212, 239
Meinertz, M. 141, 200
Mendenhall, G. 48, 50-51, 54-56, 57, 61-63
Menoud, P. 8
Metzger B., 82
Michel, O. 168, 236-237
Milligan, W. 246
Milton, H. 172

Minear, P. 177
Moessner, D. 222
Montagu, A. 22
Montefiore, C. 137, 155, 192
Montgomery, J. 141
Moore, G.F. 18, 159
Moule, C.F.D. 66-67, 124, 197, 204-206, 222, 228, 240, 245
Moulton, J.H. and G. Milligan 84, 90
Mowinkel, S. 127-128, 134
Munck, J. 3-5, 9, 13, 37, 90-91, 135, 146, 161
Murphy-O'Connor, J, 10, 76
Murray, R. 12, 96-97
Nepper-Christensen, P. 158
Neusner, J. 7-8, 36, 44, 82, 95-97, 99, 126, 129, 147-148, 154, 157
Nida, E. 28-29
Niebuhr, H.R. 7
Nock, A.D. 9
Nolan, B. 216
Noland, J. 151
Oberman, H. 34
O'Neill, J. 125
Odeberg, J. 108
Orchard, B. 163-164
Orkar, J.N. 42, 170
Outler, A. 159
Patai, R. 34-35
Pearson, B. 109, 160, 180
Pery, A. 33
Pesch, R. 199-200
Pike, K. 24, 27, 157
Plummer, A. 145
Poliak, A. 35
Pope, M. 11
Porter, S. 117
Powell, J.E. 43, 45
Przybylski, B. 99, 215-216, 250
Purvey, J. 27

Quasten, J. 98
Rabinowitz, I. 10, 59, 133
Rad, G. von 49, 55, 62, 64
Rahlfs, A. 66
Rainey, A.F. 55
Rajak, T. 83, 128
Ramsey, G. 55
Read, A.W. 28-29 246
Reicke, B. 105-106, 161-163, 166, 168, 178
Rengstorf, K. 162, 207
Richardson, C. 98
Richardon, P. 36, 137
Ridderbos, H. 131
Riesenfeld, H. 109
Ringgren, H. 128
Rist, J. 161, 166
Rivkin, E. 20-21, 125, 134, 153-154, 223-225
Roberts, C.H. 118
Robinson, H.W. 39-40, 165, 197, 242
Robinson, J.A.T. 94, 106, 144, 150, 161-162, 164
Robinson, J.M. 99, 165
Rokeah, D. 11, 152
Rood, C.S. 164
Rosenthal, E. 126
Rowley, H. 123
Rubenstein, R. 33
Sampson, G. 27
Sanders, E.P. 108-109, 154, 156, 164-165
Sanders, J. 8, 122
Sandmel, S. 8, 31-33, 36-37, 44, 64, 75, 83-85, 150, 153, 167
Sapir, E. 28
Säve-Söderbergh, T. 123
Sawyer, J. 28
Scharlemann, M. 90
Schlatter, A. 137, 139, 176-177, 227

Schmidt, K.L. 41
Schmidt, M.A. 217
Schmithals, W. 2, 195
Schoeps, H.J. 2, 67, 126, 155
Scholem, G. 127, 147, 152
Schottroff, L. and W. Stegemann 138, 190
Schram, T.L. 231
Schrenk, G. 38
Schuller, E. 80
Schürer, E. and Schürer-Vermes 9, 66, 68, 72, 81, 83, 90, 129, 135, 143, 151
Schwartz, D.R. 133
Schweitzer, A. 88, 196
Schweizer, E. 36, 135, 154, 170, 185, 194, 202, 209, 220, 231, 232, 238
Scobie, C. 90, 108, 142, 144
Seeberg, R. 12
Segal, A. 86
Segelberg, E. 41
Sevenster, J.N. 34, 117
Sigal, P. 148
Simon, M. 10, 146, 152
Smith, A.D. 39
Smith, M. 109
Smithies, B. and P. Fiddick 45
Speiser, E.A. 57-58
Spiro, A. 90
Spitta, F. 140
Stanton, G. 150, 160, 162, 241
Stauffer, E. 219
Stegemann, H. 172, 175
Steinmetz, D. 249
Stendahl, K. 18-19, 170, 176-177, 180
Stone, M. 129
Stonehouse, N.B. 167
Strack-Billerbeck 18, 107, 159
Strecker, G. 12, 103, 158, 159, 171, 176, 182, 214-215

Sundberg, A. 121-123
Sundkler, B. 5, 137, 141, 218
Tagawa, K. 112, 159
Tatian 98
Tertullian 179
Thackeray, H. 67
Theissen, G. 91, 94, 106-107, 135, 159, 163, 198, 204-205, 207-208, 209
Theron, D. 158
Thierry, J. 98
Thiselton, A. 19-20
Thomson, J.E.H. 133, 141
Tilbourg, S. van 147
Toy, C.H. 8
Torrance, T.F. 143, 246
Trier, J. 28
Trilling, W. 158, 162, 187
Troeltsch, E. 7
Tutu, D. 44
Ullmann, S. 27, 29
Vander Meer, P. 7
Vermes, G. 33, 80, 132, 136, 138, 197, 199
Verseput, D. 214
Vincent, J. 109, 200
Visser't Hooft, W. 178-180
Vööbus, A. 97
Waetjen, H. 168-169, 171, 176, 178, 227, 247

Wagner, C.P. 43, 45
Waismann, F. 7, 14, 20, 22-23, 33
Walbank, F.W. 42
Walker, R. 162
Warneck, G. 232
Warnock, G.J. 23
Weber, M. 62
Weingreen, J. 116
Weizsäcker, C. von 3
Wellhausen, J. 47, 68
Wenham, D. 120
Wilder, A. 200-201
Williamson, H. 64, 69, 173
Wilson, R.R. 42, 170
Wilson, S. 17, 108, 111, 229
Windisch, H. 44
Wink, W. 142
Winter, P. 78, 222, 224
Wittgenstein, L. 21-22, 41, 99, 205
Woods, C.F. 204
Wrede, W. 37, 125
Wright, R. 132
Yamauchi, E.M. 142
Young, R. 31
Zahn, T. 176
Zeitlin, S. 134
Zimmerli, W. 63, 123, 183

C. SUBJECTS

Abraham, 35, 48-50, 55, 59, 72, 81, 85-86, 171-172, 208, 251
acephalous, 62n54
adoption, 42, 59-60, 81, 176, 181
alternative to mission, 81
anachronism, 37, 98, 159, 250
anonymous missionaries, 87, 92, 93
antisemitism/anti-Judaism, 33-37, 43, 154-155, 223, 231
Ascension, 91, 113, 238, 245-246
Aseneth, 81-82
atonement, 126, 216-18, 220-221, 237

back-formation, 29-30
baptism, 106, 115, 143-144, 181-183, 190, 214, 236-237

covenant, 50, 54, 58, 72, 74, 77, 80-81, 86, 97, 155, 173, 220, 251
cross/crucifixion, 188, 191, 213, 219-223

date of composition,
    Matthew's Gospel, 87, 160, 163, 250
David, 54, 60, 63-64, 74, 132, 134n123, 158, 171-172, 174
diachronic, 24, 27-28, 98, 103, 159, 162-163, 246

early Israel as missionary religion, 61-62
Elijah, 64, 65, 72, 74, 122
End/eschaton, 110-111, 128-129, 133-134, 138, 143, 147, 152, 154-155, 168, 189, 191, 198, 212, 238
Exile, 48, 65, 70, 177, 217, 251
Exodus, 49-53, 61, 97, 219, 251
    Passover, 220

genealogy, 42, 168, 170-171

generation
    apostolic/1st Tannaim, 4, 13, 128, 152, 198, 207, 222,
    evil, 207, 212, 214n5, 223
gentiles, *cf.* nations/foreigners *etc.* 29-31, 41-42, 100, 208-210
    Gentile mission, 1, 17n1
    Gentile Christianity (*Heiden-Christen*) 13n65, 193

Hebrews/'Apiru, *cf.* Samaritans 8, 10, 32-36, 49-55, 61, 78-79n7, 81, 84, 89-90

Israel-centric mission, 137-138, 144, 191, 208, 210, 217

James, brother of Jesus, 92
James, son of Zebedee, 93n48
Jerusalem, 91-92, 212, 216-218
Jews, 32-35, 70, 127
    in Matthew's Gospel, 231n70
John the Baptist, 124, 126, 143-144, 181-185, 194, 215, 251
Judea, 91, 188n5, 195

Khazars, 35, 151

Magi, 177-180
Messiah/Christ, 21, 107, 119, 129, 158, 171, 188
    messianism/Christology, 21
mystery, 14, 87-88, 152, 202-203, 247, 252

nations and Israel,
    aliens, foreigners, heathen, pagans *etc.* 33, 40, 47, 76-77, 106-107, 135, 146, 153n29, 173, 227
nationality, ethnicity, 37, 39, 44, 58, 60n45, 66, 69, 153, 174, 192-193

particularity/particularism, 2, 13, 40, 78, 169, 205-206
Paul/Saul, 3, 5, 7, 13, 86-87, 91
Pentecost, 91-92, 244-247
Peter/Simon, 5-6, 13, 91-92, 161, 195-196
Philip, 92
Phinehas, 72, 74, 77
proselytes, proselytism, 9-11, 73, 81, 85-86, 131, 133n118, 145-155

race, seed *etc.*, 22-23, 34-36, 77
    racial purity, 35, 79, 173, 174n79
rejection of Israel, arguments, 218n21
remnant, 60, 65, 214n5, 218, 222
    (women), 225
resurrection/death and, 107, 124-126, 198, 212, 226

Jesus' death and resurrection as End event, 191
    sayings of risen Jesus, 112-113, 240-244

Samaritans, Observers, 7-8, 63n60, 72, 84-85, 90, 97, 122n68, 131, 134, 139-42, 144, 217
    Samaria, 91-92, 139-141, 144, 188n5, 195
Son of Man, 110n24, 196-200, 213
Stephen, 90-91

universality/universalism, 2, 5, 78-79, 169, 200-201, 216, 230, 239, 242n67, 252

zeal, zealots, 72-74, 77-78, 82, 85-86, 97, 99, 223

www.ingramcontent.com/pod-product-compliance
Lightning Source LLC
Chambersburg PA
CBHW070234230426
43664CB00014B/2296